The Catastrophic Imperative

The Catastrophic Imperative

Subjectivity, Time and Memory in Contemporary Thought

Edited by

Dominiek Hoens
Jan van Eyck Academy, Maastricht, Netherlands

Sigi Jöttkandt
Jan van Eyck Academy, Maastricht, Netherlands

and

Gert Buelens
Department of English, University of Ghent, Belgium

First published 2009 by
PALGRAVE MACMILLAN

Palgrave Macmillan in the UK is an imprint of Macmillan Publishers Limited,
registered in England, company number 785998, of Houndmills, Basingstoke,
Hampshire RG21 6XS.

Palgrave Macmillan in the US is a division of St Martin's Press LLC,
175 Fifth Avenue, New York, NY 10010.

Palgrave Macmillan is the global academic imprint of the above companies
and has companies and representatives throughout the world.

Palgrave® and Macmillan® are registered trademarks in the United States,
the United Kingdom, Europe and other countries

ISBN-13: 978-0-230-55285-2   hardback

This book is printed on paper suitable for recycling and made from fully
managed and sustained forest sources. Logging, pulping and manufacturing
processes are expected to conform to the environmental regulations of the
country of origin.

A catalogue record for this book is available from the British Library.

A catalog record for this book is available from the Library of Congress.

10 9   8   7   6   5   4   3   2   1
18 17 16 15 14 13 12 11 10 09

Contents

Notes on Contributors

Alain Badiou is Chair of Philosophy at the Ecole Normale Supérieure, Paris, France. His works in English include *Being and Event* (2005), *Ethics: An Essay on the Understanding of Evil* (2002), *Manifesto for Philosophy* (1999), *Metapolitics* (2006) and *The Concept of Model* (2007).

Benjamin Biebuyck is professor of German Literature at Ghent University, Belgium. He authored *Die poetische Metapher: Ein Beitrag zur Theorie der Figürlichkeit* (1998) and co-authored a collection of essays on the relationship between literature and ethics (*Negen muzen—tien geboden: Historische en methodologische gevalstudies over de interactie tussen en ethiek*, 2005). He has published on Nietzsche, on literary theory as well as on 19th and 20th century German literature in books and journals such as *Philologus*, *Germano-Slavica*, *Style* and *Nietzsche-Studien*.

Gert Buelens has edited *Deferring a Dream: Sub-Versions of the American Columbiad* (with Ernst Rudin, 1994), *Enacting History in Henry James* (1997) and written *Henry James: Style, Ethics and History* (1996) and *Henry James and the "Aliens": In Possession of the American Scene* (2002; recipient, American Studies Network Book Prize). Essays in *American Studies in Scandinavia*, *Henry James Review*, *Modern Philology*, *Texas Studies in Literature and Language*, *PMLA*. He is currently working on the sense of the canny in Henry James and other writers in English.

Gil Chaitin is Professor Emeritus of French and Comparative Literature at Indiana University, Bloomington, USA. He has published books and articles on French fiction, narrative theory, psychoanalysis and cultural theory, including *Rhetoric and Culture in Lacan* (1996). In his latest work, he takes a Lacanian look at politics and the novel—a recently completed manuscript entitled *Fictions of Universal Education in the French Third Republic* and a new project on George Sand and the Thesis Novel.

Justin Clemens is a Senior Lecturer at the University of Melbourne, Australia. His recent books include *The Romanticism of Contemporary Theory* (2003) and, with Dom Pettman, *Avoiding the Subject* (2004). He has co-edited the collection *Jacques Lacan and the Other Side of Psychoanalysis* (2006) and Alain Badiou's *Infinite Thought* (2003).

viii *Notes on Contributors*

He teaches psychoanalysis, and is a founding member of the Lacan Circle of Melbourne.

Tom Cohen is Professor of American literary, critical, and cinematic studies at the State University of New York, Albany, USA. He is the author of *Anti-Mimesis: From Plato to Hitchcock* (1994), *Ideology and Inscription* (1998) and *Hitchcock's Cryptonymies: Secret Agents and War Machines* (2005). He edited *Jacques Derrida and the Humanities* (2002) and, with J. Hillis Miller, Barbara Cohen and Andrzej Warminski, co-edited *Material Events: Paul de Man and the Afterlife of Theory* (2000).

Ortwin de Graef (1963) is Professor of English Literature and Literary Theory at Katholieke Universiteit Leuven, Belgium. He is the author of two books on Paul de Man, and has published widely on Romantic and Post-Romantic literature and criticism. His current research involves aesthetic ideologies of sympathy and the State.

Dominiek Hoens is an advising researcher at the Jan van Eyck Academy, Maastricht, and lecturer at the Royal Academy for Fine Arts in Ghent, Belgium. He has published on psychoanalysis (affect, logical time, sinthome), Badiou (subject, love) and literature (Musil, Duras), and has edited collections of essays on Alain Badiou and Gilles Deleuze. He is currently writing a book on the Lacanian logic of love.

Joanna Hodge is Professor of Philosophy co-ordinating research at Manchester Metropolitan University, UK. Her doctoral work, done in Oxford and Germany, was called Martin Heidegger's Account of Truth; a Study of *Sein und Zeit*. In 1995 she published *Heidegger and Ethics*, and she has forthcoming a study entitled *Time in the Name of the Other: Reading Derrida*. She has published articles on Kant, Nietzsche, Husserl, Benjamin, Levinas and Nancy.

Sigi Jöttkandt is a researcher at the Jan van Eyck Academy, Maastricht, Netherlands, where she is co-editor, with Dominiek Hoens, of *S: Journal of the Circle for Lacanian Ideology Critique*. Author of *Acting Beautifully: Henry James and the Ethical Aesthetic* (2005), she has also published essays on James, Turgenev, Beckett and Pater. She is currently completing a book titled *First Love: A Phenomenology of the One*.

J. Hillis Miller is UCI Distinguished Research Professor of English and Comparative Literature at the University of California at Irvine, USA. His most recent books are *Literature as Conduct* (2005), *Others* (2001), *Speech Acts in Literature* (2001), *Black Holes* (with Manuel Asensi) (1999).

Patience Moll received a PhD in comparative literature from the University of California, Irvine and is currently Teaching Fellow in Philosophy at the University of Dundee, UK. She has published essays on multiplicity in Derrida, Heidegger, Proust and Plato, and is currently completing a book entitled *Hegel and Romanticism: Inscribing the Multitude*.

Dany Nobus is Head of the School of Social Sciences and Professor of Psychoanalytic Psychology at Brunel University, UK, where he also directs the MA Programme in Psychoanalysis and Contemporary Society. He is the author of *Jacques Lacan and the Freudian Practice of Psychoanalysis* (2000) and (with Malcolm Quinn) of *Knowing Nothing, Staying Stupid: Elements for a Psychoanalytic Epistemology* (2005), alongside numerous papers on the history, theory and practice of psychoanalysis.

Aaron Schuster lives and works in Brussels, Belgium. He is a graduate of Amherst College (USA), and is currently completing his PhD in philosophy at KU Leuven, where he is preparing a dissertation on the concept of pleasure in Greek philosophy and psychoanalysis. He lectures and publishes regularly on twentieth century continental philosophy, psychoanalysis, legal theory, and contemporary art.

Sjoerd van Tuinen is a researcher in the Department for Philosophy and Moral Science at Ghent University, where he is currently conducting his PhD research on Gilles Deleuze's concept of the fold. He is the author of *Peter Sloterdijk—Ein Profil* (2006).

Erik Vogt is Associate Professor of Philosophy, Trinity College, Hartford, USA; Universitaets-Dozent for Philosophy, University of Vienna, Austria; author of *Sartre's Wiederholung* (Vienna: Passagen Verlag, 1994) and *Zugaenge zur politischen Aesthetik* (2003); editor and co-editor of books on American continental philosophy, Derrida, Žižek, Sartre, Adorno; general editor and translator of the book series *Neue Amerikanische Philosophie* (six volumes); numerous book translations.

1
Introduction

Benjamin Biebuyck, Gert Buelens, Ortwin de Graef,
Dominiek Hoens, Sigi Jöttkandt

> "It affected him as the sequel of something of which
> he had lost the beginning."
> —Henry James, *The Beast in the Jungle*[1]

Henry James's much discussed tale *The Beast in the Jungle* relates the story of John Marcher's lifelong wait for an experience that he believes is uniquely destined for him. His friend, May Bartram, describes it as a sense of impending catastrophe, a sense of "being kept for something rare and strange, possibly prodigious and terrible, that was sooner or later to happen" (James, p. 744). The two friends spend their whole lives in anticipation of this enormous event, imagining the possible shapes this "ignominy" or "monstrosity" might take, which Marcher names his Beast in the Jungle. It is only at the end of the tale, following May's untimely death, that Marcher finally realizes the truth of his life: by waiting for the catastrophe, he has all along been living the catastrophe itself, namely, the catastrophe of being the man to whom nothing will ever happen.

Such a sudden shift in perspective—the realization that one "is" precisely what one is waiting for (or waiting to become)—recalls what Hegel in the *Phenomenology of Spirit* calls the "cunning of reason." In the guise of something to be awaited, the event is already occurring unseen and unremarked by conscious reason. Believing that the "Beast" will spring upon him from the outside, Marcher is unable to perceive that it has already sprung, and is eviscerating his life from within. James's historical insight is thus fully modern: insofar as we imagine we stand somehow outside the grander forces that are shaping the world, we are blind to precisely how far we are implicated in them or, to put it in more conventional Kantian terms, our perceptual apparatus determines what

1

we are able to "see." If James's insight speaks particularly eloquently to us today, it is because we find ourselves in multiple different ways attending our own "Beast in the Jungle," whether in the form of a global version of the catastrophic conflagration currently engulfing the Middle East, in the cataclysmic environmental destruction and mass starvation predicted as a consequence of human-induced climate change, or in the shape of the new devastating illnesses that are being spawned by industrialized farming practices, pollution, technological "advances" such as cloning, and so on. As these examples from our contemporary catastrophic horizon cannot help but bring home to us, although one customarily thinks of catastrophe as something massive that strikes us from the outside in typically spectacular, unpredictable "natural" events, today we are increasingly being forced to face up to the extent to which we (both individually and collectively) bear a certain responsibility for them—particularly to the extent that we, like Marcher, position ourselves subjectively as passively "awaiting" them.

In the aggressively resurgent theoteleological routines that are upon us now, such waiting has always had its place as the middle of the story whose end is in its beginning: eschatology locates its subjects in the meantime of the penultimate and transmutes impending catastrophe into the rapture of revelation that always already legitimizes the mean as a means to itself. The catastrophe is already there, we are only waiting for it to occur. Which is to say that occurrence itself, a rupture in the real, is no longer material and therefore need not even take place. Such is the logic of catastrophism, the fully fledged ideological levelling of the contradictions of the catastrophic in which rapture replaces responsibility to, and for, rupture. Catastrophism is the denial of catastrophe as the original downturn to death effected by the trace instituting the time of performative response. It inverts the downturn to an upbeat banging away till constative Kingdom come. All will be revealed. All writing erased.

It is thus all the more urgent to state today that the routines of theory require resistance to theodicy. Suspending theoteleology, theory demands the assumption of at least a heightened sensitivity to one's responsibility, or "subjective implication" as we propose to call it, in immense or catastrophic events. The recent focus on trauma is perhaps the most visible performance of such sensitivity in contemporary theory. As is well known, trauma studies are concerned with the way certain inassimilable events nevertheless manage to enter and inscribe themselves on an individual's consciousness. To account for this process, trauma theory elaborates a counter-logical or at least a-chronological temporality that recalls that of James's tale. In a move that parallels the belatedness of Marcher's realization, theorists of trauma explain that it is only once the event has been inserted into a meaningful context or "Symbolic" system that it takes on its proper resonance as "traumatic." As an "unclaimed experience," Cathy Caruth reminds us, the traumatic event can never be experienced as such, but must always be re-constructed after the fact.[2] To qualify as a trauma, the event must be subjectivized: retroactively inserted into a narrative and imbued with a specific representational and affective character. All traumatic events are thus literally "post-traumatic." In this aspect, they recall the backward-facing orientation of Walter Benjamin's Angel of History: traumatic events are only ever lived in the mode of "after." Yet as the contributors to this volume indicate, the imperative to think subjectivity, memory and time as tied together in a Borromean way will require the resources not just of Benjamin but also Heidegger, at least the Heidegger of "Hölderlin's Hymn" for whom "The most violent 'catastrophes' in nature and in the cosmos are nothing in the order of *Unheimlichkeit* in comparison with that *Unheimlichkeit* which man is in himself."[3] Marcher's—and by implication our own—catastrophic realization will transpire not out of any incapacity to act "in time" to avoid the cataclysmic future. Indeed, if the ignominious event is inevitable, this will not be because of any "failure of political will," as our pundits have already in advance decided, but because we are failing, collectively, to think ourselves as James's Marcher, subjectively the very catastrophe we are awaiting and therefore denying.

The Catastrophic Imperative attempts to think this other, "subjective" causality of the catastrophe from a non-belated temporal horizon. From this perspective, contemporary ethical and political imperatives are enacted not through the preventative self-denials urged by an increasingly despairing left, but as a certain inevitability, as irreducible as it is still unmapped. Evoked by the essays collected here, catastrophe holds us accountable through a "memory" of the future, that is, through the imperceptible, always contingent ways we as individual and social subjects have already, unconsciously decided it. Far from eliciting strategies for "changing" the trajectory of this pre-written future, the task for thinking a post-global politics therefore lies, in Jean Dupuy's immortal words, in inscribing the catastrophe "in a much more radical way."[4] The essays collected here suggest what catastrophe might look like once it has been shorn of its eschatological foundation. Removed from the necessity of delivering anthropological meaning—of what, in a collective version of Marcher's hubristic delusion, it might mean "for us"—catastrophe starts to become accessible as a critical concept for tracking non-linear networks of memory regimes and their orders of reference as they are and have always been lived co-incident with eschatology in "the mean time."

J. Hillis Miller's essay, "Who or What Decides For Derrida: A Catastrophic Theory of Decision" opens up the terms of the discussion by asking whether decision itself is or can be catastrophic. The critical term derives from Kierkegaard's famous claim in *Fear and Trembling* that the moment of decision is madness.[5] All decisions rely on a previously given knowledge, but Miller explores the ways decision itself is made in a moment of madness—at a point where theoretical and historical knowledge inevitably fail. Whether madness or foolishness—that is to say, immaterial of whether it lacks knowledge, or is supported by existing laws—decision precludes the supposition of an autonomous or self-conscious ego. Instead, as Miller argues through his explorations of the above mentioned Henry James and Anthony Trollope, decision overcomes us, like a catastrophe, seemingly forcing itself on us from the outside.

The closing sentence of Erik Vogt's essay reiterates Slavoj Žižek's germane question, "Are we still able to commit the act proper? Which social agent is, on account of its radical dislocation, today able to accomplish it?" The author's query emerges from his careful prior exposition of the apparent total capture of the social that Adorno, Heidegger and Agamben detect in catastrophic thought, troped as instrumental reason, Gestell, and sovereign biopolitics, respectively. With Žižek, and implicitly Lacan, Vogt ventures the thought of the exception not as something external and constitutive of a totality but as something inherent to that totality. Totality, he suggests, is not determined by an exception but rests on an antagonism that is both internal and foundational.

Sjoerd van Tuinen's essay, "Breath of Relief: Sloterdijk and the Politics of the Intimate," begins with a catastrophic quotation (in the other, Shakespearean sense suggested by Falstaff, in *Henry IV*, meaning "behind")[6] where Peter Sloterdijk flatly states that culture must be thought from its rupture with nomadism, from the moment we become saddled with our own shit (and its smell). This recalls Lacan's famous "la culture, c'est l'égout." What should be expelled lies not outside us but is located in the "sphere" in which we live. Both Žižek and Baudrillard have reflected in their own ways on the obscene, particularly in the context of contemporary politics. For these, the obscene is defined by what remains off-stage, the ob-scene, that has no say in (democratic) representation. Analyzing these thinkers' different approaches to the obscene, van Tuinen foregrounds Sloterdijk's call for some fresh air in the form of new psycho-political scenes of communication not exclusively determined by obscene terrorism or a psychoanalytically inspired passion for the real. Can such a new psycho-political scene be represented? This is the question Justin Clemens poses in his essay. To the different ways "man" has historically been described, Clemens adds his own Lacanian-inspired definition: "Man is a swarm animal." For Clemens, the contemporary social can no longer be conceived as bound by a unifying, representational signifier (traditionally: nation, race, identity, etc.) but as a post-symbolic "swarm."Clemens pursues this swarm through an in-depth reading of the Lacanian notion of S1. The homonyms essun (S1) and essaim (swarm) comprise what Clemens calls a "puncept." In its various permutations as swarm and Schwärmerei, this revised S1 hints at the possibility of thinking a non-representational multiplicity whose autotaxic political ramifications remain unpredictable.

Tom Cohen takes these ramifications to their outermost reaches in his close reading of Hitchcock's "The Birds." For Cohen, the "cinematic" marks itself as an historial event that threatens to destroy the ocularcentric program of the human as a construct. Cohen detects in Hitchcock's birds a non-referential force, a nanoswarm he terms a "bird war," that brings the twin poles of the program of the visible into violent collision. Cohen's predictions of coming wars of reinscription confront us with the necessity for thinking memory post-globally, that is, as capable of attending to other, non-anthropomorphic temporalities invoked by inscription. Patience Moll's rhetorical reading of the section on physiognomy and craniology from Hegel's *Phenomenology of Spirit* suggests one way of seizing upon Cohen's challenge. Moll finds in the transformation of consciousness into spirit the traces of a redoubled katastrephein. In this catastrophic downturn, consciousness is confronted with its own materiality in the form of the post-Enlightenment "pseudosciences" of physiognomy and craniology. Tracing the move from the former to the latter, Moll identifies a shift from the materiality of meaning (the facial expression of a thought) to facing materiality as such—the skull, or pure "thing." Pursuing the catastrophic rhetoric of this turn, Moll argues that the concept of "action" it produces must be understood in terms of survival; action's imperative is neither moral nor idealistic, but both temporal and material.

In "Catastrophe, Citationality and the Limits of Responsibility in *Disgrace*," Gert Buelens argues that J. M. Coetzee's disturbing post-Apartheid novel is structured around catastrophic events that produce "subjects" through acts of citation and allow injury to set borders to identity. Concentrating on Lucy Lurie's remarkable response to being raped by a gang of black men (she refuses to prosecute them and decides to become the common-law wife of a member of their extended family), the essay shows how this response must be understood as an act of political performativity that relies on citationality so as to turn the aggressor's force in a different direction from the intended one. That Lucy makes this choice is linked to her acceptance of her own responsibility for her place in history. Rather than living as a white owner on what contemporary history morally regards as black turf, while citing all the time the behavioral norms of her group in a manner of which she is largely unaware but that is brought home to her in the detail of how the rape takes place, she will henceforth live as a tenant-farmer on land she no longer owns, and will be fully dependent on the protection offered by her black landlord—her new common-law husband. Her responsibility will thus be limited by a wholly new set of norms that she will have to learn to cite correctly. Lucy accepts that she has been part of the problem, and that the only solution for a future South Africa lies in white people's recognition of the extent to which their identity too must be marked by the cut of history.

Dany Nobus's essay reaches right into the heart of the volume's exploration of the intricacies of catastrophic causation. A report by one of the victims of the London bombings of 7 July, 2005 serves as Nobus's point of departure for a meditation on the status of the victim from the perspective of psychoanalysis. Nobus shows how psychoanalysis opts for the difficult position of neither denying victimhood nor refusing to acknowledge the ways such a position can have a number of uncomfortable—and discomforting—results. For Nobus, the *skandalon* of psychoanalysis—that man is an animal marked by a perverse and distorted relation to sexuality—reminds us of another scandal propounded by psychoanalysis: every trauma conceals an unconscious choice that is as unimaginable as it is unavoidable. In a period when ethics is being reduced to victims' rights, Nobus's is a far from obvious and difficult claim.

In his meditation on Nietzsche Alain Badiou asks: "Who is Nietzsche?" This is not a biographical question but one which enquires into the relation between philosophy as crime and as proper name. For Badiou, Nietzsche's gesture is both anti-philosophical and arche-political, meaning that Nietzsche offers neither a theory, nor an analysis nor an interpretation of the world but, on the contrary, he changes the world. To claim that one's thought "breaks the world in two" is not philosophy but antiphilosophy. It is only later that a philosophy capable of thinking

Nietzsche's truth comes into play, enabling us to leave Nietzsche behind. In "Is Pleasure a Rotten Idea?" Aaron Schuster returns to the all-too-hastily answered question of whether it is now time to dispense with the psychoanalytic model in favor of a Deleuzian paradigm that is not obsessed with lack. Classically, pleasure has been conceived as the (fulfilment of a) lack but desire—Deleuze's preferred alternative—is witness to an excess. This choice stems from a discussion with Lacan for whom desire also holds a central place, albeit as "lack." The author notes that Deleuze's alternative conception of desire posits no mediating Other. Insofar as this is possible within Deleuze's Spinozan system, however, it becomes difficult to conceive of accidents or catastrophes. The philosophy of plenitude and non-limitation is found to have its own problems in conceiving ways of demarcating the excesses of desire.

Regarding the question of where catastrophe occurs, Gil Chaitin claims that, neither rational nor irrational, Barrès's proto-fascism can be best understood in light of Lacan's notion of "extimacy." Barrès's *The Novel of National Energy* exemplify his neologistic mode of escaping from the polar opposition of the interior and the exterior that so often haunts the discourse of identity at the heart of republican, nationalist and fascist ideology. The text juxtaposes the ethic of acceptance and that of energetic action in the persons of the two main protagonists, Roemerspacher and Sturel, a conflict that raged in Barrès's heart as he struggled to come to terms with the death of his father, an event that precipitated his plunge into right-wing nationalism and the center of the anti-Dreyfus movement. A denial of death and the consequent nothingness of the self, his nationalist ideology asserts that the core of our inner being is nothing but the sum of our ancestors. As Sturel eventually discovers, we can reconcile determinism and autonomy only by bowing to the internal compulsion of our ancestral identity. On one level, this entails xenophobia and anti-Semitism. Yet the description of the foreign Astiné and the plot of the novel reveal another, "extimate" appeal to the movement, a covert enjoyment of the sadistic incorporation of the Other within the self. Closing out the volume, in her essay, "Topography of the Border: Derrida Rewriting Transcendental Aesthetics," Joanna Hodge presents an incisive analysis of the problems connected with Kant's forms of pure intuition, that is, space and time. Making use of Derrida's analyses in "Truth and Painting" (1978) and other texts, she amends Kant's transcendental aesthetic with a "topography of the border."

We are grateful to the contributors to this volume. We would also like to thank the Flanders Research Foundation (FWO-Vlaanderen) for its generous support of the research project on Rhetoric and Literary Ethics out of which this volume emerged. Thanks, as well, to Universiteit Gent, KU Leuven and the Jan van Eyck Academie, Maastricht for their institutional support, and to Palgrave Macmillan for their support of the project. Permission to reprint Alberto Toscano's translation of Alain Badiou's "Who is Nietzsche?" which originally appeared in *Pli: The Warwick Journal of Philosophy* is gratefully acknowledged. Versions of the chapters by Gil Chaitin and J. Hillis Miller are due to appear with Ohio State UP and Fordham UP respectively; we are grateful to those presses for granting the authors permission to publish their work in our collection.

Notes

1. Henry James, *Collected Stories*, selected and edited by John Bayley, 2 vols (NY: Knopf, 1999).
2. Cathy Caruth, *Unclaimed Experience: Trauma, Narrative and History* (Baltimore: Johns Hopkins University Press, 1996).
3. Martin Heidegger, "Hölderlins Hymne 'Der Ister'," *Gesamtausgabe*, 53 (Frankfurt: Klostermann, 1984), p. 94. Cited in Slavoj Žižek, *The Puppet and the Dwarf: The Perverse Core of Christianity* (Cambridge, Mass.: MIT Press, 2003), p. 187n12.
4. Jean-Pierre Dupuy, *Pour un catastrophisme éclairé* (Paris: Editions du Seuil, 2002), p. 164.
5. Søren Kierkegaard, *Fear and Trembling*, translated by Alastair Hannay (NY: Penguin, 2005).
6. William Shakespeare, *King Henry IV, Part Two*, Act II, Scene 1, 26.

2
Who or What Decides For Derrida: A Catastrophic Theory of Decision

J. Hillis Miller

> Who? Who? Who? What?
> A summer evening?
> —William Carlos Williams, *Paterson*

> This duty of irresponsibility, of refusing to reply for one's thought or writing to constituted powers, is perhaps the highest form of responsibility. To whom, to what? That's the whole question of the future or the event promised by or to such an experience, what I was just calling the democracy to come.
> — *An Interview with Jacques Derrida*[1]

Can a decision be a catastrophe? If so, in what sense? In everyday language we speak of a catastrophic decision, as when we discuss "Isabel Archer's catastrophic decision to marry Gilbert Osmond" (in Henry James's *The Portrait of a Lady*[2]), or George W. Bush's "catastrophic decision to invade Iraq." I claim, however, that Jacques Derrida's theory of decision is catastrophic in a more precise sense. This sense is related to what is called, in mathematics and climatology, "catastrophe theory," that is, the theory that a tiny change in one part of a dynamical system, for example, in a famous version, the flapping of a butterfly's wings in Guatemala, can, through a series of rapid relays, produce a sudden wholesale rupture, a gigantic and "catastrophic" change in the whole system, for example, a hurricane in the Gulf of Mexico. The butterfly's wing-flapping tips the balance, as we say, in a system that is precariously poised. Mathematicians have mapped the way this happens. The online encyclopedia, Wikipedia, defines a catastrophe, additionally, as a disaster, sometimes an unusually severe disaster, as the solution of the plot in a Greek tragedy, and, in the field of sociology, "as social change of an outstanding radical and rapid character, with highly magical explanations by victims and others." The word "catastrophe" means, etymologically, "to turn down, overturn," from Greek *kata*, down, and *strephein*, turn. *The American Heritage Dictionary* stresses the suddenness of a catastrophe by defining it as "a great and sudden calamity; disaster" and as "a sudden violent change in the earth's surface; cataclysm." An example, I suppose, would be an earthquake or a volcanic eruption. How can a decision be like an earthquake, like a volcanic eruption, or like that hurricane caused by a butterfly?

The reader will see the equivocation on my title. It may be read in three ways. (1) In Derrida's view, who or what decides? (2) This essay is for Derrida, dedicated to his memory. (3) Who or what, one might ask, decides in favor of Derrida, swears allegiance to him, as I hereby decide to do. But Derrida, "who, he?" Or perhaps I should say, "what, he?"

A decision seems a straightforward, even paradigmatic, speech act. I say, "I decide so and so," or a judge issues a judicial decision. Such an utterance acts to bring about the decision by making it enter the circumambient social realm. The utterance involves the first person singular pronoun and a present tense indicative verb. The "who" is the "I" who speaks, a self-conscious ego or subject in full possession of his or her faculties. That "who" is embedded in a social situation and within established institutions that give him or her the responsibility for deciding in this particular case. The "what" enters into a decision as a name for the contingent factors that make me decide in a certain way.

Like all paradigmatic speech acts, however, a decision has its peculiarities. For one thing, people do not usually, in ordinary language, say, "I decide." They say, "I have decided." That suggests that the decision is taken as an inward and spiritual act of conscience that is then later on reported, constatively, by saying, "I want you all to know that I have decided." J. L. Austin criticizes such a claim as a high-minded but false spiritualizing. "Accuracy and morality alike," he says, "are on the side of the plain saying that *our word is our bond*" (Austin, p. 10, and see the preceding sentences). A decision, like a promise, Austin, I imagine, would want to argue, takes place when the decision is put in words.

Matters are not quite so simple with decisions, however, as examples of life-determining decisions dramatized in literature indicate. One such example is Anthony Trollope's report, in *Phineas Finn* (1869), of how Marie Goesler decided to refuse the Duke of Omnium's offer of marriage. A woman's decision to accept or refuse an offer of marriage was perhaps the crucial form of decision, for women at least, in Victorian middle and upper class society as represented by its novelists. The reader looks in vain for a moment when Madame Goesler says or could say, "I decide." What Trollope's narrator gives is rather several days of agonized indecision marked by a painful awareness that nothing on earth or beyond it can help her decide. This is then followed by the report of a time when she has already decided and needs only write her letter of refusal to the Duke.

What does Jacques Derrida have to say about the moment of decision? Does he confirm or put in question Trollope's view of decision? Derrida's discussion of the aporias of decision comes in the context of a distinction he makes between law (*droit*) and justice. This is expressed most eloquently in the long preparatory introduction to his reading of Benjamin's "Zur Kritik der Gewalt" in *Force de loi*.[3] This section is entitled "Du droit à la justice" (From Law to Justice). On the one hand, what Derrida says seems straightforward enough. On the other hand, some features of it are more than a little obscure and perhaps also hard to accept. My goal is to read what he says as accurately as possible, that is, to do it justice. I want also to identify the presuppositions that lead him to say what he says.

The distinction between law and justice that is Derrida's starting point seems fairly straightforward and unexceptional. Law is the institutionalized body of regulations within a specific culture. Though laws are particular, in the sense of being instituted within a given history and culture, they are universal in the sense that "everyone is equal before the law," and in the sense that laws are general rather than specific. They do not take account of the singularity of each special case. Laws are immanent, this-worldly. Justice, however, is transcendent and ineffable. Just to apply the laws is by no means necessarily to be just.

Isabel Archer, in Henry James's *The Portrait of a Lady*, at one point soon after she has inherited a large fortune, says to Ralph Touchett that she doesn't want to be "liked too much" by everybody, as Ralph says is the case. She says, "I want to be treated with justice; I want nothing but that" (James, p. 318). She wants a lot. In fact she wants too much. How would you know you were treating another person with justice? Do we ever treat other people with justice? Certainly, if we ever do, it is not by applying mechanically to them a general law, moral or legal. Each person makes a particular demand on us for justice that no appeal to rules or laws will help us much fulfill. It is all very well to say we should love our neighbors as ourselves, but just how do you do that and know that you are doing it in a particular case? How can we as readers of *The Portrait of a Lady* render justice to Isabel Archer? That's all she asks, but it may be an infinite, unfulfillable request.

In the context of his distinction between law and justice, Derrida turns to three aporias of decision. An aporia is, etymologically, a blind alley, an impasse, a no thoroughfare, in a sequence of logical thinking. You follow through a perfectly rational line of argument, one depending on clear and self-evident distinctions and definitions. Suddenly (or gradually) you hit the wall and can proceed no further. There seems no way out.

The first aporia Derrida calls "l'*épokhé* de la règle (*épokhé* of the rule)" (*Force*, pp. 50–2/pp. 22–4). "*Epokhé*" is a Greek word meaning "suspension". More particularly, it is a Husserlian word naming the suspension of epistemological questions about "what is really out there" in order to describe with minute accuracy just what consciousness is conscious of, without reference to the objective existence or non-existence of those contents of consciousness. In Derrida's use of the word, *épokhé* names the necessary suspension of rules in the application of justice, while at the same time the one who does the suspending must recognize the necessity of rules. This is the first aporia. Throughout Derrida applies his three aporias to the situation of someone making a decision, whether it is an ethical decision in relation to another person, or a legal decision, for example, one made by a judge in a criminal case, or a legislative decision, such as a decision to vote for or against a proposed law.

No one would deny that a just decision would need to be made freely, not by someone who is coerced. "We would not say," says Derrida, "of a being without freedom, or at least one without freedom in a given act, that its decision is just or unjust" (*Force*, pp. 22–3). If, on the one hand, the decision, of whatever kind, is made by mechanically following pre-existing rules or laws, it is preprogrammed and therefore neither free nor just, though it may be "legal," that is, lawful. On the other hand, justice requires that the decision conform to rules, that it not be wildly willful and arbitrary. That is the impasse, the aporia.

Here is part of Derrida's expression of this aporia, in Mary Quaintance's very just translation. Is a translation, however, ever wholly just or justifed? Is it not always to some degree a free and unjustified interpretation of the original, not fully justified, that is, by the original? "But this freedom or this decision of the just, if it is one," says Derrida, "must follow a law or prescription, a rule. In this sense, in its very autonomy, in its freedom to follow or to give itself laws, it must have the power to be of the calculable or programmable order, for example as an act of fairness. But if the act simply consists of applying a rule, of enacting a program or effecting a calculation, we might say that it is legal, that it conforms to law, and perhaps, by metaphor, that it is just, but we would be wrong to say that the decision was just" (*Force*, p. 23).

When a logician encounters an aporia in his or her train of thinking, he or she has been taught to assume that there must be something wrong with the primary definitions or presuppositions, the theorems or positings that make the whole train of logical thinking possible. We ought not to be taken in too easily by an aporia or too easily enchanted by the claim that an ineluctable one has been found. Could it be that there is something wrong with Derrida's presuppositions? Perhaps following out a logical application of the law is not a loss of freedom, just as we do not feel unfree when we follow a line of mathematical reasoning. Is Derrida barking up a wrong tree or inventing a problem, an aporia, that does not really exist? Is there not, finally, something a little fuzzy about the meaning of "just" when he says "we would be wrong to say the decision was just?" Why is it not just to mete out justice rigorously, according to a strict application of the law? How else would you, or could you, or should you do it?

In what follows Derrida makes more plausible or perhaps even irresistible what he wants to say by appealing to two additional plausible factors. One is the claim that no formulation of the law is wholly transparent. All laws require an act of interpretation. An example would be the endless minuitiae and controversies in constitutional law in the United States. There is the United States Constitution. It was intended to be wholly unambiguous and was carefully framed to allow of no misunderstandings. Nevertheless, it has given rise to a special field among lawyers and law professors, with conflicting schools of thought and different traditions of interpretation about just what a given phrase in the Constitution ought to be taken to mean.

Every decision made by a judge requires not just a blind or mechanical application of the law but what Derrida, following Stanley Fish, calls, a "fresh judgment" (*Force*, p. 23). The judge must not just follow the law but "must also assume it, approve it, confirm its value, by a reinstituting act of interpretation, as if ultimately nothing previously existed of the law, as if the judge himself invented the law in every case" (p. 23). Here is a good example of Derrida's penchant for hyperbole. Into the tiny crack of a logical problem he inserts a tool of hyperbole that widens that crack immeasurably and leads within a few phrases and by way of an "as if" to the claim that the judge in all cases of decision invents the law. This, however, is just what the more temperate and ironic J. L. Austin says: "As official acts, a judge's ruling makes law."[4] The judge does this by a speech act that declares some law or other applies in this particular case. "I sentence you to six months in jail," or "I sentence you to be hanged by the neck until dead." "The 'fresh judgment,'" says

Derrida, "can very well—*must* very well—conform to a preexisting law, but the reinstituting, reinventive and freely decisive interpretation, the responsible interpretation of the judge requires that his 'justice' not just consist in conformity, in the conservative and reproductive activity of judgment. In short, for a decision to be just and responsible, it must, in its proper moment if there is one, be both regulated and without regulation: it must conserve the law and also destroy it or suspend it enough [this is the *épokhé*: JHM] to have to reinvent it in each case, rejustify it, at least reinvent it in the reaffirmation and the new and free confirmation of its principle" (*Force*, p. 23).

The first additional factor stressed by Derrida, then, is this ever-renewed need for an act of interpretation that may by a hyperbolic sleight of hand be defined as making the law. This is reinforced elsewhere in Derrida, for example, in *Specters of Marx*, where he stresses the inaugural and therefore in a sense unjustified feature of every act of reading, for instance, his reading of Marx. Every reading is truly inaugural:

> This dimension of performative interpretation, that is, of an interpretation that transforms the very thing it interprets, will play an indispensable role in what I would like to say this evening. 'An interpretation that transforms what it interprets' [*une interprétation qui transforme cela même qu'elle interprète*] is a definition of the performative as unorthodox with regard to speech act theory as it is in regard to the 11th Thesis on Feuerbach ('The philosophers have only *interpreted* the world in various ways; the point, however, is to *change* it' [*Die Philosophen haben die Welt nur verschieden interpretiert; es kömmt aber drauf an, sie zu verändern*]).[5]

The other newly stressed feature is the claim that every case is "other," that is, other to all other cases, singular, unique. If that is true, then it would follow that no general law (and all laws must be general in order to be laws) fits perfectly any particular case. There are always special or mitigating circumstances. The law is like a pair of shoes that is supposed to fit every foot, and obviously such a presumption is absurd: "Each case is other, each decision is different and requires an absolutely unique interpretation, which no existing, coded rule can or ought to guarantee absolutely" (*Force*, p. 23).

Law, lawyers, and judges, the whole institution of the law, has invented a clever way around this aporia between the singular case and the general law, or at least a way to sidestep it or to shift the incompatibility between the conceptually general law and the specific case to a somewhat different aporia. Derrida does not mention this expedient. It is the use of precedent, as in the use of Roe vs. Wade to re-establish a woman's right to choose. If a new case can be shown to be analogous to the precedent that has been, always more or less arbitrarily or accidentally, chosen as the proper one to refer to, then the law or the court decision that derived from the precedent can be applied. The problem, it is easy to see, is that this has done no more than redefine the impasse, not only because the choice of a precedent is always to some degree accidental, therefore in a sense unjustified, but also because no new case, if every case is "other," is really "like," or analogous to, the case taken as precedent. The claimed "analogy" is really a legal fiction turning a metaphorical similarity into a quasi-identity.

Derrida makes two final moves in the two paragraphs that expound the first aporia. One is prepared for in that ominous phrase that speaks of the "proper moment if there is one" of a just decision. Derrida always uses this formulation when he wants to indicate that something is radically unknowable or undecidable, as when he says, in *Donner le temps*, "*le don peut être, s'il y en a* (the gift may be, if there is any)."[6] Every decision is made in a moment, hence a phrase I have used elsewhere: "moments of decision," but whether that moment of genuine or just decision does or does not exist cannot be told or decided. It may or it may not. The moment of just decision is undecidable. Derrida comes back around by a circuitous route to that suspension or *épokhé* of the Heideggerian presentness of the present that has been the beginning the basis for his critique of Heidegger. It is also the basis of his development of an alternative notion of human temporality, by way of the concept of *la différance*. *La différance* differs from the Heideggerian "ecstasies" of temporality that are the basis of Heidegger's notion of decision. In Derrida's case, the justice or not of a given moment of decision can never be known. "It follows from this paradox," he says, "that there is never a moment that we can say *in the present* that a decision *is* just (that is, free and responsible), or that someone *is* a just man—even less, '*I am* just'" (*Force*, p. 23). Justice is not a matter of presence or of the present. "Instead of 'just,' we could say legal or legitimate, in conformity with a state of law, with the rules and conventions that authorize calculations but whose founding origin only defers the problem of justice" (p. 23).

A consequence of this non-presence of decision is that, as the subsequent two aporias make clear, the moment of decision is, paradoxically, unpresentable. James's *The Portrait of a Lady* gives striking examples of what this means in practical terms for the representation of moments of decision in literature, whether ethical, juridical, or political. None of Isabel's crucial moments of decision are directly represented in the novel, only what comes before and after each of them. The reader sees Isabel before she has decided. The reader sees her after she has decided. James does not show her actual instants of decision.

The reference to "founding origin" is the final move in these tightly knit two paragraphs. To take the founding origin of the law as a solid ground, says Derrida, is a mistake. The act of founding a law, for example, by the "framers" of the United States Constitution, was just as arbitrary, capricious and subject to this first aporia as any attempt to apply the law in a moment of decision once it has been laid down. "Here the best paradigm," says Derrida, in concluding this first aporia, "is the founding of the nation-states or the institutive act of a constitution that establishes what one calls in French *l'état de droit*" (*Force*, pp. 23–4). On what is that "state of law" founded? On nothing but the ungrounded say so of those who establish the law, as in the transition from British law to United States law when the United States was founded.

The second aporia is named, in English, "the ghost of the undecidable," in French "*la hantise de l'indécidable*," which more properly means the haunting of the undecidable. Moments of decision are always haunted by the undecidable. Decision is "based on," that is, abysmally undermined, by the undecidable. The undecidable is here spoken of as a ghost that haunts decision and that may not be exorcised. A ghost is neither here nor there, neither present nor non-present, neither material nor immaterial, neither bodily nor disembodied. Derrida's *Specters of Marx* presents itself as a "hauntology," a theory of ghosts or of haunting.

The undecidable, Derrida says, is usually taken as a feature of so-called deconstruction. The undecidable is taken to mean "the oscillation between two significations or two contradictory and very determinate rules, each equally imperative (for example, respect for equity and universal right but also for the always heterogeneous and unique singularity of the unsubsumable example)" (*Force*, p. 24). This has been the topic of the first aporia. The judge or the maker of a moral decision must respect the rules, (e.g., "Honor thy father and thy mother," one of the Ten Commandments [Ex. 20: 12]), but at the same time he or she must respect the singularity of a situation that never fits the rules: "And every one that hath forsaken houses, or brethren, or sisters, or father, or mother, or wife, or children, or lands, for my name's sake, shall receive an hundredfold, and shall inherit everlasting life" (Matt 19: 29), said Jesus. It is impossible to decide between these two equally compelling obligations. The conflict is undecidable, though in a given situation one *must* decide.

Derrida, however, in a characteristic gesture of upping the ante, says that's not at all what he means in this case by "undecidable." What he does mean takes the reader into a realm that is essential to Derrida's theory of decision. At the same time it is both difficult to understand and difficult, for many, to accept, in its scandalous rigor and even irrationality, its madness, its *folie*. What Derrida means by the undecidable as a feature of true decision, he says, "is the experience of that which, though heterogenous, foreign to the order of the calculable, is still obliged—it is of obligation that we must speak—to give itself up to the impossible decision, while still taking account of law and rules. A decision that didn't go through the ordeal of the undecidable would not be a free decision, it would only be the programmable application or unfolding of a calculable process. It might be legal; it would not be just" (*Force*, p. 24). Just what in the world does this mean? It means that justice is "something" that makes an implacable demand on us to decide, obliges us to decide, while at the same time being so foreign, so wholly other, so alien to existing law and its rational calculations, that it does not give clear directions for just what we should decide, even though it obliges us to decide. That's what Derrida means by "the impossible decision." I am obliged to decide, by an irresistible call, something like Heidegger's "call of conscience," but I don't have any rational grounds for decision. Derrida calls this the "undecidable," something very different from the undecidable oscillation between two significations in the interpretation of a text. If you happen to think what Derrida says is just irrational hooey, if you have never heard that demand, obligation, or call, then your notion of moments of ethical or political decision will be very different from Derrida's. Whether or not any literary texts say anything like what Derrida says would require further careful investigation.

Derrida is in this second aporia affirming that, for him, "justice" is another name for that "*tout autre*," the wholly other, that is a central motif of *The Gift of Death*, and "Psyché: l'invention de l'autre." In the latter, "invention" means more "find" than "make up" or "concoct," and we do that in response to a call from the wholly other. Or, the structure of our relation to justice is said to be like the structure of the gift as Derrida has analyzed it in *Donner le temps*. Language that echoes those works appears a little latter in the development of this second aporia when Derrida says "the deconstruction of all presumption of a determinant certitude of a present justice itself operates on the basis of an infinite 'idea of justice,' infinite because it is irreducible, irreducible because owed to the other, owed to the other, before any contract, because it has come, the other's coming as the singularity that is always other (*la venue de l'autre comme singularité toujours autre*)" (*Force*, p. 55/p. 25).

In the further development of this idea of justice as something that comes as an implacable demand from the "wholly other," Derrida is led rapidly to the idea that justice is mad, "*une folie*," or that it makes those subject to it mad, insane. "This 'idea of justice'," says Derrida, "seems to be irreducible in its circulation, in its demand of gift without exchange, without circulation, without recognition or gratitude, without economic circularity, without calculation and without rules, without reason and without rationality. And so we can recognize in it, indeed accuse, identify a madness. And perhaps another sort of mystique. [This is a reference to Montaigne's phrase about 'the mystical foundation of authority,' cited earlier in Derrida's essay, and in the subtitle of the book.] And deconstruction is mad about this kind of justice. Mad about this desire for justice" (*Force*, p. 25).

This notion of a justice that is wholly other explains why Derrida, a little earlier in this section, develops further the idea that the moment of decision is not present. You can follow what leads up to it. You can know afterward that the decision has been made and what the decision was, but you can never know or be present at the moment of decision itself. "But in the moment of suspense of the undecidable, it is not just either, for only a decision is just (in order to maintain the proposition 'only a decision is just,' one need not refer decision to a structure of a subject or to the propositional form of a judgment)." Just what this means and what the stakes of saying this are I shall explain later. Derrida continues with his hollowing out or making ghostly of the present moment of decision: "And once the ordeal of the undecidable is past (if that is possible), the decision has again followed a rule or given itself a rule, invented it or reinvented, reaffirmed it, is no longer *presently* just, fully just. There is apparently no moment in which a decision can be called presently and fully just: either it has not yet been made according to a rule, and nothing allows us to call it just, or it has already followed a rule—whether received, confirmed, conserved or reinvented—which its turn is not absolutely guaranteed by anything; and, moreover, if it were guaranteed, the decision would be reduced to calculation and we couldn't call it just" (*Force*, p. 24).

This is really weird, if you think of it. You can identify or experience the time right up to the decision, and all the time after it has been made. The moment of decision itself, however, vanishes from direct experience.

It does not exist as a moment of which consciousness can be conscious. It's jam yesterday, jam tomorrow, but never jam today. Derrida's calls this "ordeal of the undecidable," a "ghostliness" that inhabits the act of decision before, during, and after. Because apparently no moment exists in which a decision can be called presently and fully just, because the moment of decision is not experienced as a present moment in which I say, "I decide so and so," "the ordeal of the undecidable that I just said must be gone through by any decision worthy of the name is never past or passed, it is not a surmounted or sublated (*aufgehoben*) moment in the decision" (*Force*, p. 24). The undecidable that presides over the non-phenomenal moment of decision is a kind of ghost, neither present nor not present, neither embodied nor wholly disembodied. It haunts and undermines the whole temporal process of decision. The result is that one can never speak of a decision as an "event." A decision never takes place or can never certainly be said to have taken place: "The undecidable remains caught, lodged, at least as a ghost—but an essential ghost—in every decision, in every event of decision. Its ghostliness deconstructs from within any assurance of presence, any certitude or any supposed criteriology that would assure us of the justice of a decision, in truth of the very event of a decision. Who will ever be able to assure us that a decision as such has taken place?" (*Force*, pp. 24–5).

It follows from this impossibility to experience decision in the presence of the present that it is no longer possible to think of a decision as the act of an I, ego, or subjectivity. In a passage added for the French version of *Force de loi*, but not present in the English, Derrida asserts, with proper care, this shocking detachment of decision from the deciding subject: "*D'une certaine manière, on pourrait même dire, au risque de choquer, qu'un sujet ne peut jamais rien décider: il est même ce à quoi une décision ne peut arriver autrement que comme un accident périphérique qui n'affecte pas l'identité essentielle et la présence à soi substantielle qui font d'un sujet un sujet—si le choix de ce mot n'est pas arbitraire, du moins, et si on se fie à ce qui est en effet toujours requis, dans notre culture, d'un 'sujet'* " (*Force de loi*, pp. 53–4) ["In a certain way, one could even say, at the risk of shocking, that a subject can never decide anything: a subject is even that to which a decision cannot happen except as a peripheral accident which does not affect the essential identity and the presence to itself which makes a subject a subject—if the choice of this word is not arbitrary, at least, and if one has faith in what is in effect always required, in our culture, of a subject" (my translation)]. If decision makes a cut, a division between before and after, it goes strikingly against received opinion to say this is not because someone, being of sound mind and with authority to do so, utters a performative statement that effects the decision, but rather because the decision happens to someone, from the outside, as the coming of the other.

One result of this is spelled out by Derrida: It puts in question the axiomatic of responsibility that is used in the courts, by medical authorities, and so forth to determine responsibility or premeditation. If a decision is not something that I "take," in sovereign freedom, but something that happens to me, something that is "owed to the other, before any contract," then the conventional legal rules for determining malice prepense, malice aforethought, for example premeditated murder, as opposed to accidental manslaughter, are seriously flawed. "The whole subjectal axiomatic of responsibility," says Derrida, "of conscience, or intentionality, of property that governs today's dominant juridical discourse and the category of decision right down to its appeals to medical expertise is so theoretically weak and crude that I need not emphasize it here" (*Force*, p. 25).

Derrida makes it sound as if this conclusion is so obvious that it goes without saying, but a lot is at stake at this point in Derrida's exposition of his theory of decision. If he is right, then, for example, J. L. Austin's attempt to use speech act theory to keep law and order by holding people to performatives they have uttered is destined to fail. Law and order, it may be, can only be secured by unjustified force, by "*Gewalt*" or violence, as Benjamin's "*Kritik der Gewalt*" affirms. Law and order, both Benjamin and Derrida, though in different ways, affirm, are fundamentally opposed to justice.

Finally, as a transition to the third aporia, Derrida says that he resists relating this "idea of justice" to a Kantian regulatory idea or to any sort of messianism. Why does he resist this? It would seem that his idea of an "infinite justice" that implacably commands decision, so that decision is more something that happens to a self than a choice made by that self, is without question a form of a transcendental, something either like a Kantian regulatory idea that irresistibly presides from on high or like those many forms of messianism that dominate from the future as a horizon of hope toward which decision is oriented. The third and last aporia, "the urgency that obstructs the horizon of knowledge," shows that this is not the case.

It is difficult to present a "reading" of this third aporia of decision, since though it is only four paragraphs (in the English), every sentence counts. A number of remarkable moves are economically made. They are, moreover, to some degree not all that easy to grasp and accept, just as the notion of an infinite idea of justice that is never present but that is irresistibly commanding is hard to grasp and accept.

Derrida begins by explaining that he resists associating the infinite idea of justice that demands decision with the horizons of the Kantian regulative idea or the messianic advent (in whatever religious tradition: Jewish, Christian, or Islamic) precisely because these are horizons, "far off divine events," in Tennyson's phrase, that are supposed to govern present action and judgment as their telos. This happens in a species of prolonged waiting or anticipation, as Christians are still waiting for the Second Coming. Decision, however, does not wait. It is urgent, precipitous. I must decide now, or sooner or later, usually sooner. The deadline comes, and I must decide one way or the other. Caspar Goodwood or Lord Warburton or Gilbert Osmond proposes to Isabel Archer, and she must decide whether or not to accept. She must say yes or no. You never have time enough to get all the facts, or even if you did have "world enough and time," "the moment of *decision, as such,* always remains a finite moment of urgency and precipitation, since it must not be the consequence or the effect of this theoretical and historical knowledge, of this reflection or this deliberation, since it always marks the interruption of the juridico- or ethico- or politico-cognitive decision that precedes it, that *must* precede it" (*Force,* p. 26). You have an obligation to think it out as best you can, but when the moment comes, all that thinking does not really help, and you rush blindly into a decision. The relation between decision and cognition is consonant with what Trollope says about Madame Goesler's decision to reject the Duke's proposal, but it is not quite the same as what James says of Isabel's decisions in *The Portrait of a Lady,* as a detailed reading would show. In all three cases, however, the relation is not that of a careful thinking out that leads to a reasoned decision, such as we have been taught to believe characterizes a good decision.

This incongruity between knowledge and decision leads Derrida to remember what Kierkegaard says about decision: "The moment of decision is a madness, says Kierkegaard. This is particularly true of the just decision that must rend time and defy dialectics. It is a madness *(folie)*" (*Force,* p. 26). The French version adds two sentences in explanation of why the moment of decision is a madness: "*Une folie car une telle décision est à la fois sur-active et subie, elle garde quelque chose de passif, voire d'inconscient, comme si le décider n'était libre qu'à se laisser affecter par sa propre décision et comme si celle-ci lui venait de l'autre. Les conséquences d'une telle hétéronomie paraissent redoubtables, mais il serait injuste d'en éluder la nécessité*" (*Force de loi,* p. 58) ["A madness because such a decision is at once super-active *and* submissive, it retains something of passivity, even of the unconscious, as if the decider were not free to allow itself to be affected by its own decision and as if that decision came to it from the other. The consequences of such a heterogeneity appear redoubtable, but it would be unjust to elude the necessity" (my translation)]. The madness of decision derives from the fact that it is not the result of a conscious deliberation on the part of the decider, but something that happens to him or her, something he or she passively endures, as though the decision were made somewhere else, as though it came from the other. The decider is as it were not free to decide, but is "affected" from the outside by his or her decision, just as a mad person is not in control of what he or she thinks, does, or decides. We are all mad when it comes to making decisions.

Derrida goes on to relate this "decision of urgency and precipitation, acting in the night of non-knowledge and non-rule" (*Force*, p. 26) to the opposition between constative and performative utterances in standard speech act theory. Though Derrida makes it clear, as have his earlier writings on speech act theory, that he cannot accept at face value the opposition between constative and performative as developed by Austin, nevertheless he goes on to use this opposition in order to set the madness of decision, which he correctly sees as in one way or another a performative, against the presumed rationality and truth-value, or at any rate testability, of constative statements. You can, at least so it seems, find out whether or not it is raining and so verify or disqualify the constative statement, "It is raining." (I note in passing that matters are not quite so simple. Marcel, in Proust's *À la Recherche du temps perdu*, is never able to get a satisfactory answer to what looks like a verifiable question: "Is or is not Albertine lesbian?") If constative statements are at least in principle verifiable, this is not the case with performative utterances, like "I promise" or "I bet." Such statements are neither true nor false. They are, rather, either felicitous or not felicitous. They either succeed in making something happen or they do not. The problem is that it is exceedingly difficult, perhaps impossible, to find out whether a given performative has worked or, if it has worked, just what it has made happen. Performative utterances are not of the order of the cognizable. They belong to the night of non-knowledge. Here is Derrida's way of putting this congruence between decision and performatives in general:

"If we were to trust in a massive and decisive distinction between performative and constative—a problem I can't get involved in here—we would have to attribute this irreducibility or precipitate urgency, at bottom this irreducibility of thoughtlessness and unconsciousness, however intelligent it may be [an amazing characterization of decision: thoughtless, unconscious, however intelligent!], to the performative structure of speech acts and acts in general as acts of justice or law [he means, for example, that the judge does not have to speak to condemn a man to death, but just appear with a black hood], whether they be performatives that institute something or derived performatives supposing anterior performatives. A constative can be *juste* (right), in the sense of *justesse* [in the sense, that is, that a margin is 'justified' when it matches a straight line], never in the sense of justice. But as a performative cannot be just, in the sense of justice, except by founding itself on conventions and so on other anterior performatives, buried or not, it always maintains within itself some irruptive violence, it no longer responds to the demands of theoretical rationality"

(*Force*, pp. 26–7).

In the beginning was the performative, and it's more performatives all along the line. Even the most banal and easily testable constative statement, such as "it is raining," presupposes a prior performative: "I swear that I believe it is raining." Derrida's expression of this is characteristically exuberant and hyperbolic: "'I tell you that, I speak to you, I address myself to you and tell you that this is true, that things are like this, I promise you or renew my promise to you to make a sentence and to sign what I say when I say that, or try to tell you the truth,' and so forth" (*Force*, p. 27). Derrida goes on to express this through appropriation or misappropriation of a sentence from Levinas: *"La verité suppose la justice"* ("Truth supposes justice") (p. 27). Justice comes before truth and guarantees or supports or underlies it as its presupposition. Derrida transforms this into his own extravagant manipulation of French idiom, "dangerously parodying the French idiom," as he puts it (p. 27). The sentence is cited incorrectly in the English version. It should be, *"La justice, il n'y a que ça de vrai"* (*Force de loi*, p. 60). Justice: there is nothing of truth but that, or nothing but justice is the truth.

Two additional important moves are made in the two final paragraphs. In the first Derrida asserts that it is, paradoxically, just because decision is a species of performative characterized by excessive urgency, haste, and precipitation, just because it cannot be characterized as having a regulative or messianic horizon, that it perhaps (since justice is always a matter of perhaps, never of certainty) has a future or rather acts to bring about an unforeseen future, perhaps a future that is more just: "Justice remains, is yet, to come, *à venir*, it has an, it is *à-venir*, the very dimension of events irreducibly to come. It will always have it, this *à-venir*, and always has. [...] There is an *avenir* for justice and there is no justice except to the degree that some event is possible which, as event, exceeds calculation, rules, programs, anticipations, and so forth.

Justice as the experience of absolute alterity is unpresentable, but it is the chance of the event and the condition of history" (*Force*, p. 27).

The final paragraph is of great importance as a counter to claims sometimes made by his critics that Derrida is a political quietist, lost in the abstractions of speculations about "infinite justice" and detached from everyday politics. In the clearest way Derrida asserts here the contrary: "That justice exceeds law and calculation, that the unpresentable exceeds the determinable cannot and should not serve as an alibi for staying out of juridico-political battles, within an institution or a state or between institutions or states and others" (*Force*, p. 28). Derrida ends by listing a whole series of specific responsibilities where the adjudication between justice and law, which belongs to neither domain because it exceeds each in the direction of the other, is urgently necessary: "the teaching and practice of languages, the legitimization of canons, the military use of scientific research, abortion, euthanasia, problems of organ transplant, extra-uterine conception, bio-engineering, medical experimentation, the social treatment of AIDS, the macro- or micro-politics of drugs, the homeless, and so on, without forgetting, of course, the treatment of what we call animal life, animality" (*Force*, pp. 28–9).

Prior to saying this, however, Derrida had, early in this last paragraph, made an extremely important admission. Left to itself, the appeal to an unpresentable justice, however necessary and legitimate it may be, puts one in danger of the bad or the worst: "Left to itself, the incalculable and giving (*donatrice*) idea of justice is always very close to the bad, even to the worst, for it can always be re-appropriated by the most perverse calculation" (*Force*, p. 28). It is for this reason that we must always enter into the realms of politics, of legislation, of activism, and "calculate" in the most radical way possible as we negotiate between law and justice: "Not only *must* we calculate, negotiate the relation between the calculable and the incalculable, and negotiate without the sort of rule that wouldn't have to be reinvented there where we are cast, there where we find ourselves [an oblique echo of Heidegger's *Geworfenheit*], but we *must* take it as far as possible, beyond the place we find ourselves and beyond the already identifiable zones of morality or politics or law, beyond the distinction between national and international, public and private, and so on" (*Force*, p. 28). Far from being a political quietism, Derrida's idea of justice in its relation to law demands the most strenuous, difficult, innovative, and responsible engagement and activism. Fulfiling this demand is a neat trick if you can do it, but we (professors) are required every day to face up to this demand in one way or another, even in the most everyday acts of teaching or in our relations to students, family, and friends.

Derrida emphasizes the "madness" of decision, the irruptive violence of decision, the way a genuine decision is always a "decision of urgency and precipitation, acting in the night of non-knowledge and non-rule," the way a decision is irresponsible and at the same time exigently responsible, the way a decision is an anomalous kind of performative speech act, the way a decision has unpredictable and incalculable consequences. A decision is a decisive break in the continuity of things. It cannot be explained by what came before it. Nor are the results of a decision commensurate with the decision itself. Nothing but her "misreading" of Gilbert Osmond justified Isabel Archer's decision to marry him, just as nothing in the intelligence reports, far from it, justified George W. Bush's decision to invade Iraq. The results of these catastrophic decisions, however, were far-reaching and not what either decider anticipated or intended.

All these features of Derrida's notion of decision mean, I claim, that it can be defined, in a more or less technical sense modeled on climatological theory, as a "catastrophic theory of decision." The butterfly's wing "causes" the hurricane. Isabel's decision causes her (and Osmond) lifelong misery. Bush's decision "causes," so far, the deaths of toward 3000 Americans, a 100, 000 Iraqis, and civil war in Iraq. The longer term effects are still hidden in the future, the *à-venir*, the to come.

Notes

1. Jacques Derrida, *Acts of Literature*, edited by Derek Attridge (NY and London: Routledge, 1992), p. 38.
2. Henry James, *The Portrait of a Lady, The Novels and Tales*, 26 vols (Fairfield, NJ: Augustus M. Kelley, 1971), vols 3 and 4.
3. Jacques Derrida, *"Force de loi: Le 'Fondement mystique de l'autorité'"* (Paris: Galilée, 1994); "Force of Law: The 'Mystical Foundation of Authority'," translated by Mary Quaintance, in *Deconstruction and the Possibility of Justice*, edited by Drucilla Cornell, Michel Rosenfeld, and David Gray Carlson (NY and London: Routledge, 1992). Henceforth cited in the text as *Force*. Unless indicated otherwise, page numbers refer to the English translation.
4. J. L. Austin, *How To Do Things with Words*, edited by J. O. Urmson and Marina Sbisa (Oxford: Oxford University Press, 1980). Henceforth cited in the text.
5. Derrida, *Spectres de Marx: L'État de la dette, le travail du deuil et la nouvelle Internationale* (Paris: Galilée, 1993), p. 51; *Specters of Marx: The State of the Debt, the Work of Mourning, and the New International*, translated by Peggy Kamuf (NY and London: Routledge, 1994), p. 89. Henceforth cited as *Spectres*. Unless indicated otherwise, page numbers refer to the English translation.
6. Derrida, *Donner le temps: I. La fausse monnaie* (Paris: Galilée, 1991), p. 53; *Given Time: I. Counterfeit Money*, translated by Peggy Kamuf (Chicago: The University of Chicago Press), p. 35.

3

Catastrophic Narratives and Why the "Catastrophe" to Catastrophe Might Have Already Happened

Erik M. Vogt

In *Le Siècle*, his marvelous account(s) of the twentieth century, Alain Badiou remarks at some point that those who are under the spell of history or memory count the twentieth century as the site of such unspeakable and horrible catastrophes that the only category adequate to the formulation of its unity is that of crime. That is, for those who claim that the parameters of the twentieth century are those of the extermination camps, the gas chambers, and state-organized atrocities, the balance sheet of the century requires immediately the counting of the dead.[1] As Badiou suggests further, this notion of the twentieth century as catastrophic excess, whose numbers (the millions of dead) function as a kind of real for a certain rhetoric of (a kind of aesthetico-ethical) turning, has formed the horizon for much of the seminal philosophical thought attempting to come to terms with that very century. Since Badiou's claim—fully shared and endorsed by Slavoj Žižek—seems to be particularly pertinent in regard to the philosophical accounts of the twentieth century by Theodor W. Adorno, Martin Heidegger, and Giorgio Agamben,[2] a brief survey of these three well-known, different but also similar, narratives on the catastrophe that was/is the twentieth century will be followed by their reexamination in light of some questions that Žižek has critically raised apropos of their (quite explicit) messianic (post) politics.

While, for Marx, the anatomy of Western (bourgeois) society still held the key for the construction of history according to progressive societal formations, history presents itself to a twentieth century—which, according to Adorno and Horkheimer, has been marked by total domination—in an entirely different light. In the preface to their *Dialectic of Enlightenment* they note: "What we had set out to do was nothing less than explain why humanity, instead of entering a truly human state, is sinking into a new kind of barbarism"(p. xiv). The *Dialectic of*

Enlightenment thus formulates its task as identifying the spell cast over the twentieth century not simply in terms of a mere symptom of decline of bourgeois society; rather, this very decline is to be reconstructed in terms of a catastrophe that has been effective since primordial times.

In this way, the *Dialectic of Enlightenment* arrives at a radical critique of the self-delusion of all previous notions of enlightenment, progress, emancipation, and so on. These notions were not able to recognize and dissolve the spell. It is well-known that Adorno and Horkheimer emphasize three phases of Western civilization and its "tireless self-destruction of enlightenment":[3] the first signs of instrumental reason announce themselves already in the initial detachment from myth as domination of nature, as self-preservation through rational practices that, precisely in their rationality, remain trapped in deception: cunning, sacrifice, exchange, and so on. The formation of the (rational) subject is owed to a rupture between itself and the nature that has to be understood in terms of a negative identification; however, this rupture is redoubled into the subject itself and this doubling provides the basis of an ideally conceived subject that elevates its supposed selfsameness to its standard against the lacking other of nature in order to enforce its identity principle in the name of some "universality." This negative attachment of the identity principle to the devalued other finds its categorical expression not only at the level of the subject, but also at that of the commodity and of domination in general. Since, however, nature as the representative of the negatively conceived attributes forms the basis for the positive self-positing and self-definition of the subject, it continues to haunt the subject fixated on identity as its nonidentical—a nonidentical that has to be suppressed. All so-called progress only increases this suppression.

Adorno and Horkheimer locate a second phase of that process in the amalgamation of (early) capitalism and modern science:

> With the spread of the bourgeois commodity economy the dark horizon of myth is illuminated by the sun of calculating reason, beneath whose icy rays the seeds of the new barbarism is germinating. Under the compulsion of power, human labor has always led away from myth and, under power, has always fallen back under its spell.
>
> (Adorno and Horkheimer, p. 25)

This phase reaches its theoretical conclusion at the point of enlightened thought's perversion to a technological rationality that is utterly functional and instrumental. This reduction of reason is generated by the reduction of all things to exploitable objects. In the light of technological rationality the world can only appear as a collection of exploitable and disposable objects; that is, objects are, as a matter of fact, nothing but this exploitability and disposability without remainder, casting their image on calculating thought. Adorno remarks:

> Things, under the law of their pure purposiveness, take on a form which limits intercourse with them to pure manipulation and which tolerates no surplus, either of freedom of conduct or of the thing's independence, which would survive as the core of experience because it would not be consumed by the moment of action.[4]

This reduction of all things to pure purposiveness dialectically affects at the same time the status of the subject-pole: that is, human subjects find themselves reduced to the status of exploiters and disposers, without remainder. Reifying enlightened reason turns out to be reified itself by this same reduction, and this self-reification of technological rationality culminates in the third phase: "culture industry" or "administered society." That is, culture industry or administered society completes a process of rationalization through which human beings become mere secondary appendices of a machinery of calculation and instrumentalization—they become mere exploitable material reflecting the material they exploit.

Adorno and Horkheimer draw a panorama of history according to which progress appears as the triumphal procession of permanent disaster. They short-circuit the historically particular objects between the poles of mythical, primordial history and mythical present. Moreover, in one of the most well-known paragraphs from his *Negative Dialectics*, Adorno continues to write the picture of catastrophe:

> After the catastrophes that have happened, and in view of the catastrophes to come, it would be cynical to say that a plan for a better world is manifested in history and unites it. Not to be denied for that reason, however, is the unity that cements the discontinuous, chaotically splintered moments and phases of history—the unity of the control of nature, progressing to rule over men, and finally to that over men's inner nature. No universal history leads from savagery to humanitarianism, but there is one leading from the slingshot to the megaton bomb. It ends in the total menace which organized mankind poses to organized men, in the epitome of discontinuity.[5]

It is the spell of the identity principle that dominates the development of Western civilization by means of a quasi-natural force. Its dialectics of instrumental rationality—a form of rationality characterized by a reductionist calculus of means and ends—carries within itself something desperate, insofar as it is to be conceived as a catastrophic grand narrative. History is, for Adorno, a negative teleological continuum. Although he does not deny the "discontinuous, chaotically splintered moments and phases of history," he insists nonetheless that "the One and All that keeps rolling on to this day—with occasional breathing spells—would teleologically be the absolute of suffering" (*Negative Dialectics*, p. 320). Thus Adorno states:

> History is the unity of continuity and discontinuity. [...] The world spirit, a worthy object of definition, would have to be defined as permanent catastrophe. Under the all-subjugating identity principle, whatever does not enter into identity, whatever eludes rational planning in the realm of means, turns into frightening retribution for the calamity which identity brought on the nonidentical.
>
> (*Negative Dialectics*, p. 320)

That is, Adorno's catastrophic history ineluctably rushes headlong toward its negative point of culmination, thereby projecting a universal-historical narrative of disaster.

But at the same time, this negative point of culmination—which Adorno designates metonymically as the catastrophe of "Auschwitz"—may contain the possibility of a turning: that is, a turning that Adorno attempts to conceptualize as "a new categorical imperative [that] has been imposed by Hitler upon unfree mankind" (*Negative Dialectics*, p. 365). It is this perspective of the "new categorical imperative" that opposes to the destruction of remembrance the remembrance of destruction, the remembrance of the "pathological" and the "somatic," thus turning philosophy into a philosophical-materialistic practice that, for the sake of the remembrance of the traces of past, unfulfiled historical possibilities, amounts to a rummaging through the trash-bins of culture.

This "catastrophe" or "decisive turn" in/of philosophical thought attempts to open up a space for the non-identical that has always already formed a part of the philosophical project, although in the form of its denial; but this does not signify a new and nonidentifying thought, but rather the demonstration of the insufficiency of identification itself. After all, thinking is identification; that is, the nonidentical can never appear as such, but only in the form of contradiction that can be grasped as the nonidentical under the aspect of identity. This means that the thinking of catastrophe is, for Adorno, not simply exhausted by the designation of some unfathomable or sublime terror that could never be assimilated to memory and for which no concept could ever be found; rather, Adorno insists that the nonidentical is always implicated in the logic of identity; consequently, it carries the marks of the very rationality it attempts to oppose. Adorno's attitude of remembrance does not reduce this position to a traumatized, passive witnessing that, in the face of the supposedly unfathomable character of the catastrophe, would have to remain silent. Instead, Adorno insists on an analysis of those historical, social, political, and philosophical conditions that rendered the catastrophe (of Auschwitz) possible, since this catastrophe shows a continuity and intelligibility with that which preceded it and that which occurred after it. Thus, he does not invoke a simple conservative nostalgia whose "search for the past" would bring it fully into the present, but rather a remembrance of those limits that are imposed by the law of the catastrophe (of Auschwitz) on each action in the present—a remembrance that functions, at the same time, as an affirmation of the demand for the justice for the multiple, the heterogeneous, and the nonidentical.

This affirmation of justice for the heterogeneous and nonidentical has as its normative core the affirmation of the potential for democratization aimed against any attempt at "totalitarian" closure. That is, it is before the background of Adorno's politics of remembrance that "democracy" becomes the name for politics as such. This democratic and democratizing politics in the shadow of the permanent catastrophe refuses to proclaim the arrival of political or even revolutionary possibilities; but at the same time, it allegedly does not exhaust itself in mere reformism, insofar as it attempts to do justice to the gap in the heart of democracy that has to be conceptualized in terms of the "paradox of the possibility of the impossible." That is, Adorno's attempt at a rethinking and re-conceptualization of philosophy in the shadow of the catastrophe, his "new categorical imperative," ultimately implies the necessary deferral of its actualization into a coming future that is characterized by the impossibility of its actualization.[6] As "Vorschein" of redemption (and its proper site is, in Adorno, precisely "advanced art"), it cannot be detached from the impossible actualization of that redemption:

> The only philosophy which can be responsibly practiced in face of despair is the attempt to contemplate all things as they would present themselves from the standpoint of redemption. Knowledge has no light but that shed on the world by redemption: all else is

reconstruction, mere technique. Perspectives must be fashioned that displace and estrange the world, reveal it to be, with its rifts and crevices, as indigent and distorted as it will appear one day in the messianic light. To gain such perspectives [...]—this is alone the task of thought. It is the simplest of all things, because the situation calls imperatively for such knowledge, indeed because consummate negativity, once squarely faced, delineates the mirror-image of its opposite. But it is also the utterly impossible thing, because it presupposes a standpoint removed, even though by a hair's breadth, from the scope of existence, whereas we well know that any possible knowledge must not only be first wrested from what is, if it shall hold good, but is also marked, for this very reason, by the same distortion and indigence it seeks to escape. [...] Even its own impossibility it must at last comprehend for the sake of the possible. But beside the demand thus placed on thought, the question of the reality or unreality of redemption itself hardly matters.

(*Minima Moralia*, p. 247)

Possibility and impossibility are held together precisely by the (imperative regarding the) preservation of the gap between them: that is, the suspension of (actual) redemption in terms of its impossibility renders intact its possibility. The impossible redeemed world seems to occupy the position of the exception from which the totality of the administered society can be grasped and illuminated. It is for this very reason that the possibility of redemption as impossible ideal has to be articulated in a negative messianic manner.

The demand for justice for the heterogeneous and nonidentical turns out to be an exceptional demand (in relation to what is considered possible within the status quo of social catastrophe) whose possibility consists paradoxically in its own impossibility. If one were to close this gap and to realize reconciliation or justice in a positive manner, one would, at least from Adorno's perspective, subscribe to a politics that is subject to the danger of "totalitarianism." It is, perhaps, also for this very reason that art and artworks—those artworks refusing closure and totality by insisting on and exhibiting the gap that prevents *"erpresste Versöhnung"*—become, in Adorno, models for politics; after all, he states somewhere that, today, politics has migrated into artworks.

Incidentally, does Adorno's "impossible" radical politicization—that includes its own failure in advance—not also exhibit a certain affinity to Derrida's politics of the trace, his "coming democracy?" For the "coming democracy" constitutes, for Derrida, likewise an experience of the impossible, insofar as the futurity of its "coming" belongs to another order:

> For democracy remains to come; this is its essence insofar as it remains: not only will it remain indefinitely perfectible, hence always insufficient and future, but, belonging to the time of the promise, it will always remain, in each of its future times, to come: even when there is democracy, it never exists, it is never present, it remains the theme of a non-presentable concept.[7]

Is democracy thus not always deferred and to-come? And should it not also always remain open and spectral, for otherwise it would open the door for the terror of ontology and "totalitarianism," particularly in the form of collective and organized revolutionary politics? But would this then not imply that both Adorno's and Derrida's definition of democracy is a "reactive" one: one which conceives of "democracy" primarily as the avoidance of the "totalitarian" catastrophe and as the ban against revolutionary "ontological" politics?[8] Thus, in the face of Adorno's and Derrida's linkage between an absolute singularity of remembrance/trace and the spectral-messianic of democratic or reconciled society to come, would one not have to heed Badiou's warning regarding the hegemonic role of "'memory' as the guardian of meaning and of historical consciousness as a substitute for politics"[9] in contemporary political discourses addressing the catastrophe of recent history? Badiou points to certain decisive limits of memorial discourse in the following passage:

> For it is certainly true that memory does not prevent anyone from prescribing time, including the past, according to its present determination. I do not doubt the necessity of remembering the extermination of the Jews, or the action of Resistance fighters. But I note that the neo-Nazi maniac harbors a collector's memory for the period he reveres, and that, remembering Nazi atrocities in minute detail, he relishes and wishes he could repeat them. [...] Whence the obvious conclusion that "memory" cannot settle any issue. There invariably comes a moment when what matters is to declare in one's own name that what took place took place, and to do so because what one envisages with regard to the actual possibilities of a situation requires it.
>
> (*Saint Paul*, p. 44).

For Martin Heidegger, the catastrophe that has taken on its ultimate figure in the *Ge-stell* of the twentieth century can only be rendered fully legible by re-inscribing it into the history of Western metaphysics, that is, the history of (thinking) being. "That which makes our history 'Western,' according to Heidegger, is metaphysics, and metaphysics culminates in the age of technology. The truth of our Western conception of what it means to know is revealed in modern science, and is completed as techno-science."[10] It is the *Ge-stell* as the essence of modern technology that points to the particular form of rationality having characterized and determined the history of Western metaphysics. To be more precise, it is the principle of reason codified by metaphysics that authorizes planetary technology:

> Modern technology pushes toward the greatest possible perfection. Perfection is based on the thoroughgoing calculability of objects. The calculability of objects presupposes the unqualified validity of the *principium rationis*. It is in this way that the authority characteristic of the principle of reason determines the essence of the modern, technological age.[11]

Thus, the essence of modern technology reveals itself as calculative thinking that, similar to Adorno and Horkheimer's account of instrumental rationality, points to a fundamental transformation of the nature of man's relation to beings, and to the world as a whole, in that entities are reduced to mere standing reserve. Planetary technology involves not only the reduction of entities to objects to be mastered, administered and controlled, that is, to exploitable and disposable objects, but, more radically, they are ultimately transformed into mere raw material vanishing into objectlessness. That is: "Now, the object has dissolved into the merely available, into the stockpile. It is entirely on hand. The subject-object dualism [...] underwent its own dissolution" (*The New Heidegger*, p. 110).

Moreover, this dissolution of the subject-object dualism indicates clearly that the human being can no longer maintain a distance toward the process of technology, but rather becomes subjected to its challenging and summoning. The following two quotations attest to Heidegger's claim that this processing has fundamentally transformed the being of man: "As soon as what is unconcealed no longer concerns man even as object, but does so, rather, exclusively, as standing-reserve [...] then he comes to the brink of a precipitous fall; that is, he comes to the point where he himself will have to be taken as standing-reserve."[12] And:

> The subject-object relation thus reaches, for the first time, its pure "relational," i.e., ordering, character in which both the subject and the object are sucked up as standing-reserves. That does not mean that the subject-object relation vanishes, but rather the opposite: it now attains to its most extreme dominance, which is predetermined from out of Enframing. It becomes a standing-reserve to be commanded and set in order.
>
> (*The Question*, p. 173)

But it is precisely at this extreme point of danger—the stance of technological Enframing that articulates itself, as Heidegger famously notes, in the manufacturing of corpses in the camps together with mechanized agriculture and the manufacturing of hydrogen bombs—that he repeatedly invokes Hölderlin's words: "But where danger is, grows the saving power also" (*The Question*, p. 28). As is well-known, it is because of the demand imposed on us by the *Ge-stell* to think the essence of (the hidden truth of) technology that Heidegger can identify this danger itself as the saving power (p. 42). He writes: "The experience in Enframing as the constellation of Being and man through the modern world of technology is a prelude to what is called the event of appropriation."[13] This "decisive turning" concealed in the *Ge-stell* announces a different kind of gathering designated as *Gelassenheit*:

> In *Gelassenheit*, it is a different kind of gathering, and of cohesion, that prevails: not that of the total capture and seizure of all things actual, but that of letting-be and releasement of such things from out of their essence (the essence of truth). *Gelassenheit* signals an attitude and comportment towards the world that is altogether different from that of *Ge-stell*. It is an attitude of releasement of beings for their being, of letting beings be in their being.
>
> (*The New Heidegger*, p. 120)

It is precisely the calculability of the *Ge-stell* that, similar to the instrumental reason of Adorno's administered society, casts the shadow of the incalculability of *Gelassenheit*; thus one possibility would be to draw the conclusion that the *Ge-stell* ultimately dissolves even the modern "world picture" into a multiplicity of images that correspond no longer to some objective truth, but rather to an infinity of interpretations. This would be, for instance,

Gianni Vattimo's "weakening" rendition of Heidegger's attempt to intimate a "free" relation to technology. Vattimo remarks: "We can recognize in the *Ge-stell* a first flashing of the new event of Being to the extent that it brings with it a dissolution of the realistic traits of experience, in other words what I think we might call a weakening of the principle of reality."[14]

However, although Vattimo's technological "optimism" opens up a novel reading of Heidegger's reflections on technology, Heidegger himself seems to emphasize more that aspect which is "akin to the essence of technology and [...] fundamentally different from it"—art. It is from the—not technological, (regarding the *Ge-stell*) exceptional—position of art that one can gain a distance to calculative thought, technology, and technological devices. "We must learn to leave them in their right place, to let go of them as something inessential, as something that does not affect us in any decisive manner. In letting go of them, we turn to the world, and to the beings in its midst" (*The New Heidegger*, p. 125). That is, the catastrophe of the *Ge-stell*, when turned decisively in the right manner, harbors the saving power of a poetic thinking that, via its position of exceptionality, can prepare for *Gelassenheit* that is supposed to lay the ground for the possible arrival of the gods.

Finally, Giorgio Agamben's account of Western metaphysics in terms of the catastrophic unfolding of sovereign biopolitics might be understood, at least to a certain extent, as one of the latest variations on Adorno's administered society and Heidegger's *Ge-stell*. *Homo Sacer, State of Exception*, and *Remnants of Auschwitz* constitute the "*Wegmarken*" in a historico-philosophical project on the Western biopolitical paradigm culminating in Auschwitz and permeating contemporary politics. In *Homo Sacer*, a multi-layered reading of Carl Schmitt, Hannah Arendt, and, above all, Michel Foucault, Agamben traces the limit-figures of sovereign power and bare life throughout the history of Western political thought. By means of this tracing, he establishes a conceptual link between sacredness, sovereignty, and life that is to demonstrate how, with the rise of sovereignty, one witnesses the rise of a form of life that corresponds to it.

Agamben's elaboration of sovereign biopolitics extends Foucault's analysis in two directions. First, he claims a structural analogy between the classical and the modern, insofar as an examination of the Aristotelian distinction between *zoē*, the bare life common to all beings, and *bios*, the mode of life proper to individuals or groups, can demonstrate that the inclusion of bare life within the political life always already constituted the hidden center of sovereign power. In fact the production of a specifically biopolitical body is "the original activity of sovereign power."[15] That is to say, sovereignty is constituted in its power over bare life, in its production of bare life. Agamben thus "corrects" Foucault's supposed denial of the continuing significance of sovereign and legal power—as Foucault allegedly sets sovereign and legal power in opposition to biopower, ultimately subordinating the former to the latter—by revivifying a persistent and illimitable sovereign power.

By resituating biopolitical life at the center of its network of power relations, modernity is simply the expression and the rendering visible of the "secret tie" uniting power and bare life, thereby inscribing the modern and the archaic into a common, continuous horizon. This return to a classical model is accomplished via a certain appropriation of Carl Schmitt's thought on sovereignty and exception: the emergence of biopolitics has to be read together with the reconstitution of politics through a structure of exception that simultaneously includes and excludes bare life from the political order. This structure of exception can already be found in Aristotle's definition of polis in terms of an opposition between bare life and good life, whereby bare life is included in the latter only to be excluded from political life. Thus Agamben can conclude: "The fundamental categorical pair of Western politics is [...] that of bare life/political existence, zoē/bios, exclusion/inclusion. There is politics because man is the living being who, in his own language, separates and opposes himself to his own bare life and, at the same time, maintains himself in a relation to that bare life in an inclusive exclusion" (*Homo Sacer*, p. 8).

Although the sovereign and homo sacer, the two figures of inclusive exclusion, were already implied in the classical political order, they are radicalized in the modern political order insofar as "the state of exception comes more and more to the fore as the fundamental political structure and begins to become the rule"(*Homo Sacer*, p. 20). The state of exception, as the zone of indiscernibility between inside and outside, becomes the *nomos* of modernity, functioning within and in place of the "normal" political order. It is in this "absolute indistinction of fact and law" that the exception becomes the norm, and the paradigmatic site and materialization of this indistinction is the Nazi concentration camp: it attests to the final absorption of politics into biopolitics. "Insofar as the inhabitants were stripped of every political status and wholly reduced to bare life, the camp was also the most absolute biopolitical space ever to have been realized, in which power confronts nothing but pure life, without any mediation" (*Homo Sacer*, p. 171).

Agamben thus seems to suggest an almost straight line of progression between the ancient figure of the homo sacer and the inhabitants of concentration camps (including their most extreme figure, the Muselmann), as well as contemporary forms of zones of indistinction marked by the very same logic of inclusion through exclusion. The intelligibility of the Nazi concentration camp is that it fulfills, exemplifies, and is utterly continuous with that very metaphysical logic that has been prepared from the beginning of the classical political order.

It is this representation of Western history as "uniform, one-directional, and rectilinear, [...] as uninterrupted historical and philo-sophical continuity,"[16] that allows Agamben in an Adornian manner to signify Auschwitz as the essential completion of biopolitics, a totality in which the pall of bare life is about to encompass all in a "catastrophe" (*Homo Sacer*, p. 20). It marks the point at which politics has been totally transformed into biopolitics, so much so that a differentiation "between our biological body and our political body" seems no longer possible (p. 171). Yet this very moment of catastrophe contains in itself and at the same time the revelation of a mutation of the existing situation, which is also something like its redemption: "In the state of exception become the rule, the life of homo sacer, which was the correlate of sov-ereign power, turns into an existence over which power no longer seems to have any hold" (p. 153).

Agamben's essential reading of biopolitics in terms of its epochal situ-ation thus posits Auschwitz as the turning "where bare life must instead be transformed into the site for the constitution and installation of a form of life that is wholly exhausted in bare life and a *bios* that is its own *zoē*" (*Homo Sacer*, p. 188).

However, the site of Auschwitz is not only the apotheosis of biopolitics and its turning, but it marks also a certain turning toward poetry, simi-lar to that found in Adorno and Heidegger. For it is ultimately poetry, says Agamben in *Remnants of Auschwitz*, that, precisely as remaining language, is capable of bearing witness by bearing witness to the impos-sibility of bearing witness.[17] Agamben writes: "Poets—witnesses—found language as what remains, as what actually survives the possibility, or impossibility, of speaking."[18]

It is in and through poetry that one can bear witness to Auschwitz (and the Muselmann), for, as Agamben suggests, poetry renders exactly the experience of desubjectivization and subjectivization (the figures of the Muselmann and of the survivor) in the medium of language:

> The experience of the poet [...] affirms that [...] poetry and life [...] become absolutely indistinct at the point of their reciprocal desubjectivization. And—at that point—they are united not immedi-ately but in a medium. This medium is language. The poet is he who, in the word, produces life. Life, which the poet produces in the poem,

withdraws from both the living experience of the psychosomatic individual and the biological unsayability of the species.

(*Remnants of Auschwitz*, p. 93)

Of course, the kind of poetry that Agamben evokes is one that, as in Heidegger, has somehow remained/survived as the exceptional locus for thinking historicity—a locus that is, perhaps similar to what Schmitt calls a borderline concept, situated at the limit of the completion of the aesthetic itinerary. Agamben's (Heideggerian) claim is that aesthetics has not only approached a kind of completion, but that this completion marks at the same time a turning point: "And if it is true that the fundamental architectural problem becomes visible only in the house ravaged by fire, then perhaps we are today in a privileged position to understand the authentic significance of the Western aesthetic project."[19] This "privileged" or exceptional position from which poetry/art reveals a "surpassing" of aesthetics is, once again, effected by the rhetorical figure of an extreme position revealing its opposite: the moment of (aesthetic) danger is where the saving power (of poetry/art) grows.

Furthermore, it is at this catastrophic point that poetry/art gives back to man "the very space in which he can take the original measure of his dwelling in the present and recover each time the meaning of his action" (*Man Without Content*, p. 114). Agamben locates this *"Umkehr"* for instance in Kafka's reversal of Benjamin's image of the "angel of history": "The angel has already arrived in Paradise" (*Man Without Content*, p. 112). Hence what is announced here is a replacement of the idea of history as empty continuum with the image of a history in which the state of exception—the perpetual day of the Last Judgment—has become history's rule. Thus Agamben's examination of both the completion of sovereign biopolitics and of aesthetics presents two streams of argument that coincide or mirror each other in this moment of catastrophic turning. That is, in the moment of catastrophe it is poetry/art that disrupts progressive history in its sovereign-biopolitical and aesthetic completion, and messianically sets in motion another kind of history. If poetry/art authorizes history in such a messianic sense, then it can recover itself, as if it had not been sundered by biopolitics/aesthetics. Poetry/art as the possibility of the real state of exception can (continue to) depose in a messianic manner the logic of sovereign biopolitics.

Thus one could, perhaps, say that the catastrophes of Adorno's administered society, of Heidegger's *Ge-stell*, and of Agamben's sovereign biopolitics receive their respective figures from the position of some messianism as some kind of ultimate horizon, of some however spectralized "big Other." Moreover, these messianisms seem to be driven by the urge to "catastrophize"; Slavoj Žižek describes this even as a "favorite twentieth-century intellectual exercise" that, for him, characterizes Adorno's, Heidegger's, and Agamben's different philosophical endeavors:

> Whatever the actual situation, it had to be denounced as "catastrophic," and the better it appeared, the more it encouraged this exercise—in this way, irrespective of our "merely ontic" differences, we all participate in the same ontological catastrophe. Heidegger denounced the present age as that of the highest "danger," the epoch of accomplished nihilism; Adorno and Horkheimer saw in it the culmination of the "dialectic of enlightenment" in the "administered world"; Giorgio Agamben defines the twentieth-century concentration camps as the "truth" of the entire Western political project.[20]

And he then proposes the following "radical reading of this syndrome": "What if what these unfortunate intellectuals cannot bear is the fact that they lead a life which is basically happy, safe, and comfortable, so that, in order to justify their higher calling, they have to construct a scenario of radical catastrophe?" (*Puppet and Dwarf*, pp. 153–4). Of course, as Žižek himself points out, these things cannot be explained in such an easy manner by what seems to be a mere argument ad hominem; rather, the ambiguity presented by all three thinkers regarding the relationship between the ontological catastrophe and ontic catastrophes is to be taken seriously. Žižek thus claims that what has to be examined first is the notion of historical time that is operative in traditional catastrophic narratives. In order to do so, he suggests distributing the notion of catastrophe along the two axes of "impossible but not real" and "real but no longer impossible".

Either it is experienced as impossible but not real (the prospect of a forthcoming catastrophe that, however, probable we know it is, we do not believe will really happen, and thus dismiss it as impossible) or as real but no longer impossible (once the catastrophe happens, it is "renormalized," perceived as part of the normal run of things, as always-already having been possible) (*Puppet and Dwarf*, p. 160).

And he concludes:

> What is unthinkable within this horizon of linear historical evolution is the notion of a choice/act that retroactively opens up its own possibility: the idea that the emergence of a radically New retroactively changes the past— not the actual past, of course (we are not

in the realms of science fiction), but past possibilities, or, to put it in more formal terms, the value of modal propositions about the past.

(p. 160)

In order to account for the retroactive transformation of the past through the act, Žižek takes recourse to Jean-Pierre Dupuy's concept of the "time of a project" that constitutes a break with the traditional "historical" notion of temporality. Dupuy's notion describes a "closed circuit between past and future: the future is causally produced by our acts in the past, while the way we act is determined by our anticipation, and our reaction to this anticipation"(*Puppet and Dwarf*, pp. 160–1). In order to conceptualize catastrophe, one has therefore to inscribe it "into the future in a much more radical way. One has to render it unavoidable" (p. 162). Consequently, the inscription of catastrophe in terms of the "closed circuit between past and future" means adopting the standpoint of a catastrophe that is projected as unavoidable in such a way that one can retroactively inscribe into the past of the future catastrophe counterfactual possibilities that then form the basis for the actions in the present (p. 164).

What is, then, the relationship between this conceptualization of catastrophe and the closed circuit that is operative in the wide-spread phenomenon of conspiracy theories that attempt to think or cognitively map the impossible totality of the catastrophic contemporary system of late capitalism? As Fredric Jameson has claimed, conspiracy theories are to be understood as responses to what is perceived as impersonal forces and diffuse structures generated by contemporary late capitalism.[21] Jameson demonstrates that conspiracy theories can constitute "an unconscious, collective effort to figure out where we are and what landscapes and forces confront us in a late twentieth century whose abominations are heightened by their concealment and their bureaucratic impersonality" (Jameson, p. 3). Moreover, conspiracy theories often contain implicitly a broader account of politics as a totality: "For it is ultimately always of the social totality itself that it is a question in representation, and never more than in the present age of a multinational global corporate network" (Jameson, p. 4).

Žižek, too, holds that the dismissal of conspiracy theories as "irrational," "anti-modernist" or even "proto-Fascist" accounts of catastrophe might be too simple, insofar as "they function, rather, as a kind of floating signifier which can be appropriated by different political options, enabling them to obtain a minimal cognitive mapping."[22] Moreover, an easy dismissal of conspiracy theories might overlook real "conspiracies" in the age of the virtual realities of late

capitalism. That is: "the dismissal of the 'paranoid' ideological dimension of conspiracy theories (the supposition of a mysterious all-powerful
Master) should alert us to actual 'conspiracies' going on all the time.
Today, the ultimate ideology would be the self-complacent critico-
ideological dismissal of all conspiracies as mere fantasies."[23] Thus, Žižek
seems to suggest that conspiracy theories can sometimes render the
world more complex by focusing on hidden and contradictory logics,
and by proposing alternative conceptual means. In this, he echoes Jodi
Dean's contention that conspiracy theories can help us to "think glo-
bally and act locally."[24] That is to say:

> The so-called distortions and imaginative leaps of conspiracy theo-
> ries may be helpful tools for coding politics in the virtual realities of
> the techno-global information age. Not least because we've lost the
> conditions under which we can tell the difference: the increase in
> information brought about by global telecommunications disrupts
> the production of a normalized, hegemonic field of the normal
> against which distortions can be measured. The accusation of distor-
> tion is thus revealed as a play of power, one often made on the part
> of a dominant group against those who may perceived themselves as
> threatened, marginalized, or oppressed, as harmed by the devices of
> associations so inaccessible they may as well be secret. [...] Without
> theorizing conspiracy it may not be possible to confront political
> actions, to realize that struggles have already begun.
>
> (Dean, pp. 144–5)

Žižek recognizes the significance of conspiracy theories for a diagnosis
of the decline of symbolic efficiency in the "paranoiac reality" of late
capitalism: conspiracy theories invoke catastrophic scenarios so as to
respond to the nonexistence of the big Other by installing an "Other
of the Other":

> The paradoxical result of the mutation in the nonexistence of the big
> Other [...] is [...] the proliferation of different versions of a big Other
> that actually exists, in the Real, not merely as a symbolic fiction. [...]
> The distrust of the big Other (the order of symbolic fictions), the
> subject's refusal to "take it seriously" [today], relies on the belief
> that there is an "Other of the Other," that a secret, invisible and all-
> powerful agent actually "pulls the strings" [...]: behind the visible,
> public Power there is another, obscene, invisible power structure.
> This other, hidden agent acts the part of the "Other of the Other" in

the Lacanian sense, the part of the meta-guarantee of the big Other
(the symbolic order that regulates social life).

(*Ticklish Subject*, p. 362)

To return to Adorno, Heidegger, and Agamben, could one thus suggest that Adorno's "administered society," Heidegger's "*Ge-stell*" and
Agamben's "sovereign biopolitics" represent different versions of the
way conspiracy theories install some kind of "Other of the Other?"
That is, is their claim that the contemporary social order presents a kind
of closed totality not precisely dependent on the implicit assumption
of a "possibility of conspiracy?" Not entirely: while all three deploy
catastrophic narratives that seem to be very close to suggesting some
invisible power structure pulling the strings in the background, they
supplement to the vision of a closed totality characterizing conspiracy
theories the exceptional place of some messianic Otherness that,
although no determinate political agent acting its part must be allowed
to occupy it, nonetheless somehow keeps open and alive the promise
of some redemptive leap. It is precisely here that Žižek adds a Lacanian
twist to the way in which one should relate to catastrophe: reminding
us of Lacan's *l'objet petit a*, he stresses that one has to take into account
precisely the unforeseeable—grace, the event of the act—as that very cut
that "prevents the full closure of the circle" (*Puppet and Dwarf*, p. 162).
And precisely here lies the crux of the catastrophic narratives of Adorno,
Heidegger, and Agamben: that is, how do they relate to the (possibility
or the "miracle" of the) act enacting what, from the messianic perspective, must remain impossible?

Adorno's democratic politics of remembrance is characterized by the prohibition of any revolutionary "ontological" politics, insofar as the latter can
only evoke the spectre of totalitarianism. However, this seems to suggest
that "totalitarianism" functions here as an ideological notion that wants to
dismiss in advance any attempt to show how the liberal-democratic order
participates in those very phenomena that it officially condemns:

[T]he moment one shows a minimal sign of engaging in political
projects that aim seriously to change the existing order, the answer
is immediately: "Benevolent as it is, this will necessarily end in a new
Gulag!" The "return to ethics" in today's political philosophy shame-
fully exploits the horrors of the Gulag or Holocaust as the ultimate
bogey for blackmailing us into renouncing all serious radical engagement. In this way, conformist liberal scoundrels can find hypocritical
satisfaction in their defense of the existing order: they know there

is corruption, exploitation, and so on, but every attempt to change things is denounced as ethically dangerous and unacceptable, recalling the ghosts of Gulag or Holocaust.[25]

Regarding Adorno's gesture that aims at maintaining the spectral openness named democracy before the background of a non-violent reconciliation and at resisting the lure of an identitarian closure in the name of the nonidentical—that figures as the (im-)possibility of each identity thinking—Žižek poses the decisive question: "what if there is a need for a minimal ontological support of the very dimension of spectrality, for some inert *peu de réel* which sustains the spectral opening?" (*Ticklish Subject*, p. 238). From this, Žižek then draws the decisive conclusion against Adorno's democracy—formulated on the basis of a negative messianism—and its attempt to forever keep at a distance the monstrosity of "absolute abstract negativity," one of the names of Žižek's act: "[...] this monstrous moment of absolute abstract negativity, this self-destructive fury which washes away every positive Order, has always-already happened, since it is the very foundation of the positive rational order of human society" (p. 238). The impossible, Žižek wagers, has always-already happened.

Moreover, Adorno's emphasis on the spectral-messianic of a democratic, redeemed society whose effect is the blockage of any radical break betrays, perhaps, also a certain blindness to the fact that the spectrality of democracy might be complicit with spectral capitalism. For could one not claim that Adorno's all too totalizing account of late capitalism might actually be the description of the fantasy of capital itself? That is, is Adorno's presentation of late capitalism as a fully monolithic economic and societal structure not the very mirror-image of the way late capitalism wants to appear to itself? Adorno's all too great proximity to the "self-understanding" or fantasy of capitalism could then be further explained in terms of his suspension of the (political) significance of the economic realm: that is, Adorno dismisses economy as the site of struggle and political intervention. What therefore eludes him due to his suspension of (Marx's) critique of political economy is that (liberal) democracy is nothing but the political form of capitalism. This is the price that Adorno has to pay for giving up the analysis of the antagonistic logic of the economico-political process in favor of his philosophico-anthropological reading of instrumental reason as the quasi-transcendental principle of the catastrophe that is Western civilization. Moreover, it is precisely this displacement from a socio-political analysis of the concrete social relations in late capitalism to some kind of negative anthropology that accounts also for the "scandal" of Adorno's—and the Frankfurt School's—reductive interpretation of Stalinism as simply a version of a bureaucratic, administered society with "totalitarian" character. Žižek remarks:

> "Stalinism" (that is, Really Existing Socialism) was thus, for the Frankfurt School, a traumatic topos apropos of which it had to remain silent—this silence was the only way for them to retain the inconsistency of their position of underlying solidarity with Western liberal democracy, without losing their official guise of "radical" leftist critique. Openly acknowledging this solidarity would have deprived them of their "radical" aura, changing them into yet another version of Cold War anti-Communist leftist liberals, while showing too much sympathy for Really Existing Socialism would have forced them to betray their unacknowledged basic commitment.[26]

Žižek formulates a similar critique of what he considers to be Heidegger's renunciation of the constitutive dimension of the political. While he points out that one crucial difference between Adorno and Heidegger is that, in contrast to Adorno, Heidegger's concern seems to be exclusively with the ontological catastrophe and not with mere ontic catastrophes, he quickly reminds us that, in contrast to Adorno's suspension of any political engagement, Heidegger's involvement with National Socialism has to be understood as the attempt to identify a concrete ontic political engagement that would best suit and is closest to the ontological truth (of the catastrophe) of the essence of technology:

> Until about 1935, he thought that Nazism did provide a unique solution of how, on the one hand, thoroughly to embrace modern technology, work, and mobilization, while simultaneously including them in an "authentic" political act of a people choosing its fate, acting on a decision, and so on. So we have technology, not aseptic traditionalism, but combined with roots, *Volk*, authentic decision, not *das Man*—in contrast to the Russian and American versions, which, each in its own way, betrays this authentic dimension (either in liberal individualism or in mass mobilization).[27]

And as Žižek immediately adds, even after 1935, when Heidegger no longer ascribed some kind of transcendental "dignity" to Nazism, he continued to appreciate it "as the most radical version to enable modern man to confront technology" (*Parallax View*, p. 284). What is more, even Heidegger's famous turn toward *Gelassenheit*, supposedly marking his philosophical disentanglement and turn away from his former involvement with National Socialism as the culmination of the metaphysics of subjectivity, remains complicit with what it attempts to overcome. Similar to Adorno's notion of the instrumentally closed administered society, Heidegger's concept of the *Ge-stell*, of technology, also conceals the antagonism of capitalism; in Heidegger's case, however, this concealment is brought about by the reduction of economy to the closed realm of the oikos:[28]

> When Heidegger talks about technology, he systematically ignores the whole sphere of modern "political" economy, although modern technology is not only empirically, but in its very concept, rooted in the market dynamics of generating surplus-value. The underlying principle which impels the unrelenting drive of modern productivity is not technological, but economic: it is the market and commodity principle of surplus-value which condemns capitalism to the crazy dynamics of permanent self-revolutionizing. Consequently, it is not possible to grasp the dynamics of modernity without what Marx called the "critique of political economy."
>
> (*Parallax View*, p. 277)

That is to say, Heidegger's commitment to the Nazi movement must be read precisely as the commitment to capitalism-cum-community. And this commitment reveals itself as the simultaneous recognition of the basic condition of the political—that, for Žižek, is characterized by the lack of any ontological guarantee—and its disavowal by filling up the abyss of the political act via the reference to the Master-signifier of the German *Volk*. And *Gelassenheit*, "the humble subordination to and listening to the voice of Being" (*Parallax View*, p. 280), only exacerbates this problem, insofar as it functions as capitalism's perfect ideological supplement; for *Gelassenheit* is ultimately a fetishistic attitude: it suggests that one should fully accept the technological world. However, this engagement occurs on the basis of a fetish (the fetish of poetic thinking) that allows for some kind of distance, thereby not only weakening the impact of the catastrophe of technology, but also preparing silently for the possible arrival of the gods.

Both Adorno and Heidegger seem to argue that the catastrophe that instrumental reason and technological calculative thought have brought onto mankind is so total that it is no longer possible even to imagine alternatives to the current social organization. The only "alternatives" are either to surrender to a "quasi-totalitarian" administered society and *Ge-stell* on the one hand, or to wait passively for some messianic light to intrude upon contemporary closed society. What is thus tacitly acknowledged is that late capitalism is here to stay, that it has closed the space of political struggle, and any attempt to perform a critique of its political economy is presented as ultimately beside the point.

This absence of any analysis of contemporary political economy, of a radical re-politicization of the economy, also marks Agamben's homo sacer project.[29] In contrast to Foucault, who always insisted that bio-power is an indispensable element in the development of capitalism, Agamben seems not at all concerned with an analysis of the relationship between biopolitics and (late) capitalism; instead, he is content with an account of modernity in terms of a world-historical catastrophe that began with the Western state and culminated and revealed itself fully in the National Socialist concentration camps. By omitting the question of political economy, Agamben cuts the link between political economy, government and population that, according to Foucault, can help to explain how the biopolitical conditioning of both individuals and populations has been coordinated in such a way as to extract surplus-value and surplus-power from the relationships both between men and between men and things.

This may also be the reason why Agamben inscribes the political struggle no longer within the realm of (political) economy, but rather within the realm of law. I already suggested that *Homo Sacer* contains some hints as to a "new or coming politics" as an exit from sovereign biopolitics. However, these are mostly intimations regarding the notion of life-form as a life from which bare life can no longer be separated, thereby eluding external decision and the sovereign ban—represented by the homo sacer and his incarnations: the Muselmann, the outlaw, the stateless subject[30]—and the possibility of a real state of exception.

Regarding the real state of exception, Agamben remarks: "Law that becomes indistinguishable from life in a real state of exception is confronted by life that, in a symmetrical but inverse gesture, is entirely transformed into law" (*Homo Sacer*, p. 55). Bare life and the law, the two poles that are distinguished and linked by the sovereign ban (the actually existing, virtual state of exception), are abolished by the real state of exception and thus can pass into a new dimension that, from the messianic perspective, means the coincidence of the absolute fulfilment or consumption of the law and its overcoming (Geulen, pp. 102–11).

Agamben's distinction between the actually existing, virtual state of exception and the real state of exception is owed to Walter Benjamin's eighth thesis in "Theses on the Philosophy of History." It states: "The tradition of the oppressed teaches us that the 'state of exception' in which we live is the rule. We must arrive at a concept of history that corresponds to this fact. Then we will have the production of the real state of exception before us as a task."[31] However, while Benjamin still conceived the real state of exception in the political terms of the Proletarian general strike and of revolution, Agamben dissolves Benjamin's concrete political references, insofar as the real state of emergency is no longer brought about by political struggles, but rather—and exclusively—by the Messiah (*Giorgio Agamben zur Einführung*, p. 81). But this messianic hope to radically break the circle of law and violence essential to the actually existing, virtual state of exception represents, for Žižek, a kind of "abstract negation" that resembles the "utopian longing for the *ganz Andere*": that is, a complacent waiting "for the miraculous explosion of the 'divine violence'" (*Parallax View*, p. 266, p. 267). Moreover, it points to a problematic understanding of the law in Agamben. This is why Žižek turns to Agamben's reading of the Pauline account of the law in messianic time (*Puppet and Dwarf*, p. 4).

In *The Time That Remains*, Agamben establishes a structural homology between the Pauline messianic time and the (Schmittian) state of exception:[32] both are characterized by similar indeterminacies and indistinctions. In the case of the state of exception as suspension of the law, one finds an indistinction regarding the inside and the outside of the law; in the case of Paul's conception of messianic time, the indistinction emerges in the relation between the Pauline law of faith that holds in messianic time and the existing law that is precisely suspended, insofar as the law of faith uses the latter without being held by its legal obligations.[33] Žižek then poses the decisive question regarding the "pure potentiality" of the law of faith: that is, does Agamben "not thereby delineate the opposition between Law and its superego excess-supplement?" (*Puppet and Dwarf*, p. 110). That is to say, is Pauline love just the other side of "the obscene superego Law that cannot be executed and specified into particular regulations?"(*Puppet and Dwarf*, p. 111).

In contrast to Agamben, Žižek then claims that what the "Pauline emergency suspends is not so much the explicit Law regulating our daily life, but, precisely its obscene unwritten underside" (*Puppet and Dwarf*, p. 113). Ultimately it is his contention that Agamben's account of Pauline love as supplementing, completing and thereby overcoming law remains stuck in the double of law as external imposition and of the exception as the space located outside the law. In short, Agamben's reading perpetuates the "masculine" version of the state of exception in that he neglects how Pauline love "is a stance toward law from within law, from a place that posits no outside into which one might fantasize escape. [...] Such an immersion transforms law from a field held in place by an exception into a field that is non-all (in the sense that it cannot be totalized or completed)" (*Žižek's Politics*, p. 164). In this respect, Pauline love can even be rendered in terms of Benjamin's "pure" revolutionary violence because both insist that "the rule of law is 'non-all,' that is to say, not everything is subject to the rule of law, precisely because there is no exception, no outside to the law to ground universality" (*Iraq*, p. 160).

And the same goes for the field in which, according to Žižek, the "true" political struggles have to be fought. If the Law does not exist, then the same goes for late capitalist society. Following Laclau and Mouffe, Žižek holds that society also cannot be rendered in terms of a (catastrophic) totality because any supposed totality could only be guaranteed from some point of exception. Thus, it does not suffice to simply inscribe the exception into the frame of totality, for this would leave that frame unchanged and, by securing some place and right (of difference) for that exception, perpetuate identity politics. Rather, what has to be affirmed through the recognition that late capitalist society "does not exist" is the very vertical antagonism cutting through late capitalist society: an antagonism that is constitutive of the latter and that Žižek designates as—class struggle.

Late capitalist society is thus "non-all"; there is no outside to it in the form of a messianic, catastrophic breakdown; rather, the "catastrophe" has already occurred "in" capitalism. Therefore, "it is not only a question of the 'universality' of capitalism but that of an even wider 'universality'— let us call it class struggle—of which capitalism is only a part, and which renders it 'not-all'."[34] This means that the notion of class struggle is, first, "the perfect example of what Lacan means by not-all, no exception but precisely for this reason you cannot totalize it."[35] Furthermore: "What does class struggle mean? Every position we assume towards the class struggle, even a theoretical one, is already a moment of the class struggle. [...] In this precise sense, we can say [...] class struggle doesn't exist since there is no exception, no element eluding it" (*Interrogating the Real*, p. 73). This can explain Žižek's rendition of the concept of class struggle in terms of the Real, compelling him to the conclusion that "there is no class struggle 'in reality': 'class struggle' designates the very antagonism that prevents the objective (social) reality from constituting itself as a self-enclosed whole" (*Interrogating the Real*, p. 263).

As there is thus no objective logic to Capital, there can also be no objective logic to the catastrophic account of capitalism, insofar as "complications arising from the intricate texture of concrete situations and/or from the unanticipated results of 'subjective' interventions always derail the straight course of things" (*Interrogating the Real*, p. 105). In other words, what the catastrophic narratives of the administered society, of the *Ge-stell*, and of sovereign biopolitics accept in advance is some inherent crisis logic of Capital that has managed to subsume class struggle under itself, and in the face of which they can then only invoke some messianic turning. Against these appeals to some exceptional messianic position (represented by some Other "agency" to the administrative society, the *Ge-stell*, or sovereign biopolitics) that has, allegedly, not been ravaged by late capitalism, Žižek suggests a re-conceptualization of class struggle that no longer falls prey to an ontologization of both Capital and class (struggle). He writes:

> Although there is a link between the working class as a social group and the proletariat as the position of the militant fighting for universal Truth, this link is not a determining causal connection, and the two levels are to be strictly distinguished. To be proletarian involves assuming a certain subjective stance [...] that, in principle, can occur to any individual; [...] any individual can be touched by grace and interpellated as a proletarian subject.
>
> (*Universal Exception*, p. 199)

What is more, class struggle is already present in (late) capitalism precisely in its "utopian" dimensions. This is the reason why he draws the political lesson "to summon up the strength [...] to practice utopia" (*Iraq*, p. 179), to remain faithful to the antagonism that traverses late capitalism and renders it "non-all." To remain faithful to the antagonism that class struggle means, ultimately, to insist on the collective struggle to discern (and identify with) those "symptomal" points that mark the cracks within the late capitalist edifice. It is only from these cracks—those "social groups" excluded from the contemporary socioeconomic order—that light can fall on the possibility of the mobilization toward the act, toward a point from which concrete universality can be asserted. Therefore, our contemporary political plight might be decided by the way in which we relate or stand to the following two questions: "Are we still able to commit the act proper [...]? Which social agent is, on account of its radical dislocation, today able to accomplish it?" (*Universal Exception*, p. 118).[36]

Notes

1. See the section on "methodological questions" at the beginning of Alain Badiou's *Le Siècle* (Paris: Éditions du Seuil, 2005).
2. The philosophical discourse on the twentieth century as catastrophe is, of course, not limited to those three seminal figures. One could, for instance, also refer in this context to the works of Jean Baudrillard and of Paul Virilio.
3. Max Horkheimer, Theodor W. Adorno, *Dialectic of Enlightenment*, edited by Gunzelin Schmid Noerr; translated by Edmund Jephcott (Stanford: Stanford University Press, 2002), p. xiv.
4. Theodor W. Adorno, *Minima Moralia*, translated by E. F. N. Jephcott (NLB, 1974), p. 44. Henceforth cited in the text as *Minima Moralia*.
5. Theodor W. Adorno, *Negative Dialectics*, translated by E. B. Ashton (NY/London: Continuum, 2003), p. 320. Henceforth cited in the text as *Negative Dialectics*.
6. I follow here the first chapter in Josh Cohen's *Interrupting Auschwitz: Art, Religion & Philosophy* (London, NY: Continuum, 2002).
7. Jacques Derrida, *Politics of Friendship*, translated by George Collins (London, NY: Verso, 1997), p. 306.
8. On this point, see my "Auschwitz-Politik," in *Derrida und Adorno: Zur Aktualität von Dekonstruktion und Frankfurter Schule*, edited by Eva Waniek-Laquiéze and Erik M. Vogt (Vienna: Turia + Kant, 2008), pp. 37–69.
9. Alain Badiou, *Saint Paul: The Foundation of Universalism*, translated by Ray Brassier (Stanford: Stanford University Press, 2003), p. 44. Henceforth cited in the text as *Saint Paul*.
10. Miguel de Beistegui, *The New Heidegger* (London and NY: Continuum, 2005), p. 106. Henceforth cited in the text as *The New Heidegger*.
11. Martin Heidegger, *The Principle of Reason* (Bloomington and Indianapolis: Indiana University Press, 1991), p. 121.
12. Martin Heidegger, *The Question Concerning Technology and Other Essays*, translated and introduced by William Lovitt (NY: Harper & Row, 1977), pp. 26–7. Henceforth cited in the text as *The Question*.
13. Martin Heidegger, *Identity and Difference*, translated by Joan Stambaugh (NY: Harper & Row, 1969), pp. 36–7.
14. Gianni Vattimo, *Nihilism and Emancipation: Ethics, Politics, and Law*, edited by Santiago Zabala; translated By William McCuaig (NY: Columbia University Press, 2004), p. 16.
15. Giorgio Agamben, *Homo Sacer: Sovereign Power and Bare Life*, translated. by Daniel Heller-Roazen (Stanford: Stanford University Press, 1998), p. 6. Henceforth cited in the text as *Homo Sacer*.
16. Andreas Kalyvas, "The Sovereign Waver: Beyond the Camp," in *Politics, Metaphysics, and Death: Essays On Giorgio Agamben's Homo Sacer*, edited by Andrew Norris (Durham and London: Duke University Press, 2005), pp. 107–34 (p. 111).
17. On this reduplication of the catastrophic in politics and aesthetics see my "S/Citing the Camp," in *Politics, Metaphysics, and Death* (see Kalyvas above), pp. 74–106.
18. Giorgio Agamben, *Remnants of Auschwitz: The Witness and the Archive*, translated by Daniel Heller-Roazen (NY: Zone Books, 1999), p. 161. Henceforth cited in the text as *Remnants of Auschwitz*.

19. Giorgio Agamben, *The Man Without Content*, translated by Georgia Albert (Stanford: Stanford University Press, 1999), p. 6. Henceforth cited in the text as *Man Without Content*.

20. Slavoj Žižek, *The Puppet and the Dwarf: The Perverse Core of Christianity* (Cambridge, Mass.; London: MIT Press, 2003), p. 153. Henceforth cited in the text as *Puppet and Dwarf*.

21. See Fredric Jameson, *The Geopolitical Aesthetic: Cinema and Space in the World System* (Bloomington and Indianapolis: Indiana University Press, 1992).

22. Slavoj Žižek, *The Ticklish Subject: The Absent Centre of Political Philosophy* (London, NY: Verso, 1999), p. 362.

23. Slavoj Žižek, *Iraq: The Borrowed Kettle* (London, NY: Verso, 2004), pp. 78–9. Henceforth cited in the text as *Iraq*.

24. Jodi Dean, *Aliens In America: Conspiracy Cultures from Outerspace to Cyberspace* (Ithaca and London: Cornell University Press, 1998), p. 162. Henceforth cited in the text.

25. Judith Butler, Ernesto Laclau, Slavoj Žižek, *Contingency, Hegemony, Universality: Contemporary Dialogues on the Left* (London, NY: Verso, 2000), p. 127.

26. Slavoj Žižek, *The Universal Exception: Selected Writings, Volume Two*, edited by Rex Butler and Scott Stephens (London, NY: Continuum, 2006), p. 100. Henceforth cited in the text as *Universal Exception*.

27. Slavoj Žižek, *The Parallax View* (Cambridge, Mass.; London: MIT Press, 2006), p. 284. Henceforth cited in the text as *Parallax View*.

28. Arguably, Heidegger's reduction of economy to the domain of the "domestic"—based, perhaps, on an untenable reading of ancient Greek economy (when one compares it, for instance, to the very different account that one finds in the writings of Alfred Sohn-Rethel whose interpretation of ancient Greek economy deeply influenced Adorno)—marks a fundamental opposition to Adorno's insistence on the omnipresence of commodity society; nonetheless, both operate with an account of economy in terms of a closed positive totality.

29. Perhaps, then, one central aspect of Žižek's critique of Adorno, Heidegger, and Agamben can be condensed into his admonition: "It's the *political* economy, stupid!" See his *Ticklish Subject*, pp. 347–59.

30. Incidentally, Heidegger's *Dasein* is another important reference for Agamben's life-form, insofar as *Dasein* designates a unity characterized by the impossibility of maintaining the separation or distinction between being and mode of being, subject and predicate, life and world. I follow here Eva Geulen's incisive remarks in her *Giorgio Agamben zur Einführung* (Hamburg: Junius, 2005), pp. 102–111. Henceforth cited in the text.

31. Quoted in Agamben, *Homo Sacer*, p. 55.

32. Giorgio Agamben, *The Time That Remains: A Commentary on the Letter to the Romans*, translated by Patricia Dailey (Stanford: Stanford University Press, 2005).

33. This brief account of Žižek's critique of Agamben is deeply indebted to Jodi Dean, *Žižek's Politics* (NY and London: Routledge, 2006), p. 161.

34. Rex Butler, *Slavoj Žižek: Live Theory* (NY, London: Continuum, 2005), p. 120.

35. Slavoj Žižek, *Interrogating the Real*, edited by Rex Butler and Scott Stephens (London, NY: Continuum, 2005), p. 73. Henceforth cited in the text as *Interrogating the Real*.

36. Žižek, *The Universal Exception*, p. 118. Again, Žižek does not simply sever the tie between "social group" and "revolutionary collective"; rather, he interprets certain contemporary forms of societal organization—slum dwellers, the *favelas* etc.—in terms of their potential as "proletarian subject": that is, as sites for concrete universality. Of course, this does not denote some kind of social romanticism but rather requires the actualization of that potential through hard (theoretical) work and engaged struggles.

4
Breath of Relief: Peter Sloterdijk and the Politics of the Intimate

Sjoerd van Tuinen

There is a small section in *Sphären II: Globen* (*Spheres II: Globes*) titled "Merdocracy: On the Paradox of Immunity in Sedentary Cultures" in which Sloterdijk summarizes, *cum grano salis*, the fundamental tension, or "moral enigma," of all high cultures: "The atmospheric dilemma of sedentariness manifests itself in the fact that groups of humans that have bound themselves to houses and territories cannot avoid their own faeces and its aura of smell to the extent that seemed natural to prehistoric nomads."[1] Anthropologically speaking, a direct consequence of the "immune strategy" through which a sedentary population creates its own atmospheric comfort in artificial inside spaces of solidarity—"global spheres"—is that the source of immunological "stress" no longer resides only outside culture but also within. This misanthropic "paradox" between "community" and "immunity" is one of the pivotal points around which Sloterdijk's *magnum opus* titled *Sphären*, as well as many of his other recent books such as *Im Weltinnenraum des Kapitals* (*Inside the World Interior of Capital*) and *Zorn und Zeit* (*Rage and Time*), revolve.[2]

The whole of spherology must be read as a meditation on Heidegger's "existence contains an essential tendency towards proximity."[3] It is both an anthropology and a phenomeno-ontology of the *immersive intimacy* of being together (*Mit-Sein*):

> For [spherology], the following applies: the spirit of the place and the law of the latrine converge. [...] What phenomenologists have always characterized as *Lebenswelt*, following the late Husserl, must in fact—before the revolutionary deodorization of the last two centuries—be understood as a phenomenon of odour—to such an extent that the modern subject lacks the criteria for understanding it. [...]

The world of the living is a world of breathing, well said.[4] Yet what is the "sense" of breathing as long as the shared air of the sedentaries is under the ban of the midden? (*Sphären I*, p. 343). Not the night, which Heidegger honoured in linguistically and factually problematical ways, is the seamstress of being; it is the common cloaca which refers the village and the district self-inclusively to itself as a self-emanating and self-smelling "undivided, total world" and which rounds it off in itself.

(p. 348)

In an ever more densely populated, mediatized and urbanized world, in which "life equals the inhabitation of a gas-palace animated by entertainment poisons" (*Sphären III*, p. 187), it becomes the task of phenomenology to describe how the intimate has been "explicitated" and "domesticated" in the house of Being.[5] The hygienizing revolutions of modernity must be seen as a process which has resulted, for better or for worse, in the *explicit* receiving priority over the *implicit*, and in nature progressively being absorbed by culture. For Sloterdijk, the essence of modernity lies in its radical constructivism, which has led us not to a dangerous neglect of Being, but rather from "the human condition" to "air conditioning" and consequently to the realization that nowhere can it smell as bad as it does at home. If our faeces were indeed the first mass medium of sedentary culture, then what is needed now, in today's thoroughly mass-mediatized and informatized lifeworld, is a "critical theory of air" (*Sphären II*, p. 353). It is no coincidence that the words for rumors (*Gerüchte*) and smells (*Gerüche*), odium and odor, are etymologically related. Had Nietzsche not already explained to us, with exceptional olfaction, how the mass-medial latrine organizes the cohering smells of universally contagious resentment? (*Sphären II*, p. 350; see also *Nicht gerettet*, p. 93).

Socio-politically speaking, this means that if the mass-media today make an ever more irreplaceable and "unignorable smelly contribution to social synthesis as we know it today" (*Sphären II*, p. 350), it is of the utmost importance that the overtly manifest presence of intimate affections is also acknowledged *en plein publique*.[6] And in fact this presence has already become the shared concern of many politically orientated media theorists, by whom it is usually labeled "obscene" as opposed to the proper "scene" of what should be true politics. The aim of this essay is to distinguish Sloterdijk's position in the wider area of continental media theory by opposing his work to that of two authors who have most dominantly shaped the discourse on obscenity and with whom he is often compared, namely, Jean Baudrillard and Slavoj Žižek. For all three authors, obscenity is not a problem of too little communication, but rather of too much of a certain kind. Yet the conclusions they draw and the theoretical substrata from which these conclusions follow cannot be more different as they depend —as will be demonstrated—on their diverging theoretical assessments of the intimate.

Postpolitics and the obscene object of postmodernity

In "The Future of Politics," Žižek argues that a new public or collective space has appeared in which the standard opposition between private and public is no longer valid: this is the paradoxical space of "shared, collective privacy."[7] What we call privacy today has nothing to do with a small and well-protected sphere of authenticity. Traditionally, critical theory teaches us that the more we claim our right to privacy, the less there remains of it. And indeed, today the ultimate withdrawal into privacy is a public confession of intimate secrets on a television program: "Be yourself!," "Express yourself!"[8] Foucault's lesson that the experience of subjective freedom is already a subjection to disciplinary mechanisms is ultimately the obscene fantasmatic underside of the official "public" ideology of freedom and autonomy (*Desert of the Real*, p. 96). Žižek calls this paradoxical situation, in which self-expression becomes self-repression, "interpassivity," a substitute notion for the far more common and politically legitimating notion of interactivity. Far more than mere passivity, interpassivity critically reflects the lack of subjective distance that is essential to any position in-between.[9]

Yet this new, collective privacy is not old-fashioned exhibitionism. Rather, it slides ever more into a state resembling Leibniz's ontological vision of monadology.[10] Baudrillard interprets this state as "the end of the social," while Sloterdijk describes it as a world of "foams," where every bubble is an egocentric and asocial "dyad" within an aggregate condensed by mass-media and information technology. Any direct encounter with the Other has been supplanted by what Žižek, with Rancière, terms post-politics: a depoliticized politics based entirely on pragmatic negotiations, "obscene mathematics" (*Desert of the Real*, p. 52), and singular strategic compromises that neglect real and ideological antagonisms, and which simply exclude the Other from its own expanding obscenity. Another definition of obscene politics is, therefore, the wide-scale "zombification" of European social democracy.[11] It is the price the Left pays for renouncing any radical political project and for accepting market capitalism as the only game in town. If politics is the art of the impossible, as Žižek claims, post-politics is a negation of the political—a political indifference. What remains, then, are "exotic" and violent methods for making politics, in which the rational public sphere and the irrational private sphere intertwine. Hooliganism and terrorism are brought together as obscene phenomena that lack "rational" antagonism. A real or authentic act can now only be understood as an irrational act. Any renewed interest in civil society is also delusive. For Žižek, civil society is not a gentle, neutralized social movement but a legitimating network of a conservative moral majority. He criticizes the reaction of transparency in politics, the assumption of a firm ideological stance, claiming that "precisely in such moments of clarity of choice, mystification is total" (*Desert of the Real*, p. 54). However, while Neocons and Rightists openly engage in obscene politics, Leftists and Critical Theorists, Feminists and Anti-Globalists are scarcely any different when they plead for more open and rational communication in artificial environments devoid of power relations. Thus Žižek wonders if the opposition between Rightist populism and liberal tolerance actually exists, or whether they are only "two sides of the same coin," that is to say, indifference.

Such indifference is reflected in today's chief political fetish, democracy as the "Master-Signifier," which serves to render harmless all "real" social antagonisms in a new, radical mediocrity.[12] One of the great insights of Žižek's Lacanian dialectics is that obscenity is the great Counter-Signifier of democracy, and thus, in a dialectical sense, its own negative constituent. Between McWorld and Jihad is the "embarrassing third term": regimes such as those of the Saudis or the Pakistanis. They stand for the vanishing mediator, "the obscene object of postmodernity," which can no longer be denied but rather forces us to explicitly "acknowledge the primacy of economy over democracy" (*Desert of the Real*, p. 43).[13] In our culture of obscene permissivism and indifference, the superego has closer links with the id than with the ego. The Dutch populist politician Pim Fortuyn could play up his homosexuality to an almost preposterous level of camp, but what appears to be a carnivalesque subversion, this eruption of obscene freedom, really serves the *status quo*. Žižek detects an obscene underside to language, law, and politics that cannot be repressed and which continually returns to the surface (*Desert of the Real*, p. 27). He subscribes to Badiou's thesis when he states that the mark of the twentieth century was its "passion for the Real," its longing for an undeniably true experience. "The very core of the 'passion for the Real' is this identification with—this heroic gesture of fully assuming—the dirty obscene underside of Power: the heroic attitude of 'Somebody has to do the dirty work, so let's do it!,' a kind of mirror-reversal of the Beautiful Soul which refuses to recognize itself in its result" (*Desert of the Real*, p. 30). This cannot be called a "banality of evil" in Hannah Arendt's sense, where bureaucrats uncritically do whatever is asked of them. Rather, obscenity means that the dark underside is in no way kept discreet or secret (*Desert of the Real*, p. 136). Terrorism, like sexual privacy, is everywhere.

Transpolitics and the end of representation

Žižek has suggested that the absence of the Real cannot simply be asserted, nor can one take the attacks on, say, the World Trade Center as unambiguously real. If the modern passion for the Real ends up with the pure semblance of the political theater, in an exact inversion, the "postmodern" passion of the semblance (the indifference of Nietzsche's Last Man) ends up in a kind of Real. Terrorism does not confront us with the Real, but rather makes us identify with the fantasy or allows us to "traverse" it. This is also Baudrillard's understanding of the hyperreal: because the Real, in the society of the spectacle, has turned entirely into simulacrum, we postmodernists now know that reality is, in fact, only an improved appearance of itself. Modern media and information technologies serve to produce a hyperreality, a reality that is more real than the Real. The thrill of the Real is today's ultimate special effect. Reality does not produce the image; rather, it is the image that produces reality.

It is this demise of the scene or theater of the symbolic between the imaginary and the real that Baudrillard's notion of the obscene expresses.[14] Baudrillard defines the obscene as a full presence, without representation, and as a lack of spectatorial distance. "As in porn, a kind of zoom takes us too near the Real, which never existed and only ever came into view at *a certain distance*."[15] However, this must not be understood as voyeurism—as Žižek comes close to suggesting with his notion of collective privacy. The gaze is seductive only at a certain distance. Instead, we are dealing with an immanent, pre-subjective space of communication, the pornocratic realm of the masses. For Baudrillard, the overtly manifest presence of the political or the intimate in mass-media is the unambiguous sign of their disappearance. The contemporary swelling of both populist and technocratic political discourses, as well as globalized terrorism, is characterized by the fact that they do not represent anyone or anything. They therefore cannot constitute political acts in any traditional sense. In his earlier work, Baudrillard utilized the leading metaphor of obesity to denote this unbridled "proliferation" of the political. The more politics swells up, the more transparent it becomes until it finally ceases to exist. It has become, in other words, "transpolitical." A typical manifestation of this transpolitical state was found in the Dutch and French referenda on the constitution of the European Union. It illustrated our seduction by transpolitics, our immersion in it but, at the same time, it clearly showed how we are rendered completely politically inarticulate because of it. "The mass is dumb like beasts, and its silence is equal to the silence of beasts" (*In the Shadow*, p. 28).

Every attempt to reinstate a political scene, whether through governmental reorganization or terrorism, is doomed to exacerbate the situation, because symbolic exchange is no longer possible. If, as Žižek argues, terrorism is one of the sole potentially political acts remaining to us today, this is not only because it is completely irrational but also because, to the impotent hegemonic system, it is a gift that cannot be refused. It offers a "situational transfer" that covers up its own disfunctioning, such as in the so-called "war on terror." It provokes counter-reactions that, due to their hyperreal nature, can only lead to more terrorism. Baudrillard paraphrases Clausewitz: "war [Afghanistan, Iraq] is continuation of the absence of politics by other means" (*In the Shadow*, p. 34), concluding that "He who stakes his all on the spectacle will die by the spectacle."[16] Terrorism is contaminative, it is everything: political, criminal and religious; and everywhere: public and private. In dialectical terms of psychoanalysis, terrorism is obscene precisely because it puts an end to the scene of prohibition and its violation, and thus transcends the criminal act. It is not an old-fashioned power of force—remember, Baudrillard wants to "forget" the Foucauldian perspective[17]—but is rather a symbolic challenge and outbidding of the other with fatal consequences. Abu Ghraib and all the "incidents" that followed demonstrate for Baudrillard and Zizek the obscene way in which democracy, by publicizing its own vices, restores its virtue. Therefore, far beyond ideology and politics, terrorist acts deconstruct the metaphysics of presence that has dominated modern democracies. "It is the tactic of the terrorist model to bring about an excess of reality, and have the system collapse beneath that excess of reality. The whole derisory nature of the situation, together with the violence mobilized by the system, turns back against it, for terrorists are both the exorbitant mirror of their own violence and the model of a symbolic violence forbidden to them, the only violence they cannot exert—that of their own death" (*In the Shadow*, p. 18). The consequence of the new hyperreality is that the politics of force has given way to a transpolitics of obscene images. We are no longer dealing with a "theatre of cruelty" (*In the Shadow*, p. 30), for the stage has long since evaporated. Rather, we are dealing with what Virilio calls "the exhibitionism of a total terrorist war" (*Ground Zero*, p. 25). Contemporary international politics has become "like an 'automatic writing' of terrorism, constantly refueled by the involuntary terrorism of news and information" (*In the Shadow*, p. 33). Baudrillard observes: "there isn't even a need for 'embedded journalists' any more; it's the military itself that is embedded in the image" (24).

Hyperpolitics and the disdain of the last man

Both Žižek's analysis of multiculturalist indifference and Baudrillard's analysis of mass-medial indifference bear strong resemblances to Sloterdijk's early analysis of cynicism, which appeared in the same year as Baudrillard's *The Fatal Strategies*. In his *Critique of Cynical Reason*, Sloterdijk speaks of a similar lack of distance which renders us indifferent.[18] He traces modern critical consciousness's fall into an "enlightened false consciousness" (*Cynical Reason*, p. 3), understood as participation in a "collective, realistically attuned way of seeing things" (p. 5) that follows after "naive ideologies and their enlightenment" (p. 3). Yet in fact the Enlightenment is blinded by its own light: a collective "realism" and an institutionalized "rationalism" have led to an exhausting self-preservation that leaves all idealistic or utopian critique in its wake. If the twentieth century was marked by our "passion for the Real," the success of enlightening and consciousness-raising critical interventions have led us to a premature resignation in the face of an overwhelming realism. In our world, "disburdened catastrophic and apocalyptically comfortable," only "the tonal keys of livability (*Lebbarkeit*) have become dominant."[19] Pragmatic paradoxes are the modus operandi of both our politicians and of philosophical critique. At worst, philosophical critique has become part of the same "alarm economy" and "text book gothic" that dominates mass medial rationality.[20]

Indifference ("*Beliebigkeit*," originally translated as "arbitrariness," *Cynical Reason*, p. 307) is the final outcome of what Habermas has labeled the structural transformation of the modern public sphere. This transformation consists of a transition from a medieval system of news gathering to a civil society based on novels, newspapers and salon culture. Today, this civil culture is progressively degrading into an "extremism of fatigue" (p. 308) where the zero-point of articulation is governed by new mass media "whose democratic mission it is to generate indifference." Sloterdijk distinguishes between a "twofold disinhibition": "the disinhibition of the portrayal (*Darstellung*) vis-à-vis what is portrayed, as well as of the disinhibition of the currents of information in relation to the consciousnesses that absorb them" (*Cynical Reason*, pp. 307–8). The first disinhibition is the old-fashioned, systematic exploitation by journalists of the catastrophes of others; the second is a far-reaching threat in the "anthropological sense" similar to the one we started out with: urbanization and information overload have resulted in a cynical world, that—in Sloterdijk's Marx-inspired formulation—"brings things into false equations, produces false samenesses of form and false samenesses of values (pseudo-equivalances) between everything and everyone, and thereby also achieves an intellectual disintegration and indifference" (*Cynical Reason*, p. 314).

It is this indifference that Sloterdijk also criticizes in *Die Verachtung der Massen* (*The Disdain of the Masses*). He first gives an historical account of the development of the notion of the masses. For Hobbes, being part of the mass is a question of the individual's subjection of himself and his self-esteem to an omnipotent sovereign. This implies a certain silencing of the individual's pride (*thymos*), along with his need to spontaneously confess to anyone willing to listen. Subjection, becoming a subject, means becoming a private person while leaving the making of history to others. Modernity, however, according to the usual Hegelian interpretations, has resulted in the emancipation of the masses, with the result that everything in mass culture has become public. And it is this modern mass-mediatized subject that now simply absorbs its surroundings into its opaque immanence, having become completely indifferent to history. Indifference is "the one and only principle of the masses," it is a "differential indifference" that forms "the formal secret of the masses and a culture that organizes a total middle" (*Die Verachtung*, p. 87), which always threatens to become "totalitarian" (p. 95). Instead of employing the concept of cynicism, Sloterdijk now distinguishes between two kinds of disdain to describe this suffocating indifference: one is a subjective kind of disdain, as formulated by "that great anti-journalist" Spinoza (*Die Verachtung*, p. 43), whereas the other, formulated by Nietzsche, "the thinker on stage" is objective (*Nicht gerettet*, pp. 28–9). Sloterdijk paraphrases a passage from Spinoza's *Ethics*: "Disdain is the imagining of some mass that makes so little impact on the mind that the presence of the mass motivates the mind to think of what is not in the mass rather than of what is in the mass" (*Die Verachtung*, p. 45). The masses embody everything that is not particular, everything that is unworthy of being taken note of. What we are used to calling mass culture will thus always be forced to turn the uninteresting into what is most interesting. From this perspective, the "disdain of the masses" concerns the subjective disdain of everything that is not indifferent. As Sloterdijk argues, so-called human rights are first of all rights to *indifference*, according to which all essential differences between high and low have been abolished (*Die Verachtung*, p. 71). The other important theorist of disdain is, of course, Nietzsche, who was the first to show that disdain is not something that disappears when subjective disdain ceases, but rather that it is something objective. Indeed, what is objectively disdainable is precisely the Last Man's obscene satisfaction with himself and his insignificant desires. Thus, Nietzsche's own disdain, his famous "revulsion" (*Ekel*), has as its object the disdain of the masses for everything that transcends their horizon.[21]

Both versions of the obscene—cynicism and the disdain of the masses—characterize the indifferent mode of the Last Man's thinking. We are condemned not to freedom, as Sartre claimed, but rather to mediocrity. The failure of the international community merely reflects the obscene consequences of the substitution of "grand politics" and the "grand scene" by "mood fluctuations" (*Im Weltinnenraum*, p. 468; *Zorn und Zeit*, p. 82) and "the informational Pest" (*Die Sonne*, p. 25). Politicians live in a semantic brothel: not only do they have to listen to and speak the twaddle of their own caste, a twaddle carried on by the sterilized discourse of sociologists and political scientists, they also have to deal positively with the immediate presence of the lie. To propose even more "transparent" communication as a solution to this would be absurd.

In his recent works—*Sphären III: Schäume, Im Weltinnenraum des Kapitals* (*Spheres III: Foams*) and *Zorn und Zeit*—Sloterdijk uses the concept of (tele)communication in a strong sense, as any *actio in distans* in a world that is thoroughly globalized, mediatized and densified. In the globalized West, a continuous and direct, that is, pre-subjective, interaction and inter-passion or "intercourse" (*Verkehr*) subjects every action to reciprocal feedback (*Im Weltinnenraum*, p. 277). As distance disappears, everyone involuntarily becomes a neighbor. It is only natural then that in today's intimacy each obscene disinhibition strengthens misanthropic sympathies and it is precisely this new "telerealism" that terrorists employ. This is why Sloterdijk substitutes the relations of the intimate and the distant for the more traditional relations of the local and the global. The political challenge of the future will be to determine and maintain the right distance. In *Im selben Boot* (*In the Same Boat*), this challenge is called a "hyperpolitics."[22] Its task is to forge out of the self-centered Last Man an individual who is still interested in the other as Other. This task manifests itself in the notion of a "between-man" (*Zwischenmensch*) who can function both spatially and temporally as a mediator or "distantiator" between different coexisting parties, between nature and culture, and between ancestors and future generations (*Im selben Boot*, p. 80).[23]

Beyond the opposition of the scene and the obscene: The affirmation of the intimate

I have tried to show how, for each of the three media theorists, the political machinery and its discourse relies on the obscene voice in order to function. Each defines obscenity as a lack of distance, which in turn entails an excessive presence. Žižek recognizes this absence of distance in a threefold disappearance: of real political antagonisms, of the distinction between the public and the private, and of the demarcation between the superego and the *id*. In Baudrillard's analysis of the demise of the scene, the lack of distance between a subject and its object has resulted in a representationless hyperreal in which everything has become political. For both Žižek and Baudrillard, terrorism is the natural result when traditional representative democracy becomes impotent. In the cynical self-contempt of the Last Man, Sloterdijk discovers a lack of distance between the political and what it represents. For him, as for Baudrillard, terrorism is defined by an excess of mass-media communication.

All three theorists regard this mass-mediatized lack of distance as the essence of a totalitarian mediocrity, a mediocrity that is characterized by the indifference of the mass-media through which terrorism and politics speak the same obscene language. Obscenity is a promiscuous presence, a presence that constantly affects us without leaving space to oppose it. This diagnosis leads Baudrillard to simply dismiss any future for contemporary politics, thereby enforcing a nostalgia for a pre-hyperreal reality. Indeed, this pre-hyperreal reality divorces his vision from anything contemporary. At best, political insight into our own impotence leads to a transformation of fatal strategies into banal strategies.[24] Sloterdijk can thus rightly qualify Baudrillard as someone who writes beyond any kind of political subversion. He is beyond the revolutionary because he is stuck in the sheer denial of the political (*Selbstversuch*, p. 53). According to Baudrillard: "It is useless to expect a positive opinion or a critical will from the masses, for they have

none: all they have is an undifferentiated power, the power to *reject*"
(*In the Shadow*, p. 72). Ironically, it is this position under the shadow
of the indifferent majorities that Baudrillard himself self-consciously
occupies.[25] Žižek, on the other hand, is happy to trade in the all-too-
human fascist Fortuyn for "the freedom fighter with an inhuman face"
(*Desert of the Real*, p. 82). As the only truly political thinker discussed
here, he pleads for a Leninist-inspired repoliticization of the economy
and a return to "real antagonisms" to overcome "repressive tolerance."[26] This does not necessarily mean having recourse to a military
model, as in extreme-right "ultra-politics." However, it is at least a plea
for a renewed interest in the transcendent scene of Symbolic economy
(*Desert of the Real*, p. 23). Yet Baudrillard has shown the fatal nature of
such recourse. A similar argument can be found in Sloterdijk, namely
that precisely insofar as the political potential is still interwoven with
the binary opposition of a world of appearances and false ideas on
top of a real, obscene world below, today's "ethics of the real"—of
which Žižek, together with Badiou, is the most important protagonist[27]—remains tied to the obscene: "In the race for the most explicit
disclosure of the real, the ontological variants of pornography had to
emerge—never did one look deeper into denuded reality. What were
called the ideologies—what were they in fact, if not fictions of the real
that intoxicated themselves with their toughness, their coldness, their
obscenity?" (*Sphären III*, p. 697; see also p. 154 and p. 421). Precisely
insofar as Žižek's militant "tarrying with the negative" is bound by the
same opposition of Real and Imaginary to the Symbolic as Baudrillard's
nihilism, it cannot help but deny the Real instead of restaging it, thus
always amplifying the obscene. As a result, are we not left with two all-
too-apocalyptic approaches to contemporary politics?

If I am defining hyperpolitics as "a politics of the *right* distance,"
this is to stress how for Sloterdijk the notion is considerably more
affirmative of the contemporary than the critical notions of post-
politics and transpolitics. Indeed, both Baudrillard and Žižek leave us
empty-handed. Those who claim we can do nothing against terrorism,
and that we should therefore resign ourselves stoically to all the bad
news, have understood that there is no real difference. However, let us
keep in mind Nietzsche's lesson that resignation and indifference are
opposed to affirmation, and thus cannot lead to any positive political
stance. Sloterdijk, drawing from his Nietzschean background, seems
to politically affirm both Žižek's obscene object of postmodernity and
Baudrillard's fatality as an *amor fati* when he seeks to reassess intimacy
as a necessary anthropological constant. This also implies a renewal

of Nietzsche's "pathos of distance" in a "theory of immersion," that must come after the opposition between active and passive has been deconstructed (*Im Weltinnenraum*, p. 16, *Cynical Reason*, p. 139). In his playful style: "Whereto one has no distance, therewith one should play," and "Where there was inconsolability, there mediaperformance shall come to be."[28] He subscribes to Baudrillard's view, as opposed to Žižek, that escalations of conflicts originate in false but mutual imitations and that any representation of violence does more harm than good. Yet, why not re-evaluate, in terms of a pathos of distance, the ontological and political status of the simulacrum and its functioning in the masses? Although the simulacrum is indeed the edge of critical modernity, Baudrillard, as Brian Massumi has rightly noted, "sidesteps the question of whether simulation replaces a real that did indeed exist, or if simulation is all there has ever been."[29] Sloterdijk, following his fellow-Nietzschean Deleuze, clearly chooses the second option by rehabilitating the mimetological microsociology of Gabriel Tarde in a refreshingly positive social ontology. What unites these "constructivist" authors is the belief that scenic simulation has always been the sole, but always-already social, production process of the Real. Accordingly, for Sloterdijk the scene of modern representative democracy—what is usually called the social—was never more than "an autogenous illusion," and from this perspective Baudrillard's lamentation that the scene of the social has disappeared in the fatal obscenity of mere simulacras becomes obsolete. Also, Žižek's militant "tarrying with the negative," which conceives of the obscene as the negative constituent of Western democracy, is countered by an affirmation of the intimate in positive terms. By following Sloterdijk in unmasking the supposedly hard core of the real departing from "soft" human forms of intimacy, I want to demonstrate how, ultimately, the difference between the scene and the obscene is based on a typically modernist cult of distance, which only allows for politics on the level of the symbolic and condemns us to oscillate between the poles of disinhibition and nihilism. As an alternative, I argue for the "psycho-political" priority of a culture of the forgotten and non-representable scenes of intimate affections that are central to all mass-mediatized politics.

The psycho-political scenes of the simulacrum

In *Die Sonne und der Tod. Dialogische Untersuchungen* (*Sun and Death*), Sloterdijk describes his use of Tarde as an "inversion of the psychoanalytical mode of thought [...] similar to Deleuze" (*Die Sonne,* pp. 77–8). His aim is no longer to explain how personal or familial psychological energies are linked to a social semantics and staged at the level of the collective and its corresponding macropolitical scenes. Rather, he aims to search for those genuine mass-dynamical energies which are articulated only on a collective level. In *Zorn und Zeit* he calls this approach "psycho-political": it doesn't explicate the psychology of historical actors, nor does it psychologize political powers. Rather, it describes politics as a capitalist process of production and accumulation of transsubjective "materials" or "energies," first and foremost that of "resentment." Unlike the conceptual framework that informs the work of both Žižek and Baudrillard, the social ontology proposed by Sloterdijk allows for no representational relation between singular members of society and mass-medial symbols. "Taking crowds as a starting point shows that already in the original scene of collective self-development there is an excess of human material and that the noble idea of developing the mass as a subject will be sabotaged by that excess *a priori*" (*Die Verachtung*, p. 13). Typical of the masses is their excessive "blackness" or what Elias Canetti calls *Menschenschwärze*.[30] However, rather than interpret this as a dangerous lack of sociability, what is necessary is a hyper- and psycho-political understanding of the excessive presence of the simulacrum. The necessity of such a paradigm shift was already underscored by Baudrillard:

No one really knows what relation can be established between two elements that are outside representation, this is a problem for which our epistemology of knowledge permits no resolution, since it always postulates the medium of a subject and of a language, the medium of a representation. We are really only acquainted with representative series, we know little about analogical, affinitive, im-mediatized, non-reference series and other systems.

(*In the Shadow*, p. 52)

Yet for Baudrillard, the advent of these non-representational series can only mean the end of the social and of the political:

And just as a positive social energy passes between the two poles of any representative system, it could be said that between the masses and terrorism, between these two non-poles of a non-representative system, also passes an energy, but a *reverse energy*, an energy not of social accumulation and transformation, but of social dispersal, of dispersion of the social, of absorption and annulment of the political.

(*In the Shadow*, p. 53)

For Sloterdijk, on the other hand, "today there is no [...] crisis of the public—rather there is a [...] crisis of the consciousness of the scene."[31] Wasn't it Tarde who, contrary to Baudrillard, for whom terrorism "propagates, by its own non-representativity, and by chain reaction [...] the apparent non-representativity of all power" (*In the Shadow*, p. 54), has already taught us how it is exactly this magnetic chain of propagation of simulacra that constitutes the social?[32] In *Sphären I* and *II*, Sloterdijk makes an inventory of historical attempts to create scenic principles for a fantasmatic image of a fluid and auratic universe, such as those that were constructed by modern forerunners of psychoanalysis like Ficino, Bruno, Hufeland and Mesmer. In *Sphären III*, this is followed by an adaptation of Tarde's monadological attempt to write a microsociology of the present on a mimetological and magnetopathic stage.[33]

Žižek's comparison of today's collective privacy with Leibniz's monadology demonstrated how the obscenity of what used to be the scene of politics now lies in the non-communicative relation between mass-mediatized subjects. Yet as soon as we accept that communication is not restricted to a representative system, the potential of precisely such a monadological understanding of the social comes to the fore. In short, for both Tarde and Sloterdijk, the social is a psycho-political continuum that is replicated by each of its participants. In overturning classical sociological holism, they dissolve the individualistic varnish and metaphysics of the socially interacting subject by accepting that prepersonal associations have their own modalities, which are already those of coexistence. It is true that nowadays the masses hardly ever gather as aggregates, but the mass character exists more strongly than ever as the collective partaking in mass-media "programmes," that is, chains of stress and self-stress. "One is now part of the mass without seeing the others" (*Die Verachtung*, p. 16). For a thoroughly psycho-political understanding of the social, each individual is already social in essence, just as a monad has no windows but reflects and envelops the whole world from its own singular perspective.[34] Long before René Girard's analysis of the conflictual play of mimesis and original appropriation, Tarde, in *Les Lois de l'imitation*, had already demonstrated how an individual is primarily a mirror of all the others.[35] What for Deleuze is the law of the eternal repetition of self-differing simulacra is, for Tarde, the immanent but purely social law of the universal imitation and propagation of contagious inventions. These inventions are ultimately nothing but further imitations of inventions themselves. Thus, a Leibnizian social ontology gives us an understanding of society in the mirror, a society which is actualized by an infinite series of reflections or imitations, "effective illusions" that immediately re-inject simulation into social reality where it sets to work. The monads continuously form and reform a world that is nothing but a chain and a theater of simulacra in the first place. Sloterdijk goes so far as to conceive of monads no longer as self-identities, but as impulses of differential potential—"dyads" or intensive "spheres."[36] Analogical sequences of self-realization explain how in many cases an individual experience is nothing but the pretense of an individual manifestation of collective flows of force and the mimicry of irreducibly collective sensations facilitated by mass-media technology. Thus, if Tarde is not interested in the symbolic interaction of individuals, but rather with "what happens within a single individual," this does not at all mean a subordination of alterity.[37] The social is not something that can either be communicated or not, but constantly reproduces itself in transsubjective processes of imitation, "resonances" or "echoes."[38]

This "parapsychoanalytic" understanding of a prepersonal social demands a dynamic concept of flows of imitation (*Die Sonne*, p. 74). Both Tarde and Sloterdijk find a model for these flows in Franz Anton Mesmer's theories of hypnosis, somnambulism and animal magnetism. Already in his *Critique of Cynical Reason* (pp. 107–18), but chiefly in his novel *Der Zauberbaum: Die Entstehung der Psychoanalyse im Jahr 1785*, Sloterdijk bases himself on the work of Henry F. Ellenberger to show how psychoanalysis, reflecting "the intensified norms of the civil and scientific rules of distance" of the nineteenth century, emerged as an individualistic and positivistic "perversion" out of this fluidizing revolution, which, as Sloterdijk suggests, even inspired by Marx and Engels' mobilizing slogan "all that is solid melts into air."[39] The eighteenth-century protagonist, the "psychonaut" Jan van Leyden, prophesied a surprisingly Deleuzo-Guattarian psychology, which was supposed to become the "true psychology" once modern, bourgeois social psychology had departed:[40]

When the self dissolves, its life transforms from the confining Over and Against to an immeasurable In and With. But the immersion in the immeasurable is not a relapse in the unconscious origin. Rather it is an upswing to the highest and most conscious production [...]. [It] would no longer speak of reflections, but of perceptions; no longer of reactions, but of inventions. [...] But most prominently this psychology would know how to stop speaking of human relationships. [...] What remains are distant salutations on the crossroads in the immeasurable—[...] an exchange from glow to glow and a careful walking side by side with the silent steps of love.

(*Der Zauberbaum*, p. 291)

Magnetism is based on a fluid ontology that does not accept identities, but only "drifting stimuli and collective drama" (*Der Zauberbaum*, p. 22), and its psychopolitical stage remains fully immanent to these symbiotic, erotic and mimetic-competetive energies. It is this mutual exchange of intimate, prepersonal flows that Tarde would later call "sociality." It knows no contract, but a "multi-micromanic constitution" (*Sphären III*, p. 817) and can only be described as a kind of mental epidemiology:

To better understand the relationality in sociality, [...] it might be helpful to hypothetically envision an absolute and complete sociality. It would exist in an urban life so tightly knit that a good idea conceived in one mind would instantly be transferred to every other mind in town.

(Tarde, p. 130)

Sociality functions like a dream—"a dream of command and a dream in action" (*Die Sonne*, p. 137)—and it is therefore the concepts of somnambulism or "readiness for hypnosis" that offer us "a social band reduced to it's most simple expression" (p. 136; see also *Die Verachtung*, p. 21; *Sphären III*, p. 617, p. 626).

Thus, although one can recognize a Lacanian inspiration in all three authors, Sloterdijk, by following Tarde, goes furthest in redefining the essence of the Real. One of spherology's explicit aims is to "supplement" the psychoanalytic breakthrough toward the representation of the constitutive separations in the domain of the unconscious with what is both a constructivist and a realist approach to a pre-subjective and pre-symbolic connectivity. It is an analysis insofar as it becomes an "analysis of the Outside" after the "real conversion from endoneurosis to exoneurosis" (*Nicht gerettet*, p. 84, p. 86) or from the intimate complex of *eros* to the external chains of, primarily, *thymos* and its economy of excess.[41] And just like psychoanalysis was interested in making manifest subconscious facts (*Traumdeutung*), it is spherology's task to explicitate or even "emancipate" the tender truths about our atmospheric places of existence into representational form ("*Schaumdeutung*," *Nicht gerettet*,

p. 32).[42] *Spheres* thus offers us a phenomenological inventory of all those social relations, contracts and ties that for us moderns have been dismissed as symbolic, magical, irrational, presocial and, ultimately, obscene. And though in *Sphären III*, Sloterdijk paraphrases Bruno Latour's "we have never been modern" with "we have never been revolutionary," it is exactly this explicitation of the intimate scenes of spherical coexistence that makes his work politically relevant. The modern understanding of the social has to be supplemented by a profound theory of intimacy, understood as "a *mise-en-abyme* in what is closest" (*Abgründigkeit im Nächstliegenden*), and through the "subversive effects" of "the sweet, the sticky" (*Sphären I*, p. 92). Despite their non-representability, there is nothing necessarily obscene about these transitive affective relations. Only from the perspective of the *ancient regime*, which allows for just a single royal scene, could psychology's grubbing in the most sticky aspects of human existence be called "a dubious knowledge, obscene and lewd" (*Der Zauberbaum*, p. 294).[43]

Baudrillard, on the other hand, denies in advance the revolutionary potential of this magneticist affirmation of the simulacrum when he treats us with his version of "the reverse of a 'sociological' understanding" of the mass, in which the mass is nothing but the "earth" of all social "electricity":

> The whole chaotic constellation of the social revolves around that spongy referent, that opaque but equally translucent reality, that nothingness: the masses. A statistical crystal ball, the masses are "swirling with currents and flows," in the image of matter and the natural elements. So at least they are represented to us. They can be "mesmerized," the social envelops them, like static electricity; but most of the time, precisely, they form an earth, that is, they absorb all the electricity of the social and political and neutralize it forever. [...] Everything flows through them, everything magnetises them, but diffuses throughout them without leaving a trace. They do not radiate; on the contrary, they absorb all radiation from the outlying constellations of State, History, Culture, Meaning.
>
> (*In the Shadow*, pp. 1–2)

His perspective remains caught somewhere between that of the restauration and that of the completely indifferent masses. Instead of affirming the phantasmatic "comedy" as a real "sociality" like Tarde (Tarde, p. 130), he interprets every invention as the tragic attempt to impose meaning through "shock waves in the media" (*In the Shadow*,

p. 27, p. 54). For Baudrillard, the only conceivable alternative order to that of representation is absolute indetermination. Terrorists are the ultimate defiance of the social, precisely because they are involved in "a process of *extermination* of the structural position of each term" (*In the Shadow*, p. 69). "It is the mirror of the social which shatters to pieces on them" (*In the Shadow*, p. 9). Yet what if sociality is something other than the social, something indeterminate precisely because it determines the social itself? Must we not rather ask, with Sloterdijk, whether "even at the symbolical level something paradoxical (*Widersinniges*) remains—for who could sharply distinguish between that, what it means, and that, what it does?"[44] For Baudrillard, if the mass has no conscience, then it must also be without unconscious (*In the Shadow*, p. 29). But though it is true that magnetism works not through meaning but through fascination, must we not accept that fascination is in fact the law of the social and rational or symbolic interpersonal communication only the exception? ("For us an untenable hypothesis: that it may be possible to communicate *outside the medium of meaning*," *In the Shadow*, p. 36). What if the theater has always been a place in which, contrary to the still common "sociologist's illusion" of "symbolical interaction," were processed not so much the semantic aspects of life as its energetic aspects? (*Die Sonne*, p. 87). What would the consequences be for a hyperpolitics, that is, a politics that is concerned with the omnipresence of the intimate and the necessity of distance?

Constructive mediation: Beyond the reality principle

Without exception, Sloterdijk's stagings of the intimate breathe a clear discomfort regarding the overly communicative constitution of our world. One of his disturbing observations is how, from the Renaissance until the nineteenth century, interest in Antiquity was confined to its high culture, whereas from the early twentieth century onwards we have been fascinated mostly by its vulgar culture.[45] With the advent of the mass onto the modern political scene, the spiritual transcendence of the semi-circular Greek theater has progressively given way to the pure immanence of the closed circle of the Roman fascistic arena (*Sphären II*, p. 326; *Die Sonne*, p. 118). But if Roman biopolitics functioned through the mimetics of rage in the medium of the arena, for us, it proliferates its *violentia in distans* through a mimetics of pure explosions in the collective privacy of our "egocentric interior designs" (*Sphären I*, p. 201). It is one of the latent strategies of modern biopolitics to maintain the original violence of selection through collisions in symbolic space.

To return to the miasmic scenery I started out with: mass-media function as transporters of "symbolically coded secondary smells or metaphorical group vapours" (*Sphären II*, p. 349). Canetti, like no other, has taught us how, with the becoming-subject of the masses, there is always the dangerous possibility of an expressionist release of suppressed tensions. Even if today the public character of these mass-mediatized subjects has progressively disappeared into the subjective privacy of infotainment, the explosive character of mass illusions—which make us the prisoners of our own "totalitarian communism of breath," whose closed-off, toxic atmosphere doesn't allow for ventilation and makes us breathe our own noxious and self-referential excrements—remains the biggest threat against democracy (*Sphären II*, p. 190).[46] Hollywood movie directors, as much as journalists and politicians, are like "narcotic doctors" who, contrary to old-fashioned macropolitical propaganda (p. 188), give us private access to intoxications with violence and who allow us "to let a good one off." Baudrillard nihistically concludes, therefore, that the hyperreal is primarily a space of deterrence (*In the Shadow*, p. 26). Sloterdijk, on the other hand, goes only so far as to say that because everything that can be said on terrorism amplifies its effect, and because at the same time it is impossible to keep silent, journalists as well as terrorists are polluters who lack an "ethic of odours" (*Sphären II*, p. 179). Yet even if terrorism is first of all a problem of "air conditioning," this doesn't mean that we can pretend air is not a political scene. It may be true that the use of poisonous gas by the Germans on the battlefield of Ypres in 1915 was the first act of terrorism in the twentieth century, yet it was only possible through an explicitation of the intimate, but social and political scene of shared air—what Canetti has called the "defence-lessness of breath" (*Sphären III*, p. 185)—which was not itself necessarily an obscene act (p. 89).[47] In a time when everybody claims the right to communicate a private opinion about the weather, the problem is therefore no longer to prevent publics from turning themselves into crowds (the problem of fascism), but to *socially create* fresh air or to distinguish new psycho-political scenes of communication and com-munality, a task which should not be left to terrorists alone.

As long as one is indifferent to the political potential of these inti-mate scenes, there will in fact be no political scene at all and the obscene will fatally contaminate the political climate. But once one accepts that the intimate is more than a sponge-like neutralizer, it can also be affirmed as the source of differentiation and distantiation.[48] In other words, once the scene of the social is supplemented with the various other, more intimate scenes of interpersonal and pre-personal communication, it becomes clear, as Tarde has pointed out, that fashion and body culture are to society what the magnet is to physics. The explicitation of these affective relationships is always constructivist because it demands the creative consciousness of a scene for something that previously could not be thought and with each explication a new community is effectively already in construction. And it is always social, because, albeit for different reasons than psychoanalysis, it depends on a dramatization: the theater knows a natural reflection because the public sees itself in its seeing and thus reflects its own inner stage *en plein publique*. The theater, contrary to Plato's metaphor of the cave and its wall of vaguely reflecting simulacra, is not in the least bit cave-like and closed off from the world. Rather, it is a public situation and communal reflection. The same goes for contemporary installation art, which has the "explicitating" task of "developing compromises between observation and participation" ("Atmospheric Politics," p. 948). Reason is never a private property, but is directly related to social practices. Thus self-confidence or the "coming-into-the-world" of the self implies world-confidence and vice versa. Ultimately therefore, scenic explicitation is always already *socio-political*, because it immediately reflects "the climatic or psycho-political conditions for social synthesis"[49] ("Atmospheric Politics," p. 944), and *critical*, because its "deep link [...]" between the polis culture and theoretical behaviour" (p. 948) depends on a public "climactic faculty of judgment" (*Sphären III*, p. 173; see also "Atmospheric Politics," p. 944) or "good sense" that starts from the insight that 'not every emission of stench can invoke the natural right of unavoidable miasma development of the type of latrine emanations" (*Sphären II*, p. 352).[50]

Because our "dense" world relies increasingly on the priority of inhibitions on action over initiatives, this critical consciousness of the public sphere is both urgent and unavoidable (*Im Weltinnenraum*, p. 277). As an antidote to the melancholy of Baudrillard and the militant Leninism of Žižek, Sloterdijk underscores the importance of a "reason of density" (*Im Weltinnenraum*, p. 27, p. 279) which lies at the basis of any sedentary culture:[51] "One could give credit to the suspicion that sedentary man was the first to be disposed towards the idea of retaliation and the return of the deed (*Tat*) to the doer (*Täter*), after the seemingly universal evidence given by the emanations from the latrine demonstrated the impossibility of a furtive act without consequences" (*Sphären II*, p. 342). Therefore, in *Zorn und Zeit*, he wonders "to what extent the sociologist's 'social tie' is always also woven of hate?" (p. 76, p. 257; see also *Sphären I*, p. 158). In short, because of the immunological paradox we started out with, sedentary history is always also the product of the institutionalization and rationalization of the pre-eminently collective feeling of resentment. It should therefore be analyzed under the aspect of its most destructive drive: *thymos*, pride or indignation. Indeed, traditional psychology's fixation on *eros* and its derivative, *thanatos*, which together constitute the libido, is far too one-sided and responsible for the ever-widening gap between social phenomena such as the *banlieu* riots in Paris and the dominant "schoolish" concepts for describing them. The reason for this gap is that the concept of pride "most often comes down to not much more than a contentless entry in the lexicon of the neurotic" (*Zorn und Zeit*, p. 29). Psychoanalysis turns humans into patients (Oedipus, Narcissus) before it ever gets interested in humans as bearers of proud and self-affirmative impulses. Thus, it is fundamentally unable to understand humans in conflict situations.[52] For Sloterdijk, contemporary politics stands or falls by its capacity to publicly learn about and explicitate a "neo-thymotic image of man" which should allow for a more adequate approach to the merits and dangers of productive dignity, self-assertion and its competitive outward presentation.

Zorn und Zeit is clearly a polemical essay written against all those "moderates" who, from the center of the liberal democratic culture of instant gratification, argue for the social indefensibility of modest and cooperative understanding. An adequate psycho-political foundation of sociality progressively depends on "democratic techniques" and "anti-misanthropic procedures" that do not establish an indifferent "tolerance," but rather the classic virtue of *kat exochen*, which Sloterdijk creatively translates as "pride-infused inter-patience between powerful individuals" ("Atmospheric Politics," p. 950). But those who prefer to create a difference in the political economy of the Real starting from an "infinite" "depository of resentment" against the actual world and who thus capitalize no longer on money but on symbols (*Zorn und Zeit*, p. 161)—as Sloterdijk ironically describes anti-capitalist political moralism on the extreme Right *and* on the extreme Left—do not offer us the means for a *political* approach to the pre-symbolic intimate either. It is no coincidence that it is exactly the "new spirit of revenge," of "I irritate, therefore I am," that unites populist politicians, Muslim terrorists and critical theorists such as Žižek (*Zorn und Zeit*, p. 75, p. 353). Despite their revulsion toward the contemporary globalized Symbolic, they want to reintroduce yet another stinking Real.[53] However, he "who only takes offence at the political and ideological costumes of revulsion at the level of the social, misses the misanthropic message as such" (p. 328). A slowdown in the obscene flow of transient and impatient discourse is necessary for any *polis* to function ("Atmospheric Politics," p. 949). Thus, if political scenes still remain, they won't be places where everyone can just link up with disinhibitive tsunamis of emotions, cynicism, disdain, hysteria and violence. They will be scenes that have laws that are different to those of the classic public domain; mediating *"Sphären"* that are not transparent, that cannot be denied and that, instead of indifferently absorbing the expressions of their inhabitants, make a difference themselves. What is needed is an understanding of the public which is adequate to the age of complete mediatization and the rapid proliferation of symbolic and non-symbolic scenes, a public whose conductive qualities allow it to function as a relay as much as a place for confrontation.[54]

It is indeed possible that art may play an important role for such political critique. Art, in its widest possible sense of culture-creating activity or the art *of* public space—rather than defined in a Habermasian way as an object of exhibition *in* public space—knows more about the scenes of the intimate than any other discipline.[55] "Culture, in the normative sense that needs now to be remembered more urgently than ever before, is the embodiment of the attempts to defy the mass in ourselves and to decide against ourselves. It is the difference for the better that—like all relevant differentiations—only exists as long as and while it is being made" (*Die Verachtung*, p. 95).[56] If it is true that today we inhabit a global *Gesamtkunstwerk* in which the intimate is progressively explicitated and from which classical politics have been banished (*Im Weltinnenraum*, p. 268), then the political impulse of art lies in providing the necessary "freedom of breath" or "breath of relief" (*Zur Welt kommen*, p. 165) that is the precondition of all shared life. Its tradition cannot be institutionalized (p. 170), but is that of a *catena aurea*, "an aspirated chain with open links [...] a tie of untying, a chain of unchaining" (p. 171). Without exaggeration, one could say that this aesthetic quest is also the *Leitmotiv* that connects the "breaks of Enlightenment" (*Cynical Reason*, p. 82) in Sloterdijk's early *Critique of Cynical Reason* to the theme of "air at an unexpected place" (*Sphären III*, p. 27) of *Sphären*. Throughout, what is at stake in his (meta-)immunological stagings of the typically human spheres of privileged *Freimut*, frivolity, relief and play, is the experiment with the tension between openness and impenetrability (*Eurotaoismus*, p. 93, p. 180, p. 264; *Die Sonne*, p. 281; *Nicht gerettet*, p. 70; *Sphären III*, p. 708, p. 722). Though sometimes only implicitly, each book makes a crucial difference between a more classical, negative understanding of the obscene and an essentially aesthetic and positive approach to the intimate. It is the difference between compelling mediocrity and aesthetic freedom.

Art is a vital precondition of any democracy because by breaking open the compelling logos of "obscene" common sense it provides the latter with the scenes without which it could not exist. In more general terms, all high cultures are defined by their capacity for *poièsis*: they are "above all scene-constructing systems" that constitute "worlds" and "gestures" with which public stages, scenes and arenas can be opened and human relations rebuilt at every level of the *socius*[57] (*Sphären I*, p. 20, p. 132; "Atmospheric Politics," p. 949). If the progressive explicitation of atmospheres forces us to keep up an attention for the breathability of air—at least in a physical sense, then increasingly also with respect to the metaphorical dimensions of breathing in all cultural spaces where collective issues are at stake (p. 168; on metaphorical warfare, see *Zorn und Zeit*, p. 67). For if the signature of our age of resignation and spectacle is an "official privatism and intimate apocalyptics" (*Zur Welt kommen*, p. 134), it is of the utmost importance for democracy to remember that "as long as people don't become aware of their poetical world contract, as long as they don't achieve the poetical sharing of the indivisible, it will be in vain to want to bind them to legal forms of social contracts" (p. 139).[58]

Notes

1. Peter Sloterdijk, *Sphären II. Globen* (Frankfurt am: Suhrkamp Verlag, 1999), pp. 340–2. Further references to this and the other *Sphären* volumes will be in the text. All translations from the German are mine, except where an existing translation is already available. The phrase "moral enigma" is from Sloterdijk's "Bilder der Gewalt—Gewalt der Bilder: Von der antiken Mythologie zur postmodernen Bilderindustrie" in *Iconic Turn: Die neue Macht der Bilder*, edited by Christa Maar and Hubert Burda (Cologne: DuMont Literatur und Kunst Verlag, 2004), p. 347.
2. Sloterdijk, *Sphären I. Blasen,* (Frankfurt am: Suhrkamp Verlag, 1998); *Sphären III. Schäume,* (Frankfurt am: Suhrkamp Verlag, 2004); *Im Weltinnenraum des Kapitals: Für eine philosophische Theorie der Globalisierung* (Frankfurt am: Suhrkamp Verlag, 2005), henceforth cited as *Im Weltinnenraum; Zorn und Zeit. Politisch-psychologischer Versuch* (Frankfurt am: Suhrkamp Verlag, 2006), henceforth cited as *Zorn und Zeit*.
3. "[...] im Dasein liegt eine wesenhafte Tendenz auf Nähe," Heidegger cited *Sphären I*, p. 336.
4. Sloterdijk makes an implicit reference to Reinhold Grether's dissertation *Sehnsucht nach Weltkultur: Grenzüberschreitung und Nichtung im zweiten ökumenischen Zeitalter* (1994), whom he also refers to in a footnote on the "tension between finite and infinite politics" in post-war French philosophy. See *Sphären II*, p. 411.
5. In his Tate lecture from December 10, 2005, Sloterdijk himself translates the German *Explikation* as "explicitation": to unfold in the sense of explicitly making things and rendering things public. <http://www.tate.org.uk/onlineevents/webcasts/spheres_of_action> [accessed May 21, 2007].

It combines Heidegger's *poièsis* (bringing forth into the open) with the "explicitating violence" of modern avant-garde art and with what Bruno Latour calls "articulation." The term "domesticated" is from Sloterdijk, *Nicht gerettet. Versuche über Heidegger* (Frankfurt am: Suhrkamp Verlag, 2001), p. 142. Henceforth cited as *Nicht gerettet.*

6. Similarly, Patrick Süskind's *Perfume* (1985) can be read as plea for a psychoso-cial ophresiology, the taking into account of "a domain that leaves no traces in history [...] the fleeting realm of scent." Because the protagonist Grenouille is born without bodily odor, he has been from the outset excluded from all social relations. All who try to engage in some social—contractual or intimate—relationship with him, including his mother, must die. Psychologically, he is able to find himself only by imitating and recreating the smells of the world, like an anamnesis through olfaction of his exogenous, socially constituted unconscious. Sloterdijk would speak of "Air Design" as the "continuation of the private use of perfume with public means," *Sphären III*, p. 178.

7. Slavoj Žižek, "The Future of Politics," in *Die Gazette*, August 2001.

8. Žižek, *Welcome to the Desert of the Real* (London: Verso, 2002), p. 85. Henceforth cited as *Desert of the Real.*

9. Žižek, "The Obscene Object of Postmodernity," in *The Žižek Reader*, edited by Elizabeth Wright and Edmund Wright (Oxford: Blackwell Publishers, 1999), p. 112. Henceforth cited as *Obscene Object.*

10. Žižek, "No Sex, Please, We're Post-Human!" <http://www.lacan.com/nosex.htm> [accessed May 21, 2007].

11. Žižek, "Why we all love to hate Haider", in *New Left Review*, 2 (March/April 2000).

12. Henk Oosterling, „Radikale Mediokrität oder revolutionäre Akte? Über fun-damentales Inter-esse" in *Über Žižek—Perspektiven und Kritiken*, edited by Erik Vogt and Hugh Silverman (Vienna: Verlag Turia + Kant, 2004), pp. 42–62.

13. The notion of the vanishing mediator is adopted from Žižek's *Tarrying with the Negative: Kant, Hegel, and the Critique of Ideology* (Post-Contemporary Interventions) (Durham, NC: Duke University Press, 1993).

14. Jean Baudrillard, *Fatal Strategies* (NY: Semiotext (e), 1990), p. 50 and passim.

15. Baudrillard, *In the Shadow of the Silent Majorities and Other Essays* (NY: Semiotext(e), 1983), p. 84. Henceforth cited as *In the Shadow.*

16. Baudrillard, "Pornography of War," *Cultural Politics*, 1.1 (2005) 23–6, p. 23.

17. Baudrillard, *Forget Foucault* (NY: Semiotext(e), 1988).

18. Sloterdijk, *Critique of Cynical Reason*, trans. Michael Eldred, foreword Andreas Huyssen (Minneapolis: University of Minnesota Press, 1987), p. 510. Henceforth cited as *Cynical Reason.*

19. Sloterdijk, *Kopernikanische Mobilmachung und ptolemaïsche Abrüstung: Ästhetischer Versuch* (Frankfurt am Main: Suhrkamp Verlag, 1987), p. 131.

20. Sloterdijk recognizes a "healthy" alternative to cynicism in "kynicism," the frivolous anti-idealism that he adopts from such vitalists as Diogenes, Heinrich Heine and Nietzsche, and presents his own text as an exten-sive "performance" and inspired by a "critical existentialism of satirical consciousness" (*Cynical Reason*, p. 535): a self-confident, watchful mim-ing of critique and a "bodily" disclosure of truth that ultimately "gives" or "provokes" a living stage on which are comprehensible, but only sec-ondarily and in a less compelling way, the discourses of abstract critique

and rationalist idealizations. See Sloterdijk, *Zur Welt kommen—zur Sprache kommen. Frankfurter Vorlesungen* (Frankfurt am: Suhrkamp Verlag, 1988), p. 20, henceforth cited as *Zur Welt kommen*. And though he later calls his initial strategy "a romanticism of dissidence," the malicious sense of irony and "compromising" thought of the kynical thinkers will remain central to his work: "Philosophers have only differently flattered society, it is now a matter of provoking it." Sloterdijk, *Die Verachtung der Massen: Versuch über Kulturkämpfe in der modernen Gesellschaft* (Franktfurt am Main: Suhrkamp Verlag, 2000), p. 62. Henceforth cited as *Die Verachtung*.

21. Peter Sloterdijk and Hans-Jürgen Heinrichs, *Die Sonne und der Tod: Dialogische Untersuchungen* (Frankfurt am: Suhrkamp Verlag, 2001), p. 49. Henceforth cited as *Die Sonne*. Sloterdijk's double understanding of disdain comes surprisingly close to how Baudrillard describes the ambiguous role of the masses in hyperreal simulation: "The mass realizes the paradox of being both an object of simulation (it only exists at the point of convergence of all the media waves which depict it) and a subject of simulation, capable of refracting all the models and emulating them by hypersimulation (its hyperconformity, an immanent form of humor)," Baudrillard, *In the Shadow*, p. 30.

22. Sloterdijk, *Im selben Boot: Versuch über die Hyperpolitik* (Frankfurt am: Suhrkamp Verlag, 1993). Henceforth cited as *Im selben Boot*.

23. See also Sloterdijk, *Eurotaoismus: Zur Kritik einer politischen Kinetik* (Frankfurt am.: Suhrkamp Verlag, 1989), p. 277 and throughout; see Sloterdijk, *Selbstversuch: Ein Gespräch mit Carlos Oliveira* (München: Carl Hanser Verlag, 1996), p. 32. Henceforth cited as *Selbstversuch*.

24. Baudrillard, *The Spirit of Terrorism* (London: Verso, 2002), p. 87.

25. Sloterdijk in *Zorn und Zeit* (*Rage and Time*) criticizes the "amorphous negativism" in Baudrillard's analysis of the banlieu-upheavals, according to which the rioters want to become part of a French political culture, which sadly no longer exists ("Nique ta mère! Voitures brûlées et non au référendum sont les phases d'une même révolte encore inachevée," in *Libération*, November 18, 2005). If society, "in its own perception, has evolved into a phantom collective," nonetheless "the capacity to regenerate is still slightly better than the ingeniously pessimistic commentators believe," *Zorn und Zeit*, p. 324.

26. Žižek, "It's all about political economy, stupid!," p. 100.

27. For a "kinetic" of Sloterdijk's relation to Badiou and the "ethics of the real," see my essay, "Critique Beyond Resentment. An Introduction to Peter Sloterdijk's Jovial Modernity," *Cultural Politics*, 3 (2007).

28. Sloterdijk, *The Thinker on Stage: Nietzsche's Materialism*, translated by Jamie Owen Daniel (Minneapolis: University of Minnesota Press, 1990), p. 80, translation modified; *Sphären I*, p. 478.

29. Brian Massumi, "Realer than Real: The Simulacrum According to Deleuze and Guattari," <http://www.anu.edu.au/HRC/first_and_last/works/realer.htm> [accessed May 21, 2007].

30. Elias Canetti, *Masse und Macht* (Frankfurt am: Fischer Taschenbuch Verlag, 2001) p. 14 and passim.

31. Sloterdijk, *Zur Welt Kommen*, p. 138. And, "When the phantasms prevail, the epoche of psychology begins," *Sphären I*, p. 234; see also Sloterdijk, *Der Zauberbaum: Die Entstehung der Psychoanalyse im Jahr 1785* (Frankfurt am: Suhrkamp Verlag, 1985) p. 96, p. 284.

32. This propagation takes place, in the words of Tarde, according to "laws of refraction" in the "inferference" of "concentric waves" spreading through the social, Gabriel Tarde, *Les Lois de l'imitation* (Paris: Les Empêcheurs de penser en rond, 2001) p. 77, p. 82. Or in the words of Sloterdijk, when what is "at first a punctual attack"—his example is that of a small scale terrorist attack—is continued in "medial magnifications," *Zorn und Zeit*, p. 93.

33. Again, Baudrillard uses metaphors that are similar to what Sloterdijk calls foams. The mass is "a nebulous fluid, shifting, conforming, far too conforming to every solicitation and with a hyperreal conformity which is the extreme form of non-participation." *In the Shadow*, p. 48.

34. If, at first sight, we inhabit an asocial world of isolated foam bubbles, this is only the consequence of a pre-personal (Tarde writes "pre-social" or "subsocial"), but mutual "crystallisation" (*Zorn und Zeit*, p. 16) of the Leibnizian continuum. This continuum was already clearly inspired by both the idea of a "public" but non-transparent affective field, and by the dynamic conceptions of attraction and possession of which private desiring subjects are nothing but epiphenomena or functions. *Sphären III*, p. 298, p. 817. As Deleuze, following Tarde, has shown, being, for Leibniz, is having. See Gilles Deleuze, *The Fold: Leibniz and the Baroque*, trans. Tom Conley (Minneapolis: University of Minnesota Press, 1993), p. 108. Sloterdijk shares this intuition when he writes that "being and attracting in this respect are the same," *Sphären I*, p. 213.

35. See René Girard, *Deceit, Desire and the Novel: Self and Other in Literary Structure*, trans. Yvonne Freccero (Baltimore: Johns Hopkins University Press, 1965). Girard taught how all mimesis is contagious, cumulative and transferential, leading to the spontaneous mechanism of autoregulation of a given community and potentially also to a hallucinatory, unanimous frenzy, especially regarding scapegoats. For him, mimesis tends to produce and regenerate differences as well as erase them, thus demonstrating how an extreme ritual conformism leads to production of the new. However, due to its focus on order and religion, his work is more adequate for understanding the reconciliation of the community and the consolidation of differences that come from the social mechanism of victimization—which makes the victim, in reality powerless and passive, the incarnation of mysterious power of mimetic metamorphosis and change—than for an affirmation of difference and its social multiplication.

36. It goes for all three that an individual is in fact always already dividual. "For the psychoanalyst the expression 'monad' refers to a form, the contents of which are determined by the being-together of 'two' related to each other in strong psychic reciprocity." Sloterdijk approvingly refers to Béla Grunberger's "psychoanalysis beyond the theory of drives," which includes a description of the "monadic pact" as a magnethopathic practice of vicinity. Grunberger uses the concept of the monad to stress that "dividuals" are unifying container forms in which content and container coincide. *Sphären I*, p. 353 and passim.

37. Deleuze, *Difference and Repetition*, translated by Paul Patton (London and NY: Continuum, 2001), p. 314.

38. Thus, we could say that the social is at work everywhere, "realizing something in illusion itself, or of tying it to a spiritual presence," for as Deleuze writes,

"hallucination does not feign presence, but [...] presence is hallucinatory," *The Fold*, p. 125. See also Tarde, p. 110.

39. "Who can doubt that electricity and love could bring about a socialist world age?" *Der Zauberbaum*, p. 188, see also pp. 185–8.

40. Following Tarde—"[n]ot majorities but multitudes" (p. 102)—and Deleuze, Sloterdijk in *The Disdain of the Masses* contrasts a "molar" "mass without potential" with "molecular masses" (p. 18, p. 87) and highlights the necessity of such a molecular turn. Though he must have been familiar with Deleuze's work to a certain extent (p. 184), however, in 1999 he admits to have missed it in his earlier works. Alliez, 2007.

41. Sloterdijk, *Zur Welt kommen*, p. 158. In *Zorn und Zeit*, Thymos (pride), not eros is for Sloterdijk the central "drive" in political psychology. It is not defined by lack, but by dissipation and demands a Nietzschean and Bataillan genealogy rather than a Freudian or Lacanian analysis, *Zorn und Zeit*, pp. 22–7 and passim.

42. Earlier he already defined it as Socrates's "poetic" task to speak as an "erotologist" or "provocateur"(see his footnote 40): "that of which he speaks, possesses a reality only within the force field of his seduction. Without devotion to this seduction 'there are' not all the phenomena of which the speech of the seducer speaks." *Zur Welt Kommen*, p. 77.

43. In *Der Zauberbaum*, in a chapter called "The Audience—An Agony of the Real" we are presented with a group of psychologists who are allowed to visit the scene of Mr von Manivaux, who is quarantined in the famous psychiatric hospital Hôpital Général de la Salpêtrière because he thinks he is Louis xv. His prison is the intimate scene of Versaille, but only on the condition that the psychologists actively participate in the patient's theater and that they promise absolute discretion toward outsiders. Yet in his role of Louis xv, Manivaux immediately senses the revolutionary potential of van Leyden's magnopathic attempts of understanding him when he exclaims: "Mister soul explorer! Your ignorance is scandalous. I hate your science that will never understand a thing—nothing of true greatness and its melancholy. A veil lies over being after great losses (*ein Schleier liegt über dem Sein nach grossen Verlusten*)—a veil which no one can lift, not you nor anybody else. It is the suffering of kings," pp. 219–20.

44. Sloterdijk, *Kopernikanische Mobilmachung*, p. 44.

45. Sloterdijk, "Bilder der Gewalt" in Maar and Burda (eds) *Iconic Turn*, p. 333.

46. On "the convergence of explosion and truth," see *Zorn und Zeit*, p. 19, pp. 95–6. For the relation between subjectivity and explosiveness, see *Im Weltinnenraum* pp. 93–107, pp. 277–91. Baudrillard, on the other hand, prefers to speak of "implosions." Precisely because information mesmerizes, it doesn't transform the mass into energy, but only produces even more mass, *In the Shadow*, p. 51, p. 100.

47. *Sphären III*, p. 96; Sloterdijk, "Atmospheric Politics," in Bruno Latour and Peter Weibel, *Making Things Public: Atmospheres of Democracy* (Cambridge, MA: The MIT Press, 2005), p. 945.

48. As Massumi puts it: "Against cynicism, a thin but fabulous hope—of ourselves becoming realer than real in a monstrous contagion of our own making."

49. In "Atmospheric Politics," Sloterdijk discerns five media-based conditions: writing, theater, agora, rhetoric, philosophy, p. 949.

50. If the philosophical definition of sovereignty says that, paraphrasing Carl Schmitt, "sovereign is he, who can let himself be represented in such a manner, as if he were present in his representatives" (*Sphären II*, p. 667) or he "who is capable of distancing oneself from epidemics of opinions" then it is "the mission of philosophers in society [...] to prove that a subject can be an interrupter and not just a simple canal for the passage of thematic epidemies and waves of stress" (*Die Sonne*, p. 85) And: "I now know that critique is practised above all as resistance against the neo-roman Feuilletoncircus," *Die Sonne*, p. 123. See also p. 262.

51. In conversation with Éric Alliez, Sloterdijk says "It teaches, not a duty of reserve, but a decision to act with reserve." See "Living Hot, Thinking Coldly," *Cultural Politics*, 3 (2007). Again, Sloterdijk directly opposes the "decisionist" "ethics of the real" in authors such as Žižek or Badiou, who teach us to trade in our solidarity with the Other in exchange for a politics of the impossible. On the contrary, "like every shared life, politics is the art of the atmospherically possible," *Im selben Boot*, p. 71. This mass medial "reason of density" was already prefigured in *The Critique of Cynical Reason*: "What we today call Enlightenment, by which we inevitably mean Cartesian rationalism, also refers, from the perspective of the history of information, to a necessary sanitary measure. It was the insertion of a filter against the flooding of the individual consciousness, which already had begun in the learned circles of the late Renaissance, with an infinity of equally important, equivalent, and indifferent pieces of 'news', from the most diverse sources. Here, too, a situation regarding information had arisen in which individual consciousness was hopelessly exposed to news, pictures, texts. Rationalism is not only a *scientific* predisposition but, even more, a *hygienic* procedure for consciousness, namely, a method of no longer having to give everything its due." *Cynical Reason*, p. 310.

52. As a consequence, formulas such as "the militant real of love" seem to be directly adopted from the tradition of Christian moralists and their "ethics of zero dignity," of which Saint Paul is of course the father. However, Sloterdijk argues in a fashion that reminiscent of Nietzsche, since the wrath of God can't be logically derived from the love of God, but only be based on faith and on not asking why, a functional explanation in terms of an economy of thymos and resentment is necessary. See *Zorn und Zeit*, p. 155.

53. Following Sloterdijk's reinterpretation, one could say that Lacanian "realism" is no different from today's "political pedagogues, including neo-conservative columnists, political anti-romanticists, angry exegetes of the reality principle, late-Catholics and disgusted critics of consumerism, who deem it their task to make accessible again the fundamental concepts of the real for a population of over-eased citizens," *Zorn und Zeit*, p. 76. Lacan and his followers, including such "political moralists" (*Zorn und Zeit*, p. 272) as Badiou or Žižek, must be criticized for mixing up Freudian *desire* with the Hegel-Kojèvian *struggle* for recognition, whereas in fact, from the capitalism of the imaginary to the romanticism of the real, it is always the same non-libidinal capitalistism of resentment that leads the way.

54. In *Zur Welt kommen*, Sloterdijk proposes the concept of a "politics of non-proliferation" against "[the] propagating flow of the national anxieties, miseries and violence [which] drives the pedantic objectivity and the cynical

veneer of the German of the newscast and of the Zeitgeist, of bureaucrats and of the media," p. 158. See also Tarde, "The patterns of courteous behaviour overcome distances better than the train," p. 432.

55. In fact, Tarde affirms that only in art the "law of imitation as the only cause of real social similarities" is applicable, p. 114. Sloterdijk discusses twentieth-century avant-gardism and installation art as two great forces of such explicitation, *Sphären III*, p. 154, p. 811. One should add shit art as a third.

56. It is with such statements that Sloterdijk's "biosophy" (*Sphären III*, p. 24) comes closest to that other "ecosophist" of the public sphere, Félix Guattari, whose concept of environmental ecology articulates with that of the psyche (resingularization) and of the city, society and mass media (dissensus). His "ethico-aesthetic" paradigm resonates with Sloterdijk's project insofar as it consists in the urgent attempt to counter the inability of traditional politics to change, if necessary through non-parliamentary aesthetic, social, economic, ecological practices. They also share the critique of Lacan, according to which fantasy and desire don't belong to individuals but to groups and the semiotics of the unconscious is radically polyvocal and heterogeneous. For both, there are no "natural" laws, because all laws are already social, beyond the nature-culture divide. Guattari's definition of "mental ecology," inspired by the work of Gregory Bateson, has clearly influenced Sloterdijk's definition of psycho-politics: "The principle specific to mental ecology is that its approach to existential territories derives from a pre-objectal and pre-personal logic," namely a "logic of the 'included middle'" and "the principle specific to social ecology concerns the development of affective and pragmatic cathexis (investissement) in human groups of different sizes," Felix Guattari, *The Three Ecologies* (London and NY: Continuum, 2000), p. 54, p. 60. Sjoerd van Tuinen, "Air Conditioning Spaceship Earth: Peter Sloterdijk's Ethico-Aesthetic Paradigm," in *Society and Space*, Vol. 27, no. 1.

57. Technically, this understanding of poièsis is a profaned and technology-mediated rendition of Heidegger's "bringing-forth-into-the-open" (*Entbergen*), *Zur Welt kommen*, p. 7 and passim; *Eurotaoismus*, p. 145; *Nicht gerettet*, p. 153, p. 210 and passim. The most important commonality between Nietzsche, Heidegger and Sloterdijk lies in the conviction that man does not enter into the *Lichtung* of being as an actor enters the stage, but that he is the stage himself as a medium for, in the case of Heidegger, the signs of Being. In *Sphären II. Globen*, Sloterdijk argues how, through the metaphysically informed panoptic power structure of macrospherical cultures and their media, "the signs of Being partake in Being"; they are for their part "in power of Being" (*seins-mächtig*) when they represent the power that sent them both representatively and "presentatively" (*präsentisch*) *Sphären II*, p. 673. As a consequence, one could conclude that cynicism and disdain, both understood as the disbelief in the power of presence that makes a difference, are contemporary renditions of what Heidegger called the forgetting of Being (*Seinsvergessenheit*). For a more thorough discussion of Sloterdijk's relation to Heidegger and ontological difference, see my forthcoming essay, "Peter Sloterdijk's 'Transgeneous Philosophy': Post-Humanism, Homeotechnique and the Poetics of Natal Difference," *Theory, Culture and Society* (forthcoming 2009).

58. One can easily recognize in this early programmatic statement Bruno Latour's strongly Heidegger-inspired Dingpolitik (see, for example, "From Realpolitik to

Dingpolitik, or, How to Make Things Public" in Latour and Weibel, p. 14). In this context it is interesting that already in 1987 Sloterdijk describes his work as the attempt to think "*Weltoffenheit* outside of the self-referential monotony of twaddle and granting the word to things, better: making the word into the sounding-board of reality." *Kopernikanische Mobilmachung*, p. 82.

5
Man is a Swarm Animal

Justin Clemens

> Socrates: What a lucky morning this is turning out
> to be! I was looking for one virtue and have found
> a whole swarm of them.
>
> —Plato, *Meno*, 72a

> It is clear that man is a social animal more than the
> bee or any other gregarious creature.
>
> —Aristotle, *Politics*, 1253a7

> For looke you vpon the face of this common wealth,
> and you shall find it in as bad or worse state, than was
> the state of the common wealth of the Israelites in the
> time of Ezechiel, or rather woorse concerning religion.
> For Atheistes. Papistes, & blasphemers of Gods holie
> name, swarme as thick as butter flies, without checke
> or controlment.
>
> —John Hooker, *A pamphlet of the offices,*
> *and duties of euerie particular sworne*
> *officer, of the citie of Excester* (1584)

A "Puncept"

In this essay, I examine a pun of Jacques Lacan. This is S_1, *essaim*; S-one, the swarm. To date, this pun has, at best, been taken as a suggestive metaphor; at worst, as just another opportunistic word-game, entirely typical of Lacan. My argument is that, if sometimes a pun is indeed just a pun, this pun is more than that. In fact, it provides a concept that bears centrally upon the relationship between technology, politics, language and psychoanalytic formalization. I trace the aetiology of this pun-concept (or "puncept"[1]), the significance of its emergence at a particular historical moment, not to mention at a very particular moment in Lacan's own conceptual development, in order to suggest what sort of problems it responds to and what sort of theoretical consequences it entails, especially in regards to the Saussurean doctrine of the signifier and the Freudian doctrine of identification. I then turn to its political and scientific freighting, and conclude with a remark about what it adds to the psychoanalytic armature.

The prepolitical

What is it about man that makes him a candidate for politics and the political? What makes human being-together a properly *political* question and not just a question of species-activity or genetic determinism? Man, says Aristotle, is the only animal with politics and language. For Aristotle, these features are integrally connected, and remain so for the tradition he founds. But such formulas still don't answer the question: what makes the human a candidate for politics at all? A *candidate* only, given that a human being can rise above or fall from politics (e.g., Aristotle's "man without community," either a beast or a god). So the question remains: what is specific about humanity's matter such that a human can come to function as a political animal, indeed, the political animal *par excellence*? Every philosopher has provided his own answer to this question. Let's provide a stupid list.[2]

Aristotle: man is a mimetic animal.[3]
Judeo-Christianity: man is a fallen animal.[4]
Machiavelli: man is a tricky animal.[5]
Hobbes: man is a fearful animal.[6]
Locke: man is a social animal.[7]
Voltaire: man is a sensible animal.[8]
Rousseau: man is a contracting animal.[9]
Kant: man is a maturing animal.[10]
Bentham: man is a useful animal.[11]
The Romantic poets: man is a baby animal.[12]
Hazlitt: man is a toad-eating animal.[13]
De Quincey: man is an addictive animal.[14]
Hegel: man is a prestigious animal.[15]
Marx: man is a laboring animal.[16]
Nietzsche: man is a herd animal.[17]
Freud: man is a horde animal.[18]

These adjectives do not provide the *essence* of what these thinkers consider to be the *political* being of man: they rather specify something that founds the *possibility* of the political in man, the conditions for man to be or become political. After all, if there's one proposition that almost every Western philosopher shares, in one way or another: man presents as a mutable being which cannot know *a priori* what it is capable of. These responses are therefore directed towards a seizure of that mutability insofar as it can be crystallized in a concept that can be articulated with the political. The problem is that the articulation is precisely the problem. There is simply no "fundamental," "categorical pair" of concepts (whether friend/enemy, as Carl Schmitt would have it, or *zoe/bios*, as Giorgio Agamben argues) that founds political thought in the West.[19] Yet the tradition also agrees that man is the only animal with politics *and* language.

It is into this tradition that Lacan intervenes when broaching his own investigations into psychoanalysis. It is why he maintains: "That the symptom institutes the order in which our politics emerges, implies, moreover, that everything that articulates itself of this order is susceptible to interpretation. This is why we are right to put psychoanalysis at the head [*chef*] of politics."[20] However serious Lacan may be about such a program, it is also the case that his position on language—and therefore also the political—develops throughout his career. I focus here on a period that lasts barely a handful of years, from about 1969–72 and which is, in any case, hardly very perspicuous. It is a transitional period for Lacan, and it is the nature of that transition that I will try to capture here under the heading of "the swarm."[21] Indeed, I want to add to the list above that, *chez* Lacan—at least for a certain period in his thought—"man is a swarm animal."

S_1 = Swarm

To my knowledge, Lacan explicitly generates a clinical significance from this pun for the first time in *Seminar XVII, The Other Side of Psychoanalysis (1969–70)*. In the opening session of November 26, 1969, Lacan introduces his four discourses, of the Master, Hysteric, Analyst and University, with their accompanying algebraic letters of (the barred subject), S_1 (the master signifier), S_2 (knowledge), and (the object). The S_1, the master signifier, is homophonic in French with *essaim*, swarm, so whenever S_1 is pronounced, that's what you hear; or, more likely, you don't, you overlook it or rather *overhear* it. That's too bad. In fact, most of those who have noted the pun seem to have taken it entirely in their strides, as an entirely typical instance of Lacan's oneiric style that doesn't have to disrupt whatever mission they're already on.

In other words, the *swarm* appears only to disappear at once. The hilarious compilation *789 néologismes de Jacques Lacan* excludes it, presumably on the basis that "With only three exceptions (*seconder*, *verge* and *soir*), the words of this glossary don't contribute to a semantic neology, that is, through adding signification to an existing word."[22] The instructions immediately proceed to confess, alarmingly, how difficult it was to decide on inclusions and inclusions to the volume given Lacan's relentless linguistic inventiveness. Whatever the reason, *essaim* doesn't make it in. Too boring, perhaps, too opportunistic, too ordinary.

Neither, to my knowledge, does "swarm" make it as a concept into any of the dictionaries, handbooks, companions or readers currently available on Lacan, and often not even into the indices.[23] To take only one recent, authoritative instance of such an omission, we find, in the index to the *Cambridge Companion to Lacan*, despite the presence of such Lacanian coinages as *linguisterie* and *parlêtre*, that the swarm is nowhere to be found—although, as I've already stated, you can't pronounce S_1 in French without hearing *essaim*.[24] As American cultural theorists like to ask, waving their hands in wheedling disbelief: "Where's the swarm in this text?"

It was therefore something of a shock to find—not swarm itself—but a cognate, *Schwärmerei*, listed in the index to the new English translation of *Écrits*, where, in the "Index of Freud's German Terms" it is referenced to page 773 (the French page numbers reproduced in the translation, not the English ones).[25] The *écrit* in question turns out to be nothing other than "Kant with Sade," and the context Lacan's discussion of how the Marquis de Sade's boudoir education provides the truth of Immanuel Kant's abstemious moral law.

Now this is a particularly odd contribution of Lacan. Unlike most of the other *écrits*, it was not delivered as a public performance before being written up for publication. Neither does it have a strictly psychoanalytic provenance. Rather, it was commissioned as a preface to Sade's tract *Philosophy in the Bedroom*, slated to appear in a new edition of his works with Éditions du Cercle. Rejected by the editors, Lacan's essay then found a home as "a review of the edition of Sade's works for which it was intended"(in *Critique*, no less!); finally, after the success of the *Écrits* themselves in 1966, the piece was "recommissioned" and "included as a postface in the same publisher's 1966 edition of Sade's *Oeuvres complètes*."[26] Phew.

Something else is significant here: this is a text on perversion. Just as Freud had treated psychosis primarily through Judge Schreber's testimony and not, like Jung or Lacan himself, in clinical settings, Lacan—though he had dealings with a surfeit of hysterics, obsessionals, paranoiacs, schizophrenics and so on—doesn't seem to have spent a lot of time with perverts. There are perhaps a number of reasons for this. Above all, as Jacques-Alain Miller says, "Few perverts ask to undergo analysis. We might conclude that perverts are unanalyzable, but the fact is that they simply don't come asking to undergo analysis. They don't come to seek out the lost object; thus, it is just plain common sense to believe that, in some way, they have found it and can expect nothing from analysis. The effect known since Lacan as the "subject supposed to know" doesn't arise with a true pervert, demonstrating that the subject supposed to know always arises in the place of sexual enjoyment."[27] The paradox here is that, if psychoanalysis is precisely the discourse that introduced the notion of perversion as basic to human sexuality *tout court*—Freud positing an infantile "polymorphous perversity" at the root of all sexuality—perverts evade the clinic of psychoanalysis more successfully than neurotics or psychotics.

I will come back to this problem of perversion later, to some of the consequences of the fact that Lacan's major published discussion of perversion emerges from an extra-clinical commission, and that it is linked to a particular problem in the theorization of *jouissance*. Indeed, "Kant with Sade" comprises one of Lacan's most extended early accounts of *jouissance*. But I first want to identify a passage determining for Lacan's later puncept of the swarm.

The passage in question is at once an exclamation and a mission statement: "But humph! *Schwärmereien*, black swarms—I chase you away in order to return to the function of presence in the Sadean fantasy."[28] Just as hysteria's peculiar structure of address enables the lineaments of *desire* to emerge with the greatest force and clarity, here the pervert's peculiar structure of enjoyment enables the lineaments of fantasy to emerge in the most scandalous fashion. Unlike desire, fantasy seems to be most clearly revealed in its inversion or perversion: according to the Lacanian matheme, the pervert's fantasy is not formalized as $\exists \& \forall$, but as $\forall \& \exists$. That is to say that the pervert, exemplified here by the Sadean masters, places himself in the position of the object, in order that the splitting of desire is visited upon the other, not himself.[29] Yet, it seems, in order to outline this fantasy, one has to avoid the philosophical confusion of *Schwärmerei*. This is more difficult than you might think.

The translator's endnotes give the following gloss: "*Schwärmerei* means fanaticism, mysticism, and enthusiasm; *Schwärme* means swarms, and the French *essaims* (swarms) is pronounced like Lacan's matheme S_1. See

Critique of Practical Reason, 94, 110, and 204."[30] The complexity doesn't stop there, however, as the book sports yet another index denominated "Freud's German Terms," which in turn includes such old favourites as *Durcharbeiten, Fort! Da!*, and *Trieb*. What's peculiar about this is that we also find listed, not really Freud's German terms at all (of which more below), but a term allegedly deriving from Immanuel Kant (who goes unnamed in the note proper), that is, *Schwärmerei*. Lest you think this is a failure of the English translator, one finds the same entry in the French version under the same heading, *sans* the reference to Kant, and initialled by "J. L." himself. A closer look at these German terms reveals others that seem to have nothing especially to do with Freud himself, but a great deal to do with late eighteenth- and early nineteenth-century German philosophy and poetry: *Aufhebung, Bildung, Dichtung* (and *Wahrheit*), and so on.

Schwärmerei und Enthusiasmus

We might say then that Lacan himself is responsible for, or at least signs off on, authorizes, the illegitimate importation of a swarm of foreign words under cover of a Freudian alibi. With respect to *Schwärmerei* in particular, it's not just any word whatsoever. In fact, it's one of the key political terms of the German *Aufklärung*. Introduced into German theologico-political discourse by Martin Luther in the 1520s, *Schwärmerei* quickly came to be distinguished from a near-synonym: *Enthusiasmus*. Whereas *Enthusiasmus* had had a glorious Greek prehistory (from Plato's *Ion* onwards), *Schwärmerei* was something a little less elevated.

As Peter Fenves remarks:

> *Schwärmerei* derives from the swarming of bees. The likeness between the aggregates of swarming bees and the congregations of swarming churchmen gives *Schwärmerei* its highly amorphous and irreducibly figural shape. A commonality between human beings and animals— not human beings and God—is implied in every use of the word. Like bees, *Schwärmer* fly through the air on erratic paths, and, again like bees, they hover there without any easily understood means of support.[31]

In fact, almost everyone who was anyone ended up contributing to the late eighteenth-century German debate around *Schwärmerei*.[32] From Cristoph Martin Wieland, who in 1775 had called on the public to try to fix the linguistically-unfixed nature of the word, to Lessing, Herder,

Kant, Hölderlin, and Schelling, *Schwärmerei* denominated a topos whose limits couldn't quite be fixed or formalized.[33] In Fenves' words, "*Schwärmerei* names the aporetic condition of a coordinated disorderliness."[34] In English, *Schwärmerei* has been translated as "fanaticism," "mysticism," "enthusiasm," "zealotry," and "exaltation," all of which seem unsatisfactory.[35] But the difficulty is irreducible, for *Schwärmerei* is an exemplarily *equivocal* term.

In his own reconstruction of the debate, Anthony La Vopa notes that "*Schwärmerei* assumed new (though still familiar) shapes in the ideological arena created by the French revolution," and that it thereafter "became a commonplace of German anti-revolutionary discourse that philosophical *Schwärmerei* was assuming especially virulent forms in the rhetoric of radical intellectuals and in the frenzy of violent mobs."[36] So the problem of *Schwärmerei* is the problem of the articulation of radical political action and abstract philosophy, of the fixing and un-fixing of the limits of reason with respect to the being-together of human beings.[37]

If Fink's note (quite rightly) sends us then to the *Critique of Practical Reason*, which is, after all, Lacan's central explicit reference in this text, the final sentence of "Kant avec Sade" clearly alludes to another of Kant's works. Lacan, in his summing up of the case of Sade, writes, "What is announced about desire here, in this mistake based on an encounter, is at most but a tone of reason."[38] Think of Kant's late text, "On a Newly Arisen Superior Tone in Philosophy" (1796), itself a response to the conservative Johann Georg Schlosser's annotated translation of Plato, *Plato's Letters on the Revolution in Syracuse with a Historical Introduction and Notes* (1795).[39] There Kant speaks of the philosophizing of mathematics as consisting in the feeling and enjoyment of swarming (*im Gefühl und Genuß zu schwärmen*), of the mistuning of heads in swarming (*Verstimmung der Köpfe zur Schwärmerei*), and so on. Lacan's implication is surely that this philosophical tone is really a *drone*.

In fact, Kant's work of this time swarms with swarms. In "Conjectures on the Beginning of Human History" (1786), he will write of the establishment of human imperialism and colonialism in the struggle between agrarian settlements and nomadic tribespeople:

> The human race could multiply and, like a beehive, send out colonists in all directions from the centre—colonists who were already civilized. This epoch also saw the beginning of human inequality, that abundant source of so much evil but also of everything good; this inequality continued to increase hereafter. So long as the nations

of nomadic herdsmen, who recognize only God as their master, continued to swarm around the town-dwellers and farmer, who are governed by a human master or civil authority, and as declared enemies of all land ownership, treated the latter with hostility and were hated by them in turn, the two sides were continually at war, or at least at constant risk of war.[40]

But this war between the swarms of nomads and the permanent settlements of the village communities is also one of the guarantees of internal freedom for Kant; after all, "perpetual peace" stinks of the grave. One can also see how the term implies a kind of historical regression on those who have succumbed to it (a sense that we will pick up on later). Moreover, a fundamental asymmetry and inequality is at stake whenever a swarm begins to form.

Speaking of his *Schema 2* in "Kant with Sade," Lacan notes that Sade's declaration of the universal rights of *jouissance* doesn't have a symmetrical structure. Rather, the commands and tortures inflicted upon sufferers are such that "it can be seen that the subject's division does not have to be reunited in a single body."[41] There is more than a hint of the swarm in this phrase: the subject's division can be distributed across 1+ bodies. In other words, perversion is something that reveals how a subject tends towards an indeterminate proliferation of bodies without any concomitant obliteration, proliferation or dispersion of the subject. It is at this point that Lacan finds himself conscious of having to "chase off" the black swarms of letters that confuse the issue of fantasy (I will try to give some reasons for this decision towards the end of this essay).

So the Lacanian swarm has almost-but-not-quite-emerged with respect to the clinical problem of perversion; to the problem of the relation between philosophy and non-pathological actions; to the problem of the theorization of *jouissance*—only to vanish nearly immediately as a term. But that doesn't mean the idea is not still active in Lacan's work.[42] Indeed, it is my thesis here that this first, fleeting, quasi-emergence of the black swarms sees them immediately disperse, only to regroup some time later, under completely different circumstances, and in a clarified form.[43]

Freudian *Schwärmerei*

If *Schwärmerei* isn't a strictly Freudian concept, why does Lacan insert it into the German glossary of *Écrits* under that heading? Is this merely another case of an arbitrary Lacanian fiat, whim, or parapraxis? I don't think so, again for good political—not to mention psychoanalytical—reasons.

For if *Schwärmerei* is not a particularly Freudian word, nor a particularly Freudian concept, it is not entirely absent from Freud's work. Certainly, it would be a surprise *not* to find it at least somewhere in Freud, not only because it is a standard German word, but because it would seem eminently appropriate to a man who traces all knowledge, even the most elevated and refined, back to its sources in infantile fantasies and biophysical drives. On the other hand, it is also a word that comes overdetermined with pre-analytic significance, enmeshed in a politico-theological genealogy that might well make it inappropriate for Freudian redeployment.

So when the word does appear—as it does at significant moments in Freud's work—it proves to be used consistently, although without ever attaining the rigor of a true concept. Symptomatically, *Schwärmerei* and its cognates receive unreliable attention in the relevant indices to the *Gesammelte Werke* (and none at all in the *Standard Edition*).[44] There is no listing for *Schwärmerei* in the indices to the key *GW* volumes x, xii, nor xiii, and only one listing in the index for v. In volume xviii, the *Gesamtregister*, however, we find a far more extensive entry.[45] Following these references is of extreme interest in the present context.

In *Three Essays on the Theory of Sexuality* (1905), we find *Schwärmerei* under the heading "Die Umgestaltungen der Pubertät" *(The Transformations of Puberty)*, where Freud remarks: "Dessoir hat mit Recht daruf aufmerksam gemacht, welche Gesetzmäßigkeit sich in den schwärmerischen Freundschaften von Jünglingen und Mädchen für ihresgleichen verrät."[46] The *Standard Edition* translates: "Dessoir [1894] has justly remarked upon the regularity with which adolescent boys and girls form sentimental friendships with others of their own sex."[47] Note the peculiarity, first, of the translation, and, second, of Freud's use of the word. As the *Vocabulaire Européen des Philosophies* explains, in a short entry, "La '*Schwärmerei*' chez Freud": "[*Schwärmerei*] does not designate, for the founder of psychoanalysis, any form of delirium, nor any belief, but the stories recounted by adolescents when they devote an exalted love towards a person of the same sex as themselves. [...] These whims or fervours generally dissolve as if by magic, as Freud says in *Three Essays on Sexuality*, and in particular when love for a person of the other sex takes form."[48] For Freud, then, the word is not used in its familiar, polemical conceptual sense, but merely in passing, as an adjectival specification, to designate a transitory inversion, a momentary swerve towards an (idealized) homosexual object-choice.

Freud will also use the word in passing in such texts as "On the History of the Psycho-Analytic Movement" in the context of the perverse eroticism of religious enthusiasts, the preparedness of martyrs to suffer for their God (and it is also noteworthy that that text is concerned with the religious backslidings of psychoanalytic renegades such as Adler and Jung).[49] If such use may seem to reunite Freud not only with the political and philosophical, but also with the physiological genealogy of the word, it remains the case that he gives the word a directly *sexual* significance that it has hitherto lacked. *Schwärmerei* emerges to designate a transitional sexual phase between the prepubescent interregnum and the full-blown emergence of adult sexuality, in which an intense yet unfulfilled homoerotic attraction manifests itself. Yet it also refers to an excessive capacity for self-sacrifice, to an extraordinary submission to an ideal.

These features remain operative in Freud's most liberal use of the word, in a famous case-study of 1920, *Über die Psychogenese eines Falles von weiblicher Homosexualität* ("The Pychogenesis of a Case of Homosexuality in a Woman").[50] The word (or cognate) appears at least seven times in this text. Let me quote liberally from both the German and the *Standard Edition's* translation:

> *Wie weit es zwischen ihrer Tochter und jener zweifelhaften Dame gekommen ist, ob die Grenzen einer zärtlichen Schwärmerei bereits überschritten worden sind, wissen die Eltern nicht.* (p. 272)
>
> The parents could not say to what lengths their daughter had gone in her relations with the questionable lady, whether the limits of devoted admiration had already been exceeded or not. (p. 148)
>
> *Es war nur klar, daß sie die Schwärmerei ihrer Tochter nicht so tragisch nahm und sich keineswegs so sehr darüber entrüstete wie der Vater.* (p. 274)
>
> All that was clear was that she did not take her daughter's infatuation so tragically as did the father, nor was she so incensed at it. (p. 149)
>
> *Bei keinen der Objekte ihrer Schwärmerei hatte sie mehr als einzelne Küsse und Umarmungen genossen, ihre Genitalkeuschheit, wenn man so sagen darf, war unversehrt geblieben.* (p. 278)
>
> With none of the objects of her adoration had the patient enjoyed anything beyond a few kisses and embraces; her genital chastity, if one may use such a phrase, had remained intact. (p. 153)[51]

What are the hallmarks of Freud's use of the word here? Above all, it refers to an a-sexual devotion, an "inversion" or "perversion." It is central in Freud's account of this case that the young woman rejects those of her sex with whom she might actually enjoy direct sexual (genital) satisfaction. Indeed, she insists on refusing or renouncing such satisfaction—with a concomitant, extraordinary idealization of her love-object—up to and beyond the point of self-sacrifice and self-abnegation, indeed, to the point of (attempted) suicide. In his own commentary on this case in *Seminar IV*—a seminar in which the interpretation of perversion is centrally at stake—Lacan doesn't hesitate to identify the young woman's love for her Lady with the intricacies of courtly love. The young woman, for Lacan, is aiming *beyond* her apparent object, at the phallus itself.[52] What I want to underline again here, however, are the triple aspects of *Schwärmerei*—transient inversion, idealization of the object, and propensity for self-sacrifice—that seem implicitly bound together for Freud in his uses of the word, which also hints at the phylogenetic regression suggested by the standard political sense of the term.

Yet what would usually go under the name of *Schwärmerei* takes another route in Freud, especially in his later theories of group behavior. Let's turn to Freud's *New Introductory Lectures on Psychoanalysis* which, though denominated "Lectures," were in fact never delivered and which, though dated 1933, in fact appeared in 1932. In Lecture xxx of that volume, titled "Dreams and Occultism" we find the following extraordinary statement:

> The telepathic process is supposed to consist in a mental act in one person instigating the same mental act in another person. What lies between these two mental acts may easily be a physical process into which the mental one is transformed at one end and which is transformed back once more into the same mental one at the other end. The analogy with other transformations, such as occur in speaking and hearing by telephone, would then be unmistakable. And only think if one could get hold of this physical equivalent of the psychical act! It would seem to me that psychoanalysis, by inserting the unconscious between what is physical and what was previously called "psychical," has paved the way for the assumption of such processes as telepathy. If only one accustoms oneself to the idea of telepathy, one can accomplish a great deal with it—for the time being, it is true, only in imagination. It is a familiar fact that *we do not know how the common purpose comes about in the great insect communities* [my emphasis]: possibly it is done by means of a direct psychical transference of this kind. One is led to a suspicion that this is the original, archaic method of communication between individuals and that in the course of phylogenetic evolution it has been replaced by the better method

of giving information with the help of signals which are picked up by the sense organs. But the older method might have persisted in the background and still be able to put itself into effect under certain conditions—for instance, in passionately excited mobs.[53]

There are a number of features of this passage to which I would like to draw your attention. First, Freud is returning to something that will prove a little embarrassing, if not for him, at least for such *bien pensant* followers as Ernest Jones: the topic of telepathy. He has brought it up several times before, most notably in 1921/1922, when completing the essays "Psychoanalysis and Telepathy" (1921, but unpublished until 1941) and "Dreams and Telepathy" (1922). What is noteworthy about its reappearance here is the direct link that Freud makes between telepathy and materiality. If thoughts are material events, then it is perhaps possible that they can be, indeed are able to be transmitted according to as-yet unknown biophysical processes. A good materialist cannot a priori exclude the possibility of telepathy.

Second, Freud's analogy here is with the telephone, a piece of relatively new communications technology. In this context, it is significant that Freud opened the entire series of "Lectures" with another famous analogy, that of his one-time "phonographic memory" (now, lamentably, not quite what it used to be, although still pretty impressive, mind you). As ever, Freud is extremely sensitive to the psychopathology of technological life (His Master's Voice, and all that).

Third, Freud not only wants to suggest that evolutionary development doesn't simply supplant archaic formations, but that these archaic characteristics of the organism are always liable to be revivified under certain extreme conditions. In this instance, Freud suggests that the enigmatic communicational powers of insect communities—which are presumably prior to any form of psychological individuation—may well account for the peculiarities exhibited by "passionately excited mobs." Freud thereby proposes that there may be a direct link between the possibility of telepathy and group-psychology.

Fourth, Freud thereby binds materialist rationalism, telepathy, modern telecommunications, mass psychology and the most archaic forms of biological organization together in a single concept. As ever, Freud sees no principled difference between human beings and other forms of life, no matter how allegedly lowly. Indeed, we find this procedure throughout Freud's later work, where the links between technology, biology, and politics are ceaselessly re-examined, and concepts developed to unite them.

Yet where else does one find such an explicit reference to "passionately excited mobs," but in *Group Psychology and the Analysis of the Ego* of 1921? (A piece that Freud is writing, moreover, just after the case of the young homosexual woman!) *Group Psychology* was itself written in the wake of a major theoretical shift. Freud had just altered his theory of the drives in *Beyond the Pleasure Principle*. This alteration had forced him to return to his existing theoretical concerns and rethink them according to the new problematic of the death drive. The basic point is this: if libidinal economy is not sufficient to account for the entirety of psychic organization, then how does the non-libidinal part contribute to such an organization? In *Group Psychology*, the central problem is to explain how psychologically complex individuals can form into larger aggregates with qualities radically different from those of the individuals that compose them. What triggers the formation of a mob? How do the individuals that comprise it communicate amongst themselves? Why is there such a serious diminution in the intellectual level of an individual's mental functioning when subsumed in a group?

Freud draws heavily on the work of Gustave Le Bon, the conservative French writer whose *Psychology of Crowds* (1895) was extremely influential in the early twentieth century.[54] For Le Bon, the crowd suppresses individuality, is irrational, and closer to a kind of racial unconscious than at other times. Le Bon gives three main reasons for the alterations in psychology in groups; 1) from sheer *force of numbers*, the individual develops a sense of personal invincibility; 2) *contagion* (for Le Bon, a phenomenon "of a hypnotic order"), which enables an individual to sacrifice "personal interest to the collective interest"; 3) the most important, the *hypnotic suppression of ego* to the point of becoming an automaton.

Now, while these reasons won't entirely wash for Freud, the problems raised by Le Bon of "contagion" and "hypnotic suppression" are preeminently psychoanalytic questions. This raises the problem of telepathy once more, and, whatever you make of Freud's speculations in this regard, there is a very good reason for him pursuing the idea in this context: how *do* groups hang together? Telepathy becomes the focus of interest for Freud at precisely the same time that he is studying group behavior ("Psychoanalysis and Telepathy" (1941/1921) and "Dreams and Telepathy" (1922), as well as "Some additional notes on dream-interpretation as a whole" (1925), and the aforementioned "New introductory lectures, xxx" (1933). But the possibility of telepathy remains mere speculation, and so Freud finds himself having to generate a new theory of identification to explain the emergence of a wide variety of groups. This theory hinges on the concept of "the unary trait" (*ein einziger Zug*). As Alenka Zupančič glosses it, the unary trait "is very different from imaginary imitation of different aspects of the person with which one identifies: in it, the unary trait itself takes over the whole dimension of identification."[55]

It is at a hinge point of this text that the word *Schwärmerei* re-emerges for Freud. In Chapter VIII, "Being in Love and Hypnosis," and Chapter IX, "The Herd Instinct" (in fact, "*Der Herdentrieb*," "the herd-drive"), the word recurs, along with the same problematic I noted above. In Chapter VIII, we read: "*Der Mann zeigt schwärmerische Neigungen zu hochgeachteten Frauen, die ihn aber zum Liebesverkehr nicht reizen, und ist nur potent gegen andere Frauen, die er nicht 'liebt,' geringschätzt oder selbst verachtet*"; ("A man will show a sentimental enthusiasm for women whom he deeply respects but who do not excite him to sexual activities, and he will only be potent with other women whom he does not 'love' and thinks little of or even despises").[56] We have met with this "universal tendency to debasement in the sphere of love" before, with its characteristic aim-inhibited drives and sexual over-valuation. Here, however, Freud is preparing a new kind of explanation.[57]

For Freud, the earlier "group psychology" of *Totem and Taboo*, in which the murder of the father founds the community of brothers is no longer enough to account for the artificial, temporary or spontaneous nature of certain group-formations.[58] Instead, Freud now has to supplement the earlier account with one better able to explain, say, mass hysteria at a girl's school. Freud thus gives the following summary:

> First, identification is the original form of emotional tie with an object; secondly, in a regressive way it becomes a substitute for a libidinal object-tie, as it were by means of introjection of the object into the ego; and thirdly, it may arise with any new perception of a common quality shared with some other person who is not an object of the sexual instinct.[59]

Instead of telepathy, then, we have a new account of identification. The aggregations made possible by the mechanism of the unary trait are no longer the primal hordes of the earlier study, but far more volatile, transient, intense, and (apparently) irrational mobs. And we also find a Freudian anticipation of just the characteristics I have tried to emphasize in Lacan's "Kant avec Sade": mob behavior is bound up with transient perversion, idealization, and self-sacrifice. In a word, *Schwarmerei*.

The place of *Seminar XVII*

If the swarm had only briefly caught Lacan's attention, by the time of *Seminar XVII*, all is flux (to invoke Heraclitus).[60] First, the political situation: May '68 has happened, which seems to have unleashed an entirely new form of political action. Second, the socio-economic situation: the law, the family, work, all seem to be in crisis. Lacan himself alludes to the events with his famous, ironical remarks about pot-smoking nudist homosexuals. Third, the institutional situation: Lacanian psychoanalysis is entering the university of the French state, then itself undergoing massive and rapid expansion (thanks, in part, to the administrative labors of one Michel Foucault). Fourth, the theoretical situation: Lacan is no longer happy with his idiosyncratic structuralist account of language that has, with constant minor divergences, sustained him until now. There are both immanent and external reasons for this unhappiness, for example, in the shift to post-structuralism then underway with Foucault, Derrida and Deleuze, all of whom are at that time elaborating serious critiques of the classical Saussurean doctrine. Fifth, the clinical situation is itself changing: psychoanalysis doesn't seem to be working as effectively as it once did.[61] Sixth, the technological situation is changing too: not only genetics, but post-WWII forms of telecommunications are now clearly shifting the relationship between humans and their environment (e.g., television and computing).

It is my contention that the "swarm" now returns, in a clarified form, as part of Lacan's attempt to respond to this situation. As such, it is a puncept that attempts to account for political, technological, social, institutional, theoretical, and clinical change *at once*. This program is entirely in line with psychoanalysis as it had been bequeathed by Freud: as we have seen, Freud himself had recourse to an insect metaphor in order to think the problem of groups in a time of political, socio-economic, institutional, theoretical, clinical and technological crisis.

As a result of this ferment what, in terms of Lacanian dogma, gets reworked in *Seminar XVII*? The nature of the unary trait, the master, identification, the object and enjoyment. The father is separated from the master. The master is now the master-signifier, and, in this mutation, can no longer be thought as: (i) the locus of law; (ii) the phallus; (iii) the father; (iv) diacritically defined. As Lacan puts it in this Seminar, the father has only "the most distant of relationships" with the master. The Oedipal complex is, moreover, a myth. The master himself doesn't give the law in knowing what he wants and in knowing what he wants to say, but in his very incoherence and opacity. Yet, this master "not only induces but determines castration." This master will later become the foundations for the doctrine of *lalangue*. But here Lacan's work of separation is beginning in earnest: $S_1 \neq$ phallus $\neq$ nom-du-père $\neq$ unary trait.

The unary trait, for instance, which had previously "filled the invisible mark that the subject draws from the signifier" (*Écrits*, p. 808), that "alienated the subject in the primary identification that forms the ideal ego" (p. 808), and which was "the mark of a primary identification that will function as ideal" (*Ornicar*, p. 10), is now given a different spin. First appearing as such in *Seminar VIII* (*The Transference*), then taken up in earnest in *Seminar IX* (*Identification*), the unary trait continues to shift its significance. In *Seminar XIV*, "the Logic of Fantasy," Lacan says the act can only be defined "on the foundation of the double loop, in other words, of repetition. [...] It is this repetition in a single line (trait) that I designated earlier by this cut that it is possible to make in the centre of the Moebius strip" (February 15, 1967). It is here that one can discern that the "one" of the "unary trait" is essentially the "one" of repetition, that is, of what I am arguing becomes the one-multiple of the *essaim*.

As for the algebra (not the concept) of S_1, it first appears, to my knowledge, in 1967, for example in the "Proposition of October 9, 1967 on the psychoanalyst of the School," where it has a rather different significance, being merely one element in the denominator of the formula of the transference.[62] But it is not until *Seminar XVII* that the S_1 achieves its canonical form as the master-signifier. Prior to this, the master had most clearly had a role in Lacan's reading of Hegel, and by which it was often associated with a major function of the ego (e.g., "Le moi est une fonction de maîtrise").

Without fully reconstructing this conceptual trajectory, it would remain difficult to determine the relation that S_1 and the unary trait bear to each other in Lacan. Indeed, the difficulties have led to dissension on the part of various authorities. Mark Bracher says that the *trait unaire*:

> is the earliest significance through which the child experiences itself—as a result of significations attributed to it by the Other (mother, father, and ultimately society at large). This constitutes the subject's primary identification. [...] But the *trait unaire* established by primary identification is supplemented and extended by various secondary identifications that serve as its avatars. It is, in fact, only through these secondary identifications that the primary identification manifests itself. And these secondary identifications, which

are certain (usually collective) values or ideals, play a crucial role in discourse. They are what Lacan calls master signifiers, S_1.[63]

Gilbert Chaitin's opinion is that "the unitary trait is a sign rather than a signifier; unlike the signifier, which can function only in opposition to other signifiers, it operates alone, without entering into relation with a 'battery of signifiers.'"[64] For his part, Paul Verhaeghe thinks that "[s]ubject formation derives from an S_1 that stems from a unary trait that needs to be repeated over an underlying absence."[65] For Ellie Ragland, "Miller has spoken of this signifier [S_1] as commensurate with the unary trait. Identification with the father is identification with him as the voice of difference."[66] Whereas Dominiek Hoens writes: "in *Seminar XVII* Lacan is again dealing with the unary trait (introduced in the final part of *Seminar VIII* and developed in *Seminar IX*), neither distinguishing it from nor identifying it with the master signifier S_1."[67] In yet another account, Lorenzo Chiesa maintains: "the one as unary trait is the '*instrument*' by means of which identification is made possible: the unary trait is not a one but an operation, a count, that constitutes 'the *foundation* of the one' of identification with the signifier."[68]

I have quoted these commentators in order to show how Lacan's text is clearly anything but clear on how the *trait unaire* and S_1 are articulated, or what their precise functions might be. I would like to suggest that the problem can be both explained and resolved by recourse to the swarm. Indeed, the difficulties experienced by commentators in deciding the precise relationship between the unary trait and master signifier are a result of the difficulty of the puncept itself. My own account is this: the S_1 derives from the originary multiplication of unary traits into a swarm, that is, an equivocal mess of foreign lines of imaginary identification that have been cut into the body: "Repetition is the precise denotation of a trait that I have uncovered for you in Freud's text as identical with the unary trait, with the little stick, with the element of writing, of a trait insofar as it is the commemoration of an irruption of enjoyment."[69] So the unary trait must be re-marked (or re-marks itself); it is only "unary," one, by being so re-marked; as it is re-marked, it becomes a swarm, the S_1, the precondition of language in the subject, what emerges between imaginary and symbolic as the trace of the real (*jouissance*).

So an S_1 is *literally* a "swarm" of unary traits that have been incised into a living body and which have acquired a kind of "critical mass." When it is no longer possible to define the foundations of signification on the basis of a primordial diacritical difference (as had previously been the case for Lacan's theory of signification), Lacan is forced to come up with a new response. This S_1-unary trait theory is an important part of his answer. For the S_1 is not a diacritically defined signifier, but emerges from an irreducibly equivocal reiteration prior to signification, inseparable from the identificatory stigmata of the unary traits.[70] The swarm *must* be prior to sexual differentiation (which is bound to the symbolic), so this "origin" cannot be a father, name of the father, or phallus. In fact, a swarm is—as recent scientific research has suggested—autotaxic (that is, without leader or external directives), non-linear, omnidirectional, transient, a one-multiple composed of indiscriminable elements.[71]

Swarms are highly unpredictable in their movements, varying in the length, scale, dimensionality, velocity and acceleration of individuals. One notable feature is that the communicational range between the creatures comprising the swarm is smaller than the swarm itself. There is no leader, organizing structure, clear aim or end to a swarm. Why, then, do creatures swarm? Usually, it's considered: a defense against predators, for example, lizard predators turn out to be averse to gregarious but not solitarious locusts, and there is less chance of any individual being eaten due to sheer force of numbers; a defense against environmental change (the phase-shifts of locusts enable rapid adaptation to different environments); there are mating and feeding swarms ("love and hunger"); etc. Yet swarms are inevitably destroyed (e.g., locust swarms starve or are blown out to sea). So there is also an adaptive problem posed by the swarm: what's the evolutionary point? Moreover, swarm creatures are diphasic-creatures, that is, "split subjects," and, if a swarm does not comprise any kind of Dionysian orgy (that is, a self-destructive melding with others), it still bears clear links to the death-drive. The swarm is thus irreducibly equivocal.

Moreover, why Lacan considers "the master" to be "a swarm" seems to me determined by the lines I have been tracing: the problem of prelinguistic foundation and the problem of pre-political community meet in the terrain of the swarm. Lacan no longer founds his theory on the phallus, but on *traits unaires*, bundles of little sticks, letter-scar-stigmata of primal identifications; meaningless and contingent in themselves, they come to constitute the S_1 as a one-multiple. Lacan therefore no longer conceives of enjoyment as transgression of the law (which now becomes a secondary phenomenon, itself just a *semblant*), but as bound to sophisticated technical apparatuses (soon denominated *lathouses* by Lacan) for extracting *lichettes*, tiny amounts of *jouissance*. The limits of existence are no longer given by primal bands of guilty brothers, nor by highly organized, hierarchical mass societies of repression, but by stochastic drifts of unleashed particles that sporadically and unpredictably erupt into vast destructive swarms that are both pre- and trans-individual.

With the swarm, then, Lacan not only rethinks traditional psychoanalytic concepts, but anticipates and formalizes a notion that is today everywhere in science, technology and cultural studies. The swarm has become a staple quasi-notion in communication-theory, a function of "a creeping shift from an era of centralized communication dominated by commercial mass communication to an emergent era of decentralized communication dominated by mobile mass communication."[72] This is one great psychoanalytic contribution to the study of technology. Contemporary technology isn't going to lead to any transcendence of consciousness, as MIT robotics researchers are idiotically wont to declare, but rather uncovers something profoundly archaic, uncanny: humans are swarm animals. Technology, as "the highest means for the lowest ends," today inserts its connections directly into the organism (that is, the inscription of unary traits), without having to pass through "language" *per se* or the mediation of the vocal apparatus. Thus the Lacanian swarm undoes the distinction between human/animal—but without a simple reduction to the natural. And where Lacan differs from many others who praise the swarm is his refusal to idealize it.[73]

One Judeo-Christian tradition considers that Nimrod—"mighty hunter before the Lord"—was the builder of the Tower of Babel, a narrative that provides a striking image of the S_1. In one Islamic tradition, Nimrod—also the enemy and oppressor of Abraham—is ultimately defeated by a swarm of gnats sent by God. One of the swarm enters Nimrod's brain and drives him mad with its buzzing.

Notes

1. A "puncept" is not a philosophical concept but an elementary psychoanalytic notion; perhaps it would be better phrased as a "puneme" or "calemboureme," on the same model as a "mytheme" or "matheme." Lacan is extremely sensitive to the use of punning as a fundamental form of thinking in others: in Freud, of course, and in Heidegger and Joyce, as well as in many other places. In *Seminar XI*, he states of the pre-Socratic investigation into knowledge, which "required a *clinamen*, an inclination, at some point. When Democritus tried to designate it, presenting himself as already the adversary of a pure function of negativity in order to introduce thought into it, he says, *It is not the μηδεν that is essential*, and adds—thus showing you that from what one of my pupils called the archaic stage of philosophy, the manipulation of words was used just as in the time of Heidegger—*it is*

not an μηδεν, but a δεν, which, in Greek, is a coined word. He did not say *εν,* let alone *ov." The Four Fundamental Concepts of Psychoanalysis,* translated by A. Sheridan, introduced by D. Macey (London: Penguin, 1994), pp. 63–4. But he also insists that the psychoanalytic (and perhaps also literary) uses of punning differ importantly from those of the philosophers. One could also think of Roland Barthes' famous "punctum" in this context. Also here, the puncept itself puns on "ponctuel," like a point, but also punctual and fleeting (as Bruce Fink translates it in *The Seminar of Jacques Lacan Book XX: On Feminine Sexuality, the Limits of Love and Knowledge (1972–1973). Encore,* edited by Jacques-Alain Miller, translation and notes by Bruce Fink (London and NY: W. W. Norton & Company, 1998)). The unconscious, as Lacan never ceases to reiterate, is arrhythmic and untimely.

2. What makes this list at once so appealing and so specious is that it utterly ignores the conceptual, procedural and institutional differences with which each thinker pursues his case, his singular elaboration of the place and status of the prepolitical element in humanity. It is also unacceptably truncated. I nonetheless present it here for its pedagogical and polemical qualities, in order to emphasize, first, the anti-anthropological tenor of such discourses (the political proper is never to be presupposed in humanity, but is always a result of a condition that must be reconstructed after the fact) and, second, the heterogeneous continuity of responses to the problem.

3. "The instinct for imitation is inherent in man from his earliest days; he differs from other animals in that he is the most imitative of creatures, and he learns his earliest lessons by imitation. Also inborn in all of us is the instinct to enjoy works of imitation," Aristotle, "On the Art of Poetry" in *Classical Literary Criticism,* translation and introduction by T. S. Dorsch (London: Penguin, 1988), p. 35.

4. Stupid as it is to say so, there are no politics in Eden, precisely because it is sexual difference as such that distributes social labor, and there is no polity. If the snake is the +1 that introduces desire into the mix, then that triangulation becomes one condition of the political.

5. For example, "One can make this generalization about men: they are ungrateful, fickle, liars, and deceivers, they shun danger and are greedy for profit; while you treat them well, they are yours." Niccolò Machiavelli, *The Prince,* translation by G. Bull, introduction by A. Grafton (London: Penguin, 2003). p. 54.

6. "The passions that incline men to peace are fear of death, desire of such things as are necessary to commodious living, and a hope by their industry to attain them," Thomas Hobbes, *Leviathan,* edited by A. P. Martinich (Ont.: Broadview, 2002), p. 97. Hobbes used to say that he and fear had been born as twins with the Spanish Armada; of the English Civil War, he was pleased to say that he was "the first of all that fled."

7. "God, having made man such a creature that, in His own judgment, it was not good for him to be alone, put him under strong obligations of necessity, convenience, and inclination, to drive him into society, as well as fitted him with understanding and language to continue and enjoy it." John Locke, *Two Treatises of Government* (London: Everyman, 1986), pp. 154–5. See also "God having designed Man for a sociable Creature, made him not only with an inclination, and under a necessity to have fellowship with those of

his own kind; but furnished him also with Language, which was to be the great Instrument, and common Tye of Society," *An Essay Concerning Human Understanding*, edited by P. H. Nidditch (Oxford: Clarendon Press, 1985), Book III, Chapter I, p. 402.

8. "Among the Romans *sensus communis* meant not only common sense, but humanity, sensibility. Since we are not up to the Romans this word means only half as much to us as it did to them." Voltaire, *Philosophical Dictionary*, translated and edited by T. Besterman (Harmondsworth: Penguin, 1972), pp. 376–7. Or, again, "the man who is not a beast and does not think he is an angel," p. 376. One can easily see why Alain Badiou recently denominated Voltaire, "one of the most considerable thinkers of humanitarian mediocrity." *Le siècle* (Paris: Seuil, 2005), p. 177.

9. Jean-Jacques Rousseau, *Discourse on Political Economy; and The Social Contract*, trans. with introduction and notes by Christopher Betts (Oxford: Oxford University Press, 1994).

10. "Enlightenment is man's emergence from his self-incurred immaturity." Immanuel Kant, *Political Writings*, translation by H. B. Nisbet, edited by H. Reiss (Cambridge: Cambridge University Press, 1991), p. 54. Another revealing essay in this regard is his "Conjectures on the beginning of human history," where he states in a note about the learning of language: "The *urge to communicate* must have been the original motive for human beings who were still alone to announce their existence to living creatures outside themselves, especially to those which emit sounds which can be imitated and which can subsequently serve as a name. A similar effect of this urge can still be seen in children and thoughtless people who disturb the thinking section of the community by banging, shouting, whistling, singing and other noisy pastimes (and often even by noisy religious devotions). For I can see no motive for such behaviour other than a desire on the part of those concerned to proclaim their existence to the world at large," p. 222.

11. Jeremy Bentham, *An Introduction to the Principle of Morals and Legislation*, edited by J. H. Burns and H. L. A. Hart (London and NY: Methuen, 1980).

12. Most of the Romantics placed an exceptionally high value on infancy, and this Romantic obsession remains legible today, in the work of thinkers such as Maurice Blanchot and Giorgio Agamben (*Infancy and History*, 2007). Carl Schmitt also picked up on this with extreme irritation in his *Political Romanticism*, where he fulminates, "Children are also bearers of the irrational profusion that the romantic has at his disposal. Not every child; as Novalis said, not 'spoiled, pampered, namby-pamby children,' but only 'undetermined children.' Like many other romantic sentiments, this one as well had already been expressed by Schiller in his essay on naïve and sentimental poetry: what is touching about a child is that it is not yet determined, not yet limited. It still has in itself all the innumerable possibilities that the man has already lost. Primitive peoples—humanity as childlike—are also bearers of these unlimited possibilities." *Political Romanticism*, translation by Guy Oakes (Cambridge, MA: The MIT Press, 1986), p. 69.

13. "Man is a toad-eating animal. The admiration of power in others is as common to man as the love of it in himself: the one makes him a tyrant, the other a slave." William Hazlitt, *Selected Writings* (Harmondsworth: Penguin, 1989), p. 378.

14. Thomas de Quincey, *Confessions of an English Opium Eater*, edited by Alethea Hayter (London: Penguin, 1986).
15. G. W. F. Hegel, *Phenomenology of Spirit*, translated by A. V. Miller, analysis and foreword by J. N. Findlay (Oxford: Oxford University Press, 1977); this, at least, would be what Alexandre Kojève takes from and extends in Hegel: the primacy of the struggle for prestige as founding the political sphere, *Introduction to the Reading of Hegel*, edited by Allan Bloom, translation by J. H. Nichols (NY and London: Basic Books, 1969).
16. See Karl Marx, *Capital*, vol. 1, translation by Ben Fowkes, introduction by E. Mandel (Harmondsworth: Penguin, 1976). As Jean-Luc Nancy comments, for Marx "the name of sense—of the sense of liberation and the deliverance of sense—was 'labor' (for him, and for an entire epoch that remains still in several respects our own) [...]. It is thus a question of labor as the *first need of life.*" *The Sense of the World*, translated with foreword by Jeffrey S. Librett (Minneapolis: University of Minnesota Press, 1997), p. 95. One should refer here also to the Master/Slave dialectic of Hegel.
17. *Twilight of the Idols*. Note that Nietzsche's utterance is itself a brilliant *imitation* of Aristotle's statement on mimesis (that is, Nietzsche is imitating Aristotle, both at the level of the signifier and at the level of meaning), but with an abyssal nuance. What is the difference between "mimesis" and "following the leader," as Nietzsche's utterance poses? Nietzsche returns the Aristotelian statement from its poetic setting to a political one. He also suggests how the leader that you follow is—yourself. A man is a herd animal because he is constantly following the pattern set by his own past; yet this repetition also introduces a multiplicity, a divergence that induces confusion into the organism.
18. Sigmund Freud, "Group Psychology and the Analysis of the Ego" in *The Standard Edition of the Complete Psychological Works of Sigmund Freud*, vol. 18, edited by James Strachey. (London: The Hogarth Press, 1955), p. 121.
19. For instance, it is here that Giorgio Agamben's work suffers from a too-rapid reduction of the *zoe/bios* distinction. Animality is not the only thing that is excluded from the polis in order to found qualified forms of life; rather, animality is itself already naturally differentiated and, moreover, man outside the polis, a man without others, is not *simply* an animal (he could also be a "god," he can make a return to human life, etc.). As Paolo Palladino says, "Strikingly, while Agamben's articulation of the common foundations of bio-power and governmentality is quite compelling, he fails to note that, while Aristotle understood the human to be a 'political animal,' he also conceded that some animals were 'social,' if not properly 'political.' In other words, the meaning of zoe was as unclear as the meaning of bios." Paolo Palladino, "Life ... On Biology, Biography, and Bio-power in the Age of Genetic Engineering," *Configurations*, 11. 1 (2003), 81–109 (p. 88).
20. Jacques Lacan, "Lituraterre," *Autres Écrits* (Paris: Seuil, 2001), p. 18.
21. My emphasis on "swarms" will mean that one cannot really give, à la Philippe Julien, a version of Lacan's development that runs from an interest in the Imaginary (1930s & '40s), then Symbolic (1950s to mid-60s), then finally on the Real (late 1960s–'80s). However useful such a schema may be for a general appreciation of Lacan's mutations, it is inadequate to comprehending the non-linear subtleties of his development.

22. Y. Pélissier, "Glossaire mode d'emploi," *789 néologismes de Jacques Lacan* (Paris: EPEL, 2002), p. x.

23. Though it has indeed become the title of a journal *Essaim*, edited by Erik Porge and others, it still seems to be deployed there in its role as pun and the mark of a doctrinal affiliation, not a carefully elaborated concept in its own right.

24. *The Cambridge Companion to Lacan*, edited by Jean-Michel Rabaté (Cambridge: Cambridge University Press, 2003); note also the absence of "swarm" in the index to *Jacques Lacan and the Other Side of Psychoanalysis*, edited by Justin Clemens and Russell Grigg (Durham: Duke University Press, 2006), where it does not appear under "master signifier," nor under "S_1," nor in its own right.

25. Jacques Lacan, *Écrits*, translated by Bruce Fink with Héloise Fink and Russell Grigg (NY: Norton, 2006), p. 870. I would also like to point out two typos in the publishing details, all the more peculiar when read together: instead of the French publisher of Lacan's texts being listed as *Éditions du Seuil* (lit. Threshold Publishing), it is here *Éditions du Deuil* (Bereavement Publishing); Lacan's name appears further down the same page, with his birth date (1901–), but no termination, as if he hadn't yet died. ... such typographical errors smack of a veritable refusal to mourn!

26. Lacan, *Écrits*, pp. 645/668.

27. Jacques-Alain Miller, "On Perversion" in *Reading Seminars I and II* edited by Richard Feldstein, Bruce Fink and Maire Jaanus (Albany: SUNY, 1996), pp. 309–10. See also his "A Discussion of Lacan's 'Kant with Sade,'" in the same volume, pp. 212–37. See Judith Feher-Gurewich, "A Lacanian Approach to the Logic of Perversion," in *The Cambridge Companion*, pp. 191–207, Dominiek Hoens, "Towards a New Perversion: Psychoanalysis" in Clemens and Grigg (eds) *Jacques Lacan*, pp. 88–103, as well as Slavoj Žižek's extensive writings, for example, *The Puppet and the Dwarf: The Perverse Core of Christianity* (London: The MIT Press, 2003). Lacan deals with perversion in a number of places, notably in *Le Séminaire IV: La relation d'objet* (Paris: Seuil, 1994), *Seminar VII: The Ethics of Psychoanalysis (1959–1960)*, translation by Dennis Porter (London: Routledge, 1992), which introduces the Kant-Sade coupling, to *Le Séminaire X: L'angoisse* (Paris: Seuil, 2004)—in addition, of course, to the previously cited "Kant with Sade."

28. Lacan, *Écrits*, p. 652.

29. This a ◊ $ has led several commentators to identify the pervert's structure with that of the psychoanalyst; after all, in Seminar XVII, the discourse of the analyst is explicitly formalized as a → $. Lacan, moreover, constantly raises the question of the analyst's desire—perhaps implying that, having himself necessarily passed through the end of analysis, he, the analyst, has, in the course of the process, come to know the secret of desire (the pervert's very conviction). If this were the whole story, psychoanalysis would truly be, as Dominiek Hoens suggests, "a new perversion." On the other hand, perversion is a *structure* for Lacan, whereas the analyst's is a *discourse*: not the same thing at all. This means, first, that the analyst only places himself in such a *position* in his role as analyst, a precarious and transient role in any case. Second, perversion is not a social link, because it is not a discourse; instead, the pervert is literally *a-social*. This is confirmed when one takes into

account the underlining of the four discourses: in the analyst's discourse, the a → $ is perched over S_2 // S_1, putting knowledge in the place of truth and the master as the product of analysis. Elsewhere, I have suggested a matheme for the "a-discourse" of the pervert, whereby a → $ is perched above S_1 // S_2, which puts the master in the place of truth (hence the characteristic aggression of the pervert, his or her undoing of social bonds). See my essay, "The Purloined Veil: Notes on an Image," *(a): The Journal of Culture and the Unconscious*, 4. 1 (2004), 75–88, esp. p. 84.

30. Lacan, *Écrits*, p. 832.
31. P. Fenves, "A note on the translation of Kant," in *Raising the Tone of Philosophy: Late Essays by Immanuel Kant, Transformative Critique by Jacques Derrida*, edited by P. Fenves (Baltimore: Johns Hopkins University Press, 1993), p. xi. As Anthony La Vopa puts it, "*Schwärmerei* [...] drew on the sights and sounds of agricultural life, and these made it resonant with images that gave contagion and mass violence a palpable presence." "The Philosopher and the *Schwärmer*: On the Career of a German Epithet from Luther to Kant," *Huntington Library Quarterly*, 60. 1–2 (1998), p. 88. The term *Schwärmerei* entered medicine in the course of the eighteenth century, and hence, as La Vopa suggests, philosophers began to use the term by analogy: doctors deal with the health of the physical body, philosophers with that of the ethico-political body.
32. The work of Peter Fenves is particularly useful in this context. See, in addition to the papers and translations quoted here, *A Peculiar Fate: Metaphysics and World-History in Kant* (NY: Cornell University Press, 1991).
33. One of Hölderlin's juvenile poems is entitled, precisely, *Schwärmerei*; there is another poem by Sophie Frederike Mereau-Brentano entitled *Schwärmerei der Liebe*. A late poem by Paul Celan reads:

> Out of the near
> waterpits,
> greygreen shoveled
> upwards with unawakened hands:
>
> the depth
> gives up its growth, inaudible,
> without resistance.
>
> To recover that
> too, before
> the stoneday blows the men-
> and animal swarms [*die Menschen-/und Tierschwärme*] empty, exactly as
> the sevenflute, that stepped in front of the mouths, the maws, demands it.

From *Threadsuns*, translation by Pierre Joris (København and Los Angeles: Green Integer, 2005), p. 93. Whether significantly or not, Hölderlin's poem is hardly discussed at all, and when it is it is often in patronizing tones, for example, "Several of the early poems and letters show the writer working deliberately at the excitation of strong feelings. In "*Schwärmerei*," for example, he revels in thoughts of his own death,' David Constantine, *Hölderlin*

(Oxford: Clarendon Press, 1988), p. 9. Though he doesn't discuss this early poem, Fenves suggests of Hölderlin's later work, that "the *Schwärmer* is the term Hölderlin uses in 'Reflections' to designate what he elsewhere calls 'the halfgods' (*Halbgötter*)," and that in *Der Rhein*, Herakles will destroy his own house because *"sein will und nicht/Ungleiches dulden, der Schwärmer"* (*wants to be and will not bear inequality, the Schwärmer*), *"The Scale of Enthusiasm,"* *Huntington Library Quarterly*, 60 (1998), p. 150. Hölderlin has sometimes been mooted as the addressee of Schelling's *Philosophical Letters*, in which Schwärmerei is discussed.

34. Fenves, "The Scale of Enthusiasm," p. 121. After all: "A host of words have been used to designate what, as an indefinite multitude, is less than a natural kind. One of these words gains particular importance because it points toward the natural—and therefore non-transcendent—origin of 'enthusiasm': the German word, *Schwarm*, 'swarm.' The members of a swarm are not only impossible to distinguish from one another but are also, for this reason, not even members of the swarm: instead of belonging to a stable collective according to which they would be recognized and named, each one is a temporary participant in an act of 'swarming,' or *Schwärmerei*. Whereas the term enthusiasm refers without ambiguity, although not without irony, to something more than humankind—less than human because animals, not human beings, aggregate into swarms; and more than human because the only animals whose multitudes turn into swarms are those that, like the gods, are able to take leave of the earth," p. 120.

35. In addition to Fink and Fenves, Nisbet provides the following footnote to his translation of "What is orientation in thinking?" (*Was heisst: Sich im Denken orientiren?* 1786): "Kant uses the term *Schwärmerei* to denote extravagant thinking in a philosophical or religious context. Its closest equivalent in English is the term 'enthusiasm' as it was used in the eighteenth century; but since 'enthusiasm' now has different connotations—predominantly emotional rather than intellectual, and positive rather than negative it is no longer appropriate as a translation of *Schwärmerei*. The term 'fanaticism' is scarcely adequate either, since it suggests rather the extreme emotional commitment with which a belief is held than the irrationality of the belief itself. 'Zealotry,' with its implication of sectarian dogmatism as well as obsessive commitment, is perhaps the least unsatisfactory term in the present context." Immanuel Kant, *Political Writings*, edited by H. Reiss, translation by H. B. Nisbet (Cambridge: Cambridge University Press, 1991), p. 284.

36. La Vopa, "The Philosopher and the *Schwärmer*," p. 91, p. 103.

37. In fact, the metaphor of the swarm extends far beyond the German scene. In *De Cive*, Hobbes announces that, "Among the animals which Aristotle calls political he counts not only *Man*, but many others too, including the *Ant*, the *Bee*, etc. For although they are devoid of reason, which would permit them to make agreements and submit to government, still by their consenting, i.e. by desiring and avoiding the same objects, they so direct their actions to a common end that their swarms are not disturbed by sedition. Yet their swarms are still not *commonwealths*, and so the animals should not be called *political*; for their government is only an accord, or many wills with one object, not (as a commonwealth needs) one will." *De Cive*, 5.5, quoted in Malcolm Bull, "The Limits of Multitude," *New Left Review*,

35 (September/October 2005), p. 32. For Hobbes, what is determining is that there is no difference in bees and ants, etc., between public and private benefit. This is due to their absence of reason and, as such, they do the public good by pursuing their private interests. Bull argues that, from Hobbes through Mandeville and Smith to Hayek to Hardt and Negri, the image of the swarm serves to found a philosophically conservative naturalization of man.

38. Lacan, *Écrits*, p. 667.

39. The title of Kant's book in German is *Von einem neuerdings erhobenen vornehmen Ton in der Philosophie*; Schlosser's is *Platos Briefe über die syrakusanische Staatsrevolution, nebst einer historischen Einleitung und Anmerkung.*

40. Kant, *Political Writings*, p. 230. Earlier in his career (indeed, as early as 1766), "Kant ha[d] criticized Boehme and Swedenborg as mystics who had fallen prey to *Schwärmerei*—wild and unaccountable enthusiasm"; Jean-Michel Rabaté, *Jacques Lacan: Psychoanalysis and the Subject of Literature* (London: Palgrave Macmillan, 2001), p. 97. Fenves notes that "After the publication of the first *Critique*, Kant's polemics against *Schwärmerei* cease to be so closely bound up with attempts to explain the phenomenon through recourse to physiology; instead, Kant almost always returns to the history of philosophy and thus alters the basis of explanation from biological causality to historical and genealogical nexes," *Raising the Tone of Philosophy*, p. 112n1.

41. Lacan, *Écrits*, p. 657, translation modified.

42. Significantly, the word *Schwärmerei* has already cropped up in Lacan's work in a tangential way, for example, in 1960 he declares that "Plato's *Schwärmerei* consists in having projected the idea of the Supreme Good on that which I name the impenetrable void," *Seminar VIII*, p. 35. As for bees on the verge of swarming, they are everywhere in Lacan, from his invocations of Mandeville to animal ethology to Benveniste, as well as in the Wolfman's *Wespe*. As Freud recalls: "The relationship between the scene with Gruscha and the threat of castration was confirmed by a particularly suggestive dream, which he was able to translate on his own. He said: 'I dreamed that a man was tearing the wings of an asp [*Espe*].' 'Asp?' I naturally asked, 'What do you mean by that?'—'Well, the insect with yellow stripes on its body, the one that can sting you. It must be a reference to Gruscha, the yellow-striped pear.'—Now I was able to correct him: 'You mean a wasp, then [*Wespe*]'—'Is the word wasp? I really thought it was asp.' (Like so many others, he used his unfamiliarity with German to conceal his symptomatic actions.) But an asp, that must be me, S. P. (his initials). An asp is of course a mutilated wasp." *Fragment of a History of an Infantile Neurosis*. In his "Postface to *Seminar XI*," Lacan writes, "*Si du butinage de l'abeille je lis sa part dans la fertilité des plantes phanérogames, si j'augure du groupe plus ras-de-terre à se faire vol d'hirondelles la fortune des tempêtes—c'est bien de ce qui les porte au signifiant de ce fait que je parle, que j'ai à rendre compte.*" *Autres Ecrits* (Paris: Seuil, 2002), p. 505.

43. This is why I don't quite agree with Ed Pluth and Dominiek Hoens when they say, "In our own view it is Badiou rather than Lacan who develops the logical and political implications of 'Logical Time.' In doing so it seems to us that he re-elaborates the Kantian distinction between enthusiasm and fanaticism." "What if the Other is Stupid?" in *Think Again: Alain Badiou*

and the Future of Philosophy, edited by Peter Hallward (London and NY: Continuum, 2004), p. 188. Their basic point is sound: that the problem of logical time is directed to the problem of action, and they are right to suggest that, in the coupling of these problems, a distinction between enthusiasm and *Schwärmerei* re-emerges. Yet Lacan is entirely aware of the necessity to rethink this too, as I am arguing; in fact, this is at least partially his motivation for his development of the S_1.

44. Indeed, the disappearance of *Schwärmerei* from English-language psychoanalysis has been close to complete. When I did a search through the Psychoanalytic Electronic Publishing archive (which, as their publicity has it, "contains the full text of the *Standard Edition of the Complete Psychological Works of Sigmund Freud* and the full text of eighteen premier journals in psychoanalysis"), I found only one occurrence of the word in the "over 50, 000 articles" available, in Eugen J. Hárnik, "Pleasure in Disguise, the Need for Decoration, and the Sense of Beauty," *Psychoanalytic Quarterly*, 1 (1932), 216–64. Even more suggestively, though the article uses the word only in passing, in the familiar non-technical sense of "passionate enthusiasm," it does so in the context of discussing a case of "perversion": "I once observed an unbounded *Schwärmerei* for the beauty of the female sexual organs in a genital hair fetishist, whose interest at times was completely absorbed by the conformation of the female pubic hair, samples of which he would procure for his private enjoyment," p. 246.

45. *Schwärmerei [Schwärmen, schwärmerische Liebe]* (s.a. *Verliebtheit*), V p. 130f.; *homosexuelle*, v, p. 130f.; xii, p. 110, p. 272, p. 278, p. 295; *hysterische beim Mann* v, p. 221 *beim Weib* v, p. 220f., p. 223f.; *bei Normalen* (s.a. *Schwärmerei*, i.d. *Pubertät*), v, p. 130f.; xii, p. 297f; f. *Künstler*, xiii, p.133; i.d. *Masse*, xiii, p. 132f.; *Mitleids-*, x. p. 325, p. 333; xiv, p. 503 f.; i.d. *Pubertät*, v, p. 130f., xii, p. 297f., xiii, pp. 123–5; *religiöse u. Mätyrertum*, v, p. 297 u. *Perversion u. Mystik* (s.a. *Mystik*), x, p. 77f;. *Soldaten*, xii, p. 100.

46. Freud, *Gesammelte Werke*, vol. v (London: Imago, 1942), p. 130.

47. Freud, *Standard Edition*, vol. v,p. 229.

48. *Vocabulaire Européen des Philosophies: Dictionnaire des Intraduisibles*, edited by Barbara Cassin (Paris: Editions du Seuil/Dictionnaires Le Robert, 2004), p. 456. Though the *Vocabulaire* gives *Psychische Behandlung* (1890), *Drei Abhandlungen zur Sexualtheorie* (1905), *Zur Geschichte der psychoanalytischen Bewegung* (1914) and *Über die Psychogenese eines Falles von weiblicher Homosexualität* (1920) as references, it does not, for reasons that are obscure, note the apparition of the term in a number of other places, including "Thoughts for the time on War and Death," and the *Massenpsychologie*.

49. See "Zur Geschichte der psychoanalytischen Bewegung," in *Gesammelte Werke* x, p. 77, and "Zeitgemäßes über Krieg und Tod" in the same volume, for example, "*die meisten Mitleidsschwärmer, Menschenfreunde, Tierschütze, haben sich aus kleinen Sadisten und Tierquälern entwickelt*," p. 333.

50. Sigmund Freud, *Gesammelte Werke*, vol. xii (London: Imago, 1947), pp. 269–302; "The Psychogenesis of a Case of Homosexuality in a Woman"(1920), *Standard Edition*, vol. xviii (1920–2), pp. 145–72. All further German and English quotations will be to these volumes.

51. See also pp. 288/160, 288/161, 295/166, 297/170. Note that the variations in the SE make it impossible to recognize—let alone reconstruct—the vicissitudes

of the word in English translation, and, *a fortiori*, whatever import it may have for psychoanalysis.

52. See Lacan, *Le Séminaire IV*, p. 109.

53. Freud, "New Introductory Lectures on Psychoanalysis" in *The Standard Edition*, vol. XXII, p. 55.

54. See B. Marpeau, *Gustave le Bon: Parcours d'un intellectuel 1841–1931* (Paris: CNRS, 2000), for some suggestive details about the circumstances in which Le Bon penned his masterpiece, including sales of his books.

55. Alenka Zupančič, "When Surplus-enjoyment Meets Surplus-value," in Clemens and Grigg (eds) *Jacques Lacan*, p. 156.

56. Freud, *Gesammelte Werke* XIII (London: Imago, 1940), p. 123; *The Standard Edition* , vol. XVIII, p. 112. In Chapter IX, Freud writes: *"Man denke an die Schar von schwärmerisch verliebten Frauen und Mädchen die den Sänger oder Pianisten nach seiner Produktion umdrängen"* (GW, p. 133); "We have only to think of the troop of women and girls, all of them in love, in an enthusiastically sentimental way, who crowd round a singer or pianist after his performance" (*SE*, p. 120).

57. Note that, soon following the passage cited, Freud realizes how problematic the situation is, and begins to run through explanatory possibilities very quickly. Is it the case that, first, *"The object has been put in place of the ego ideal"* (p. 113)? Is it that, in identification, the ego has "enriched itself" with the object, whereas, in the extreme "fascination" and "bondage" of certain loves, the object has been substituted for the ego itself? Can it be that, in identification, the object has been lost or renounced, but set up again in the ego, which now has partially modeled itself after the lost object, whereas, in fascination, there is rather a hypercathexis of the object (traces of *Mourning and Melancholia* are at play here)? Or is the question whether the object has been put in place of the ego *or* of the ego ideal? It is such questions that the new theory of identification is to resolve.

58. In an extremely interesting essay, Jean-Claude Milner provides a footnote regarding the problem of crowds: "August 14th is the material base of militarist subversion. The concept of *crowds [foules]*, such as Le Bon articulated from 1895 in explicit reference to the Commune, is its intellectual base. One can retroactively sum up its function: to construct a point from which one will not distinguish 1793 and 1914; reciprocally, the concept of *masses [masses]* has no other function than to construct a point where the distinction subsists. One sees in what sense Hitlerism is a politics of crowds and in what sense the question poses itself of knowing what Stalin made of the distinction between masses and crowds. We will note that subversion requires that one remain in the spaces organized by the conjuncture. This is what separates Freud from Hitlerians. Like them, he didn't distinguish between 1793 and 1914. But this non-differentiation, with him, is very precisely a matter of what Lacan called the Freudian indifference in politics. It is a question of a movement by which he attempted (perhaps in vain) to tear himself from the spaces of the conjunction. Among the sectarians of the classical doctrine, it would be interesting to test L. Strauss on the following point: had he the will and, having it, has he the means to distinguish 1793 and 1914? The question equally concerns C. Schmitt, Jünger and their current disciples, that is, in particular, F. Mitterand. It's legitimate to think that a political doctrine

incapable of working such a distinction would not be entirely serious." Jean-Claude Milner, *Constats* (Paris: Gallimard, 2002), pp. 49–50.

59. Freud, *Standard Edition*, vol. XVIII, pp. 107–8.

60. Is it any accident that, in the very first session of Seminar XVII, Lacan then invokes "Kant avec Sade," and in regards to the *"quart de tour,"* p. 13?

61. "Lacan's inaugural point of departure, in 1952, is the assertion, 'There is psychoanalysis.' It exists, it works. [...] His arrival point is 'psychoanalysis doesn't work,' and to ask himself why it doesn't"; Jacques-Alain Miller, "Six Paradigms of Jouissance," *Lacanian Ink*, 17, p. 41.

62. One can also find S_1 making a very brief appearance in *Seminar XI*, where it is linked with S_2 as "the first dyad of signifiers" (p. 236) along with a diagram (p. 238), where it surmounts the algebra "S(i(a, a', a", ...))" for a series of identifications, *The Four Fundamental Concepts of Psychoanalysis*.

63. Mark Bracher, "On the Psychological and Social Functions of Language: Lacan's Theory of the Four Discourses," in *Lacanian Theory of Discourse: Subject, Structure, and Society*, edited by Mark Bracher, Marshall W. Alcorn Jr, R. J. Corthell, and F. Massardier-Kenney (NY and London: New York University Press, 1994), p. 111.

64. Gilbert Chaitin, *Rhetoric and Culture in Lacan* (Cambridge: Cambridge University Press, 1996), p. 129.

65. Paul Verhaeghe, "Enjoyment and Impossibility," in Clemens and Grigg (eds) *Jacques Lacan*, p. 56.

66. Ellie Ragland, "The Hysteric's Truth," in Clemens and Grigg (eds) *Jacques Lacan*, p. 99.

67. Hoens, in Clemens and Grigg (eds) *Jacques Lacan*, pp. 124–5.

68. Lorenzo Chiesa, "Count-as-one, Forming-into-one, Unary Trait, S_1" in *The Praxis of Alain Badiou*, edited by Paul Ashton, A. J. Bartlett and Justin Clemens (Melbourne: Re.press, 2006), p. 154. Chiesa continues: "the S_1 is the unary trait as repressed," p. 173.

69. Lacan, *Seminar XVII*, p. 89. As Lacan also says, "Here I will borrow something from Freud's text and give it a sense that is not highlighted there, namely, the function of the unary trait, that is, of the simplest form of mark, which properly speaking is *the origin of the signifier*," p. 52 [my emphasis]. He immediately adds: "everything that interests us analysts as knowledge originates in the unary trait," p. 52.

70. This is brought to its apotheosis in *Seminar XX*: "What does 'There's such a thing as One' mean? From the *one-among-others*—and the point is to know whether it is any old which one—arises an S_1, a signifying swarm, a buzzing swarm. If I raise the question, 'Is it of them-two that I am speaking?', I will write this S_1 of each signifier, first on the basis of its relation to S_2. And you can add as many of them as you like. This is the swarm I am talking about.

$$S_1(S_1(S_1(S1 \rightarrow S2)))$$

S_1, the swarm or master signifier, is that which assures the unity, the unity of the subject's copulation with knowledge. It is in language and nowhere else, insofar as language is investigated qua language, that what a primitive linguistics designated with the term στοιχείον, element—and that was no accident—can be discerned. The signifer 'One' is not just any old signifier.

It is the signifying order insofar as it is instituted on the basis of the envelopment by which the whole of the chain subsists." *Seminar XX*, p. 143. The swarm of the S_1 thus at once conditions and envelops knowledge; knowledge, *pace* Kant, cannot escape *Schwärmerei*.

71. See such accounts as: E. Bonabeau, M. Dorigo & G. Theraulaz, *Swarm Intelligence: From Natural to Artificial Systems* (NY: Oxford University Press, 1999); C. M. Topaz and Andrea L. Bertozzi, "Swarming Patterns in a Two-Dimensional Kinematic Model for Biological Groups," *Siam Journal of Applied Mathematics*, 65. 1 (2004), pp. 152–74; Y. Tyutyanov, I. Senina, and R. Arditi, "Clustering due to Acceleration in the Response to Population Gradient: A Simple Self-Organization Model," *The American Naturalist*, 164.6 (2004), pp. 722–35. What's striking about the models proposed by such naturalists is that they continue to rely on a very basic Empedoclean model: a swarm is held together by both attractive and repulsive forces ("love" and "hate?"), which are themselves too fundamental to be otherwise explained.

72. Judith A. Nicolson, "Flash! Mobile mobs in the Age of Connectivity," *Fibreculture*, 6 <http://journal.fibreculture.org/issue6/issue6_nicholson.html> [accessed June 19, 2007]. Nicholson continues: "Frequent comparisons of flash mobbing to flocking and swarming were used to mark the trend as apolitical (Rheingold, 2002, 174–82; Micah, 2003; Bedell, 2003). Flocking and swarming describe the cooperative grouping of certain fish, birds and insects. Swarming was also used to describe the activities of protestors at WTO meetings who used the Internet and mobile phones to coordinate mobs to evade police (Taghizadeh, 2003). These metaphors can be used both in political and apolitical senses. Deleuze and Guattari used swarming and flocking as metaphors to describe types of decentered and leaderless political action (Deleuze and Guattari, 1987; 1980). Flash mobbers used these metaphors not to describe their actions as political but to evoke ecological narratives. In other words, these metaphors were used to propagate benign associations and obscure historical narratives of the politicized mob." In addition to the ever proliferating scientific studies of swarming, note the amazing range of contemporary research for which the "swarm" functions as a defining concept. B. Alexander, "Going Nomadic: Mobile Learning in Higher Education," *Educause Review*, (September/October 2004), 29–35 (education); V. Flusser, "The City as Wave-Trough in the Image-Flood," *Critical Inquiry*, 31 (2005), 320–28. [1988] (media theory); J. Garreau, "The age of swarming," *The Washington Post*, August 17, 2002 (sexual life); J. Arquilla and D. Ronfeldt, *Swarming and the Future of Conflict* (military affairs); J. Kennedy and R. C. Eberhart with Y. Shi, *Swarm Intelligence* (San Diego: Academic Press, 2001) (academic psychology); *Insect Poetics*, edited by E. C. Brown (Minneapolis: University of Minnesota Press, 2006) (cultural history).

73. As Jean-Luc Nancy says, "the 'unconscious' designates—and this is what Jacques Lacan understood—the inexhaustible, interminable swarming of significations that are not organized around a sense but, rather, proceed from a significance or signifyingness [*signifiance*] that whirls with a quasi-Brownian motion around a void point of dispersion, circulating in a condition of simultaneous, concurrent, and contradictory affirmation, and having

no point of perspective other than the void of truth at their core." *The Sense of the World*, pp. 46–7. Also: "The singularity of psychoanalysis—which confers on it all of its disruptive force and epoch-making scope—consists in having inaugurated a mode of thought that, in principle, dissolves all sense, that not only situates sense outside of truth and rigor [...] but in principle renders sense destitute by reducing it to a mere demand of sense, and by exposing truth as the disappointment of that demand," p. 46.

6

Notes on the Bird War: Biopolitics of the Visible (in the Era of Climate Change)

Tom Cohen

> "Why did he shoot her?" "Watching a ball game on television—his wife changed the channel"
> —Hitchcock, *The Birds*

Representations of "climate change" catastrophes only recently returned in massive ways to the American media after an effective black-out by Bush: suddenly movies and television specials and media columnists are flooded, so to speak, with bedazzled specials. Sometimes they are so titled as to be chilling for other reasons. For instance, the title of CNN's "We Were Warned"—about the end of oil—plays to the Protestant pleasure of being disciplined for one's misdeeds, which could secretly welcome catastrophic correction. And since no one hearing such material expects any real global response until "tipping points" are all passed—such would constrain competitive "global" growth or be impossible to apply locally—this news forms an interesting imaginary: it creates a spectral "present" assured of a cataclysmic future gifted to heirs, out of sight and irreal since unprecedented. Climate change proponents have been advised that too much media information risks producing not response but numb passivity. This puts the present in a Hamlet position. It knows too much from a (future) ghost, yet the knowledge does not coincide with phenomenality or experience before it in the court. It is too much—and, today, one finds new temporalities being probed. Critical force here might be thought to shift from a focus on the otherness of the (human) other to something "wholly other"; from the human-on-human model of struggle to the "threat without (human or visible) enemy." That arrives in the form of glacier meltoff, or dying seas, or biodiversity collapse. It links the artifacted present of today to other prehistorial and biopolitical time-lines.

There will likely emerge a critical discourse of *catastrophics* in the twenty-first century to incorporate the archipelago of mutations now calculated under the general rubrics of climate change. Such logics encompass various spin-offs and feedback loops (mass extinction events, resource wars, nanomutations). If the category of the "catastrophe" is temporally mobile, it is unlike that of "trauma" for being neither a faux origin to memory nor subject to allegory as we know it. These incursions on a planetary or biomorphic scale do not contribute to or further current critical agendas, cultural identity, social justice, human-on-human narratives. Like Hitchcock's birds, they *appear* as if from a certain outside.

Among the images that struck me recently, of a certain "materiality," was one from New Orleans—in the parenthesis following its deluge. Cut off from communications for days, people faced a soup of contaminates, a site where techno-poisons and a prehistorial swamp reversion opened a temporal warp. A pause of non-response and abandon, no tidal movement. Yet as an entry into the dossier of catastrophes, it is also an image of the state of the image, the seepage of the non-anthropomorphic into the spellbound frame.

Numerous histories converge about an "event" less readable than "9/11." The latter took out two symbolic buildings, the former the coming attractions of erased cities and deterritorialization of the homeland. Unlike the human against human strike, New Orleans has proven inappropriable to political or media agendas. Its incursion of *material* and spectral forces opens a rift in the anthropocentric trance. In the anarchy of several days in which the denizens of the Big Easy hung without response from the outside, a certain modernity was revoked (the abandoned as temporary "disposable humans"), and an alternate real exposed itself.[1]

New Orleans suggests a *lateral* acceleration from the staged shock of "9/11"—only without human double or aura, without face. Leave aside the subsequent militarization of the gulf zone in a clean-up peopled by troops back from Iraq for whom it looks worse, reportedly—the ban on showing corpses and so on. Leave aside the triage of a disempowered class, the racial subtext or the dubious reality TV that elicits a strange voyeurism. New Orleans suggests a counter-text to the "global" war on terror—a spectral war, without temporal or geographic horizon, which still bears the poster-face of a spectral enemy other (the terrorist, Osama, Saddam—for a while). What interests me here is the rift in the anthropomorphic bubble, temporal and perceptual, the breakdown of circuitry in which *terra* substitutes for the spectral double of the terrorist.

Hitchcock casts this assault as the "bird war" of the present—that is, it is a "war" that turns against the two sides of so-called world wars, hot or cold. Again and again, Hitchcock sees the world wars as late imperial contretemps between two extremes in the same Enlightenment epistemology. It opens and supersedes a certain "now"—call it, the era of climate change, mass extinction events, the shift from an "otherness of the (social) other" to the non-anthropomorphic. The schoolchildren in their mnemonic chat conclude, again and again, with the repetitive assertion, "now, now, *now*"—the repetition of which undoes the *present* it would somehow stamp. The birds assault the "eye" in its blind programming, in the name of its cinematic other—and against the cinematic accelerations that produce a spell.[2]

It may be that the twenty-first century critical project will involve an epistemological mutation of memory regimes and referential orders that organize perception and the ritual of thought. In this bizarre rhetorical environment, decisions made in the present, the logic runs, alter or erase prospective futures in calculable ways (tipping points passed, glaciers melts, coasts inundate, "population culling"). Hence the appeal to children, or grandchildren, like a recent commercial featuring a train which a man steps aside from, revealing a granddaughter in the way—generic and without traction, since there is no ethical contract to what does not exist yet. There is no general ethics of or toward virtual "futures"—particularly ones not appealing to contemplate. Such a global "present," in a sense, hoards or consumes temporalities as it does life forms, species, resources, and so on. Hitchcock names this scenario Bodega Bay and, when all is said and done, what is attacked in the name of these birds is above all how the visual and the eye are programed, with memory, in the mode of blind consumption. I will ask below whether Bodega Bay's "bird war" may be read—as an uprising of the trace itself from within the biopolitics of the image—as a parable of this incursion.

1.

As a *hyper* medium that absorbs others, "cinema" marks itself as a historial event producing new forms of memory and perceptual blinds. In Hitchcock, who can be read as a courier and critic for this advent, there appears a sort of Benjaminian war over two logics or definitions of the image itself. That is, the technologies of memory. This war can appear as that of the *home* state, or rote memory and mimetic spells, and that of the cinematic saboteur, or assassin, whose uprisings if successful would re-cast the MacGuffin of history and the senses. By late Hitchcock, this war shifts from being between human communities and appears as a "bird war" against the human as a construct—and against the latter's *ocularcentric* programs. These birds, black slashes or wing-beats that peck out eyes, are linked to a sheer technicity. They avenge from a *prehistorial* logic that, simultaneously, anticipates a coming "war" over these inscriptions themselves—what might be called, a war within the *archive* from which phenomenality and programs of consumption are legislated. The accord between non-auratic cinema and Hitchcock's attacking Zarathustran birds poses a *biopolitical* question: what role, in the post-global orders of today, does the cinematic image have in the ordering of the "senses," the contemporary spell of political anesthesia, and the mass manipulation of memory? What is implied by the paradox of a cinematic practice that marks its aim not as servicing a visualist culture but as violating, blinding, or dispossessing "the eye" as an artifactual construct? The "bird war" in Hitchcock brings the figure of animation and the house into collision, implying coming wars of reinscription of the senses that open upon a post-global politics of memory.

In the era of climate change, the political may migrate from a social struggle (class domination, identity positions) toward what we may call the X-factors of the now planetary and biomorphic orders impinging on geographic regions, communities, and so on. Such X-factors would include a swarm of logics incompatible with today's economic, political, and epistemographic programs—"global warming," inundated cities, a global underclass of "disposable" humans (already used to cull "organs" from), predicted oil and water wars, mass drought and what has been referred to, in a suppressed Department of Defense report, as expected "population culling."[3] Certain critical categories mutate before these twenty-first century logics. "History" is no longer that of national languages or cultures since geological and biomorphic time-lines intervene and recast the former's several millennia of writing as a sort of time-bubble linked to the oil era.[4] The "future" *narratives* of terrestrial mutation seem most brutal in their simplest implications: the triage of the least empowered, the geographically or historically unlucky—predictions of "population culling," mass migration, pandemics and so on. Current theorizations of "human rights" are unlikely to be more successful as the era of "disposable humans" expands with the catastrophic scenarios painted by the shock jocks of global warming—often resolving into both media entertainments and numb information.[5] The DoD report analyzing climate change from a military perspective, for instance, more or less anticipates a regress to hi-tech feudal states, local resource wars with nuclear prospects.

How does one address these slashes that carve up the visible, dispossess the house, empty interiors, put out a certain way of seeing? We know, there is no *time* in which to interpret this attack—nor any single *referent* to hang on these animated points allowed to evoke animation, the prehistorial, and the *mark*. Critics generally analyze the misfired scripts and psyches of the characters, grouped nonetheless without star power or narrative. How to address the birds themselves, which Hitchcock alludes to as the "stars"—shifting identification from the B-list humans, squeezed finally from the frame, to their atomizing antagonists? "No references," as is said of Marnie at her first workplace. An assault on "general semantics"—which Melanie is said to study at Berlekey—from a hypothetical *outside* that is, nonetheless, the mere points or marks out of which the visual and the screen coalesce. These small cuts or points are re-animated, militarized, rise up from the margins, drive the inhabitants out of the frame. The irreducible mark embedded in all visual constructs arises to avenge itself, or wipe clean, a sensorial program bound to hyperconsumption, anthropomorphic blinds, terrestrial eviscerations. Hitchcock never recovers.

To begin with, one must assume the action of this work occurs on the screen too, precisely when these prosthetic slashes carve up the title letters or the visible itself. Yet Hitchcock's birds avenge in the name of a certain *justice*, presented in the film as an absent cause. They peck out eyes—and assault a certain way of seeing, which is also to say, here, of eating or interiorizing. Tippi Hedren's platinum head and mannequin looks (stepped out of a television commercial) violate the visible—turning the blond as faux figure of metaphysics into its other (to become the dissembling "Marnie" as site of truth). *Melanined*, cohabited by a figure of blackness, both white and black are consumed by the same Heraclitean semioclasm—become "one." Bodega Bay's "packaged goods" recast the humans as bad copies, replicants from a B-cast, or real "models" inducted like Hedren, from TV advertisement logics into the frame—a precession of the simulacrum by itself, indicating a rupture, triggering the attack (as the hysterical mother in *The Tides* restaurant misrecognizes). In driving the children from their moment of memorization, these Zarathustran birds posit an event or possibility of *ex-scription*. It evokes nausea. Why?

The birds simulate innumerable points (as Mitch Brenner mumbles, "What's the point?"). Their swarm precedes any graphic image that might coalesce as animation on the screen—any face, but also any alphabetic sign, or hieroglyphic. Cinema in this sense precedes and supersedes the era of the Book which is also marked in Bodega Bay variably—from the post-office to the schoolhouse. The schoolteacher Annie's line about herself, spoken before a library cabinet, addresses this when she says: *I am an open book, or rather a closed one. Open*: that means, the histories of the Book are all evoked and traversed in this site, return at the atomizing assault of marks, and this by what precedes letteration itself (and the histories of alphabetic writing, hence monotheism); *closed*: that means, with this release of the cinematic mark, the era of the Book is closed, dissolved. There seems a movement here beyond twentieth-century epistemo-critical practices—the acute focus on the social other, the "otherness of the other," identitarianisms of all sort, historicisms and dominations, so-called ethics—and a shift toward what cannot quite be called the "wholly other" represented by the attacking birds. No Enlightenment, dialectical, utopist, materialist, faux nomadic or psychist discourse seems adapted for what alters the contract of temporalities and biopower. "Absolutely No Credit," says a sign in *The Tides* restaurant.

One might at this point riff on the following here: the first sign on the cinematic trolley car advertising "The Bar at the Top of the Mark" (a quote from *Vertigo*—drawing our attention to bars and marks at once). To be without "references" is not to be without violence, only to remark that the way perception is programed, reference regimented, may be structurally blind, consuming, anthropocentered. The "birds" generate reference to account for themselves, only to exceed it as cutting wings and myriad attacking points. Why?

2.

Assaulting what is alluded to as "general semantics," which includes the pecking out of eyes, the work is less a film than a template of ex-scriptions. *Interiorities* of all forms will be vacated or exposed as mere pockets or folds like the bay itself. Eyes are pecked out, stomachs emptied, the premise of the house finally abandoned. And this is accomplished by a nanoswarm, disciplined yet relentless, which is experienced on the screen as so many points, irreducible cuts and marks preoriginary to any era of the Book, to alphabetics or hieroglyphs.

The logic of attacking birds is that of cinematic "shock" carried to its formal extreme. If we view "Hitchcock" less as a part of film studies than an unread event within the prehistory of contemporary teletechnic culture, one across which the formal thinking of script and cinematechnics reflects on its destinies, certain moments or turns put the histories of the senses, memory, and the machine into question. In such sites, wars within the image from out of which the 'global' would be constructed are underway. And one finds reading models that exceed and precede old sensorial programs like *ocularcentrism*—the *auratic* programming of identification and mimeticism that remains the official ideology of the photographic image. *The Birds*, for instance, issues forth black slashing wings that carve up the visible and peck out eyes from a non-anthropomorphic and perhaps avenging prehistorial space. They gather for an attack on a jungle gym before a schoolhouse—when they are not flying past telegraph wires or attacking telephone booths, allied with machinal hums and vehicles.

Melanie's past trauma involves the shattered glass pane of media and what is obscurely called the playtime of her summer at "Rome"—that is, everything ever meant by "Rome," as *Spellbound* reminds us. *Rome*: that is, the capital or head of the empire and the church, rewritten as the streaming lights of the cinematic apparatus, programer of memories and new technology of the spirit (the movie house as inheritor of the theatrical-churchly ritual. The word "capitol" will appear on a sign at the gas station when attacked and in flames: "Capitol Oil." *Oil*, black organic waste matter of dinosaurs, ink-like, allied to the head or *capo*, engine of the teletechnic era and its vehicles of transport. It is allied to these birds—who set a gas station ablaze, fire alarms in the archive.[6] *Without references*, the birds solicit and disown in turn every interpretive program—yet, conversely, are identified with, if anything, what precedes the letter, the voice, "mother" as such, the unearthly earth and fluorescent horizons where sea meets earth and then sky as so many lines.

Why do these birds attack the eye (the most recurrent word in the film is "see")? Why are they identified *not* with animals and certainly not with an avenging "nature" (as Hitchcock pretends to Truffaut and in his trailers) but with engines and machines, telegraph wires and telephones, spatial graphs like *the jungle gym*? Why is Hedren linked to studying a course in *"General* Semantics" and why does the name Melanie, a black name, cast her platinum white screech as a blackout, as though white and black collapsed, momentarily, as the same Heraclitean semioclasm, exposing "light" itself as other than itself? The identification of the skeletal graph of the jungle gym is with the very edge, the rim of the archive or great house, lines and joints, verticals and horizontal lines, cells, frames, rows or bands—as if the avenging black flecks, attacking *eyes* and children, outside and against the "human" as such, were the uprising of the frame folding in against the MacGuffin of an imaginary content. So when one is looking for referents or tropes to rename these figures, one cannot call them animals, or nature, or apocalyptic agents. If one continued this prescribed game into the present and asked them to conform to an allegory of climate change, as I am doing, they would resist differently—being allied first of all with marks, machines, telegraphics, *technics*.[7]

The Birds solicits interpretive responses which it cuts off nonetheless in advance, a sensorial and hermeneutic war strategy. It puts some major ones in play indifferently only to dismiss each—the Oedipal (Annie), the Christo-Apocalyptic (the drunk at the tides), "science" (the ornithologists). The birds are, the ornithologist Mrs Bundy says, "impossible," the impossible—*they, these marks, were not supposed to violate the logics of the visible which they, after all, gave rise to and serviced*. Zarathustran harpies, avenging on behalf of a mnemonic backloop that always precedes the screen *present* it generates, they turn against the very construction of the "eye"—and in the name of an other that is not just without *identification*, not only prefigural, not only a convergence of technics and the province of animation. Preceding and closing the era of the Book, the birds return from the archival rim or dome. It is interesting that the site beyond relapse corresponding to leaving the house, *abandonment*, seems represented by the mute, catatonic, emptied, staring eyes of Melanie. This stare which appears elsewhere in Hitchcock as a zero-figure or so-called "psychotic" logic is actually a cinematic *apsychism* broadly—Gregory Peck's amnesiac trance with razor, Norman at the bog, are here assigned a future. It exceeds any psychologizing trope. When Lydia rushes from seeing the blinded eyes of Dan Fawcett, a summary of all literary blindings of the blind, she understands too that *no one* knows where "mother" is (as Melanie says), that she (Lydia) is from the start a simulacrum mother, a *copy* like Melanie whose hair rhymes with hers, and that one proceeds into Bodega Bay's hermeneutic traps without any familial, Oedipal, or "maternal superego" map (as Annie more or less tells us: "with all due respect to Oedipus, I don't think so"). Hence one could—since the birds are, says Hitchcock, the "stars," yet are without aura or identification—of limited interest to narrate Lydia's vanquishing of Melanie, the latter's doomed return to faux maternalism, and so on, since the characters are largely ciphers and not personalities: interpretive vortexes scanned against what may seem to be sheer *exteriority*. Melanie's stare accelerates what Lydia knew from seeing the blinded man's eyes but fussed and retreated before for advantage, playing the faux "mother" still as preprogramed role. Melanie, on the bluff, says she doesn't know where (her) mother is.

3.

We are told several times of Melanie's obscure *trauma* in Rome, of her Rome days, which she has left behind her. Something about reckless play, naked romps in fountains that made it into the newspapers, a wild past linked, less obviously, to the shattered window pane of media which brought her to the courtroom where Mitch first saw her. What Hitchcock puts in the past is the entire Christo-imperial legacy he evokes elsewhere in references to "Rome" or "empire."

In *Spellbound*, "Rome" is relocated, just after the second "world war," as New York City, the new mediatric capital of the coming global era. And we see a banner above Grand Central Station—that is, the sort of historial ground zero of the arrival and departure of all historical trace-chains, cinematic times, tropological narratives going back through the archeological capital of the old empire and the Church, of the Europe or West decimated after that war. That is, before its *coming amnesia* in the era of the global announced by moving the capital to New York City, new capital of media and advertisement, the *Empire State*. At the center of the station vault the banner advises the ticket-buyers below: "Buy More War Bonds." Grand Central appears, then, as an allegory of the screen itself—the new public space as site of endless transport devolved to a central station that is the screen. The name "empire" appears another sign, a rectangle mirroring the movement of mere traffic. The *Empire State Hotel* glosses this global empire to come allied to cinematic logics or accelerations and it is here that Hitchcock's cameo appears.

The shot of Grand Central prefigures Bodega Bay. It streams with cinematized light rays from its giant eye-like window, vaulted like a cathedral, transposing the old Rome of empire, cognition, and the Church into the implications of an artificed technology of the spirit (and memory, or amnesia) dependent on machines of transport. The cinematic bars echo those that haunt Peck's amnesiac. The non-site of arrivals and departures, a giant domed head, is where memory loops are installed and *spells* reign. Throughout *Spellbound* there is a waiting for what is called the "new head," who never arrives, or already has as an imposter. The war is over and seen beyond by a weak messianic urge undermined in advance. Thus "Buy More War Bonds." The bonds in question, echoed in the titular *Spellbound*, would be between cinema and psychoanalysis, or both and "the war" (or war as such), but it also tells the ticket buyers below that *the war* is not over, that the catastrophe of Western history just witnessed is already subject to amnesia, that the contretemps of fascists and western liberal colonial democracies was as if between two extreme doubles in the same Enlightenment episteme, a late imperialist and territorial skirmish. That is, that the real war to come, that over the earth or its prosthesis (an earth without nature, consumed and cinematized, without future), is announced already by the "global" logic cinema's arrival marks in advance. It anticipates what will be called the "bird war."

4.

How does one strike against a totalization one cannot, per definition, see? To launch a war on what is essentially *the* visible occurs in the name of what also can be said to make it possible. Or in the name simply of the "non-anthropomorphic," an assault on temporalities and sensorial programming, an intervention in and against programs of memory as such. The birds correspond to flying marks. As cinematic black holes, they withdraw from personification or anthropomorphism—no aura, no star power, no metaphoric viability. This is what the destruction of aura attributed to the advent of cinema was—the withdrawal of personification (as Benjamin defines aura in the Baudelaire essay explicitly). The birds *avenge* in the name of a nameless *techne* outside of the spell of ocularcentric culture. Gathering on the structure of the frame, no longer house or interior, allied to memory and the disruption of mnemonic bands, they totalize and dismiss a form of terror. It is an assault against an artifactualization of "life" or sight referenced to global markets (Bodega Bay) in and by the cinematic operations that have, over time, produced that relapsed or, if you like, anthropo-political regime.[8]

Hitchcock assumed "globalization" the instant there is, was, cinema or photography more generally—just as the former's advent is bound to the histories of technoweapons and twentieth-century genocides. The Shakespearean echo of The Globe is rewritten in cinematic terms, either as the newspaper of *Foreign Correspondent* or the bar of *Frenzy*. In *Blackmail*, the first British "talkie," Hitchcock depicts what might be called the cinematic *trace* (allied to shadows, mail, blackmail), as something whose logics precede all the history of writing back to hieroglyphs. Cinema precedes Egypt as a *techne* since it contains every possible mutation of the mark or pictogram. The blackmailer, named Trac(e)y, will be chased through the British Museum, through its archives, staring into the screen like the mummy case in which his cinematic reflection is cast, through the museum's papyrus displays, indeed, through its book-lined archives. The blackmailing trace, like any image, knows too much about the present that regards it, since it testifies to anterior truths that "sponge" up referential systems they pass through. It or he cannot stop traversing a frozen field of temporalities in which the cinematic image is reflected, at first, as a freezing of times, a *mummifaction* process, and finally runs out onto the outside of the museum's giant archive and universal reading room, its head-like *dome*. It or he precedes the histories of writing, passes to the outside of the historial archive it cites and sponges up—caught in a redefinition of memory chains. The museum as trope of the cinematic arrest of time is momumentalized as the fading empire's memory warehouse—an ordering of history imposed by that empire (British universalism). Yet *blackmailing* as a logic also explains the perpetually anterior and dangerous relation of the image to any "present"—it knows too much about the past and its structural crimes.[9] Thus Trac(e)y is called a "sponger," like the image itself, which *sponges* up referential and interpretive investment from the viewer, the shot-at set, the citations on the screen. Thus Trac(e)y falls back through the dome into the *Universal Reading Room*, circles within circles of readers in the central archive, caught in circular or cinematic loops. Which may be why Hitchcock in his singular cameo appears interrupted reading on a cinematic train, the *Underground*, and this by a bullying boy—reading is hyperbolized, interrupts itself on this accelerated train. It is interrupted in the same way that a biblio-centric imaginary is preceded by the shadow writing of orchestrated points coalesced into the screen's mimetic fictions, or as alphabetic writing—say, on the credit title of *The Birds*—is cut up by black wing slashes or pecks. The cinematic is not an add-on to the era of the Book or modernity, a supplemental technology to the prestige of writing here: its logics, those of sheer atomization, precede that history and hence Egypt and hieroglyphics as such.

Why does this "bird war" suggest still a transvaluative logic? It evokes an epistemological intervention that is, would be, *irreversible*. How, then, does the MacGuffin of a *cinematic uprising* that is routinely suppressed at border crossings in the espionage films, the model of early Hitchcock, resolve into a "bird war" against the "human" *in toto*? Why the Zarathustran import and exploding backloop to these black nothings, flying marks and black suns which induce nausea and vomiting in little Cathy? As if Hitchcock's term for the cinematic experience of eternal recurrence, that is, "vertigo," had simply come to this—the sheer exteriority of all, the folds and pockets of the Bodega Bay coast, *Ekel* or what exceeds it.

Hitchcock sends us back to the logics of *Sabotage* in the opening visit to the bird shop, where Melanie asks for *Mynah birds*—birds that memorize human language as sounds and repeat phrases with no subject to the repetitions. Later, when the schoolhouse is attacked, the children driven out when they are all repeating songs and phrases together, like Mynah birds, the cinematic assault on where memory is inscribed, programs of reference memorized or imprinted. The reference to *Sabotage* is the bird shop—which is a front for the bombmaker Chatman in that film, who supplies the bombs Verloc will issue from behind his front as proprietor of a movie house. The bomb is allied to a birdcage and the explosive "blast" of cinematic shock to the successive bars—the series of alternating slashes

that precedes any sign system and occurs in every Hitchcock work as a signature effect—and to the moment the birds will "sing." It would be placed
in Piccadilly Circus, what is called "the center of the world"—meaning
where phenomenality is set, the spectralization of worlding governed.
Cinema, with its memory band, mimes what de Man called the "phenomenality of inscription"—and it is by atomizing these that a moment
of disinscription is approached. "*Circus*" inscribed the circularity of a temporal backloop that the mnemonic band mimes and forgets in advance
of itself. Yet there is a biopolitical dimension to this act—as it is called in
every performative sense in the dialog. This is explicit in a visit to the *Zoo*
to visit Verloc's handler, who is not impressed with his mere turning off
of the lights in London—a caesura and blackout, displaying "light" itself
as a techne. They didn't get it. The Londoners coming from the cinematic
underworld laughed, thought it more entertainment. The *ante* must be
upped. Yet in the aquarium it is against a screen-like tank that the melt-
ing of building and structures is projected—as if this atomization occurred
before and in the name of prehistorial and premammalian sea creatures.
Like the bizarre fish that a passing couple note changes sex after laying
innumerable eggs—a shape and gender shifting life-form, as though "life"
were itself, here, the effect of a complexly mutating technics. Like animation—which supplants the mirage of "life" with what is not alive but itself
generated from cinematic graphics, a mimesis without model and copy
mutating forward.

Yet this is what is shown the one time we visit the theater itself, where
a Disney cartoon of bird-men and a bird-woman appear, the latter as
a *Mae West figure*—who is herself marked, in Hitchcock, as a female
female impersonator. When "the birds *sing*" turns out to be this croon-
ing of half-animeme half-human figures, the bomb affiliated not just
with the trope of explosion, of blasting and shock, of atomization and
artificial memory, but the "secret" that the cinematic precedes and
generates what takes itself for "life," or "the home," or the "human" for
that matter. It is, as Derrida has it, an artifact and artifiction—together
with the concept of the "present" we inhabit. It is, it accesses, other
temporalities, as the time-bomb makes clear—which explodes, too,
a prison of temporal definition, anthropomorphic. The cinematic allies
itself here, again, with the prehistorial and pre-originary, with an animation that dislocates the field of "life" into other terms—as another
effect of technicities and artifacted mnemonics. Yet here there are two
logics at war: that of the house, of mimetic cinema and anesthetiza-
tion, the spell of occularcentrism and the hyperconsumption of the
planetary—that is, the image as we know it, a blind construct—and its

other, the cinematic assault of the birds. The bird attack is one on an epistemo-anthropomorphic regime by its own premises and *techne*.
5.
Hence Dan Fawcett, the *blinded man*—who is shown with eyes pecked out. What is assaulted by the cinematic occurs at or before the core of the visible, the fiction of the consuming "eye" (whose logic Hitchcock allies to that of advertisement media). In the name of allo-anthropomorphic legibilities at once teletechnic and preoriginary to 4000 years of scriptive history and animal forms. Engine of the teletechnic era and its vehicles of transport, is allied to these birds—who set a gas station ablaze, fire alarms in the archival order. This non-origin is, was, in the preceding film, called "mother," a figure everywhere yet without gender or one "voice," without place, a *Khora*-site in the Derridean sense, a non-site of inscription precedent to *phainesthai* in its entirety. Among the avatars of these birds in Hitchcock is not only a menagerie of *animemes*, especially cats, but black suns and marbles, airplanes. Or the fly on "mother's" hand—addressed by her through Norman in his *cell*, when mother would show, by being still before the viewer, how she wouldn't hurt a fly. That *fly*, exoskeletal, cannot be hurt by "mother" in any event—since it is a flying hole or tear in representational orders, like the black sun shot at in the first *Man Who Knew Too Much* which inverts the perceptual premises of "image" in its entirety, in its "General Semantics," and opens other temporalities and wormholes. And hence the attack on the *schoolhouse*—where the herd-like children speak in unison, like Mynah birds, and would be interrupted in rote memorization, at their point of being inscribed.[10]

The schoolhouse is *spellbound*—like the last man of the mediatric era, the ocularist consumer of democratic fictions in a post-democratic horizon comically sustained by a "global" war on terror without face or temporal or geographical horizon. The burning horizons of Bodega Bay, all but electric, shift the problem of the so-called living and the *animeme* into one of animation and trace-chains that revoke any definition of earth that relies on maternal metaphors of ground. It is not the "natural" that attacks. One could call this *aterra*—and it demands a certain vengeance against the human program or artifice by what can be called an aesthetic or epistemo-political agency. Hitchcock saw the "world wars" of the last century as fratricidal contretemps played out by opposite poles in the same Enlightenment template, and anticipated (or tracked) the coming wars that would issue from, and against, the subsequent totalization of "empire"—which he locates in New York City.[11]

To inspect the *biopolitics of the image*, its many spells and blinds, what it frames and anaestheticizes, is to question the post-democratic era we have stepped, as if spellbound, into. One is aware, as an American recently, of how certain logics of the image appear totalized, a calculable zone of identifications and mimetic spells, as if with no horizon, which program or consume futures in a post-democratic era that seems visible everywhere. One can wonder whether the so-called "'global' war on terror" was connected to this media totalization of an aesthetic ideology. It gives rise to a spectral war that is supposedly totalized and against an other without face, that is without temporal or geographic borders, and that occludes and diverts seeing the greater threat to the "homeland," from the machinery within the accelerated systems itself—the predicted decimations of climate change, bio-pathogenic collapse, oil and water wars, and so on, whatever lies outside what Agamben calls "the anthropological machine." These Rovean spells or neutralizing logics of advertising and consumer identification shield the emergence of what one might call, inverting a Derridean fable, the autocracies to come. One may speak of a biopolitics of the cinematic image—in which the de-auratic trace, like so many black slashing birds, emerges in a prehistorial, avenging logic. Here, a certain justice turns against the human as a mnemonic construct.

The trope of a "democracy to come," even as a spectral logic, may prove less relevant to a time whose mediatric spell accelerates a post-democratic horizon—the beginning of a drift toward contesting fortress states once the pressures of energy depletion, climate change, and biological poisons pierce the anthropomorphic screen (as the little girl Cathy says: "Mom, I know all that democracy jazz"). It may be that the aesthetic is the missing term or agency for a transformation that is, would be, epistemographic above all.[12] One summons, unleashes these birds—"Hitchcock" does, but I am thinking of ourselves now—not in a state of emergency, but when that has itself been anaestheticized, totalized without horizon.

The birds *attack* the construct of the visible, standing reserves of reference and consumption, interiors, eyes. The interruption of mnemonic programming explains their fondness for children. Bodega Bay locates a vacant yet consuming pocket, that of hiatus or stand-still, at(r)opos, the market *bodega* a redistribution of cinematic "shock."

"All the windows are broken in Dan [Fawcett's] bedroom," says Lydia to Melanie, "all the windows." What occurs when the media glass shatters, or becomes visible as a spider-web of crack-lines drawing attention to itself when a bird strikes? The nanoswarm of these wingbeats and zero-effects inverts the logics of the MacGuffin and, with that, figuration and anthropomorphism (the birds, said Hitchcock, these blackholes, are the "stars"). One is precisely asked to negotiate what precedes letters and the spell of spelling itself, of getting one's name in print (as is said of Melanie's *scandals*). I mentioned above the "X-factors" of the twenty-first century, which arrive outside of media, without face or aura. Such a chiasmic X appears throughout Hitchcock. Taking on different forms it mutates, interestingly, in the late work. From the two Charlies of *Shadow of a Doubt* to the "criss-cross" of positions by Guy and Bruno in *Strangers on a Train*, to the "imminent Dr X" that the amnesiac Peck calls himself—linking a certain cure to this cinematic chiasmus or void. It is seen on the back of the servant Germaine in *To Catch a Thief*, a servant of the Underground ("she strangled a German general once—without a sound"). Then, as if tiring of its automatism and ubiquity, Hitchcock targets it with the single assassination shot of the second *Man Who Knew Too Much*, as the flag beneath the Hitchcock-like Prime Minister suggests (bald, rotund, infantine), as if it itself could be exceeded. And it then turns up written onto the face of the earth itself in *North by Northwest*, a giant chiasmus presented by the crossroads as the prairie stop, as if between the earth and the living. But in *The Birds* an "X" emerges on the screen in curious places. One appears on a neon sign for *Lucky X Lager* on the window of *The Tides*, for instance, where the community goes to imbibe and feed, and then it appears on the car horn that Melanie frantically strikes in her besieged Ford Galaxie. The chiasmic X seems here totalized and stuck in an irreversible limit. It no longer reverses character position or polarities within the visual but whatever is within the frame with something else. Yet in doing so, it is the program of the visible, of constitutive memory and the eye, which is brought to the point of reinvention otherwise.

Notes

1. The flooded parishes encountered a slippage of time lines reflected when the scene was compared to a primitive time (a racially inflected "heart of darkness," as it was called by a journalist).
2. As such, the birds cannot be apocalyptic. Their invasion as a warping of temporal logic implies a folding in of the frame, without outside. Nature as origin is the effect of a certain semantic or mimetic ideology, and its disarticulation accompanies that of mimetic regimes. What may seem parallel is the *nausea* of Zarathustra before the backloop of eternal recurrence (Cathy's vomit), and the biting off of the snake's head, the stepping "beyond" to a site that is not mapped yet in other terms. These birds are not animals but technemes, allied to machines, telegraph wires, pecks, the prehistorial

and post-anthropomorphic, the cinematic as such. *Earth*, after all, is what the camera will always (also) be gazing at, be recording—even when a simulacrum earth, as with sets of anthropomorphic monuments made of stone and steel. But *nature* was always other than maternal, an anthropomorphized "she," the shot's representational claim. "She" is something else, *proactively* mimetic, a mimesis without model or copy much as species which alter ceaselessly according to the technicity of an environs or for camouflage or shape shifting, adapting proleptically as an animal or coral sea creature or insect assumes camouflage before a predatory other when it cannot "see" itself to be like the mimicked twig or rock or leaf. This artifactual "earth" is the paradoxical counter-world to the passivity of "globalization." What may be called this *aterra* is allied to the birds because of the latter's refusal of mimetic laws—teleological, referential, apocalyptic.

3. See Mark Townsend and Paul Harris, "Now the Pentagon tells Bush: Climate Change will Destroy Us," *The Observer*, February 22, 2004. <www.guardian.co.uk/climatechange/story/0,12374,1153530,00.htm> [accessed July 12, 2007].

4. One could track this shift through several recent critical probes. Such would include not only Masao Myoshi's call for a turn to the "planetary," without being able to define or account for such future practice. Masao Miyoshi, "Turn to the Planet: Literature Diversity and Totality," *Comparative Literature*, 53 (2001), 283–97. Or Gayatri Spivak's attempt at a conceit of the "planetarity" in *The Death of a Discipline* (NY: Columbia University Press, 2003) that, because it remained unusable to prescribed left agendas, would be stillborn. There are numerous efforts to probe these and related borders. Judith Butler's treatment of the "face" of the terrorist, in *Precarious Life* (London: Verso, 2004) as indicating the limit, today, of the "ethical" model as a failed attempt to account for the face of the "humanities" (which the essay is designed to affirm the future of). And I would shift to Manuel de Landa's *A Thousand Years of Nonlinear History* (NY: Zone Books, 1997) to adduce the emergence of "nonlinear" histories—his involves three parallel accounts of geological, biological, and what he calls "linguistic" (or socio-linguistic) history. Here the human agent recedes and the crystallization of energies and intensities track what is referred to as biomass or "stuff"—a materiality without matter, essentially. What is missing from de Landa is an account not of "socio-linguistic" groupings of languages but the technologies of inscription of referential and memory systems—what Plato termed the *hypomnemata* and which Foucault referenced to the preoriginary "copy-books" out of which "selfhood" is constructed.

5. Media experts warn alarmists that in these matters too much news only paralyzes and creates passivity. This is a lesson "Bush" pre-empted with a prolonged media blackout, the logic of which few fully appreciate. That is, rather than the denial of "global warming" being in any way authentic, or a product of oil industry influence and its lack of electoral payback, one assumes *they know* (they have better satellites and so on, as the above mentioned DoD report on "Climate Change" confirms). That is, *they know* and consider it irreversible in fact, impossible to rewire, counterproductive to inform the populace of. Since any half-measure would only weaken them and not work across the boards, it is rather to be accelerated for the selective survival of a new hyperclass—for a while longer.

6. Indeed, references to *oil* are systematic in Hitchcock, this *black liquid* source of prosthetic energy and hence the electric light and all vehicles of transport—the fossil residue of the birds' prehistorial forebears, dinosaurs, cycling back like Norman's bog.

7. Mel Gibson's recent *Signs* inverts *The Birds* precisely—as attacking space aliens beaten off by family and faith, by the human. The exact opposite of Hitchcock—these birds are domestic, of the frame or background, invisibly visible, attacking the eye, driving from the house of metaphor, assaulting the biopolitics of the image or how it has been constructed.

8. It is the regime operative today in what Derrida has called the suicidal auto-immunitary process that accelerates the "house's" self-cancellation in a double chase of the spectral other—as in the "global" war on terror.

9. In Hitchcock's *The Lodger*, it is the faceless Avenger who is identified with "London fog," that is the chiaroscuro of cinematic light-play on suspended particles, or points.

10. The lesson of these birds involves the interruption of an education and sensorial spell.

11. In *Spellbound*, the eye of ocularcentrism would be cut, too, as in the Dali dream-sequence citing *Un chien andalou*.

12. The model for this total inversion of the "aesthetic" from a representational premise to the site of tele-technics, and inscriptions, from which phenomenality is generated—the "center of the world"—appears in *The Birth of Tragedy*, in which Kittler reads Dionysus as the "master of media," the sheer flow of data.

7

Dialectical Catastrophe: Hegel's Allegory of Physiognomy and the Ethics of Survival

Patience Moll

> katastrepho ... to turn down, trample on, ... turn
> over ... II. to upset, overturn, ... ruin, undo ... III. of
> a floating solid, right itself ... b. ... return. IV. turn
> round, direct ... katestrepsen eis philanthropian tous
> logous guided the conversations to a friendly end, ...
> hence, bring to an end, k. ten biblon, ton logon, ...
> close, ... end life, die ... V. screw or stretch tight
>
> katastropheus, ho one who ruins or spoils his work,
> bungler ... 2. subverter
>
> katastrophe, he, overturning ... II. end, close,
> conclusion, ... death ... in the drama, dénouement[1]

If Hegel, in his introduction to the *Phenomenology of Spirit*, claims that the "hard work of science" requires the liberating turn (*Wende*) of science against (*gegen*) its own appearance (*Scheine*), his description of the conclusion to the dialectic of phrenology or craniology in the middle of this work invokes the multivalent turning reflected in the Greek *katastrepho*.[2] This particular turn in the dialectic takes place according to so many divergent prepositional directions and dramatic phrasings that it seems to be a turning of turning, a dizzying, disorienting disaster instead of a movement toward intellectual liberation. Facing Franz Josef Gall's late eighteenth-century, apparent "science" of craniology, "observing reason," the figure that must perform this specific dialectical turn,

> seems in fact to have reached its peak, at which point it must abandon itself and somersault; for only what is entirely bad has, in itself,

the immediate necessity of inverting itself.[...] So is this last stage of observing reason its worst, but therefore also is its overturning necessary (*scheint ... in der Tat ihre Spitze erreicht zu haben, von welcher sie sich selbst verlassen und sich überschlagen muß; denn erst das ganz Schlechte hat die unmittelbare Notwendigkeit an sich, sich zu verkehren. [...] So ist diese letzte Stufe der beobachtenden Vernunft ihre schlechteste, aber darum ihre Umkehrung notwendig*).

(*Phänomenologie*, pp. 257–8)

But if the multiplication of turns (in terms of reaching a peak, self-abandonment, a somersault, inversion and an overturning) along with the emphasis on this moment as entirely bad and even the worst, warrants the Lacanian critic Mladen Dolar's description of the passage as a "catastrophe" or "sudden regression" for reason, what would this mean for the dialectic of consciousness?[3] Given the inscription of a turning in both catastrophe and dialectic, the multiplicity of the turns here can be taken as an emphatic description of a catastrophe inherent in the Hegelian dialectic as such, of how the liberating turn of science "against" its appearance, for example, is never unidirectional but always at least implies both a turning toward and a turning away from. While craniology appears to be the low point and dénouement in the history of what Hegel calls observing reason, in fact it also appears as a markedly necessary or imperative passage between consciousness and spirit, the two major figures structuring the *Phenomenology*. If the craniologist is a bungler of the dialectical method, he also presents the spiritual subversion of the paternal authority presumed by this text's ethereal, generically sanctioned narrator, the philosophical "us." In terms of both its location and its content, the craniological catastrophe is necessary specifically to the development of a discourse on what Hegel calls "ethicity" (*Sittlichkeit*), the explicit topic of the first chapter on spirit and foundation for the final chapters on culture, morality, religion (including the religion of art) and "absolute knowing." Hegel's craniology, in short, demonstrates the materiality articulating spirit and consciousness, the necessity of what in the introduction he calls the dialectical "advance" (*Fortgang*), and an ethics of multiplicity as the concern of his dialectical method and that, insofar as it is temporally conceived, can also be called an "ethics of survival."[4]

The ethical context of the craniological dialectic is obscured by Dolar's essay "The Phrenology of Spirit," which concludes an investigation into Hegel's material semiotics that runs at least from Pöggeler to de Man to Žižek.[5] Dolar distinguishes himself from the approaches of both de Man and Žižek (to whom his analysis also owes a great deal) by restricting his discourse to a theory of the subject and by conclusively rejecting what he describes as the contemporary appreciation of Hegel as a thinker of radical heterogeneity. Naming Derrida and Lyotard in particular as representatives of this attitude, he ends the essay by calling for a renewed appreciation of Hegelian ambivalence: "Maybe the irreducibility of Hegel's ambivalence gets much closer to the heterogeneous, which, in its 'lateral' emergence, keeps dissolving in the conceptual progression, but that progression nevertheless maintains it as its inner limit, an ambiguous condition that founds it" (Dolar, p. 81). The binarism of this conclusion, which presumes an opposition between the self-identical concepts of "heterogeneity" and "progression," is also reflected in his analysis, which approaches the discussion of craniology in terms of its immediate context of what Hegel describes as the transformation of observing reason into active reason or the "actualization of rational self-consciousness through itself."[6] But if the focus on a theory of subjectivity, along with the indifference in the ambivalence allegedly characterizing Hegel's thoughts of "heterogeneity" and "progression," both obscure the ethical implications of this section, Dolar's actual description of craniology's transformation of observation into action unwittingly preserves Hegel's own ethical concerns. This occurs in Dolar's description of craniology's production of an original, Hegelian theory of action:

At the end of "observing Reason," the subject of Reason "found itself" in a thing, a piece of senseless materiality, which pinpointed and highlighted the very impossibility of the subject's finding itself, the point that eludes the subject. [...] This is the starting point of Hegel's curious "theory of action": the theoretically produced object is not enough, the subject has to experience it by turning itself into that object and thus risking the loss of subjectivity. There is a chance of becoming "for-itself" only if it assumes the loss of itself. If the passage from the "in-itself" to the "for itself" is at the same time the passage from theory to action, this implies that paradox that what is required is not a higher state of reflection, but quite the contrary, a loss of reflection, not a new insight but a new blindedness. [...] The structure of Hegelian action is such that action cannot realize its goal. [...] *Action by its very nature perverts the goal, it always realizes something other than what was intended.*[...] The Hegelian act is thus, like the act in psychoanalysis, by its very nature a failed act, and its failure brings forth the dimension of the subject's truth ("only failed acts are really successful," was one of Lacan's favourite dictums.)

(Dolar, pp. 75–6, emphasis added)

Instead of dialectical "integration," the encounter with craniology results in the absolute disruption of theory and action, a disruption however that is at least figuratively contained by Dolar's phenomenalized subject, viewed as blinded and in "flight" (Dolar, pp. 75–6). For Dolar, the dialectical progression does not so much suddenly regress here, as it is displaced into this figure of a wounded subjectivity, which turns out to be the "truth" of this particular dialectical movement.

In its illustration of a proto-Lacanian theory of subjectivity deduced by Hegel from the encounter with craniology, Dolar's gloss, however, transcribes more or less word for word Hegel's account of the prior moment of physiognomy, which, within the latter's overall narrative, is itself supposed to give rise to craniology. The transcribed *hysteron proteron* thereby points back, in spite of Dolar's rhetoric of the subject, to the beginning of the discussion of physiognomy, along with Hegel's thematization there of the interrelations between imperative, reading, and the set of multiple relations he later describes as constituting "ethical life" (*Phänomenologie*, p. 328). For example, at the beginning of his account of the rise of late eighteenth-century, Lavaterian physiognomy, Hegel explains that

> speech and work are expressions in which the individual no longer holds onto himself and possesses himself, but instead lets the inner get completely outside and *gives it up to the mercy of the other* (*sondern das Innere ganz außer sich kommen läßt und dasselbe Anderem preisgibt*). One can therefore just as well say that these expressions express the inner too much as that they express it too little: (1) too much, because the inner itself breaks out in them, leaving no opposition between the expressions and itself; they give not only an expression of *the inner, but rather they give the inner itself immediately; (2) too little, because in speech and action the inner makes itself into an other, gives itself over to the mercy of the element of transformation (Verwandlung), which perverts (verkehrt) the spoken word and completed act and makes something else out of them than they are in and for themselves as actions of this determined individual.[...].* Acting then [...] has the double, opposed meaning of being either the inner individuality and not its expression, or as outer, an actuality that is free from and entirely other than the inner. On account of this ambiguity (*Um dieser Zweideutigkeit Willen*) one has to look around for the inner as it still is in the individual, but in a visible or external way.
>
> (*Phänomenologie*, pp. 235–6, emphasis added)

Whereas Dolar's gloss on Hegelian action stresses a truth about the subject, Hegel's own account of action emphasizes a specifically inter-subjective existence, or what throughout the discussion of physiognomy he will refer to as "being for another," "being for others," "being against (*gegen*) others," and "existing for another (*Dasein-für-Anderes*). This account of an allegorical, juxtapositional otherness disturbs any discourse of a subject, or what Hegel himself refers to throughout the chapter on reason as the "individual." Hegel's allegorical description of action furthermore indicates that ambiguity or *Zweideutigkeit* is a spiritual problem precisely because it never appears on its own, as such, but always along with what he describes as being "against" or "at the mercy of" others. In Hegel's discussion of physiognomy, ethics emerges as the relation between self and other, or identity and difference, that is experienced as antagonistic ambiguity. The impossibility of an apolitical, indifferent ambiguity furthermore accounts for the phenomenon of systematic physiognomy, which attempts to redress the antagonistic ambiguity of social existence with a restrictive typology.[7]

In this way Dolar's "Phrenology of Spirit" points back to a reading of the prior discussion of physiognomy, a discussion that none of the critics mentioned above have discussed at any length. The virtual citation of Hegel's social account of physiognomy, in order to explain the resolution of craniology, furthermore indicates why the discussion of physiognomy has proven so difficult for a student of the dialectic method to comprehend.[8] On the one hand, the discussion of physiognomy and craniology completes Hegel's narrative of observing reason. "Reason" arises from the earlier dialectic of the liberated self-consciousness as the overweening certainty (*Gewißheit*) that the entire world is its own or that it is itself "all reality," a certainty that it first of all "declares (*ausspricht*)" (*Phänomenologie*, p. 177, p. 178). In its initial shape as observing reason, it sets about seeking referential evidence of this declaration. First reason looks for itself in the natural world, which seems to reflect rational law, or analogy, but fails to reflect "reason itself," which is to say the singular, subjective force animating reason. It then turns to the inner mind or "psychology," which similarly fails to manifest what Hegel increasingly refers to as "individuality." Finally, observing reason turns to the apparent integration of "outside and inside" that is the individual, human form. The actual title of this final moment of observing reason is "Observation of the relation of self-consciousness to its immediate actuality; physiognomy and craniology (*Beobachtung der Beziehung des Selbstbewußtseins auf seine unmittelbare Wirklichkeit; Physiognomik und Schädellehre*)."

Although the dialectical shape or *Gestalt* in question here is supposed to be that of the observing, rational mind, Hegel begins his discussion of physiognomy with a description of the shape from the point of view of the object that is observed by reason, which is to say, the embodied individual, or the physiognomist's patient. While the experience of being interpreted on the basis of one's body is certainly part of the "shape" that is physiognomy, since there is no such thing, technically, as a physiognomist without a patient, Hegel's attempt in this section to cover both viewpoints and describe a dialectical shape that is inherently, spiritually divided, already has catastrophic implications for the unity of the dialectical progression that, according to the introduction, is always what should be at stake philosophically. In this chapter, the dialectic's trope of identity encounters the dialectic's description of ethical experience in explicitly material terms. The dialectical *Fortgang* accordingly has to be thought in other than unifying terms. Hegel's initial privileging of the object's viewpoint also establishes a supplement to the explicit dialectical narrative that very quickly turns into a critical examination of dialectical narrative as such. In fact the initial shift in emphasis from observing reason to its object can take place without any direct explanation for the following reason: the dialectical narrator's more or less automatic selection of the human form to represent "the relation of self-consciousness to its immediate actuality" already, implicitly, points back to and points out the embodiment of observing reason itself. By association, this turn to the human form also points out the implicit embodiment of consciousness, self-consciousness, spirit, and of all the otherwise apparently disembodied figures structuring the dialectical investigation, including that of the philosophical first-person plural relied upon to control and justify it. In short, the allegedly rational, scientific turn toward the human body and Hegel's attempt to critique it in the name of his own phenomenology calls attention to the embodiment of the *Phenomenology of Spirit* itself.

The discussion of physiognomy amounts to a discussion of the contemporary environment of the *Phenomenology of Spirit* and of the huge popularity enjoyed by a textual production—Johann Kaspar Lavater's four-volume *Physiognomic Fragments for the Promotion of the Knowledge and Love of Mankind* (1775–1778)—that lies entirely outside the one in which the science of the experience of consciousness had been laid out.[9] The explicit dialectic of how the modern, rational mind seeks to confirm its belief that it is at home or that the world is "its own" and that spirit and body are one, thereby becomes supplemented not only by a reflection on the implications of "our" embodied existence (*Phänomenologie*, p. 184). It also becomes supplemented more specifically by Hegel's own struggle to distinguish the dialectical progression of consciousness toward spirit (or the turn of science against its own appearance), from Lavater's popularly received belief in the transcendent, divinely authorized sublation of the body by the mind.

The stakes of the distinction between physiognomy and phenomenology, Lavater and Hegel, neighbor and neighbor, are both ethical and political. Lavater presents his project from the beginning not only in the hermeneutic terms of face-reading, but also in the more general terms of the improvement of "mankind," a word repeated twice in the original German title of the *Fragments*. Hegel's phenomenological project likewise can be understood as an attempt to turn against the universalist ethics of Kant's transcendentalism, a turn summed up by the following observation in his early work, *The Spirit of Christianity and its Fate* (1798):

> The love of men, conceived as having to extend to all those of whom one knows nothing, with whom one has no relation at all, this universal love is an insipid invention. [...] The love of one's neighbor is the love of men with whom everyone enters into relation. A being that is thought can not be a being that is loved.[10]

If Lavater and Hegel agree that ethical consciousness or a "love of mankind" presupposes and concerns the existence of actual, concrete relations between men, Hegel's critique of Lavater focuses on the latter's binarism that limits these actual relations in terms of a body and soul or "inside" and "outside." Lavaterian physiognomy perfectly exemplifies what Hegel calls "observing reason" insofar as its methodology is based on observation and analogical deduction. In the first chapter or "fragment" of his work, Lavater explains that he had begun to notice, for example, that more than one person he came across with a short nose would display a short temper, or that more than one person he came across with small eyes would display below-average intelligence, and so on. From these observations he deduced a necessary relation between the outer body and the inner soul, hypothesizing that his specific observations would apply to all similarly embodied souls. The engravings in his work are generally not of specific individuals, then, but either are composites of the analogies he allegedly discovered between individuals' facial characteristics, or collections of corporeal "fragments" such as noses and eyes.[11] On the one hand, Lavater's project responds to social existence with a transcendent movement from the one (encounter with an individual), to the many (repeated encounters) to the all (a scientific system based on analogy). On the other hand, the actual collagist and fragmentary form of his work retains the open-ended multiplicity of social existence that the symbolist system otherwise attempts to overcome and erase. Within the *Phenomenology*, this multiple actuality preserved by the actual, aesthetic construction of the *Fragments* emerges both as the truth of Lavaterian physiognomy and as the presumption of Hegelian dialectic.

Hegel's response to Lavater is already implied in his introductory description of action as a socially contextualized process of alienation, perversion or transformation. According to Hegel, the semiotics of the *Physiognomic Fragments* is always already deconstructed by its politics. Lavaterian symbolism, in other words, is deconstructed by its referential function: its fundamental promise that by studying the systematic relations between inside and outside, one can enter into a more certain and secure political communion. More specifically, the promising gesture of the *Fragments* is that the existing similarity between X's and Y's noses, and that between X's and Y's characters, can be transferred to the uncertain relation between X's nose and X's character. The very performance of the Lavaterian promise, in other words, acknowledges an apparent, unknown, yet imperative relation between X's nose and X's character, a relation that is curiously both contingent and necessary: on the one hand, X's nose and his character simply happen to appear in the same place at the same time; on the other hand, this contingency is necessary insofar as it also means that X's nose never appears without X's character and X's character never appears without his nose. The promise of Lavater's project is to convert what it acknowledges as a contingent necessity into analogical identity. Since logically, contingency and necessity are mutually exclusive, whereas rhetorically their relation can be named by the term metonymy, we can say that the promise of Lavaterian physiognomy is to convert the metonymical, con-tactual conditions of existence into a metaphorical, ideological system.

Hegel develops his critique of physiognomic ideology by pointing out the physiognomic rhetoric that identifies interiority with a future-oriented "capacity." He uses this rhetorical identification to argue that in fact this alleged "science" of the body is concerned with anything but the actual, apparent body or "shape" (*Gestalt*). In the process, he himself identifies self-consciousness and embodiment in terms of a shared "singularity." The identification points to both a distinction between the physiognomic and phenomenological methods, and the way Hegel's phenomenology is informed by the actual physiognomic situation to which Lavater's *Fragments* alludes but fails to grasp:

> [In physiognomy] it is not the murderer or the thief that is supposed to be known, but rather the capacity (*Fähigkeit*) to be one.

Such fixed, abstract determinations become lost in the concrete, infinite determinateness of the singular individual (*des einzelnen Individuums*), which in fact requires more artful depictions (*kunstre-ichere Schildereien*) than the qualifications presented by physiognomy. Now, such artful depictions might say more than the qualifications of murderer, thief, kind-hearted, unspoiled and so forth, but even so, for their purpose of expressing the being that is meant (*das gemeinte Sein*) or the singular individual, they are far from adequate. *They are just as inadequate as any depictions of the shape (*Gestalt*) that would try to go beyond the flat forehead, the long nose and so on. For the individual shape (*einzelne Gestalt*), just like the individual self-consciousness, is, as a being that is meant, inexpressible.* The science of knowing men, which is concerned with supposed men (*vermeinten Menschen*), or the science of physiognomy, which is concerned with man's supposed actuality (*vermeinte Wirklichkeit*) and which attempts to raise the consciousless judgment (*das bewußtlose Urteilen*) of natural physiognomy to the level of knowing (*Wissen*), is therefore without end and ground (*End- und Bodenloses*), something that can never succeed at saying what it means because it only means, or opines, and its content remains that which is merely meant (*das nie dazu kommen kann, zu sagen, was es meint, weil es nur meint, und sein Inhalt nur Gemeintes ist*).

(*Phänomenologie*, pp. 241–2, emphasis added)

Even if one were to continue refining Lavater's clumsy or "queer" quali-fications of personality and come up with ever more "artful depictions" of an individual's possible inner state, still one would never reach the actual singular individual or "being" that is meant—the referent of Lavater's system.[12] In other words, one can learn nothing from Lavater's *Physiognomic Fragments* about what it means to encounter an actual indi-vidual, and consequently nothing about what it means to exist politi-cally or among "mankind." What this means for Hegel is indicated by the comparison of the ineffability of the "individual self-consciousness" (or the "being that is meant") to that of the individual shape, within his argument that neither Lavater's qualifications of character *nor* his actual drawings approach the actuality of social existence. According to the comparison, both "self-consciousness" and the body or "shape" only appear as other than what they are. The comparison casts the singular self-consciousness as fundamentally corporeal, performative, semiotic and social. And self-consciousness is fundamentally social because its semiotic nature is, according the critique of Lavater's misprision of inef-fability, fundamentally referential rather than analogical. For Hegel, it is the contingent, necessary, lateral relations between men that should serve as the basis for thinking the relation between body and soul, or the sign and its meaning. Accordingly, the social multiplicity presumed by Lavaterian physiognomy should actually take place as critical, allegorical thought, or as the socially contextualized reading of otherness.

The allegorical description of self-consciousness, in the discussion of physiognomy, indicates the physiognomic setting of Hegel's dialectical method itself. The reference here to the ineffability of shape (*Gestalt*) rather than, say, to that of the body (*Leib*), directly and explicitly reiterates his vocabulary of the "shapes of consciousness" (*Gestalten des Bewußtseins*) that are supposed to constitute the dialectical advance.[13] The "shapes" that appear to consciousness do so, that is, only insofar as they are always already meaningful; and yet, that meaning has validity or actuality only as the process of its socially contextualized communication. This communication both implies a set of multiple viewpoints, and presumes the act of judgment as an incision into or decision about them, which then shapes their future or movement forward (*Fortgang*). The act of dialectical judgment and its peculiar temporality are alluded to in a second gesture back to the rhetoric of the introduction, Hegel's passing reference to the consciousless judgment (*bewußtlose Urteilen*) of what he calls "natural" physiognomy. Hegel does not deny or take issue with natural, "everyday" physiognomy or face-reading, which he describes as the inevitable, "more than fast" (*vorschnelle*) judgment that occurs as the "first glimpse" (*ersten Anblicke*) of an appearing, spiritual shape, and that insists on the legibility of appearance by always already viewing visibility as the "visibility of the invisible" (*Sichtbarkeit des Unsichtbaren*) (*Phänomenologie*, p. 241). His critique is directed specifically at the attempt to transform this natural, consciousless kind of judgment into the rigid universalism of a natural science, which is to say, the attempt to replace its materiality with an ideology.

A motif of consciouslessness or *Bewustlosigkeit* in fact runs through Hegel's work at least from his critique of Kant in the early essay *Faith and Knowledge* (1802), where he identifies consciouslessness with the copula of Kant's synthetic judgment, to the discussion of ethics in the *Phenomenology of Spirit*, where it is pervasive.[14] In the chapter on Kant in the earlier essay, Hegel introduces *a priori* synthetic judgment and its aesthetic version, productive imagination (*productive Einbildungskraft*), as the "most interesting part" of Kant's critical project. He then sets about glossing Kant's answer to his question "how are *a priori* synthetic judgments possible?" Hegel's version of the answer appeals to a "consciouslessness" inscribed within such judgments, in a discussion that aims generally at arguing the priority of difference over unity and that ultimately translates Kant's *a priori* into a Hegelian *a posteriori*. To cite one example:

> *A priori* synthetic judgments [...] are possible through the original, absolute identity of the dissimilar. [...] The rational or, as Kant himself puts it, the *a priori* nature of the synthetic judgment, the absolute identity as the mediating concept, does not appear in the judgment, but only in its outcome. In the judgment it is only the copula "is," something that is consciousless, and the judgment itself is only the prevailing manifestation of difference.[15]

According to Hegel, Kant's *a priori* appears after the fact and in response to a quasi-conscious act of judgment or theoretical copulation. Although Hegel's English translators generally opt for "unconscious" when it comes to *bewustlos*, Hegel's own use of the suffix -less (*-los*) over the prefix un- (*un-*) indicates the quasi-negativity of Heidegger's "unthought" (which should be understood in terms of the un*thought* rather than the *un*thought).[16] The acknowledgment, in the *Phenomenology*, of a consciousless judgment informing the physiognomic situation that at the very least overlaps rhetorically with Hegel's dialectic, suggests that Hegelian "consciousness" itself arises in quasi-negative relation to, or as the decipherment of, the expressed judgments actually shaping social existence.

The suggestion will be made explicit by the description of the imperative move from physiognomy to craniology.[17] This transition might seem to represent a move from the signifying body to something like "the body itself," one that removes the aesthetic medium of the lithograph, the word, or the flesh, and gets to the pure "thing." Hegel's introduction to craniology however is more complex. He describes it in terms of a move from the consciousless judgment in natural physiognomy—the judgment that "X (the visible) is not X (that is, is the invisible)"—to the emergence of consciousness from a consciousless past or "inheritance."[18] This occurs in a passage that appears to distinguish between the signifying value of the face, on the one hand, and the meaningless impersonality of the skull, on the other:

> [The being that is the skull does not] even have the value of a sign (*den Wert eines Zeichens*). Facial expression and gesture, tone, even a pillar or post erected on a deserted island announce right away that something else is meant than what they only immediately are. They present themselves right away as signs, since they have a determination in them that points to something other, insofar as

it does not properly belong to them (*daß sie ihnen nicht eigentümlich angehört*). All sorts of things can occur to one in the presence of a skull, as in the case of Hamlet with Yorick's, but the skull bone on its own is such an indifferent, unprejudiced thing, that there is nothing else immediately in it to see and think, than just itself. (*Man kann sich wohl auch bei einem Schädel, wie Hamlet bei Yoriks, vielerlei einfallen lassen, aber der Schädelknochen für sich ist ein so gleichgültiges, unbefangenes Ding, daß an ihm unmittelbar nichts anderes zu sehen und zu meinen ist, als nur er selbst.*)

(*Phänomenologie*, p. 251)

The passage apparently lays claim to a distinction between the positive, signifying potential of the facial expression, gesture, and tone of voice, on the one hand, and the sheer meaninglessness of the skull on the other. The former all indicate meaning as value or immediately there, if at the same time "something other" than and not properly belonging to that which appears. The skull, by contrast, presents nothing but a thing by itself (*Ding [...] an ihm [...] selbst*). A simple, life/death opposition seems to inform the passage: the face indicates life, presence, meaning, and the possibility of communication and communion, whereas the skull indicates death, absence, meaninglessness and silence.

And yet Hamlet, the stand-in for Gall, becomes anything but silent upon picking up Yorick's skull; he is beset, rather, by a multiplicity (*vielerlei*) of thoughts. In fact the series of neat, binary distinctions the passage claims to illustrate is immediately interrupted by the redoubled figure that is supposed to articulate them with each other, namely the "pillar or post" on the deserted island. While the argument explicitly aligns these architectural pronouncements with facial expression, gesture and tone of voice, their placement on an island that is deserted (*öden*) aligns them much more with the silent skull. In fact, the skull is both metaphorically and metonymically closer to the silent post and pillar, insofar as if one were to find oneself, like Defoe's Robinson Crusoe, stranded on a deserted island marked by a pillar or post, one would be more likely to come across a leftover skull than a living face. Since Hegel nevertheless associates the pillar/post with the facial expression, the example ultimately emphasizes the similarity rather than the difference between the face and the skull. It introduces a temporal and historical dimension into the initial example of the face-as-sign, disrupting the evaluative reference to a totalizing, synecdochic contemporaneity between individuals and reprising the theme of action as allegory. In this way the skull explicitly challenges rational imperialism, or "reason's" belief in its ownership of the world. If the face-as-sign reflects my rational certainty that the world is mine, that I own the significance of visibility, the skull emphasizes the pillar's indication of an otherness that questions this certainty. Comprising both the figure of the face and the sheer indication that is the pillar, the skull also points to a multiplicity that resists the rational trope of identity, thereby indicating that reason's certainty about itself is mistaken specifically with respect to its certainty about the identity of the self. The skull's disturbance of rational identity accounts for Dolar's description of this chapter's outcome in terms of a wounded or "blinded" subjectivity. The emergence of a rhetoric of multiplicity within Hegel's account of this disturbance, however, points specifically to the historical conditions of the social antagonism inscribed in the relation between reason and the skull.

If the pillar/post and its deserted island imply Defoe's Robinson (insofar as it is here a pillar/post that is observed, by someone else), Hegel's skull also, and explicitly, does not appear on its own, in spite of his description of it as "on its own" and "just itself." In the movement from face to pillar to skull, the "something other" indicated by the face becomes externalized in the form of a monologuing Hamlet. At the same time and in the other direction, the implied consciouslessness of the judgment that 'something else is meant than what [...] immediately [appears]," the consciouslessness inscribed in the judgment's copula, takes on the externalized shape of the "unprejudiced" (*unbefangenes*) skull. The reversal thereby dramatizes not only the temporal delay implied in the face-as-sign, but also what might be described as its material sociality, along with the kind of consciousness (represented by the excessively reflective Hamlet) that emerges from that sociality. Like Lysias' written speech in the *Phaedrus*, Hegel's skull, in its silence, actively demands that someone else respond, and in responding, decide on his own what the skull means.[19] The skull may not display a determinate or "prejudiced" content, such as happy, sad, brave, cowardly, and so on, but—in distinction from, say, a kneecap, wing bone or even a spine—it does "demand" meaning, whether (as in the case of Hamlet's monologue) it is that of the other's death, or more particularly Yorick, Ophelia, Alexander or Caesar, or, by reflection, the death of myself, or, by extension, death itself.[20] The skull, in other words, points to the mortality that hollows out every indication of meaning, such that its alleged indifference and lack of prejudice can only appear ironically. The skull may "be" indifferent, but its appearance is not, insofar as it always appears "for an other," an other who for its part appears historically, as the skull's survival. The skull indicates death, that is, only by also positing the survival of another consciousness, with consciousness emerging from craniology, the materiality of the apparent shape, as socialized survival. In its emergence from the skull, this consciousness is also emphatically alone, soliloquizing in the face of an antagonistic society that demands an independent, arbitrary choice between passivity, or paralysis by a multiplicity of thoughts, and action.

In his discussion of craniology Hegel continues to emphasize the paralyzing, hermeneutic multiplicity that joins Hamlet and the skull of Yorick. Unlike the physiognomist, whose failure was marked by an inability to grasp the ineffability of singular self-consciousness, the craniologist faces the problem of the sheer, material multiplicity presented by the skull. Insofar as he merely touches, as opposed to recognizing and giving shape to coherent forms (slanting forehead, narrow eyes, jutting chin and so on), the craniologist's work itself is a kind of blind, endless stumbling or stuttering over sheer material differentiations:

> On the one side there is a mass (*Menge*) of inert positions on the skull, on the other side a mass (*Menge*) of spiritual qualities, whose multiplicity (*Vielheit*) and determination will depend on the state of the current psychology. [...] If each child of Israel were to take from the sand on the shore that is supposed to correspond to them, that grain of sand (*Körnchen*) that is his own sign, then the indifference and arbitrariness according to which each grain of sand is allocated would be no more stark than that which assigns to all the capacities of soul, passions and [...] shadings of character [...] their stations on the skull and shapes of bone (*ihre Schädelstätten und Knochenformen*). The skull of a murderer has this—not an organ, not even a sign—but this bump (*Knorren*). But this murderer also has a mass of other qualities as well as other bumps, and with the bumps other depressions. One has a choice between bumps and depressions (*aber dieser Mörder hat noch eine Menge anderer Eigenschaften, so wie andere Knorren, und mit den Knorren auch Vertiefungen; man hat die Wahl unter Knorren und Vertiefungen*).
>
> (*Phänomenologie*, pp. 252–53)

Instead of reflecting on death, the craniologist attempts to organize the mass of material gradations and degradations on the skull into whatever analogical system the current psychology happens to offer. Like Lavater, he passes off arbitrariness as law. Although the explicit object of the critique is the capriciousness of the craniologist's method, Hegel emphatically describes the caprice in terms of an overwhelming numerousness, which his own prose starts to perform with the stuttering of "bumps [...] bumps [...] and depressions [...] bumps and depressions." The allusion to Genesis that is supposed to illustrate the "stark" indifference and arbitrariness of the craniological method also alludes specifically to a passage that pronounces the vast multiplication of Abraham's progeny as the divine reward for the faith displayed by his willingness to sacrifice his only (*einzigen*) son. In the Old Testament, the sands on the seashore and "stars in the sky" represent multiplicity, regeneration, survival, political power and divine blessing, not indifference and caprice.[21]

Hegel's description of the craniological predicament suggests that, in order to move beyond Enlightenment science's catastrophic conclusion that "spirit is a bone," and in order for this "end" also to serve as a "turn" in the consciousness-to-spirit plot, the rational observer must arbitrarily convert or determine the multiplicity of materiality according to a coherent content, and that survival as such is constituted by such acts of conversion. The silent, material skull requires, in other words, that the passive, analogical observer become a decisive actor, that reason cease looking for itself and begin to create itself. The prose of this passage—the skull of Hegel's own dialectic—performs the predicament as well as the solution insofar as the allusion to the Israelite, like the implicit allusion to *Robinson Crusoe* and the explicit allusion to *Hamlet*, gives shape to the otherwise indifferent, unprejudiced, bumpy skull. The Israelite's choice of this or that grain of sand may be arbitrary, but neither the self-identification as Israelite nor the allusion to the Israelite is. The reader is presumed to recognize the identity of the allusion and know what "child of Israel" designates. In this way Hegel himself performs the conversion of multiple materiality into coherent content, by alluding to a recognizable literary-cultural figure. The craniological skull converts the observer into an actor finally by exposing him as a reader, by placing upon him the imperative of reading something that cannot be verified by the analogical procedures upon which Enlightenment science or "observing reason" depends.

The conversion of multiplicity into meaning by way of allusion does not amount to a simple theoretical reduction of the many to the one. The imperative of reading the allusion instead reinscribes the multiplicity that was presumed by Lavaterian physiognomy and reflected on by Hamlet, as the horizon or goal (*Ziel*) of Hegel's dialectical advance. As he puts it in the concluding sentence of the *Phenomenology of Spirit*, each "shape" of the dialectic of consciousness is always also a "station on the skull" (*Schädelstätte*), an allegorical performance that inscribes a future multiplicity within the imperative of their reading. Our reading of the Old Testament, or of *Antigone* or *Faust* or any of the literary-allusions inform-ing the ensuing dialectic of spirit might differ from Hegel's, for example. Even the allusion to the child of Israel, which is meaningful only in terms of its reference to the figure for the vast multiplication of Abraham's progeny (a figure used by Hegel to describe "indifference"), also implicitly alludes to the children of Ishmael and thereby deconstructs the figure's illustration of indifference. The craniologist's association of borrowed psychological qualities with various bumps and depressions may be indifferent and arbitrary, but the identification of oneself with a natural referent, whether it be sand or a presumed-to-be natural "capacity," is not. The multiplication of Abraham's descendants and their struggle to identify themselves with specific sands illustrates how indifference, and indifferent multiplicity, are made impossible by their very description. Description, insofar as it is always also an act of reference beyond itself, is always an ethical event and therefore a discourse of ethicity. Hegel's face and skull, the final referents of reason's initial declaration that it is itself all reality, conclude the dialectic of observing reason by revising rational discourse into a discourse of ethicity. This latter discourse not only *describes* the antagonistic, ambiguous relation between self and other—as we saw in Hegel's account of the rise of physiognomy,—but also turns out to actually occur as the reference of all description beyond itself. Hegel's ethics of multiplicity, in other words, is always also an ethics of survival.

As indicated by Hegel's critique of physiognomy, dialectical description is never just a turn of mind to matter, but is always a turn of the mind to a material that is presumed and even required, albeit consciouslessly, to be meaningful. The dialectical turn implies the consciousless judgment that "this is not this" and therefore from the beginning implies what might be called a physiognomic situation and its attendant multiplic-ity of minds. The ethicity of the dialectical turn is legible in more than one passage in the introduction where Hegel attempts to distinguish the originality of his project from the declared rigor of Kantian critique. For example, he does not describe the advance from "being-for-conscious-ness" (or knowledge) to "being-in-itself" (or truth) as a movement from a narrow perspective a larger one. Instead, he describes this advance by referring to an undetermined but actual perspective of "being-for-an-other" that, rather than being unfolded, must be quickly erased in order for the advance to continue under the aegis of the philosophical "us":

[Consciousness] distinguishes [...] something from itself, something to which it at the same time relates itself; or as this is expressed, it is something for consciousness; and the determined side of this relating, or of the being of something for a consciousness, is knowledge. From this *being-for-an-other* however we distinguish being-in-itself; what is related to knowing is just as much distinguished from it and posited as being also outside of this relation; the side of this in-itself is called truth.

(Phänomenologie, p. 76, emphasis added)

The very distinction between "being-for-consciousness" and "being-in-itself" depends on the allusion to the relation of "being-for-an-other," which is to say, the allusion to the "object's view of consciousness. The second sentence, instead of reading "from this *being-for-consciousness* however we distinguish being in itself," reads "from this *being-for-an-other* however we distinguish being-in-itself." In the second sentence, consciousness itself is thereby turned into "an other" and the thing that is "for consciousness" takes on a perspective, that of "being for" something "other." It is emphatically this "other" perspective that leads to being-in-itself: "from this being-for-an-other [...] we distinguish being-in-itself." If being-in-itself appears here as the erasure of all individual perspective, it also is authorized only by the surreptitious pronouncement in the following paragraph of the philosophical "us" and the measuring stick (*Maßstab*) of truth that apparently lies in "our" hands: "In this investigation [knowledge] is *our* object, it is *for us*; and the *in itself* of knowledge which results from the investigation would be that much more its being *for us*." On the one hand, the movement from being-for-consciousness to being-in-itself is characterized by the displacement of a rhetoric of viewpoint by one of measure and scientific "investigation." On the other hand, this rhetorical displacement is authorized only by the actual displacement of the object's viewpoint (that regards consciousness as "other") into that of the philosophical "us"; both of these viewpoints share the quality of being something other than consciousness, and of regarding consciousness as something other than themselves. The displacement of being-for-an-other into being-for-us furthermore makes explicit as the authorial-editorial "we" the plurality that is always implied in the lateral, allegorical relation of being-for- (or "against")-an-other.

The relation of "being-for-us" takes on the role of ensuring the coherency of the dialectical advance, by announcing, describing and explaining it, even if it insists that the movement takes place within "consciousness itself." And each of "our" philosophical pronouncements about the meaning of the dialectic has to refer to the relation of being-for-an-other in order actually to maintain the dialectical advance. The relation of being-for-an-other must be both implied and erased by every transition from knowing (being-for-consciousness) to the truth (being-in-itself). In the discussion of physiognomy, the viewpoint of being-for-an-other takes over the prescribed linearity of the movement from apparent knowledge to truth, disrupting the presumed authority and above all the identity of the first-person plural that calls itself philosophy and distinguishes itself from mere "consciousness." The physiognomist looks at the body, and should be able to progress to the realization that "the true being of man is much more his act" than his face (*Phänomenologie*, p. 242). Insofar as this is not all that happens, however, Hegel's physiognomy makes explicit what is implicit from the beginning of his science of consciousness, with the physiognomist's patient emerging as a critical reading of the phenomenologist's "shapes," always called upon to indicate meaning without actually speaking it themselves. The story of the catastrophic "ending" of Enlightenment science in the form of craniology furthermore turns the dialectic of consciousness into an allegory of a Hegelian ethics of survival, one that describes "being-for-an-other" in terms of the necessary advance we call history.

The allegory becomes pronounced in Hegel's attempt to reflect directly on the relation between the dialectical method and ethical existence, in the beginning of the chapter on spirit, where consciousness turns out to always have been the process of spirit's dividing. For example, after having finished off the chapter on reason with a critique of the Kantian identification of ethics with non-contradiction—("It is not [...] because I find something is not self-contradictory that it is right; it is right, rather, because it is what is right"), he begins the section on "the ethical world; human and divine law, man and woman" by explaining that

the simple substance of spirit divides as consciousness (*teilt sich als Bewußtsein*). In other words, just as consciousness of abstract, sensuous being passes over into perception, so too does the immediate certainty of real, ethical being. And just as simple being becomes a thing of many qualities for sense-perception, so too, for the perception that is ethical, does action as such (*der Fall des Handelns*) become an actuality (*Wirklichkeit*) of many ethical relations.

(*Phänomenologe*, p. 322, p. 328).

This description of consciousness as the division of spirit contradicts the view of the *Phenomenology* as a story firstly of a psychologically informed "consciousness," which then gives rise to the historically and socially informed "spirit." This view is fundamental to the traditions both that regard the *Phenomenology* as an expression of idealism, and that regard it as an expression of an irreducible and indifferent ambivalence.[22] In spite of Dolar's impressive and much needed analysis of the chapter on reason, his conclusion regarding Hegel's ambivalence appeals to the latter tradition, which in distinction from "The Phrenology of Spirit" has generally acted as if the middle chapter on reason had never been written. But according to its outcome, the chapter on ethics, consciousness is never just "itself" insofar as it is always the dividing of spirit. Hegel does not say that spirit divides "as consciousness does," but simply that it divides "as consciousness." The multiplication of being in sense-perception and of action in ethics are examples of spirit's dividing into consciousness. To reduce the ethical multiplicity exemplifying Hegel's account of consciousness as an effect of spiritual division, to the concept of an ambivalence wavering between the thoughts of heterogeneity and progression, is to avoid the actuality of reference and the ethical decision that Hegelian multiplicity requires. It is to avoid, in other words, the ethical examination of the relation of "self-consciousness to its immediate actuality" that is performed by the dialectic of physiognomy and craniology. Far from being an obscure lapse in the dialectic of consciousness, the passage through physiognomy and craniology unfolds a Hegelian ethics of multiplicity in terms of the phenomenality of dialectic and the spirituality of consciousness, which is to say, in terms of the interrelations of image and speech, reference and dialog. This dialectic can be called catastrophic insofar as it turns over the linearity of the method, along with the binarism of "science and its appearance," into a reflection on the multiplicity implied by the dialectical advance. As with all catastrophes, the survival here occurs by virtue of a necessity that replaces theoretical ideals of progression with an awareness of the historical conditions of spirit.

The overturning is a subversion, the dénouement an undoing and revising of the laws of the genre itself.

Notes

1. Henry George Liddell and Robert Scott, *A Greek-English Lexicon* (Oxford: Clarendon Press, 1996).
2. "Science must liberate itself from [...] appearance, and it can do this only by turning against it" (*Die Wissenschaft muß sich [...] von [dem] Scheine befreien, und sie kann dies nur dadurch, daß sie gegen ihn wendet*). G. W. F. Hegel, *Phänomenologie des Geistes*, edited by Eva Moldenhauser and Karl Markus

Michel (Frankfurt am: Suhrkamp, 1970), p. 71. Henceforth cited in the text as *Phänomenologie*. Unless otherwise noted, translations in this essay are my own, and throughout I have translated what Hegel calls *Schädellehre* as "craniology." In his chapter on this section of the *Phenomenology*, David Verene explains how Gall (1758–1828), a respected anatomist who frowned upon the association of his science with Lavaterian physiognomy, also disapproved of the term *Phrenologie* to refer to it, preferring instead the more literal *Schädellehre*. It was Gall's student and colleague, Johann Georg Spurzheim (1776–1832), who quickly and effectively replaced *Schädellehre* with *Phrenologie*, in order to lend the science more philosophical weight at least within public perception. David Verene, *Hegel's Recollection: A Study of Images in the* Phenomenology of Spirit (Albany: SUNY Press, 1985), p. 82, p. 88. The Greek *phren* designates "the heart, mind, understanding, reason," and "the heart and parts near the heart, the breast," *Liddell and Scott's Greek-English Lexicon, Abridged* (Oxford: Clarendon, 1991). Presumably Gall and Hegel alike favored *Schädellehre* in order to underscore the materialism of this "teaching of the skull" that offers a theory of "the mind" only on the basis of a topography of the skull.

3. "So after examining outer and inner nature, Reason arrives at a 'higher synthesis' of the two, their 'dialectical integration,' which it happens to find in, of all things, phrenology. Is Hegel pulling our leg? Is he parodying his own method? Is he playing a joke at our expense? Does the progress of Reason suddenly regress, ending in catastrophe?" Mladen Dolar, "The Phrenology of Spirit," in *Supposing the Subject*, edited by Joan Copjec (London: Verso, 1994), p. 65.

4. The reference to the necessity of the dialectical *Fortgang*, usually translated as dialectical "progression," reads: "The completion of the forms of the unreal consciousness itself arises through the necessity of their advance and interconnection" (*Die Vollständigkeit der Formen des nicht realen Bewußtseins wird sich durch die Notwendigkeit des Fortganges und Zusammenhanges selbst ergeben*) (*Phänomenologie*, p. 73). Paul de Man refers in passing to a Hegelian "ethics of survival" that characterizes the work of the critical poet, in "Hegel on the Sublime," *Aesthetic Ideology*, edited by Andrzej Warminski (Minneapolis: University of Minnesota Press, 1996), p. 117.

5. In the 1961 essay "Zur Deutung der *Phänomenologie des Geistes*" (Toward an Interpretation of the *Phenomenology of Spirit*), Otto Pöggeler analyzes the material genesis of the *Phenomenology* in order to argue that the text's ambivalence is not accidental, but rather is philosophically irreducible and hermeneutically productive. His analysis circles without facing directly the middle section on physiognomy and craniology. See Otto Pöggeler, "Zur Deutung der Hegels *Phänomenologie*," reprinted in *Hegels Idee einer Phänomenologie des Geistes* (Freiburg: Alber, 1973). Pöggeler's ambiguity or *Zweideutigkeit* is reprised by Paul de Man's analysis of Hegel's aesthetics in the 1980s. De Man describes the ambiguity in terms of the opposition between Hegel's prosaism and his poetics, diverging from Pöggeler's open-ended appreciation by arguing that Hegel's "political legitimacy" lies specifically in the former and its opposition to the latter. The implicit recommendation of de Man's analysis that future readings of Hegel be concerned with the unaesthetic, problematic moments in the dialectic is taken up Slavoj Žižek, who concludes *The Sublime Object of Ideology* (London: Verso, 1989) with

a discussion of the *Phenomenology*'s grotesque and dialectically troubling section on physiognomy and craniology. Like de Man, Žižek focuses on the political implications of Hegelian dialectic and like de Man, he argues that Hegel presents one of the most rigorous accounts of a politics of the "small" or provisional as opposed to a politics of the grand or sublime. The Lacanian influence of Žižek's analysis, along with the focus on the craniology discussion, is then taken up by Dolar, who, with his conclusive call for an appreciation of Hegel's ambivalence, brings the lineage full-circle back to Pöggeler.

6. "Die Verwirklichung des vernünftigen Selbstbewußtseins durch sich selbst" is the title of the chapter immediately following the discussion of craniology, which itself is the last part of the larger chapter on "Observing Reason."

7. See Terry Pinkard's gloss of Hegel's discussion of physiognomy in terms of what he calls "social space": "Individual self-consciousness is one's taking oneself to be located in a determinate 'social space'; an individual's self-identity is made up of his actions in that 'social space' and how those actions are taken by others. The 'social space' is both the basis of the principles on which actions are taken and the basis of the interpretations of those actions by others." Terry Pinkard, *Hegel's* Phenomenology: *the Sociality of Reason* (Cambridge: Cambridge University Press, 1996), p. 89.

8. Findlay refers to its tortuous organization as repulsive, while Pöggeler refers to it and the entire chapter on reason as an unnecessary shattering. See J. N. Findlay, "Foreword," *Hegel's* Phenomenology of Spirit, translated by A. V. Miller (Oxford: Oxford University Press, 1977), p. xix.

9. The original, German title of Lavater's major work is *Physiognomische Fragmente zur Beförderung der Menschenkenntniss und Menschenliebe*, the standard English translation of which is *Essays in Physiognomy*. Johann Kaspar Lavater *Physiognomische Fragmente zur Beförderung der Menschenkenntniss und Menschenliebe*. Leipzig, 1775–8.

10. Cited in Jean Luc-Nancy's *The Birth to Presence*, translated by Brian Holmes (Stanford: Stanford University Press, 1993), p. 127.

11. Engravings of individual paintings and of famous figures such as Socrates, Jesus Christ, Descartes and Goethe are also included and used to exemplify the method established by the more general depictions.

12. In a letter to Reverend John Sibree (February 1846), George Eliot similarly if inversely bemoans "Lavater's queer sketches of physiognomies and still queerer judgments on them." Cited in Graeme Tytler's *Physiognomy in the European Novel: Faces and Fortunes* (Princeton: Princeton University Press, 1982), p. 98.

13. See for example the concluding paragraph of the introduction in *Phänomenologie*, p. 80.

14. For example, *Phänomenologie*, p. 265, p. 330, p. 341, p. 344. The complete title of the 1802 essay, originally published in the second issue of Hegel's and Schelling's co-edited *Critical Journal of Philosophy*, is *Faith and Knowledge, or the Reflective Philosophy of Subjectivity in the Completion of its Forms as Kantian, Jacobian and Fichtean Philosophy*. G. W. F. Hegel, *"Glauben und Wissen oder die Reflexionsphilosophie der Subjektivität in der Vollständigkeit ihrer Formen als Kantische, Jacobische ud Fichtesche Philosophie," Jenaer Schriften 1801–1807*, edited by Eva Moldenhauser and Karl Markus Michel (Frankfurt am: Suhrkamp, 1986).

15. "Synthetische Urteile a priori [...] sind möglich durch die ürsprungliche absolute Identität von Ungleichartigem. [...] Das Vernünftige, oder wie Kant sich ausdrückt, das Apriorische dieses Urteils, die absolute Identität als Mittelbegriff stellt sich aber im Urteil nicht, sondern im Schluß dar; im Urteil ist sie nur das Kopula 'Ist,' ein Bewußtloses, und das Urteil selbst ist nur die überwiegende Erscheinung der Differenz" *G. W. F. Hegel, Jenaer Schriften 1801–1807*, edited by Eva Moldenhauser and Karl Markus Michel (Frankfurt am Main: Suhrkamp, 1986), p. 307.

16. The attribution of "quasi-negativity" is borrowed from Jacques Derrida's discussion of Heidegger's unthought, in his essay "Désistance," in *Psyché: Inventions de l'autre* (Paris: Galilée, 1987). I discuss Derrida's commentary on the unthought in my essay, "Dislocating Derrida: Badiou, the Unthought and the Justice of Multiplicity," in *Encountering Derrida: Legacies and Futures of Deconstruction*, edited by Allison Weiner and Simon Morgan-Wortham, (London: Continuum Books, 2008), pp. 152–167.

17. The imperative of the move from physiognomy is pronounced by Hegel's description of it in terms of what observation "must do" (*machen muss*), *Phänomenologie*, p. 244.

18. Hegel discusses the relation of consciousness to its inheritance or "what is born" (*angeboren*) to it at the beginning of the chapter on physiognomy, *Phänomenologie*, p. 234.

19. The silent face is uncanny and therefore disruptive of paternity: "Writing, Phaedrus, has this uncanniness, and is very like painting; for the creatures of painting stand like living beings, but if one asks them a question, they preserve a solemn silence. And so it is with written words; you might think they spoke as if they had intelligence, but if you question them, wishing to know about their sayings, they always say only one and the same thing. And every word, when once it is written, is bandied about, alike among those who understand and those who have no interest in it, and it knows not to whom to speak or not to speak; when ill-treated or unjustly reviled it always needs its father to help it; for it has no power to protect or help itself." Plato, *Phaedrus*, translated by Harold North Fowler (Cambridge: Harvard University Press, 1990), p. 275d (translation modified).

20. See William Shakespeare, *The Tragedy of Hamlet, Prince of Denmark* (London, 1603) V. i. Hegel comments on the particular significance of the skull bone in the following terms: "When anyone thinks of the proper location for the existence of spirit, it is the not the back but only the head that comes to mind," *Phänomenologie*, p. 247. The skull is not sheer matter or a mere "thing," but is specifically the material existence of spirit; it does in fact signify.

21. "Because you have done this and have not spared your only son I will bless and multiply your race like the stars in the sky and the sands on the sea shore, and your descendants will possess the gates of their enemies; and all the peoples on earth will be blessed through your race, because you have hearkened my voice" (*Weil du solches getan hast und hast deines einzigen Sohnes nich verschont, will ich dein Geschlecht segnen und mehren wie die Sterne am Himmel und wie den Sand am Ufer des Meeres, und deine Nachkommen sollen die Tore ihrer Feinde besitzen; und durch dein Geschlecht sollen alle Völker auf Erden gesegnet werden, weil du meiner Stimme gehorcht hast), Lutherbibel*

Standardausgabe mit Apokryphen (Stuttgart: Deutsche Bibelgesellschaft 1999), p. 22; 16–18.

22. A relatively recent example of the old tradition that attributes Hegel's idealism to his consciousness-to-spirit narrative, and that implicitly excises the chapter on reason, appears in Judith Butler's chapter on the *Phenomenology* in her book *The Psychic Life of Power*. The chapter on Hegel describes the *Phenomenology* in terms of a direct transformation of "self-consciousness" into "spirit" as if the passage through reason (and its reflection on "the body") were not part of that movement. Judith Butler, "Stubborn Attachment, Bodily Subjection: Rereading Hegel on the Unhappy Consciousness," *The Psychic Life of Power* (Stanford: Stanford University Press 1997), p. 53.

8
Catastrophe, Citationality and the Limits of Responsibility in *Disgrace*

Gert Buelens

This essay argues that J. M. Coetzee's *Disgrace* (1999) dramatizes how all responsibility is limited in character through what Judith Butler has anatomized as the inevitably citational basis of social agency.[1] I will turn to Butler's theory in a moment, but first want to rehearse the basic elements of the novel's plot.

David Lurie is a middle-aged professor of English at Cape Technical University, where he is forced to spend most of his time teaching courses in communication. He is divorced, with one grown-up daughter, and is introduced to us as a man who believes he has "solved the problem of sex rather well" (p. 1), spending one afternoon a week with Soraya, a hostess selected from the range offered by an escort service. But it becomes clear very quickly that Lurie is nonetheless a frustrated man in many respects. He hates his professional existence—being allowed to teach one literature course only, and having a hard time getting through to the students that do opt for his Romantics course—and he cannot resist the urge to follow up on a chance meeting with Soraya in the street, when he sees her together with her two young sons, an urge that will result in Soraya's withdrawing her services in the face of this breach of her privacy. Nor can he stop himself from wooing Melanie, a student of his, persisting in his pursuit when she has made it clear she does not want him, and having sex with the young woman on several occasions, at least one of which is presented in terms that do not suggest mutual consent. Lurie is driven by passions, including that of Eros, which he invokes when challenged to give an account of his actions to a university committee, following a complaint lodged by Melanie. Refusing to repent, Lurie instead agrees to resign, in public disgrace. He embarks on a prolonged stay with his daughter Lucy, who has a smallholding in the Eastern Cape, where, with some assistance from a man called Petrus, she grows vegetables and flowers for sale at a local market and runs boarding kennels. Here Lurie manages to retrieve a measure of equanimity, though Lucy and he see eye-to-eye on few things. This relative stability is completely destroyed when two men and an adolescent, in broad daylight, lock Lurie into the lavatory of the house, rape Lucy, kill all the dogs present in the kennels, set fire to Lurie, and drive off in his car. The rest of the novel is taken up first and foremost with the widely divergent reactions this attack provokes in Lucy and in her father.

Before examining this point in more detail, I must go into one aspect that I have wholly—and somewhat studiously—ignored up to now, but which many critics have concentrated on: the novel's striking racial dynamics. Lurie and his daughter are evidently white, Soraya is what would be called "coloured" in South Africa, as is Melanie, probably; the gang-rapists are black; so is Petrus, who is related to one of them. As Derek Attridge usefully summarizes:

> The overriding question for many readers is: does this novel, as one of the most widely disseminated and forceful representations of post-apartheid South Africa, impede the difficult enterprise of rebuilding the country? Does the largely negative picture it paints of relations between the communities hinder the steps being made toward reconciliation? Is it a damagingly misleading portrait of a society that has made enormous strides in the direction of justice and peace?[2]

Attridge adds that even readers like himself "whose view of the artist's responsibility is less tied to notions of instrumentalism and political efficacy than these questions imply [...] may find the bleak image of the 'new South Africa' in this work hard to take" (p. 164). Yet he goes on to demonstrate, in the course of one of the most persuasive and comprehensive readings of *Disgrace*, that the novel's appraisal of South African society in many respects possesses little specificity. For instance, its condemnation of how the teaching of literature is displaced by that of communication studies rings true across the globe; the series of references to how the contemporary attitude toward sex has become viciously moralistic can be contextualized easily for US society, say, at a time of publication when the Clinton-Lewinsky relation had just been the stuff of scandal. To the extent that the novel does address uniquely South African problems, Attridge argues that its critique "explores, by means of one invented life, some of the pains and strains of a social and economic order reinventing itself against this background," of "a new global age of performance indicators and outcome measurement, [...] of a widespread prurience that's also an unfeeling puritanism" (p. 173).

Attridge's point is well taken, and enables him to show, as he does throughout his book on Coetzee, that an allegorical reading—one which would in this case insist on the social and political realities that *Disgrace* stages—misses the singularity of the literary work of art by either reducing its meaning to the specifics of the context in which it took shape or attempting to derive from it universal truths about "the human condition." However, while Attridge knows that one can never wholly escape the seductions of allegory, the alternative take that he proposes does not do as good a job of resisting this allure as it might had his reading been less focused on the figure of the male protagonist, whose allegorizing tendency Attridge ultimately replicates in developing an allegory of grace. I will show that, by attending more closely to Lucy as an "alternative center" of consciousness—a suggestion of Gayatri Spivak's that Attridge considers but does not take up,[3]—and by examining her response to events from the perspective of Butler's theory of performativity, we can more successfully meet Attridge's call for a non-allegorical mode, that is, an attempt to avoid reading literature merely for reminders "of what we already know" (p. 43).

Let me first consider the rape, about which Lurie reflects: "So it has come, the day of testing. [...] His child is in the hands of strangers. In a minute, in an hour, it will be too late; whatever is happening to her will be set in stone, will belong to the past. But *now* it is not too late. *Now* he must do something" (p. 94). The moment is clearly presented as a crucial turning point in the protagonist's life, a moment, too, when he will in fact prove totally unable to do anything, except undergo what the black men do who have locked him into the bathroom (such as surrender his car keys and witness through the bars of the window how they kill Lucy's dogs after they have finished their business with her). Lurie appears completely undone by the event—catastrophe: an overturning, ruin, conclusion; from *katastrephein*: to ruin, undo (*American Heritage Dictionary*). And he tries to make up for his powerlessness during the event by displaying a near-frenzied level of activity in its wake. That activity is organized around the question of responsibility: first and foremost, the black men's guilt. The text vividly represents the devastation that the rapists wreak on Lucy, and on her father. There can be no question that narration and focalization (through an indignant David Lurie) make the reader feel moral outrage at the violence of their acts, at their choice of victim, and at Petrus's (passive) role in their getting away with it all (it is soon suspected that he knows the rapists, though it takes a while before it is clear he is distantly related to Pollux, the adolescent). Throughout the scenes that follow Lucy's rape, the debate between father and daughter centers on the issue of who is responsible (is David, too, for failing to protect Lucy, for instance? is Petrus, by being suspiciously absent on the day? is Lucy, for living out there in this way?). That is to say: this is the debate that David Lurie keeps going. Lucy tries to avoid having this type of discussion altogether. Through Lurie's eyes, we see Lucy's insistence that nobody be told as either a form of withdrawal into the private self (her failure to manage her farming business as she had done before is an instance of this withdrawal) or a form of undergoing as a private person what is really a public settling of historic scores (Lurie voices this idea and tries to persuade Lucy that this is not the way forward). We are not made privy to the full depth of Lucy's reaction, which is rarely expressed in explicit words, and even those only uttered in response to David's challenges. Spivak has cogently pointed out how our inability to get real access to Lucy's thoughts frustrates us to the point of participating much more actively in the text than we otherwise might. "When Lucy is resolutely denied focalization, the reader is provoked, for he or she does not want to share in Lurie-the-chief-focalizer's inability to 'read' Lucy as patient and agent. No reader is content with acting out the failure of reading. This is the rhetorical signal to the active reader, to counterfocalize" (Spivak, p. 22).

When Lucy does speak, it is to resist Lurie's pressure (my unconscious choice of words here makes me better aware of how his psychological effect on her is indeed akin to that of the actual rape) that she make some form of public statement: bringing charges with the police, exposing Pollux in the community. "You wish to humble yourself before history," David writes in a note to Lucy (p. 160). You are "meekly accepting what happened to you," he tells her earlier, asking: "Is it some form of private salvation you are trying to work out? Do you hope you can expiate the crimes of the past by suffering in the present?" (p. 112). "No, you keep misreading me," she replies. "Guilt and salvation are abstractions. I don't act in terms of abstractions. Until you make an effort to see that, I can't help you"; "what happened to me is a purely private matter. In another time, in another place it might be held to be a public matter. But in this place, at this time, it is not. It is my business, mine alone" (p. 112). And later: "What if [...] what if *that* is the price one has to pay for staying on? [...] Why should I be allowed to live here without paying?" (p. 158). From Lucy's response, insofar as we are provoked into reading her, we can derive an interpretation of the black men's responsibility as limited by space and time. In post-Apartheid South Africa, the rights and wrongs of acts cannot be divorced from racial relations, which makes it particularly significant that we are not given a clear picture of Melanie's racial status: David Lurie, the story's focalizer, is blind to this dimension, which, in another place and time would endear him to us: he "just" loves "pretty girls" (p. 218), no matter what race they are, but which, in his South Africa, can only count as irresponsibility. They cannot be divorced from the historical catastrophes whose authors have been the white dominant class; whose subjects have been the black and colored population.

To thus qualify the rapists' responsibility as limited is not to do the same as Lurie in his abstracting summary of Lucy's response, whereby she allegedly undergoes "history speaking through" these black men's deeds (p. 156). To accept such a summary would amount to a dismissal of any responsibility on the part of the individuals, which is neither suggested by Coetzee's novel, nor by the theoretical perspective of Butler's on which I base my reading of Lucy's stance. Rather, Butler identifies a specific responsibility that is citational in character. I am working here mainly with *Excitable Speech: Towards a Politics of the Performative*, which is the most relevant text of Butler's, in that it focuses on rhetoric and the question of responsibility in legal contexts, just as this novel, not only in the debate between David and Lucy about publicly testifying to the rape but also in how it portrays David Lurie's unwillingness to speak the right phrases as stipulated by the university committee.[4] The expression "excitable speech" refers to "utterances [...] made under duress, usually confessions that cannot be used in court because they do not reflect the balanced mental state of the utterer" (p. 15). Butler's argument is that all speech "is always in some ways out of our control" (p. 15), because our utterances are provoked by a language that transcends us and that was already there before we were. The human subject is not a "sovereign subject" (p. 16) that can calmly send forth its dictates into the world, in full mastery and confident autonomy. Yet, the human subject is nonetheless an acting subject that performs deeds in the world for which it is responsible. The force with which it acts and the responsibility it carries for this acting are limited, however, by the fact that they are provoked by the givens of a language that has been passed down to us:

> [T]he subject is constituted in language, [...] what it creates is also what it derives from elsewhere. [...]. The one who acts (who is not the same as the sovereign subject) acts precisely to the extent that he or she is constituted as an actor and, hence, operating within a linguistic field of enabling constraints from the outset.

(p. 16)

Butler's key point is that we are always constrained by something that lies outside our control but that this something is also the motor of our ability to act. With regard to the system of gender norms, she had shown in earlier works, such as *Gender Trouble* and *Bodies That Matter*, that we are bound to cite the terms of a heterosexual matrix, which treats as abject all the bodies that fail to conform.[5] Yet, all of us are compelled to engage in such citation, a finding which shows up the lack of inborn naturalness of all gender or sexual classification. And since it is very hard to cite word perfectly, miscitations inevitably occur, most of which get to be promptly corrected by the coercive character of heteronormativity; some of which escape such punitive intervention, hence becoming available for subsequent citation, and thus, perhaps, contributing to social change—to the institution of modified norms.

Against this theoretical background, what the rapists are doing can be understood as a citing both of the norms of a heterosexual matrix that subjugates women (and of which the opening scenes show Lurie himself to be a particularly pernicious exemplar, it could be argued) and, inversely, of the norms of a racially stratified society in which one race subjects another (or even others) through violent events that bring catastrophe into the lives of their victims. That such citational processes are at stake is strikingly illustrated in the novel when the men use the gun that Lucy was keeping in the house (as a half-hearted gesture of self-defence) to shoot the dogs she was caring for—"[w]atchdogs, all of them" (p. 61), watchdogs, that is, "in a country where dogs are bred to snarl at the mere smell of a black man" (p. 110). The citationality is curiously doubled here in that Lucy's own decision to have a gun in the house (she bought it from a neighbor) also cites one of the practices that have enabled a white dominant class to keep a black majority in check. So too does her main chosen occupation (looking after watchdogs) constitute a citational act with regard to the power matrix that has organized this particular society (symbolized in her neighbor Ettinger, whose farm is a fortress), however gentle and unassuming her presence in this world is; however respectful her attitude to the black people she shares a community with. In showing how the black men take command of the gun and dispose of the dogs, the text may be said to demonstrate one of the key points of the theory of citationality: the norms that we are forced to cite in order to become subjects of a social system will occasionally become miscited or hypercited. Such miscitation can happen accidentally or (less easily, given the strength of social constraints) on purpose, as when the black men turn the white person's gun against that person. In both accidental and deliberate cases, room is created for the subversion of norms. Through such subversion, social change can and does occur: black South Africans take control over the land from which they had been dispossessed. The chiastic link between Lurie's abusive relation to (non-white) women and the rapists' to his (white) daughter is similarly available for interpretation as "mis"citation of the norms of the long-time dominant class in South African society (even if, under Apartheid policy, it would have been illegal for white men to have sexual intercourse with non-white women).

Why does Lucy insist on the "purely private" nature of what she was submitted to? How can we account for her resistance to Lurie's attempts to tie up her experience with the public realm if such a Butlerian social reading is to make any sense? Returning to *Excitable Speech*, we must note that Butler takes issue with those on the American left who believe in pursuing certain minority rights in court. Not only does the record, in Butler's eyes, prove them misguided in their faith in the legal system, she is also sure that the very attempt to prosecute, say, perpetrators of hate speech (those heaping abuse on lesbians, for instance) on the grounds that it "produces a 'victim class'" performs the victimization that it seeks to counteract (Butler, p. 41). Such attempts, Butler argues, "deny critical agency and tend to support an intervention in which agency is fully assumed by the state," an assumption of power that she is deeply suspicious of (p. 41). What she proposes instead of such "state-sponsored censorship" is "a social and cultural struggle of language [...] in which agency is derived from injury, and injury countered through that very derivation" (p. 41). "The political possibility of reworking the force of the speech act against the force of injury consists in misappropriating the force of speech from those prior contexts. The language that counters the injuries of speech [...] must repeat those injuries without precisely reenacting them" (pp. 40–1).

While Butler addresses possible rhetorical responses to hate speech, her theory takes as its point of departure the dual idea that all speech constitutes an act and that all agency is ultimately rhetorical. It therefore causes no surprise that her take on hate speech resonates meaningfully for Lucy's response to physical injury in *Disgrace*. Here, too, "hate" is a crucial aspect of the injury she suffers: "It was done with such personal hatred. [...] The rest was [...] expected. But why did they hate me so?" (Coetzee, p. 156). The suggestion is that when hatred is so personal, the way to deal with it must be personal too; when the injury is so personal, the agency that can counter it must inevitably be personal. To turn to the police, to a "state-sponsored censorship" of acts of hatred, would be to surrender the personal to the public in a defeatist move that is of a piece with the other honorable course of action David Lurie proposes: packing up and moving back to the city, or even all the way to Holland, where Lucy's mother lives. To pursue either of these avenues would be to resign oneself to victimhood. It would also be tantamount to running away from the limited responsibility that we carry in whichever sociohistorical context each of us functions in. Such an act of escape could only take the subject into a realm of abstract morality, where, rather than being limited, all responsibility becomes paralyzingly absolute in that it can only be referred to a transcendent authority capable of deciding rights and wrongs. Lucy's response to her humiliation, "[s]ubjection," "[s]ubjugation" by the black rapists refuses to appeal to such an authority (p. 159), on hand in the novel in the form of her father (ever ready to avenge her) and the police. An appeal to authority of this type would take away from her the need and the ability to act, assigning her instead to a passive, victimized role. Lucy's rejection of moral absolutes can hardly be dismissed as a moral relativism that would somehow equal a failure to assume responsibility. Rather, Lucy insists as strongly as one can imagine on her own accountability: "In another time, in another place it might be held to be a public matter. But in this place, at this time, it is not. It is my business, mine alone" (p. 112).

Lucy's response to being raped must also be read more specifically as an act of political performativity that relies on citationality so as to turn the aggressor's force in a different direction from the intended one. This reading is facilitated by Spivak's fascinating analysis of how the word "nothing" precisely operates in the conversations between Lurie and Lucy, and how there is a manifest intertextual link to (or, in Butler's terms, citation of) the dialog between Lear and Cordelia in the opening act of Shakespeare's play (Spivak, p. 20).[6] Lucy is very clear about the fact that she was "nothing" to the rapists (Coetzee, p. 158). This, she cannot change: raped she was—reduced to nothing. What she can attempt to do, though, is resignify the meaning of nothing, by quoting it in another context, "misappropriating" the negating force of the rape from how it was used in its original context (Butler, p. 40). Lucy first of all decides to keep the child that is growing inside her as a result of the rape. And she insists on staying put. But since she is convinced the men have marked her as theirs and will return, she needs a strategy. She goes on to accept the self-serving offer Petrus makes that she "marry" him—even though he is already committed to two separate households (Coetzee, p. 202). "Then it is over all this badness," Petrus tells Lurie in making the offer, since Lucy would henceforth be under his protective wing (p. 202). And of course he would become the outright owner of all of Lucy's coveted land. "Say I accept his protection," Lucy instructs her father. "Say he can put out whatever story he likes about our relationship and I won't contradict him. [...] But then the child becomes his too. The child becomes part of his family. As for the land, say I will sign the land over to him as long as the house remains mine. I will become a tenant on his land" (p. 204). Lurie objects that this is "humiliating," which his daughter admits, but in terms that Spivak interestingly picks up on. Here is what Lucy says: "Yes, I agree, it is humiliating. But perhaps that is a good point to start from again. Perhaps that is what I must learn to accept. To start at ground level. With nothing. Not with nothing but. With nothing. No cards, no weapons, no property, no rights, no dignity" (p. 205). Spivak comments: "I do not think this is an acceptance of rape, but a refusal to be raped, by instrumentalizing reproduction. [...]. It is not 'nothing but,' Lucy insists. It is an originary 'nothing,' a scary beginning" (Spivak, p. 21). This, I would say, is a refiguring of the meaning of nothing that wrests the sense of that concept away from the rapists' way of treating Lucy. It is, in light of Butler's performative framework, a way of proceeding "in which agency is derived from injury, and injury countered through that very derivation" (Butler, p. 41). It is not, as Attridge claims in what strikes me as an echo of Lurie's misreading of Lucy, a "survival strategy of pragmatic accommodation at any price" (p. 182). This is to reduce the near-impenetrable otherness of Lucy's response to a version "of what we already know" (Attridge, p. 43).

> Of Petrus there is no sign, nor of his wife or the jackal boy who runs with them. But Lucy is at work among the flowers. [...] Field-labour; peasant tasks, immemorial. His daughter is becoming a peasant. [...] There is a moment of utter stillness which he would wish prolonged for ever: the gentle sun, the stillness of mid-afternoon, bees busy in a field of flowers; and at the centre of the picture a young woman, *das ewig Weibliche*, lightly pregnant, in a straw sunhat. [...] She is flushed from her labours and perhaps a little sunburnt. She looks, suddenly, the picture of health
>
> (pp. 217–18).

Though the idyllic quality of the scene is implicitly qualified as the product of Lurie's aestheticizing impulse ("A scene ready-made for a Sargent or a Bonnard," p. 218), it is still the final image of Lucy that the text presents us with, and nothing in the context denies the strength of the constructive force that Lucy is able to muster at this point of relative narrative closure. Rather than dwelling on those who carry personal responsibility for the hurt Lucy suffered, the description focuses instead on how she is taking control of her existence. And there is no break, but a clear continuity between the injury and the agency. The reference to Petrus, Petrus's wife, and Pollux reminds us, as does the pregnancy, that Lucy will only be able to take up a fulfiling peasant's life by the grace of the protection that belonging to Petrus's extended family might bring her. In the midst of the idyllic, the counterfocalizing reader will never forget that "Lucy is a figure that makes visible the rational kernel of the institution of marriage—rape, social security, property, human continuity" (Spivak, p. 23).

Crucially, she *chooses* this dependent way of life. There were alternatives available to her: turning to a prosecuting authority (the Law, her father), having an abortion, and moving away. Lucy, though, opts for a form of moving on with her life that accepts the limited responsibility each of the actors carries in the drama that has occurred: the rapists' responsibility is real (they and no one else committed the rape), and it is limited by the citational character their act possesses vis-à-vis the matrices of heterosexual and racial abuse that dominate the world the novel evokes; Petrus's responsibility is real (he could have stopped the rape from happening), and it is limited by his understanding of a man's prime duty to be loyal to the members of his family, a category to which, in a further move, he is able and willing to admit Lucy in an act of assumption of responsibility that is available to him; Lucy's responsibility is real (she was owning black land, looking after watchdogs and keeping a gun), and it is limited by the citational character that links her acts to the white tradition represented more starkly by her neighbor Ettinger and by her father's response to the rape. The course of action she ultimately adopts is in line with this dual insistence on the limited nature of our responsibility and on the need nonetheless to assume this responsibility. We could reformulate her decision as a choice—and a much more conscious one this time—for a different limitation on her responsibility; or to put it slightly differently: for a different circumscription of the realm within which her personal responsibility can be held to account. Rather than living as a white owner of what contemporary history morally regards as black turf, while citing all the time the behavioral norms of her group in a manner of which she is largely unaware but that is brought home to her in the detail of how the rape takes place, she will henceforth live as a tenant-farmer on land she no longer owns, and will be fully dependent on the protection offered by her black landlord. Her responsibility will thus be limited by a wholly new set of norms that she will have to learn to cite correctly. Some miscitation will inevitably occur, which may or may not be punished. Within this matrix, she will hold herself personally accountable for the success of her life—for the fruits of her labors, for the health of her child, for the happiness she does or does not enjoy. She will not hold herself responsible, least of all in an abstract sense, for the fate of black people at this juncture in history, as her father has mistakenly charged her with doing.

How does this take on responsibility in terms of the citationality of speech acts help us make sense of the main protagonist's actions and development? My argument here is that *Disgrace* shows how Lurie's initial brand of Romanticism makes him blind to the limited but real nature of accountability. By the end of the novel, though, he has attained an understanding that is much more similar to that of his daughter, and that lifts his morality to a higher plane altogether.

Let us first consider Lurie's desire for Soraya. We could say that, as long as Lurie observes the rules that govern a sexual relationship of the type he enjoys with her, there is a contractual correctness about his actions, assuming that prostitution is accepted as a fact of social life, which is what Soraya herself is presented as doing, strictly keeping apart her professional life as a hostess from her private life as a wife and mother. His responsibility is to that extent in effect limited by the whole system and history of prostitution. This is not something that Lurie himself is able to see, as becomes evident from his response to finding out more about Soraya's life beyond their commercial relationship. As soon as their meetings take place, at first accidentally, then through Lurie's design, outside the bounds of the space contractually allocated to them, Lurie could be said to be misciting the rules of commercial sex, imagining himself, for instance, in a parental relationship to Soraya's sons (p. 6). His miscitation—his attempt to assign a personal romantic meaning where the system allows only for the offering of sex and possibly tenderness in return for money—is experienced by the woman as abusive, and his phoning her at home on a number secured by a private detective is decisively resisted as an act of "harassing" (p. 10). One way of formulating Lurie's miscitation is to say that he turns a public relation—that is, one governed by marketplace economics—into a private one—that is, governed by the rhetoric of romantic love.

With Melanie, the miscitation is built into the very relationship. The norms that govern relations between teachers and students do not allow for sexual contact between members of the two groups. Lurie knows "he ought to let her go" (p. 18), and there is only a weak suggestion that he actively enjoys transgressing such rules, let alone that this would be the main attraction Melanie holds for him. Rather, "he is in the grip of something. Beauty's rose: the poem drives straight as an arrow. She does not own herself; perhaps he does not own himself either" (p. 18). At the university hearing, this idea is reiterated, Lurie insisting that he "became a servant of Eros" the moment he met Melanie Isaacs outside of the classroom context—a modification that again reminds us that he has no fundamental quarrel with the rules of propriety that are observed in teacher-student interaction (p. 52). What he does, rather, is to assert the absolute value of romantic love, and to claim for it a power that ought not to be resisted ("I have denied similar impulses many times in the past, I am ashamed to say," p. 52), whatever the context, whatever the consequences. He thus conceives of his responsibility in terms that are absolute and, as Lucy would put it, merely abstract. Any challenge to his actions is essentially dismissed as incommensurate with the call of the transcendent authority, Eros, that he has been obeying. While Lurie's refusal to accept any of the compromises proposed by the members of the hearing at first comes across as little short of heroic—the narrative (thanks to the consistent focalization through Lurie) carefully casting subtle ridicule on those suggesting ways out of the problematical situation—the fundamental continuity between Lurie's principled stand here and his wholly unhelpful advice to Lucy after the rape, as well as his fraught visit to the Isaacs home, ultimately make us reconsider his earlier unwillingness to negotiate.

What we see then is that Lurie is in thrall to a Romantic belief in the impregnability of his private persona and in the sanctity of what motivates him as a thinking-feeling human being, even where these emotions lead him into conflict with the rules and regulations that organize society and its morality. A clear illustration is presented by the inability of Lurie and Melanie's father to achieve any real communication, Lurie attempting to explain the transcendence of his desire, Mr Isaacs urging the stronger claims of his God. Lurie's absolute understanding of morality—shame attaching to a denial of the law of desire; honor to the steadfastness with which one undergoes the punishment (the disgrace) society imposes on those who are true to their own deep self—is a geographical and chronological miscitation of the ideology of Romanticism, which does not differ all that much in its essential outlines from that of the deeply religious Mr Isaacs. It makes the protagonist unable to understand, let alone accept, that his guilt vis-à-vis Melanie, her parents, and society is real, but also limited. It is limited, because Lurie's act does not exist in isolation, but forms part of a social history that his critics here cast as that of the powerful abusing the powerless, men abusing women, and whites abusing non-whites. As this part of the novel compellingly demonstrates, however, to point out that Lurie's responsibility is *limited* is not to say that it is therefore *diminished*. Rather, his amorous affair with Melanie derives its full meaning from public forces that exceed whatever private intentions or even feelings the individual agent(s) may assign to the act. The limitation on individual responsibility may thus in fact *augment* the weight an act carries. But the social production of an act's moral significance does make it an artificial business to assign sole accountability for an act to one agent only, just as it is artificial to believe that one can safeguard one's private actions from public censure, as Lurie avers, rejecting all calls for him to make a public apology. Significantly, only the equally unconditional Mr Isaacs is able finally to shame Lurie into apologizing, a moment that hardly comes across as cathartic for the protagonist, proving only that one moral absolutism can easily lord it over another.

In the course of the latter part of the novel, Lurie is exposed to a number of forces that gradually change his understanding of the nature of subjectivity and responsibility. While the scene with the Isaacs parents occurs late in the plot, it does not yet show a Lurie who has fully taken to heart the lessons that are taught first and foremost by women: his daughter Lucy, as we have already seen, her friend Bev Shaw, and Teresa, Byron's mistress, and their daughter Allegra, the latter two women whose suffering Lurie imagines in the act of attempting to compose an opera, *Byron in Italy*. Work on this opera enables Lurie to open up to the feelings of others, which is something that, for all his Romanticism, he had been incapable of doing. Whereas his earlier Romanticism seemed to admit only of his own relation to love and desire, the music that is now taking shape inside of him possesses a polyphonic quality through which the emotional life of others makes itself felt, in particular that of women, who swiftly displace the Byron planned as the opera's protagonist. Yet, by novel's end, Lurie must admit to himself that "the truth is that *Byron in Italy* is going nowhere. There is no action, no development, just a long, halting cantilena hurled by Teresa into the empty air, punctuated now and then with groans and sighs from Byron offstage" (p. 214). What the opera teaches Lurie is to become more attentive to those that history, including the romantic history of Byron and of himself, has abused. What it cannot do is offer the basis for an alternative existence. Indeed, to believe that it somehow could, would be to remain stuck in exactly that Romantic conception of Art in which the latter becomes a substitute God—the locus of transcendence, the absolute basis for morality. Regarded from such a perspective, an individual's responsibility is limitless, and once a sense of guilt sinks in—as it does with Lurie—there is no way of dealing with it: the voice of one's personal conscience, too, becomes "just a long, halting cantilena" to which the only response can be one's own "groans and sighs" (p. 214).[7]

The novel does not end on this unproductive note, though. Lurie's work at the animal welfare clinic is allowed to occupy the position of closure—however relative that closure may prove to be. Lurie had initially been smugly dismissive of his daughter's appreciation for her friend Bev Shaw's efforts to help as best she can the animals brought to or abandoned at the clinic. "As for animals," he preaches to Lucy, "by all means let us be kind to them. But let us not lose perspective. We are of a different order of creation from the animals. Not higher, necessarily, just different. So if we are going to be kind, let it be out of simple generosity, not because we feel guilty or fear retribution" (p. 74). That we might be kind to animals out of a sense of responsibility, love or care, rather than guilt, fear or generosity, is not a possibility that he is able to entertain at this early point of the plot. Yet by the close of the narrative Lurie has come to respect both Bev Shaw as a person and the animals that she treats with loving care. He takes it upon himself to help her when she puts down those unwanted animals the shelter cannot accommodate either. "He has learned by now, from her, to concentrate all his attention on the animal they are killing, giving it what he no longer has difficulty in calling by its proper name: love" (p. 219). And he ensures that the corpses are disposed of respectfully at the local incinerator. What Lurie displays here is an acceptance of the limited nature of the responsibility we carry. He is willing now to engage in what we may call, not quite adequately, compromise, in an effort to bring out the contrast to his moral response to the earlier events. He knows it is impossible, for lack of resources, to look after the two dozen-odd newly abandoned animals the clinic receives each week. The ideal of offering each animal the care that would sustain its life cannot be reached. All that Shaw and Lurie can do is to acknowledge this limitation on their power to act, yet at the same time refrain from using this constriction as an excuse not to act at all.

Lurie has moved beyond such evasions of responsibility, a fact that is demonstrated strikingly by his willingness to part with one dog he had grown particularly fond of. Giving up the invalid dog with an ear for music, Lurie reveals a new grasp of how he is accountable to others.

He could have chosen to adopt this one dog, placing himself as a screen between it and the harshness of the world in a move similar to how he urged himself upon Lucy, intervening in her relation to the world by punishing Pollux, say. To do so would be to select one particular corner of the universe and then assume full responsibility for it in a Romantic-heroic vein. What he has developed toward is a very different moral stance, in which the limited character of all proper responsibility is recognized. Bringing love to these abandoned animals by ensuring that their final moments are spent in tender care is to take up a real responsibility that is not restricted to just a happy few selected for adoption, yet is at once to concede that one's power to act is not limitless.

Returning to the novel's title, we can now assess how far the state of disgrace still pertains that David Lurie had experienced even more in the wake of the catastrophe that struck—and disgraced—his daughter than in that of the public exposure of his abusive relationship with Melanie. As we saw, the final image of Lucy is an emphatically positive one. Indeed, as she bends over, even "the milky, blue-veined skin and broad, vulnerable tendons of the backs of her knees" become charged with significance: "the least beautiful part of a woman's body, the least expressive, and therefore perhaps the most endearing" (p. 217). Lurie is allowing himself to be stirred by that which is "vulnerable"—stirred not in a sexual sense (as was perhaps the case with Melanie), but in a caring one, warming to what is "endearing" in this particular woman of his. He goes on to reflect on the new life that Lucy is carrying—Lucy, who, not that long ago, was "only a little tadpole in her mother's body": her child, his grandchild, too will hopefully prosper and bear fruit, and so on, and each time "his share, his gift, will grow inexorably less and less, till it may as well be forgotten" (p. 217). He has come to realize that he can only submit himself to this process that is larger than himself, that exceeds him. He is nothing, ultimately, yet he has been all—or at least all of his necessary half of a process of conception.

What is more, if he has given life, and knows that the most caring thing he can do is to let this life go, to relinquish control over Lucy, he now also gives death, in the same knowledge that doing so lovingly is the most caring thing he can do for the animals at the clinic, even to the extent of "giving up" Driepoot, the limping dog that had so attached itself to him. Having listed the things he will do for the dog (for instance, "caress him and brush back the fur so that the needle can find the vein"), he concludes: "He will do all that for him when his time comes. It will be little enough, less than little: nothing" (p. 220). We find here the same tension between everything and nothing that Spivak outlined for Lucy and that I indicated with regard to Lurie's limited role in the life-giving process that has produced Lucy and, now, her off-spring. If both life and death are presented with a measure of starkness that is quite arresting, what we retain above all from these moments is the newly won emphasis on the protagonist's real yet limited ability to assume agency and responsibility in each process. David "will do all that" for the dog—agency, to be sure; yet, it will be "nothing": what has he truly been able to do, except for allowing the operating room to act as the "hole where one leaks out of existence" (p. 219)? *Pace* Attridge, it seems to me that Coetzee, ultimately, is too politically committed a writer to want to leave us with an upbeat picture of a man's discovery of the true path to grace in the midst of disgrace. The terrible constrictions under which we must labor, the catastrophes that strike day in, day out, whether they form the legacy of well-recognized repressive political systems like Apartheid, or comprise the largely unacknowledged fate of animals under a human-centerd regime, make it impossible to achieve more than a very limited ability to act for change.

Notes

1. J. M. Coetzee, *Disgrace* (1999; London: Vintage, 2000).
2. Derek Attridge, *J. M. Coetzee & the Ethics of Reading* (Chicago and London, University of Chicago Press, 2004), p. 164.
3. Gayatri Chakravorty Spivak, "Ethics and Politics in Tagore, Coetzee, and Certain Scenes of Teaching," *Diacritics*, 32.3–4 (2002) 17–31.
4. Judith Butler, *Excitable Speech: Towards a Politics of the Performative* (NY: Routledge, 1997).
5. Judith Butler, *Gender Trouble: Feminism and the Subversion of Identity*, (NY: Routledge, 1990); *Bodies That Matter: On the Discursive Limits of "Sex"* (NY: Routledge, 1993).
6. In *King Lear*, Cordelia's use of the word "signifies the withholding of speech as an instrument for indicating socially inappropriate affective value. In Cordelia's understanding, to put love in the value-form—let me measure how much—is itself absurd" (Spivak, p. 20). "Lucy's 'nothing' is the same word but carries a different meaning from Cordelia's. It is not the withholding of speech protesting the casting of love in the value-form *and* giving it the wrong value. It is rather the casting aside of the affective value-system attached to reproductive heteronormativity as it is accepted as the currency to measure human dignity" (Spivak, p. 21). Spivak's article goes on to argue, quite suggestively, that *Disgrace* faces up to the true difficulty of the postcolonial situation in a country like South Africa. Reformulating lines from *Lear* and applying them to Lucy and her negotiation with Petrus, Spivak rhetorically wonders "What does it mean, in the detritus of colonialism, for one from the ruling race to call for interpellation as 'unaccommodated woman, a poor, bare,

forked animal,' and hold negotiating power without sentimentality in that very forkèdness? [...]. Is it a gendered special case, or can it claim generality, as making visible the difficulty of the postcolonial formula: a new nation?" (Spivak, p. 21). Can the new nation be born any other way than as the result of a rape?

7. Attridge risks reproducing Lurie's absolutist stance, emphasizing as he does the absolute value of "an excess, an overflow, an alterity that no calculation can contain, no rule account for" (p. 182).

9
Unpredictable Inevitability and the Boundaries of Psychic Life

Dany Nobus

The face of our era

"It has been a rollercoaster. I don't remember hearing any noise or blast. But I could see a strange nasty yellow light and then it all went black. I was on the floor and I felt my face was wet with blood. I did not know what had happened and I thought it was just me. I couldn't see very well without my glasses—they had been blown off—and I rolled over to ask someone to help me. Then I saw people lying covered in blood and I knew it was a major event that had affected the whole train." These are the words of Professor John Tulloch, my colleague in the School of Social Sciences at Brunel University, spoken from his hospital bed shortly after he was lifted from the wreckage of an underground train at Edgware Road station in London on July 7, 2005, as reported by the *The Mail on Sunday* in an article entitled "A Survivor's Story: 'So Good to be Alive'."[1] Unlucky to be traveling in the doomed carriage of a hell-bound train on that fateful Thursday morning, yet lucky to escape relatively unscathed from the massive impact of the terrorist bomb, Professor Tulloch tried to reconstruct the circumstances and the immediate after-math of the blast which had left so many people dead, providing a level of detail that leaves nobody indifferent. And if one knows that here we have a man who has spent prolonged periods of time as a researcher working under the most insecure conditions and in the most dangerous situations, the event of him being at the center of a suicide-bombing while traveling home from London to Cardiff one summer morning becomes all the more tragic, unbearable, unthinkable.

The young history of the twenty-first century has already taught us that violence, death and destruction can appear at any given moment, in any given place—an office tower-block, an underground train, a holiday resort, a university campus—the likelihood of its occurrence no longer being a matter of "if" but quite simply a question of "when." Indeed, however much the "short" twentieth century may have been an "age of extremes," as Eric Hobsbawm put it, the "extremes" have always been somehow "explicable" as culminations, artifacts or fallouts of specific socio-political configurations.[2] If the twentieth century will forever be associated with the horrors of the Holocaust, the latter has nonetheless been "explained" and "situated" with reference to historical developments, whether the technocratic rationalism of high-capitalist production processes (Horkheimer and Adorno) or the submissive nature of the German soul (Goldhagen). By contrast, our new age promises to be radically different, if only because it seems to be turning, quite paradoxically, unpredictability into a central organizing principle of the human condition and inevitability into a new law of social awareness. Politicians, government officials, intelligence and security agencies, law enforcers and public opinion makers are constantly telling people to prepare themselves for the occurrence of catastrophe—an event which no one is able to prevent, and no one is able to predict—without therefore changing our daily business and altering our course of life.

As a survivor of a terrorist attack, Professor Tulloch is the face of our new era, a face he not only shares with people in the Middle East, but also with people in South-East Asia, Western Europe and North America. His experiences, his story and his attempts at reconstructing the events are recognizable for health care practitioners in every part of the globe, and it is to be expected that his will become an ever more iconic condition and an increasingly paradigmatic case as time goes on and the "unpredictable inevitability" of our catastrophic world takes its toll on an increasingly larger scale. In this essay, I propose to explicate, in the etymological senses of "unfolding" and "unraveling," the relationship between the "unpredictable inevitability" of catastrophe that is endemic to our current living conditions, and the status of the protective boundaries that characterize the development and maintenance of psychic life. In this way, I will attempt to show that the only way to think catastrophe is by allowing catastrophe itself to enter the realm of thought, not in order to control it, even less in order to abdicate rational power in the face of its "irrational" emergence, but with a view to locating it as an energy-laden event endowed with the potential of creative reorganization.

Trauma and its consequences

There is no doubt in my mind that my colleague has suffered from trauma, both in terms of the etymological meaning of the word as "wound" and "rupture of a protective boundary," and in terms of the DSM-IV's definition of it as an "actual or threatened death or serious injury, or a threat to the physical integrity of self and others" which produces "intense fear, helplessness, or horror."[3] It is not at all certain, however, that the physical trauma which he has sustained will also lead to the emergence of uncontrollable psychological symptoms such as recurrent nightmares, intermittent flashbacks, blunted emotion and attention and memory disturbances—in short, to the kinds of symptoms the compilers of the DSM have grouped under the heading of "Post-traumatic Stress Disorder" (PTSD). For if one thing can be concluded from the massive body of psychological literature on trauma and its consequences, it is that there is no direct, one-to-one relationship between a traumatic event, regardless of its seriousness, and psychological symptoms of post-traumatic stress.

As Nice et al. reported in an influential paper from the mid-1990s, only a minority of US soldiers who had been subjected to torture as POWs in Vietnam subsequently experienced symptoms of post-traumatic stress disorder.[4] Puzzled by their findings, and seeking to offer an explanation for what they regarded as a clinical conundrum, the researchers postulated that the POW's psychological integrity had remained more or less intact, owing to their age, education and extensive military training, which would have mentally prepared and therefore hardened them against the traumatic effects of capture and torture. To make matters more complicated, and definitely more interesting, it has also been reported that some patients show clear symptoms of PTSD without recalling any traumatic event whatsoever, and that objectively innocuous events such as giving birth to a child or accidentally running over some frogs while mowing the lawn can also trigger PTSD.[5] As could be expected, this observed discordance between "objective event" and "subjective reaction" has given rise to a vast amount of research into so-called "risk factors," ranging from low IQ and neurological defects to a dysfunctional social environment, which are believed to increase the likelihood of someone developing PTSD following a relatively harmless, ostensibly trivial occurrence, or even *sui generis*, subsequent to a non-event.

Mental "buffering" is considered to be the key, here, for our understanding of clinical symptoms of traumatization. The person who develops PTSD after accidentally mauling a frog with the lawnmower may just not be as psychologically robust as the POW who is subjected for days on end to the most horrific forms of torture, and who has been carefully prepared for the circumstances of his arrest. Of course, the problem is that one can never be fully prepared for everything that will come to pass, precisely because it is impossible to know what will happen and at what time, under any given circumstance. Military instructors no doubt have a good degree of knowledge of what will happen when a soldier is captured by enemy forces, yet in preparing their trainees for this event, they are building a mental buffer against a known eventuality, which can be relatively well located in space and time and is therefore more or less predictable. However, there is no evidence that these fortifications will hold against all "other" events, that is, those that were not predicted because they were unknown.

Understanding the relationship between an event and its (traumatic) consequences is not only important theoretically, as a reflection upon the epistemological status of "objective causes" and the psychological nature of "subjective effects," but also clinically, since it is likely to contribute to the development of more effective strategies for preventing the occurrence of trauma-related symptoms, and more adequate models of intervention for treating those who are already showing the symptoms. In addition, in light of the "unpredictable inevitability" that characterizes our age and the exponential increase in risk situations that it brings about, "trauma studies" are also destined to become a salient feature of the political agenda, which is currently already reflected in the deployment of more rigorous health and safety policies, the creation of specialized ethical committees to protect the public against potentially abusive practices, and the formulation of more stringent codes of conduct for professionals working with human subjects. As such, the Western world has also witnessed a progressive externalization and visualization of the protective boundaries of psychic life, in many cases with a view to abdicating liability and preventing litigation, yet sometimes also to protect individuals against the "unpredictable inevitability" of themselves. Funny as it may be to observe that bottle-caps now come with a "guideline" saying "only open with your hand," and that the operating instructions for a steam-iron regularly state "do not use when wearing your clothes," and regardless of the potential legal consequences of self-inflicted trauma, these identified non-risks have come to obfuscate the non-identifiable real risks. And the more we observe that manufacturers and policy-makers feel the need to warn us, also and perhaps primarily against ourselves, the more vulnerable and the less prepared we appear to be, leaving us seemingly all the more at risk of becoming wounded, victimized and traumatized by our own fragile state of mind when the non-identifiable real risk becomes a material reality.

Tickle your trauma!

In what follows, I shall address some of the issues with which contemporary trauma-researchers are confronted from a distinctly unusual and rather controversial perspective, notably that of Lacanian psychoanalysis. The perspective is unusual, because much like any psychoanalytic outlook it is rarely employed these days by researchers and health professionals in the field of trauma-studies, who generally prefer the evidence-based practices of cognitive neuroscience and cognitive-behavioral therapy to the "strictly speculative," "seriously outdated" and "demonstrably false" assumptions of psychoanalysis. This is not to say that psychoanalysts themselves have steered away from contributing to current discussions of trauma. The fact that the International Psychoanalytic Association's 44th Congress, held from 28 to 31 July, 2005, in Rio de Janeiro, was organized around the topic of "Trauma: New Developments in Psychoanalysis" may even serve as an example of how psychoanalysts (at least those belonging to the mainstream) are extremely keen to investigate and debate the new theoretical and clinical challenges that are posed by our current age of trauma. However, for reasons I shall detail further on, psychoanalysis is rarely taken seriously within the field of trauma-research itself, which is mainly populated by cognitive psychologists, hypno-therapists, child psychologists, research psychiatrists, clinical psychologists and neuroscientists. However, when the name of the psychoanalyst is Lacan, skepticism often turns into outrage—and this is true outside as well as within the realm of psychoanalysis—because Lacan is still widely regarded as a theoretical nonsense-monger and a clinical charlatan, whose work should be relegated to the dustbin of history, or simply remembered as a historical instance of pseudo-science, much like astrology, alchemy and the theory of phlogiston. Opening a Lacanian perspective on trauma thus poses a dual challenge, because this type of approach not only needs to address the criticisms on psychoanalysis formulated by the anti- or non-psychoanalytic research community, but also be aware of the anti- or non-Lacanian factions within the psychoanalytic community itself.

As a matter of fact, the challenge is even a triple one, because it is not at all easy to extract an original theory of trauma from Lacan's writings and seminars. Not until 1964, when Lacan conducted his famous Seminar on *The Four Fundamental Concepts of Psychoanalysis*, did the first signs of an innovative outlook on trauma appear on his intellectual horizon.[6] Perhaps we should not minimize, here, the precipitating impact on Lacan's conceptual elaborations in this Seminar of a traumatic event that had occurred in his own life a couple of months earlier. On November 19, 1963, a majority of members of the "*Société française de Psychanalyse*," the professional organization to which Lacan belonged and for which his seminars during the 1950s had become an intellectual beacon, decided to adopt a recommendation from the International Psychoanalytic Association that they "release" Lacan from his function as a training analyst and teacher if they wish to maintain their status as a Study Group. The decision effectively meant that the members of the SFP, many of whom had been or were still in analysis with Lacan, were happy to defrock and abandon their guide in return for an institutional favor. Shocked by this sudden, peculiar twist of fate, yet accepting its implications for his own position, Lacan presented the first and last session of his Seminar *The Names-of-the Father* the day after, ending with the words "I have never, at any moment, given any pretext for believing that there was not, for me, any difference between yes and no."[7] When Lacan resumed his Seminar at the "*École normale supérieure*" (ENS) in January 1964, where he was invited to teach by virtue of the interventions of Claude Lévi-Strauss and Louis Althusser, he was no more and no less than an independent analyst, a renegade intellectual and a lone scholar, without any institutional affiliation and no official sanctioning from a professional body. In the opening session of his new series of lectures at the ENS, which became the platform for his seminar on *The Four Fundamental Concepts of Psychoanalysis*, Lacan therefore compared his position to that of Spinoza after he was made the subject of a major excommunication by the synagogue on July 27, 1656.

Within this context, and perhaps reminded by his own recent experiences, Lacan posited in his seminar-session of February 12, 1964 that a traumatic event can be understood psychoanalytically in terms of Aristotle's notion of "*tuchè*," which can be found in the sixth section of the second book of the *Physics*.[8] Aristotelian scholars generally render "*tuchè*" as "chance," yet the problem with this translation is that it may convey an intrinsically positive, beneficial quality, whereas "*tuchè*" can be either bad or good, positive or negative. I would therefore prefer to translate it as "accident," "coincidence," "luck," "fortune" or even "happening"—a sudden, unexpected and unforeseeable occurrence which could not have been prevented and which completely escapes one's control. When presenting this notion to his audience, Lacan was careful to emphasize that psychoanalysts are generally reluctant to accept that such a thing as "pure chance" exists: "This is something that we analysts never allow ourselves to be taken in by [*ne nous laissons jamais duper*], on principle. At least, we always point out that we must not be taken in [*il ne faut pas nous laisser prendre*] when the subject tells us that something happened to him that day that prevented him from realizing his wish [*sa volonté*] to come to the session" (*Four Fundamental Concepts*, p. 54). The principle is strictly Freudian, of course, because

Freud constantly warned his readers not to take "coincidences" at face value and encouraged analysts always to search for the unconscious determination behind apparently random occurrences. The principle is also highly contentious, because it implies that a subject to whom something happens is never "innocent" and is always somehow implied in the "happening." As such, the principle forces a subject to somehow take responsibility for everything that happens to him. To exemplify the scope of this directive, let us imagine, for a moment, that my colleague John Tulloch was on his way to see his analyst on the morning of July 7, 2005, and let us also imagine that after having been admitted to hospital he called his analyst to explain the circumstances which had prevented him from coming to the session. If we follow the Freudian principle that nothing ever happens by chance but only ever *"as if* by chance," the upshot is that my poor colleague would have to start "tickling his trauma," thus exploring the vicissitudes of his death drive and the unconscious reasons for his symptomatic self-destructive compulsion to expose himself to dangerous, potentially lethal situations. "After all," the Freudian analyst would say, "let us not forget that for many years you have been dispatching yourself to some of the most unstable regions of the planet. You better start thinking why you are so keen to seek out risk situations." When hearing this type of comment, few people will disagree that it is not only ludicrous, but also cruel and inhumane. And yet, as I shall try to argue, something about the principle, which prompts subjects not to regard themselves purely as innocent victims of circumstance but to assess and recognize their subjective implication in the circumstances, may be beneficial for overcoming the pathogenic effects of a personal catastrophe.

But let us return to Lacan's theory of trauma and the notion of *"tuchè."* When trauma is defined as the sudden eruption of something that could not have been anticipated, that is radically unexpected and therefore inassimilable and inexplicable, the notion acquires a much broader meaning than that provided by its etymology ("wound" and "rupture of a protective boundary") and the *DSM-IV* ("actual or threatened death or serious injury, or a threat to the physical integrity of self and others" which produces "intense fear, helplessness, or horror"). The advantage of Lacan's emphasis, here, on the unexpected, not immediately understandable and momentarily shattering quality of the event—which also prompted him to designate it as "a missed encounter with the Real"—is that any event can function as a trauma and that no event is by definition traumatic for each and every subject. In Lacan's view, the traumatic quality of an event does not depend upon the actual, "objective" threat that it poses to a subject's physical and/or mental survival (much like the phobic quality of an object is not dependent upon its "objective" dangerousness), but rather on the extent to which it imposes itself unavoidably and pervasively upon a subject's existence, which is as much an "objective" as a "subjective" criterion.

If all of this seems rather obvious and trivial, it still constitutes only half of Lacan's theory of trauma in his Seminar of 1964. Apart from the notion of *"tuchè,"* Lacan also re-activated Aristotle's concept of *"automaton,"* which appears in the same chapter of the *Physics*, in order to explain how a traumatic event becomes the object of a process of repetition. *"Automaton"* is usually translated as "spontaneity," which may make it difficult to understand how the term differs from *"tuchè."* Aristotle's aim was to distinguish between "chance-events," which are as such uncontrollable, and "spontaneous operations," which may also occur suddenly but which moreover operate according to their own self-perpetuating mechanisms, and are as such equally uncontrollable. The transliteration of *"automaton"* as "automatism" or "automation" gives a good idea of what Aristotle was trying to convey: a mechanism that follows its own course without any external intervention.

When juxtaposing *"tuchè"* and *"automaton,"* Lacan endeavored to explain how a traumatic event acquires a pathogenic quality, that is to say, he attempted to account for the way in which some traumatic events in some subjects become the object of a symptomatic process of repetition. Or, to put it in yet another way, the difference between *"tuchè"* and *"automaton"* accounts for the manner in which certain traumatic events are more than sudden eruptions of the unexpected, and become incorporated as a traumatizing nucleus into a pathological series of symptoms such as recurrent nightmares, "spontaneous" debilitating flashbacks, emotional bluntness and memory disturbances—those symptoms that are currently clustered together under the heading of PTSD.

In his reading of Aristotle, Lacan collapsed the notion of *"automaton"* (spontaneity) onto his own concept of the "network of signifiers," which serves to designate the intricate set of relationships between endless series of acoustic images that make up the fabric of a natural language (*Four Fundamental Concepts*, p. 52). In other words, Lacan's "network of signifiers" stands for the sum-total of symbolic connections that simultaneously link and separate the sounds (of letters and words) within a spoken language, thereby constituting its uniqueness and differentiating it from other spoken languages. The reason as to why Lacan felt he could identify Aristotle's *"automaton"* with the "network of signifiers" is no doubt related to the fact that the symbolic connections that govern and define a spoken language indeed appear to deploy and develop themselves following a self-regulating, "autonomous" mechanism. No one knows, for example, when, how and why the English language came to accept and integrate the sounds of "l" and "r" as phonemes, that is, as linguistic units for differentiating meaning, whether these phonemes will continue to be part of the English language, and why they do not occur, for example, in Mandarin and Japanese, to the great amusement of the Anglophone visitor to the Chinese restaurant who is being asked by the waiter whether he would like more lice. It is true, of course, that the vocabulary of a language is constantly enriched with new words that are invented on the street and in the media (much more than in honorable cenacles of scholars, such as the *Académie française*), but the structures of sounds in which these words are integrated operate beyond individual control and remain largely unaltered, despite multiculturalism and the cacophony of accents it brings along.

Repeat after me, put it into words!

How, then, does the "network of signifiers," a linguistic structure, account for the pathogenic effect of a traumatic event? Why is a linguistic structure necessary for an original "accident," a contingency, to be transformed into the source and origin of the aforementioned list of so-called "post-traumatic symptoms?" And more importantly, perhaps, if the transformation of a traumatic contingency (in the Lacanian sense) into a traumatizing, pathogenic experience crucially depends on the spontaneous intervention of a symbolic structure, why is it that not all subjects who are confronted with traumatic events (all of us, from time to time) develop post-traumatic symptoms, given that all of us employ and therefore relate in one way or another to language? Don't we run the risk, here, of having recourse again to the identification of risk and vulnerability-factors, which would explain why some people's relationship with language is "less robust" than others?

The second question is definitely more difficult to answer than the first one, so I shall leave it in a state of suspension for the moment, in order to concentrate first of all on the significance of language (the "network of signifiers") for the "pathologization" of a traumatic event. Language is a necessary precondition for a traumatic event becoming pathogenic, because it is the only way in which an event can be registered and encoded in a meaningful way and operate as a point of reference in the mind of the patient. However, the encoding process itself does not need to occur around the time of the traumatic event, which would seem altogether difficult if we accept that the event cannot be directly assimilated when it happens, meaning that there are no words to express, describe, explain and understand it in the actual moment of happening. As Freud suggested in his analysis of the Wolf Man, the trauma in a sense always occurs twice: once when the actual event takes place and once again (after the original event) when it is semantically encoded.[9] This is the famous Freudian principle of *"nachträglichkeit"* (deferred action), which entails that an event is not traumatizing when it happens, but only becomes pathogenic with hindsight, in retrospect, when it is historicized and endowed with meaning from a subsequent vantage point in the subject's life. Outside psychoanalysis, the principle has rarely been discussed in trauma-research, yet it might very well explain why it is not at all necessary for trauma-victims to remain conscious during their predicament in order for them to develop symptoms of PTSD. I am referring here to a remarkable study by Mayou, Black and Bryant, published in the "British Journal of Psychiatry," which found that of 309 survivors of traffic accidents, there was a higher incidence of PTSD among those who had lost consciousness during the accident than among those who had not, 48 percent compared to 23 percent respectively.[10] In his admirably comprehensive survey of recent findings and outstanding issues in trauma-research, the Harvard professor of psychology Richard J. McNally commented on these (and similar) observations as follows: "The most intriguing recent finding [with regard to remembering trauma and developing PTSD] concerns individuals who lost consciousness during the trauma, but who developed re-experiencing symptoms for events they had never consciously experienced. Whether these emotional reactions in the absence of autobiographical memory for trauma reflect conditioning without awareness or the acquisition of frightening knowledge about the traumatic event remains to be seen."[11] I am not entirely sure how "conditioning without awareness" would work—although the fact that Pavlov (to the best of my knowledge) never attempted to elicit a conditioned response of salivation in an unconscious dog of course does not mean that consciousness is a prerequisite for being Pavlovized—yet I am fairly sure that McNally's willingness to consider "the acquisition of frightening knowledge" was partly instilled by the vicissitudes of the recovered memory movement, which tragically demonstrated that human beings are quite capable of remembering things that never (f)actually happened to them, as long as there are enough authoritative people out there to convince them that they did.

Freud's principle of "deferred action" proposes that a trauma does not actually happen when it happens or, to put it less paradoxically, that an event only ever becomes truly traumatic, that is to say pathogenic, "after the facts." In this sense, it does not matter whether a subject remained conscious during the time of the trauma for it to become pathogenic; what matters is the subject's subsequent encoding of it. And for this encoding to take place it is by no means necessary for a subject to consciously remember the event, insofar as the event can precisely be encoded as a "*non licet,*" as something one has been deprived of, and which can therefore only be approximated tangentially, by tracing its boundaries and defining its limits. This is exactly what seemed to have happened with the PTSD patients who had been unconscious during their road traffic accidents in the aforementioned study by Mayou, Black and Bryant: one of their symptoms involved the recurrent, intrusive recollection of things that had taken place immediately prior and just after the accident.

Freud's principle of "deferred action" is presumably ignored by trauma-researchers because they regard it as part and parcel of his so-called "hydraulic model" of repression, and its underlying dynamics of forgetting and remembering, which has been widely exposed as a fallacious theory, with highly disputable clinical implications. The story is well-known, yet purely for the sake of recollection, it is perhaps worth recalling its key features. A traumatic experience, so the Freudian story goes, imposes itself upon the mind in the form of a combined representation and affect (emotion). Inasmuch as it is traumatic, the representation is inadmissible into consciousness, that is, it cannot partake of the current of representations that reign over one's conscious experience, and therefore it is repressed. The process of repression itself occurs as a result of the detachment (disconnection) of the affect, which constitutes an energetic quantum, from the representation, and the upshot is that the latter "sinks" into the unconscious, whereas the former is displaced onto another, less painful and more neutral representation. Yet the repressed representation, so the story continues, does not lie dormant in the unconscious, but returns from its dwellings with a symptomatic vengeance. Clinically, this theory suggests that psychoanalytic practice must be geared toward "recovering" repressed memories, re-connecting them with the displaced affects, and venting the energetic quantum (the painful emotion) through narrative expression. For inventing this model, Freud has been vilified as the father of the recovered memory movement and its numerous fads.[12] Yet he has also been attacked for assuming that "talking about things," especially those things that cannot be talked about, may bring relief. The former Lacanian Dylan Evans, for example, has discarded the clinical implications of Freud's "hydraulic model" as "too simplistic," for which he mustered "evidence" produced by Jo Rick and Rob Briner, who found that victims of trauma who had received "stress debriefing" (a supposedly therapeutic form of psychological assistance whereby the victims are encouraged to talk through all the emotions that the event has instilled in them) by professional counselors subsequently experienced more symptoms of PTSD than those who had been left to come to terms with the event all by themselves. Evans concluded: "When left unexamined, bad memories do not fester like some untreated wound, as Freud thought. Rather, they tend to fade away, a process known as 'extinction.' By contrast, if the neural circuits encoding memories are continually reactivated by recounting the original experiences, extinction is prevented. Talking about memories does not help them to go away."[13]

The fact of the matter is that Evans is quite right: the "hydraulic model" is far too simplistic. But instead of being a remarkable finding, this observation is actually merely a regurgitation of something Freud himself had already discovered shortly before World War I: the hydraulic model of repression and its associated ideas of forgetting and remembering do not do justice to the complexity of the mental processes at stake. Freud's seminal article on the topic is "Remembering, Repeating and Working-Through" and it marks his abandonment of any type of psychoanalysis that could still reek of "recovered memory therapy."[14] I am not sure whether I can agree with Lacan's assertion, in *Seminar XI*, that "of all psycho-analytic texts ['Remembering, Repeating and Working-Through'] is certainly the one that has inspired the greatest amount of stupidity," but it is definitely the text which inspired the greatest amount of theoretical and clinical revisionism in Freud himself (*Four Fundamental Concepts*, p. 49). After rehearsing the basic precepts on which psychoanalytic practice had been conducted until then, Freud adduces three reasons as to why the dynamics of remembering and forgetting do not capture the complexity of the mental phenomena he is dealing with. First, it happens on a regular basis that when a patient "remembers" something she has "forgotten," she puts things into perspective with the words, "As a matter of fact I've always known it; only I've never thought of it" ("Remembering," p. 148). Hence, rather than a question of forgetting and remembering, it seems to be a question of knowing and not-knowing and perhaps even of a not-wanting-to-know. Second, Freud claims that whenever something is "forgotten," it is not "really forgotten," because it is always somehow present in the form of "screen memories," which as such already constitute a compromise between the psychic motives of forgetting and the unconscious forces that strive toward remembering. Finally, and most importantly, Freud admits that the process of "remembering" can only be accepted on the grounds that something has indeed been forgotten, that is to say, on the grounds that something was initially present at the level of consciousness and subsequently lost, obliterated, canceled out. Strictly speaking, one cannot remember something one could not have forgotten on account of the fact that it was never consciously acknowledged. And for Freud, this is true for all experiences happening during the first years of life: "There is one special class of experiences of the utmost importance for which no memory can as a rule be recovered (*läßt sich eine Erinnerung nicht erwecken*). These are experiences which occurred in very early childhood and were not understood at the time but which were *subsequently* understood and interpreted" (*nachträglich aber Verständnis und Deutung gefunden haben*) ("Remembering," p. 149). As James Strachey remarks in a footnote to his translation of the text, Freud must have been thinking of the processes he had observed in his analysis of the Wolf Man, whose treatment he had recently completed yet whose case-study he would only publish after the war.

Following this triple nuance of the "remembering vs forgetting" paradigm, Freud introduced the new notion of repetition ("*Wiederholung*")—although it had already been foreshadowed at the very end of his 1912 technical paper "The Dynamics of Transference"—which he characterized as the patient's unconscious reproduction in acts of what cannot be remembered, a process which not only serves the purpose of resistance, but which also contaminates the transference and thus the entire course of the psychoanalytic treatment.[15] Although in 1914, Freud still believed in the possibility of curbing repetition psychoanalytically in the direction of remembering, the worm had definitely entered his theoretical fruits and six years later, in the conceptual watershed of "Beyond the Pleasure Principle," Freud had to concede to the existence of a new fundamental psychic force which challenges psychoanalytic practice in the most radical way, and which he now dubbed the "repetition compulsion" ("*Wiederholungszwang*").[16] It is within this context, rather than that of remembering and forgetting, that the term "*nachträglichkeit*" (deferred action) needs to be situated.

Let us return, then, to the aforementioned idea that a trauma only ever becomes pathogenic "*nachträglich*," "after the facts." If we accept Freud's perspective in "Remembering, Repeating and Working-Through" that some original events cannot be remembered, because they could never have been forgotten on account of their never having been consciously present, then the implication is that they can only be repeated—endlessly, compulsively, ineluctably. In other words, when a traumatic event is encoded by deferred action, the encoding itself is not tantamount to its remembering—as Freud says, it is an understanding and interpretation (*"Verständnis und Deutung"*) rather than a remembering—but signals the start of its repetition.

We can now begin to understand why Lacan felt justified in regarding the "network of signifiers" (the *automaton*) as the necessary precondition for the retroactive (secondary) assimilation of the traumatic event, for it is only possible to "understand" and "interpret" something with the tools of a symbolic system. In addition, we can also grasp why in *Seminar XI* Lacan put the "network of signifiers" on a par with the notion of repetition (and repetition compulsion), for this is merely an extension of Freud's argument that the retroactive interpretation of an event constitutes the start of its integration within a compulsive movement of reproductive action. Yet in his definition of the traumatic event as an unassimilable accident, Lacan clearly intended to go beyond Freud's restriction of traumatic experiences to those which occur in very early childhood: although a child may be less capable of understanding and interpreting things than an adult, the latter is by no means entirely protected against experiences for which the words are lacking and which can only be grasped retroactively, long after they have happened.

Should all of this seem very abstract and austere, it is by situating the process of "traumatization" outside the dimensions of forgetting and remembering that some clinical observations may appear in a new light and some therapeutic strategies may acquire a different color. When defining symptoms of PTSD in terms of repetition, the implication is that they maintain themselves "spontaneously," purely by virtue of being conditioned by a linguistic structure, and independently of any type of memory function. Remembering a traumatic event, whether or not it is associated with speech and narration, neither precludes nor relieves symptoms of PTSD, and symptoms of PTSD neither presuppose nor maintain the forgetting of this event. Helping a traumatized patient to recover "lost memories" of the original event can by definition do nothing to curb the repetition that governs the symptoms. And if some form of "spontaneous" remembering does occur, it is never a crucial step on the pathway to healing, but by definition a symptomatic component of the repetitive action which maintains the state of traumatization. Furthermore, because the original event is by definition unassimilable, *all* memory of it must necessarily be false, insofar as it can only be a retrospective approximation of what "really" happened. And when traumatized patients do find relief—at least if we believe the advocates of recovered memory therapy—when recalling the circumstances of a "long-forgotten" traumatic experience, it is therefore not because the recovered memory cancels out their suffering, but rather because they are under the spell of the seductive and suggestive therapeutic authority which has helped them to overcome their misery.

The fantasy of catastrophe

At this point of my explication, one question remains and a new one emerges. The new question is of a technical nature, which does not make it less significant, on the contrary: if the symptoms of traumatization are governed by the fundamental psychic force of repetition, rather than by (flawed) remembering, what can a clinician working with traumatized patients do in order to tackle this force? The issue needs to be addressed, yet before I engage with it I wish to concentrate first on the question I formulated above and which has not been given a satisfactory resolution, inasmuch as that would be altogether possible. The problem presents itself as follows: if the network of signifiers (the structure of language) is a necessary precondition for a traumatic event (an "unassimilable accident") to be retroactively understood and interpreted, because it makes its encoding possible, thereby initiating its transformation into the pathogenic nucleus of a process of repetition compulsion, how can we explain that not all human beings, to the extent that they operate with and within the symbolic order, display symptoms of PTSD, since we can reasonably assume that all human beings have at one point in their lives been confronted with "unassimilable accidents?" Or do we need to assume that by virtue of its mere dependency upon the structure of language the repetition of traumatic events does indeed occur in all of us, but that only in some of us the repetition is pathological, insofar as it elicits symptoms of PTSD? After all, Freud himself argued in "Beyond the Pleasure Principle" that the repetition compulsion is an intrinsic component of human psychic functioning. What would be the difference, then, between a pathological and a non-pathological form of repetition?

A pragmatic, and perhaps slightly circular answer could be: pathological repetition is repetition someone complains about. The answer seems trivial in light of the complexity of the question, yet it nonetheless captures an essential characteristic of the symptom, as defined from a psychoanalytic perspective: a symptom does not exist until it appears as a complaint in the speech of a subject who addresses himself to an analyst. Hence, despite its inane simplicity, the pragmatic does have its value. If it somehow dodges the issue, it is less because it misses the point, but rather because in its oblique generality it avoids the specificity of the problem. What may be true for the symptom is not necessarily true for repetition. And if there is anything both Freud and Lacan are clear about it is that repetition is not a formation of the unconscious, and should therefore not be understood psychoanalytically in the same way as symptoms, dreams, slips of the tongue etc.

So, if we assume that the repetition compulsion is an essential feature of being human, why is it that in some human beings this repetition compulsion becomes pathological and in others it remains within the boundaries of mental health? Why is it that some people remain traumatized by traumatic events whereas others manage to overcome them and return to their daily lives? For all I know, Freud and Lacan did not tell us, which does not necessarily mean that they did not have the answer, even less that the answer does not exist and that we should not bother trying to formulate one. Freud, of course, was notoriously reluctant to exercise his mind on problems of what could be designated as "psychic bifurcation." Why is it that someone becomes neurotic in confrontation with a certain course of events, whereas someone else manages to stay shy of pathology? Why is it that someone, Freud's Little Hans for example, developed a phobia instead of becoming a fetishist?[17] The problem, which Freud baptized as the issue of *"Neurosenwahl"* (choice of neurosis), seemed to completely defy his acumen, as exemplified in the following famous passage from his 1927 paper on "Fetishism": "Probably no male human being is spared the fright of castration at the sight of a female genital. Why some people become homosexual as a consequence of that impression, while others fend it off by creating a fetish, and the great majority surmount it, we are frankly not able to explain. It is possible that, among all the factors at work, we do not yet know those which are decisive for the rare pathological results."[18] Here, Freud admitted to his ignorance. At other points, as in his discussion of the reasons why some girls overcome their Oedipus complex in the direction of motherhood and others choose the path of a masculinity complex, he could find no better answer than that of a "constitutional factor."[19]

My own answer will be different and I shall leave it up to others to judge whether it is better. Insofar as the network of signifiers facilitates the encoding of a traumatic event, which cannot as such be understood, interpreted and explained, the latter indeed becomes the nucleus of a "spontaneous" process of repetition. As such, repetition transforms contingency into necessity, yet this transformation does not in itself account for the mutation of the traumatic event into the pathology of traumatization. The example that Freud gives in the second chapter of "Beyond the Pleasure Principle," of the young boy (his own grandchild) who compulsively repeats the coming and going of his mother in a game of throwing away and pulling back a reel, sufficiently reminds us of the fact that repetition is not inherently pathological.[20] On the contrary, we might say, the encoding of a traumatic event and its subsequent repetition may be a productive way of "recycling," of "processing" and "re-processing" the event in order for it to become somehow "assimilable" within a subject's mental economy.

It thus appears that the network of signifiers is a necessary but not a sufficient condition for the emergence of a "traumatic neurosis." Something else is required for the repetition compulsion to mutate into an infernal cycle of fixated representations. It may also be worth recalling, here, that Freud's notion of repetition compulsion does not exclude variation; the theme may always be the same, yet its expression may change from one instance to another, or the theme may reoccur in a different guise depending on the circumstances. What differentiates this type of "normal" repetition from its "pathological" version is that in the latter case an event always returns in the same way. The theme has no variations and always expresses itself in exactly the same form, regardless of the circumstances.

In addition, from the 1920s, Freud started to realize that the repetition compulsion governs the patient's unconscious wish to hold on to his symptom, despite the pain and suffering it induces. Beyond the antagonistic dynamics of the pleasure principle, the symptom is animated by a force which fuels the patient's satisfaction. This is exactly what Lacan tried to capture with the notion of enjoyment (*jouissance*). Enjoyment functions beyond the pleasure principle; it is not incompatible with pain and is not necessarily pleasurable. As Lacan put it in an oft-quoted passage from *Seminar VII*: jouissance is pain and pleasure in a single packet.[21] This mixture of pain and pleasure is often already noticeable at the level of the complaint. On the one hand, the complaint is rooted in an experience of suffering, yet on the other hand patients may find it quite pleasurable to complain about their ailments. One of the main tasks of the psychoanalytic treatment consists, then, in bringing this satisfying mixture of pain and pleasure, which pervades the texture of the symptom, to light. This does not mean that a symptom ought not be interpreted, yet beyond its interpretation, and the concurrent crystallization of meaning (desire), another assignment awaits, which is much more delicate and onerous. The entire endeavor even seems to be intrinsically futile, for the satisfaction which the symptom incorporates operates beyond the boundaries of the symbolic, which is precisely why Lacan referred to it as real, whereas the psychoanalytic process is entirely embedded in language. How could we possibly use language to reach what remains fundamentally beyond it? In a programmatic paper from the mid 1980s, Jacques-Alain Miller phrased the issue as follows: "the symptom is not all signifier, and what this formal envelope of the symptom evokes as negative is what it envelops of *jouissance*, of *jouissante* matter. Thus, what is carried out in analysis, in some way naturally, that is to say logically, is a labor on the formal envelope [...]."[22] What Miller, with reference to Lacan, terms "the formal envelope of the symptom," here, is nothing but the narrative structure which the symptom acquires in the patient's account of his problem.[23] Yet Miller argues that this narrative structure is wrapped around *jouissance*, and that psychoanalytic treatment should be geared toward emptying out the container, or at least toward separating the symptom from the satisfaction it contains.

It seems to me that the transformation of a "normal," varied repetition into a "pathological," fixed repetition is based on a de-randomization or, better still, a hypostatization of the encoding of the traumatic event, and this can only be conditioned by the subject's fantasy. For if there is one "de-randomizer" at work in the human mind, it is the sexuo-erotic template that provides an answer to the desire of the Other, governs the subject's desire vis-à-vis this Other, and regulates our experiences of satisfaction. All human beings operate with a certain "matrix," which is as idiosyncratic as it is static, through which they understand and interpret events, including those that are traumatic. What type of fantasy, then, could be responsible for turning repetition into the engine of a traumatic neurosis? Here, my answer is that it can only be the fantasy of being victimized by the Other, a fantasy of catastrophe, of being singled out, unpredictably yet inevitably, by a nameless agency who can neither be identified nor controlled and whose only purpose is to obtain satisfaction. It can only be this fantasy, because this is the only fantasy which attributes total and totalizing power to the traumatic event as a catastrophic occurrence, in such a way that it is allowed to repeat itself in exactly the same form after it has been encoded. However, it should be noted, here, that this type of fantasy, which also functions as a newly constituted boundary of psychic life, does not imply that the subject who operates with it puts himself in a completely passive position. As Freud has indicated, it is entirely possible to actively pursue passive pleasures.[24] Someone may be completely at the mercy of the Other at the level of the fantasy, yet not at all passive in manoeuvering himself into the position whereby he is indeed at the Other's mercy. In addition, it should be noted that the fantasy of victimization is not inherently painful. As I pointed out above, the fantasy regulates experiences of satisfaction and may in this way maintain itself as fundamental source of enjoyment, however "objectively painful" its contents may seem.

Folding the fantasy

Bearing these features of the fantasy in mind, let me return now to the vexed issue of how symptoms of PTSD, insofar as they are determined by pathological repetition rather than (flawed) remembering, can be approached within a clinical setting. Freud's technical answer to the question as to how repetition can be handled psychoanalytically was the infamous process of working-through (*"durcharbeiten"*). As he pointed out at the end of his 1914 paper: "One must allow the patient time [*Man muß dem Kranken die Zeit lassen*] to become more conversant with this resistance with which he has now become acquainted [after the compulsion to repeat has entered the transference], to *work through* it, to overcome it, by continuing, in defiance of it, the analytic work according to the fundamental rule of analysis" ("Remembering," p. 155). Working-through, for Freud, "effects the greatest changes in the patient and [...] distinguishes analytic treatment from any kind of treatment by suggestion," yet unfortunately Freud did not seem to know what exactly happens in working-through, nor how the analyst could facilitate it ("Remembering," pp. 155–6). "One must allow the patient time" is pretty much the only technical guideline Freud provided in his 1914 paper, and the other mention of working-through, in the first addendum to "Inhibitions, Symptoms and Anxiety" is equally devoid of supplementary glosses.[25]

Remarkably, however, Lacan reactivated the notion of working-through at the very end of *Seminar XI*, when elaborating on his famous idea of the traversal or crossing (*"traversée"*) of the fantasy. Talking about the "cycle of the analytic experience," Lacan stated: "The loop [*'boucle'*] must be run through several times. There is in effect no other way of accounting for the term *durcharbeiten*, of the necessity of elaboration, except to conceive how the loop must be run through more than once" (*Four Fundamental Concepts*, p. 274). Although it would certainly be possible to interpret Lacan's notion of loop, here, with reference to the schema of the "interior eight" with which he had graphically represented the process of analysis earlier on in this session of the Seminar, I wish to read it instead with reference to his algebraic representation of the fantasy, as a "lozenge" with two complementary vectors, one vector (that of alienation) connecting the subject to the object and the other vector (that of separation) re-directing the subject away from the object, onto himself.[26] Interpreted in this sense, Lacan's "running through the loop several times," which he explicitly identified with the process of working-through, takes place simultaneously at the level of the fantasy and in response to repetition. In light of what I argued earlier on, concerning the role of a certain type of fantasy for the crystallization of pathological repetition, Lacan's suggestion of "running through the loop several times" may now also be regarded as a technical recommendation, notably that clinicians approach the pathological repetition which governs the traumatic neurosis (the symptoms of PTSD) indirectly, via concentrated work on and with the fantasy. Similar to the process of facilitation (*Bahnung*), which Freud adduced in his *Project for a Scientific Psychology*, working-through the fantasy involves path-breaking—not of the neurones, but of the logic underpinning the re-constituted boundaries of psychic life.

For the purposes of this essay, I will not enter into a discussion of how the traversal of the fantasy functions as a precondition for analytic training, but limit myself to an exploration of the relationship between the technical procedure of working-through, the associated traversal of the fantasy, and its effect on the status of the symptoms in traumatic neurosis. The link between the symptom and the fantasy seems to be of fundamental importance, here, for if working-through is a necessary operation within the analytic process of disentangling the symptom, and working-through is a pre-condition for the traversal of the fantasy, then the separation of symptom and jouissance must depend on this traversal of the fantasy or, vice versa, the fantasy must somehow be responsible for keeping symptom and jouissance together.

How should we interpret the relationship between the symptom and the fantasy? How does the symptom feed on the fantasy, and how can the fantasy constitute a bridge between the symptom in its narrative form of complaint and the nonsensical satisfaction that perpetuates it? These questions open up onto some of the most complex and advanced developments within psychoanalytic theory, and I shall therefore only be able to scratch their surface. Nonetheless, I hope to demonstrate how the symptom, by virtue of its indebtedness to the fantasy, is never purely an individual accident, but follows a logical trajectory through which the subject adopts a particular position vis-a-vis the Other.

Relying on clinical experience, it is much easier to differentiate the symptom and the fantasy than to pinpoint the areas where the two forces meet each other. In general, if most patients enter the treatment with their symptom as a complaint, the fantasy is rarely complained about, even when it includes scenes of sexual debauchery that are strictly illegal and that have acquired a high degree of fixity. If patients complain about their symptom, they generally comply with their fantasy. Partly because of this compliance, or rather complacency with the fantasy, patients do not even tend to talk about it—a silence which is often exacerbated by feelings of guilt or shame at the perverse nature of this "private theatre."[27]

What, exactly, is the function of the fantasy? First of all, the fantasy is an answer to the desire of the Other. It is an answer to the question, forever mysterious and unresolvable, as to what the Other wants, which place one occupies in the desire of the Other, what the Other has in store for us. In this sense, the fantasy constitutes the subject's most intimate *Weltanschauung*, a subjective ideology which guarantees psychic continuity, regulates our intersubjective space, and provides stability and reassurance. The fantasy governs our so-called "object-relations" and sustains our desire, which is precisely why Lacan defined it as *"désir de"* (desire for).[28] Yet the fantasy is also the psychic architecture which makes us experience an event as a source of satisfaction, and which may therefore prompt us to actively seek its continuation or return. The classic example is the sexual act, whose satisfaction crucially depends on the consistency of the fantasy. Whether practised alone, with a partner or in a group, human sexual activity is never intrinsically satisfying, inasmuch as satisfaction only ensues if a particular fantasy, which may be very different from the sexual act itself, is operative. And one does not need to be a psychoanalyst to understand this function of the fantasy. Behavioral therapists working with sex offenders know very well that the criminal behavior may extinguish if the satisfaction-generating fantasy with which it is paired is altered or replaced.

The fantasy also connects the "button" of *jouissance* to the "fabric" of the symptom. The symptom's *jouissance* is dependent upon the fantasy; without the fantasy, the symptom would not be enjoyable. Therefore, disconnecting the symptom from its enjoyment relies on a decomposition of the fantasy which is responsible for keeping the contents in the envelope. Rather than operating directly on the patient's enjoyment, the analyst thus works with the fantasy. This analytic labor is difficult, yet it is not impossible because the fantasy does not live beyond speech and language. In Freud's most elaborate contribution to a psychoanalytic theory of the fantasy, his 1919 paper "A Child is Being Beaten," he made it perfectly clear that the fantasy exercises its power according to precise linguistic rules.[29] Yet unlike the symptom, and because the fantasy is not a coded message but an intricate circuit of interconnected components, the fantasy cannot be interpreted and needs re-construction instead. Hence, before the fantasy can be decomposed, traversed, worked-through, it needs to be assembled first, and this constitutes the most advanced aspect of the psychoanalytic treatment. Its effect is not that the fantasy disappears, but that it loses its grip on the subject's symptom and the latter's enjoyment is emptied out.

Questions remain as to what exactly should be understood by Lacan's "running through the loop several times," how a clinician can facilitate this type of work, and why it can be taken as an effective intervention strategy for people suffering from traumatic neurosis. The latter issue is easy to address, at least from a theoretical point of view: if we assume that symptoms of PTSD are governed by pathological repetition, which is itself conditioned by a certain type of fantasy, the restructuring of this fantasy must necessarily lead to a modification of the symptoms. The other questions are more difficult to answer, if only because Lacan himself was rather vague in elaborating on his own principles. In my understanding, Lacan's recommendation by no means entails that the patient is encouraged to assume more strongly the role of the victim, or the survivor—the latter term is slightly more appreciative of the patient's self-empowerment, but is nonetheless constructed against the background of victimization—although this is of course precisely what many therapeutic models set out to do. From a Lacanian perspective, assuming (and identifying with) the role of the victim is not the solution, but the problem. Likewise, assuming (and identifying with) the role of the survivor perpetuates the problem because it is simply another way of substantiating the victim role. And it would be equally futile to consider, assuming that therapists would indeed be brave enough to do so, the possibility of encouraging the patient to assume (and identify with) the role of the aggressor, because this role would still maintain that of the victim as its dialectical opposite. The point, therefore, is neither to consolidate nor to dismantle the victim-role (and the fantasy supporting it), but to redefine it in such a way that it becomes less fixed, more flexible, less petrified, more malleable. Hence, traversing the fantasy of the victim does not entail its eradication, even less its substitution for another fantasy (which could only ever be that of the analyst), but its reorganization into a less rigid, more negotiable template. If I were to introduce a new idea here, I would say that this reorganization takes place as a process of folding and re-folding, through the development of a layering structure which does not cover up anything, but which allows the material to be represented in a different way. And this is exactly why it can be beneficial for a patient to "tickle his trauma" and explore his own unconscious implication into the traumatic event that he has experienced. For instead of purely looking at the world through the eyes of someone who is always victimized by the Other, it may prompt him to look again through the eyes of someone who also victimizes himself. The victim is still a victim, but a victim who is less rigidly defined in his relation to the Other and who can therefore operate more freely within the terms of his own position. As should be clear by now, this form of newly acquired subjective freedom does not depend on a fortification of the boundaries of psychic life, nor on the progressive undoing of their sclerotic structure and the restoration of some form of healthy elasticity, but on the continuous localization and integration of trauma and catastrophe as such within these very boundaries, through which the unpredictable inevitabilities of our current living conditions, whether actually experienced or anxiously imagined by the dominant ideologies of our time, can be perceived as forces requiring the constant creative reorganization of thought.

Notes

1. "A Survivor's Story: 'So Good to be Alive'," *The Mail on Sunday*, July 14, 2005. <http://www.mailonsunday.co.uk/pages/live/articles/news/news.html?in_article_id=355761&in_page_id=1770> [accessed May 2, 2006].
2. Eric Hobsbawm, *The Age of Extremes: A History of the World, 1914–1991* (London: Vintage, 1994).
3. American Psychiatric Association, *Diagnostic and Statistical Manual of Mental Disorders-IV* (Washington DC, American Psychiatric Press, 1994), pp. 427–8.
4. D. S. Nice, C. F. Garland, S. M. Hilton, J. C. Baggett and R. E. Mitchell, "Long-term Health Outcomes and Medical Effects of Torture Among US Navy Prisoners of War in Vietnam," *Journal of the American Medical Association*, 276 (1996), pp. 375–81.
5. See J. Briere and J. Conte, "Self-reported Amnesia for Abuse in Adults Molested as Children," *Journal of Traumatic Stress*, 6 (1993) 21–31; J. Czarnocka and P. Slade, "Prevalence and Predictors of Post-traumatic Stress Symptoms following Childbirth," *British Journal of Clinical Psychology*, 39 (2000) 35–51; B. A. Thyer and G. C. Curtis, "The Repeated Pretest-Posttest Single-Subject Experiment: A New Design for Empirical Clinical Practice," *Journal of Behavior Therapy and Experimental Psychiatry*, 14 (1983) 311–15.
6. Jacques Lacan, *The Four Fundamental Concepts of Psychoanalysis* (1964), edited by Jacques-Alain Miller, translated by Alan Sheridan, with a new introduction by David Macey (Harmondsworth: Penguin, 1994). Henceforth cited in the text as *Four Fundamental Concepts*.
7. Lacan, "The Names-of-the-Father" (1963), in *Television/A Challenge to the Psychoanalytic Establishment*, translated by Jeffrey Mehlman (London and NY: W. W. Norton & Company, 1990), p. 95.
8. Aristotle, *Physics*, translated by Robin Waterfield (Oxford: Oxford University Press, 1996), pp. 46–8.

9. See Sigmund Freud, "From the History of an Infantile Neurosis" (1918b [1914]), *The Standard Edition of the Complete Psychological Works of Sigmund Freud*, vol. 17, edited by James Strachey (London: The Hogarth Press, 1955), p. 45, footnote 1. Hereafter *Standard Edition*.

10. R. A. Mayou, J. Black and B. Bryant, "Unconsciousness, Amnesia and Psychiatric Symptoms following Road Traffic Accident Injury," *British Journal of Psychiatry*, 177 (2000), pp. 540–5.

11. Richard J. McNally, *Remembering Trauma* (Cambridge MA-London: Harvard University Press, 2003), p. 124.

12. See especially Frederick Crews, *The Memory Wars: Freud's Legacy in Dispute* (London: Granta Books, 1997).

13. Dylan Evans, *Emotion: The Science of Sentiment* (Oxford: Oxford University Press, 2001), pp. 84–5.

14. Freud, "Remembering, Repeating and Working-Through (Further Recommendations on the Technique of Psycho-Analysis II)" (1914g), *Standard Edition*, 12, pp. 146–56. Henceforth cited in the text as "Remembering."

15. In the final paragraph of "The Dynamics of Transference," Freud wrote: "The unconscious impulses do not want to be remembered in the way the treatment desires them to be, but endeavor to reproduce themselves [*sie streben danach, sich zu reproduzieren*] in accordance with the timelessness of the unconscious and its capacity for hallucination." See Freud, "The Dynamics of Transference" (1912b), *Standard Edition*, 12, p. 108.

16. Freud, "Beyond the Pleasure Principle" (1920g), *Standard Edition*, 18, pp. 1–64.

17. See Freud, "Analysis of a Phobia in a Five-Year-Old Boy" (1909b), *Standard Edition*, 10, pp. 1–147.

18. Freud, "Fetishism," *Standard Edition*, 21, p. 154.

19. Freud, "New Introductory Lectures on Psycho-Analysis. Lecture 33: Femininity" (1933a), *Standard Edition*, 22, p. 130.

20. Freud, "Beyond the Pleasure Principle," pp. 14–15.

21. Lacan, *The Seminar of Jacques Lacan. Book VII: The Ethics of Psychoanalysis* (1959–60), edited by Jacques-Alain Miller, translated by Dennis Porter (London-NY: W. W. Norton & Company, 1992), p. 189.

22. Jacques-Alain Miller, "Reflections on the Formal Envelope of the Symptom" (1985), translated by J. Jauregui, *Lacanian Ink*, 4 (1991), p. 20.

23. Lacan uses the expression "the symptom's formal envelope" in "On My Antecedents" (1966), *Écrits*, translated by Bruce Fink (London-NY: W. W. Norton & Company, 2006), p. 52.

24. Freud, "Instincts and their Vicissitudes" (1915c), *Standard Edition*, 14, pp. 110–40.

25. Freud, "Inhibitions, Symptoms and Anxiety" (1926d), *Standard Edition*, 20, p. 159.

26. See *The Four Fundamental Concepts*, pp. 209–15.

27. "Private theatre" is how Anna O described her compulsive day-dreaming. See Joseph Breuer and Sigmund Freud, "Studies on Hysteria" (1895d), *Standard Edition*, 2, p. 22.

28. Lacan, "Kant with Sade" (1962), *Écrits*, p. 653.

29. Freud, "A Child is Being Beaten": A Contribution to the Study of the Origin of Sexual Perversions (1919e), *Standard Edition*, 17, pp. 175–204.

10
Who is Nietzsche?

Alain Badiou

What is the true center of Nietzsche's thought? Or: what is it that Nietzsche calls "philosophy?"

I believe it is essential to understand that, for Nietzsche, what he calls "philosophy" is not an interpretation, is not an analysis, is not a theory. When philosophy is interpretation, analysis, or theory, it is nothing but a variant of religion. It is dominated by the nihilist figure of the priest. In *The Antichrist*, Nietzsche declares that the philosopher is "the greatest of all criminals." We should take this declaration seriously.

Nietzsche is not a philosopher, he is an anti-philosopher. This expression has a precise meaning: Nietzsche opposes, to the speculative nihilism of philosophy, the completely affirmative necessity of an act. The role that Nietzsche assigns himself is not that of adding a philosophy to other philosophies. Instead, his role is to announce and produce an act without precedent, an act that will in fact destroy philosophy.

To announce the act, but also to produce it: this means that Nietzsche the anti-philosopher is literally ahead of himself. This is exactly what he says in the song from *Thus Spake Zarathustra* entitled: "Of the Virtue that Makes Small." Zarathustra introduces himself as his own precursor:

> Among these people I am my own forerunner, my own cock-crow through dark lanes.

Thus what *comes* in philosophy is what the philosopher bears witness to. Or, more accurately: the philosophical *act* is what philosophy, which nevertheless coincides with it, can only announce.

Straight away, we are at the heart of our examination of Nietzsche. For his singularity is entirely contained in his conception of the

195

philosophical act. Or, to use his language, in his conception of the power of philosophy. That is to say, of anti-philosophy.

In what do this act and this power consist?

It is by failing to place this question at the threshold of any examination of Nietzsche that both Deleuze and Heidegger partially missed his absolute singularity, the one that ultimately both fulfills and abolishes itself under the name of *madness*.

Deleuze begins his book, *Nietzsche and Philosophy*, with this declaration: "Nietzsche's most general project is the introduction of the concepts of sense and value into philosophy." Now, I believe that the philosophical act according to Nietzsche does not take the form either of a project or of a program—rather, as in Sarah Kofman's title, it could be called an *explosion*. Neither is it a question for Nietzsche—of introducing concepts. For the name of the philosophical event can be nothing other than a figure, and ultimately a proper name. The proper of the event deposes the common of the concept. To do this, it supports itself on the opacity of the proper name. Nietzsche's philosophical thought is given in a primordial network of seven names: Christ, or the Crucified, Dionysus-Ariadne, Saint Paul, Socrates, Wagner, Zarathustra, and finally the most obscure of all the names, the name "Nietzsche," which recapitulates the others.

Of course, Deleuze is aware of these names, the meaning of which he interprets. One can, as he does with virtuosity, read in these nominal series the coding of types of force, and analyze them according to the grid of the active and the reactive. But in this case, the network of proper names is brought back to the commonality of sense, and Nietzsche is absorbed into the stream of interpretation. What is lost in Deleuze's strong reading is this: it is through the opacity of the proper name that *Nietzsche constructs his own category of truth*. This is indeed what assigns the vital act to its nonsensical, or invaluable, dimension. Nietzsche's last word is not sense, but the inevaluable.

The common name of the supreme act, the one that puts an end to Christian enslavement, is "the reversal of all values," or the transvaluation of all values. But the reversal of all values does not itself have a value. It is subtracted from evaluation. Certainly, it is life itself against nothingness, only that, as Nietzsche will say in *The Twilight of the Idols*, and it is a decisive axiom:

The value of life cannot be estimated.

To enter into Nietzsche, one must therefore focus on the point where evaluation, values, and sense all come to falter in the trial posed by the act. Thus where it is no longer a question of values or of sense, but of what actively surpasses them, what philosophy has always named "truth."

In my view this is what Heidegger fails to grasp when he thinks that Nietzsche's program of thought is the institution of new values. We know that Nietzsche analyzes the old values as a triumph of the will to nothingness. They exist in virtue of a principle that for Nietzsche is the supreme principle, which is that man prefers to will the nothing, rather than not to will at all. For Heidegger, Nietzsche, in reversing the old values, in proposing the noon of affirmation over against the will to nothingness, actually intends to overcome nihilism. Now, Heidegger will say that by so doing, by willing to overcome nihilism, Nietzsche's thought separates itself from the very essence of nihilism, which is not in fact the will to nothingness. This is because for Heidegger, if nihilism is the will to nothingness, it is then intelligible in its essence on the basis of the figure of the subject. But in truth nihilism is not a figure of the subject; nihilism is the history of the remaining-absent of being itself, as historiality. Nihilism is a historial figure of being. It is this that comes to be concealed within a Nietzschean program of thought, which consists in the overcoming of nihilism. As Heidegger will say: "The will to overcome nihilism [which he attributes to Nietzsche] does not know itself, because it excludes itself from the evidence of the essence of nihilism, considered as the history of the remaining-absent and thus prohibits itself from ever knowing its own doing."

Is Nietzsche really so ignorant of his own doing? We find ourselves brought back to the question of the act. We must begin by asking if this Nietzschean doing represents itself as an overcoming, in the metaphysical form of the subject. It seems to me that there is here, on Heidegger's part, a critique which Hegelianizes Nietzsche before judging him. Because I believe that for Nietzsche the act is not an overcoming. The act is an event. And this event is an absolute break, whose obscure proper name is Nietzsche.

It is to this link between an act without concept or program and a proper name, a proper name that is his own only by chance, that one must refer the famous title of one of the sections of *Ecce Homo*: "Why I am a Destiny." I am a destiny because, by chance, the proper name "Nietzsche" comes to link its opacity to a break without program or concept.

I am strong enough to break up the history of mankind in two.
(Letter to Strindberg of December 8, 1888)

I conceive the philosopher as a terrifying explosive that puts the entire world in danger.

(Ecce Homo)

Nietzsche's anti-philosophical act, of which he is at once the prophet, the actor, and the name, aims at nothing less than at breaking the history of the world in two.

I would say that this act is *archi-political,* in that it intends to revolutionize the whole of humanity at a more radical level than that of the calculations of politics. Archi-political does not here designate the traditional philosophical task of finding a foundation for politics. The logic, once again, is a logic of rivalry, and not a logic of foundational eminence. It is the philosophical act itself that is an archi-political act, in the sense that its historical explosion will retroactively show, in a certain sense, that the political revolution proper has not been genuine, or has not been authentic.

It follows from this that, in Nietzschean archi-politics, the word politics is sometimes reclaimed and validated, and sometimes depreciated, in a characteristic oscillation. In the draft of a letter to Brandes from December 1888, Nietzsche writes:

We have just entered into great politics, even into very great politics [...]. I am preparing an event which, in all likelihood, will break history into two halves, to the point that one will need a new calendar, with 1888 as Year One.

Here Nietzsche proposes an imitation of the French revolution. He assumes, as a fundamental determination of philosophy, the word "politics." Moreover, this imitation will go so far as to include images of the Terror, which Nietzsche will adopt without the least hesitation. Many texts bear witness to this. Let us cite the note to Franz Overbeck from January 4, 1889, where Nietzsche declares:

I am just having all anti-Semites shot

On the other hand, in the letter to Jean Bourdeau from December 17, 1888, the word politics is subjected to critique:

My works are rich with a decision with regard to which the brutal demonstrations of calculation in contemporary politics could prove to be nothing more than mere errors of calculus.

And, in a draft letter to William II, Nietzsche writes this:

> The concept of politics has been completely dissolved in the war between spirits, all power-images have been blown to bits,—there will be wars, like there have never been before.

The Nietzschean anti-philosophical act, determined as archi-political event, thinks the historico-political, sometimes in the figure of its broadened imitation, sometimes in the figure of its complete dissolution. It is precisely this alternative that gives legitimacy to the act as *archi*-political. If the act is archi-political then the philosopher is an over-philosopher.

Letter to Von Seydlitz of February 1888:

> It is not inconceivable that I am the first philosopher of the age, perhaps even a little more. Something decisive and doom-laden standing between two millennia.

Nietzsche is first of all the chance name of something, something like a fatal uprising, a fatal, archi-political uprising, which stands between two millennia. But what then are the *means* of such an act? What is its point of application? And finally, what is an anti-philosophical event that would be archi-political in character?

To address this problem, we must examine the Nietzschean critique of the Revolution, in its political sense. This critique consists in saying that, essentially, the Revolution did not take place. What we should understand by this is that it has not happened as revolution, in the sense that archi-politics conceives it. It has not taken place, because it has not truly broken the history of the world in two, thus leaving the Christian apparatus of the old values intact. Moreover, the equality to which the Revolution lay claim was nothing more than social equality, equality as the idea of being the equal of another. And this equality, in Nietzsche's eyes, is always commanded by *ressentiment*.

In *The Antichrist* we can read the following:

> "Equality of souls before God," this falsehood, this pretext for the rancune of all the base-minded, this explosive concept which finally became revolution, modern idea and the principle of the decline of the entire social order—is Christian dynamite.

It is not at all for Nietzsche a question of opposing some sort of wisdom to Christian dynamite. The fight against Christianity is a fight amongst artillerymen, or amongst terrorists. In October 1888, Nietzsche writes to Overbeck:

> This time—as an old artilleryman—I bring out my heavy guns. I am afraid that I am blowing up the history of mankind into two halves.

Archi-politics is thus the discovery of a *non-Christian explosive*.

Now, it is at this juncture that Nietzsche will have to pay with his person, for it is clear that he will apply himself to the radical impasse of any archi-politics of this type. But he will apply himself the more deeply and the more sincerely because he has defined archi-politics not as a logic of foundation, but as the radicality of the act. Here everything rests on Nietzsche's conception of the archi-political event, of the event in which anti-philosophy breaks the history of the world in two.

At this point it must be said that this event does not succeed in distinguishing itself from its own announcement, from its own declaration. What is declared philosophically is such that the possibility of its declaration alone proves that the history of the world is broken in two. Why is this? Because the truth at work in the archi-political act is exactly what is prohibited, and prohibition is the Christian law of the world. To pass beyond this prohibition, as the declaration attests, is enough to make one believe in an absolute rupture.

> One day my philosophy will win, because until now no one has, in principle, prohibited anything but truth.
>
> (Ecce Homo)

But all of a sudden, since what Nietzsche declares is also the event itself, he is caught, ever more manifestly, in a circle. I pointed out, above, that Nietzsche says: "I prepare an event." But the declaration concerning the preparation of an event becomes progressively more indiscernible from the event itself, whence an oscillation characteristic of Nietzsche between imminence and distance. The declaration will shatter the world, but that it is going to shatter it is precisely what it declares:

> Foreseeing that I will shortly have to address to humanity the gravest challenge that it has yet to receive, it seemed to me indispensable to say who I am.
>
> (Ecce Homo)

This book belongs to the very few. Perhaps none of them is even living yet.

(The Antichrist)

On one side, the radical imminence that constrains me, as the only living proof, to declare who I am. On the other, a stance that leaves in suspense the question of knowing whether a witness of this act has been born yet or not. I think that this circle is the circle of any archi-politics whatsoever. Since it does not have the event as its condition, since it grasps it—or claims to grasp it—in the act of thought itself, it cannot discriminate between its reality and its announcement. The very figure of Zarathustra names this circle and gives the book its tone of strange undecidability with regard to the question of knowing whether Zarathustra is a figure of the efficacy of the act or of its prophecy pure and simple. The central episode in this respect is the song entitled "On Great Events." This song is a dialog between Zarathustra and the fire-dog. But who is the fire-dog? Rapidly, it becomes clear that the fire-dog is nothing but the spokesperson, the agent, or the actor of the revolutionary political event itself, of revolt, of the collective storm. Let us read a passage of the dialog with the fire-dog. Zarathustra speaks:

"Freedom," you all most like to bellow: but I have unlearned belief in "great events" whenever there is much bellowing and smoke about them. And believe me, friend Infernal-racket! The greatest events—they are not our noisiest but our stillest hours. The world revolves, not around the inventors of new noises, but around the inventors of new values; it revolves inaudibly. And just confess! Little was ever found to have happened when your noise and smoke dispersed. What did it matter that a town had been mummified and that a statue lay in the mud!

The opposition here is between din and silence. The din is what attests externally for the political event. The silence, the world pregnant with silence, is instead the name of the unattested and unproved character of the archi-political event. The archi-political declaration misses its real because the real of a declaration, of *any* declaration, is precisely the event itself. Thus it is at the very point of this real, which he lacks and whose presence and announcement he cannot separate, that Nietzsche will have to make himself present. And it is this that will be called his madness. Nietzsche's madness consists in this, that he must come to think of himself as the creator of the same world in which he makes his silent declaration, and in which nothing proves the existence of a break in two. That in some way he is on both sides; that he is the name, not only of what announces the event, not only the name of the rupture, but ultimately the name of the world itself.

January 4, 1889, Nietzsche situates himself as "Nietzsche," as a name:

> After [and this after is necessary] it has been averred as irrevocable that I have properly speaking created the world.

A sincere archi-politics madly unfolds the *phantasm of the world*, because it is the process of the undecidability between prophecy and the real. It mimics, in folly, the intrinsic undecidability of the event itself; it is this undecidability turning upon itself in the figure of a subject. Whence this harrowing declaration from the last letter, the letter to Jakob Burckhardt of January 6, 1889, after which there is nothing more:

> Actually, I would much rather be a Basel professor than God; but I have not ventured to carry my private egotism so far as to omit creating the world on his account.

Yes indeed, this statement is a statement of madness, but of madness coming at the real point of a lack, when the announcement fails. This ordeal takes place in three stages: the ambition of radical rupture, of archi-politics, is indeed that of creating a world, of creating the *other* world, the world of affirmation, the world which in fact is no longer the world, or the man that is no longer man, and whose name is "overman." But to create this world, the everyman must also be seized by its creation. Only this everyman can *certify* the appearance of the overman. And what would have been preferred, or preferable, is that the professor, in Basel, be seized as such and traversed by this unattested event. But since this is not the case, since this legitimate preference is not verified, the anti-philosophical hero is forced to declare that he *will* create this world. That he will create it, and not that he has been seized by its triumphal appearance. This world is thus a program, but one that antecedes itself. And so one is a captive of the circle. And in the end to break this circle one needs the disinterested fiction of an integral creation, not only of a new world, but of the old world as well.

At this point, nothing but madness.

Upon what does archi-politics itself come to break? Upon the unavoidable necessity of politics. Of politics, which demands patience. Which knows that it is pointless to announce the event. That one must think and act with chance, and in circumstances that one does not choose. Of a politics which has had to renounce the idea of breaking the history of the world in two. A politics that is content—which is already a lot, and very difficult—with being faithful to a few new possibilities.

Equally, anti-philosophy comes to break upon the permanence, upon the resistance, of philosophy. Philosophy, which knows that its act, as an act of truth, does not have the power of abolishing the values of the world. And that the labor of the negative may not be dissolved in the great Dionysian affirmation.

Is this to say that Nietzsche's force, his sincerity, his sacrifice, are of no use? That the idea of an archi-politics is a vain folly? I do not think so. For there is in Nietzsche an extremely precious indication, an indication concerning a decisive question for any philosophy whatsoever, the question of the relationship between sense and truth. On this question of sense and truth there are, I think, three primordial stances. First, there is the stance that holds the idea of a rigorous continuity between truth and sense. I call this stance religion. There is a stance that unilaterally establishes the supremacy of sense and attempts to destroy the religious stance. This is Nietzsche's struggle. And finally there is the philosophical stance. It is in rupture with anti-philosophy because it both retains and develops, by means of a rational critique, the idea of truth. But it is also in rupture with religion, because it refuses to identify truth with sense; it even willingly declares that in any truth there is always something of the nonsensical.

But what happens historically is that the second stance, the anti-philosophical stance, is almost always what points the third stance, the philosophical stance, toward its own modernity. Anti-philosophy puts philosophy on guard. It shows it the ruses of sense and the dogmatic danger of truth. It teaches it that the rupture with religion is never definitive. That one must take up the task again. That truth must, once again and always, be secularized.

Nietzsche was right to think that his primordial task could be named the Antichrist. He was right to call himself the Antichrist. And in his role as radical anti-philosopher he pointed philosophy to the very place of its modern task. From Nietzsche, we need to retain what he designated as the task of philosophy: to re-establish the question of truth in its rupture with sense. Nietzsche puts us on guard against hermeneutics.

Therefore, I believe that Nietzsche is someone that one must at once discover, find, and lose. One must discover him in his truth, discover him in the desire of the act. One must find him, as he who provokes the theme of truth toward a new demand, as he who forces the philosophical stance to invent a new figure of truth, a new rupture with sense. And finally, of course, one must lose him, because anti-philosophy must, when all is said and done, be lost, or lost sight of, once philosophy has established its own space.

This discovery, this find, this loss: I often feel them with regard to all of the century's great anti-philosophers; with Nietzsche, with Wittgenstein, and with Lacan. I think that all three—but Nietzsche's case is without doubt the most dramatic—in the last instance sacrificed themselves for philosophy. There is in anti-philosophy a movement of putting itself to death, or of silencing itself, so that something imperative may be bequeathed to philosophy. Anti-philosophy is always what, at its very extremes, states the new duty of philosophy, or its new possibility in the figure of a new duty. I think of Nietzsche's madness, of Wittgenstein's strange labyrinth, of Lacan's final muteness. In all three cases anti-philosophy takes the form of a legacy. It bequeathes something beyond itself to the very thing that it is fighting against. Philosophy is always the heir to anti-philosophy.

This is why I am so touched, in one of the last notes to Brandes, by this very Pascalian phrase of Nietzsche, which immediately speaks to me of this singular and intricate relationship to the great anti-philosophers of the century.

> Once you discovered me, it was no great feat to find me: the difficulty is now to lose me.

And it is true that the great difficulty for us all, that which demands of us a creation, is not to discover and to understand Nietzsche. The difficulty is to know, philosophically, how to lose him.

Translated by Alberto Toscano

11

Is Pleasure a Rotten Idea?
Deleuze and Lacan on Pleasure and Jouissance

Aaron Schuster

> Pleasure is the only thing worth having a theory about
>
> —Lord Henry, *The Picture of Dorian Gray*

In his seminar of March 26, 1973 Deleuze claims that pleasure is a "rotten idea," a notion totally spoiled by the Platonic-Schopenhauerian tradition with its negative ontology of lack.[1] "I can scarcely tolerate the word pleasure," Deleuze writes in a collection of notes dedicated to Foucault.[2] Better simply to cede the word to the enemy, and begin thinking with a different one: namely, desire. Desire, Deleuze tells us, lacks nothing and is tormented by no vain aspiration or melancholy impasse; it is experimentation, creative power, the movement of multiple flows and becomings. The central problem of desire is not one of impossible fulfilment, but the dis-organization and breakdown of already sedimented patterns and connections (life is a process of breaking down, as Deleuze liked to quote F. Scott Fitzgerald). What is rejected here is the age-old theme of transgression—think of the litany of crimes attributed to eros "the tyrant" in the *Republic*—in favor of an immanent conception of desire with no aim outside its own active deployment and renewal. Desire is constructive, not transgressive; an affirmative force, not a reaction to pain and loss; a vagabond movement, not the striving to reach some goal (whether attainable or not).

This idea of "desire without lack" is central to the criticism of psychoanalysis that Deleuze developed with Félix Guattari in the 1970s and '80s. According to Deleuze, whether it is Freud's pleasure principle demanding the extinction of drive tensions or Lacan's jouissance that is barred for the speaking being, psychoanalysis remains stuck in a Platonic framework. It misses the "joy immanent to desire"[3] best theorized by that dissident tradition in philosophy including Spinoza, Nietzsche, and Bergson. To reconceive psychoanalysis on the basis of this tradition, and thus to replace its "rotten" foundations, is one of the primary aims of the new discipline Deleuze and Guattari dub schizoanalysis.

The purpose of this paper is to offer a critical perspective on this familiar polemic. In doing so, I will not pretend to offer a global account of the relationship between Deleuze's thought and psychoanalysis, a subject that, despite growing interest and the recent appearance of some significant scholarly commentaries, still remains far from being properly understood.[4] Instead I will focus on one key aspect of this relationship: Deleuze and Guattari's concept of desire, or "desiring machines," as a challenge to (*and* reformulation of) the psychoanalytic notions of drive and desire, pleasure and enjoyment (jouissance).

A few general remarks at the outset. The rhetorical force of Deleuze and Guattari's criticism turns on the equation of lack and negativity with impotence, pessimism, sadness, "bad conscience," and so forth. Lack and negativity, along with the prohibiting (castrating) power of the Law, are, so they repeat, maledictions wrought on desire by a guilt-ridden crypto-Christian theoretical edifice. Now, it is not difficult to imagine the flipside of this argument. Why not view lack as something "good" and plenitude, positivity, chaotic multiplicity, etc. as the real terror? This is precisely what Lacan does when he stands on its head the received wisdom regarding the pre-oedipal period: what traumatizes the child is not the loss of the mother, her absence, but rather her over-proximity. Instead of starting with the supposition that the subject is afflicted by some kind of deficiency, Lacan argues that it is originally caught in the grip of an overwhelming and suffocating presence (*la jouissance de l'Autre*). Lack signifies in the first place "breathing room," the installation of symbolic boundaries which separate the subject and the Other, and thus create space for desire—to effect this separation is the primary role of the father in Lacan's refashioned Oedipus complex. Conversely, when the object of desire comes too close, when the "lack lacks," the subject's borders threaten to dissolve and it is flooded with anxiety.[5] This is, ironically, exactly the charge laid by the analyst Serge Leclaire against *Anti-Oedipus*: "The book puts your more perceptive readers in the situation of a single and unique perspective that leaves them feeling absorbed, digested, bound, even negated by the admirable workings of your so-called machine! [...] It seems to put the reader in the situation of feeling cornered, by the simple fact of speaking and asking a question."[6] Swallowed up by the (maternal?) anti-Oedipal machine? One will object that this remark is rather facile, and that Deleuze and Guattari's desiring machines, far from being totalizing, explicitly include breakdowns and malfunctions, gaps and misfires. However, these are all "positive" failures, part of the larger workings of the apparatus. For Leclaire what is missing is the shattering power of negativity as opening up a space for the subject.

That is not to say that Deleuze and Guattari's critique is unfounded. There does seem to be a more or less straight line leading from Hegel's "unhappy consciousness" to Sartre's "man is a useless passion" to Lacan's "jouissance is forbidden to whomever speaks as such" (the influence of Hegel here is arguably more indebted to Jean Wahl than Alexandre Kojève). Commentators often define jouissance as a fantasy of "total enjoyment," an impossibly delightful, unreachable fulfilment which haunts our actual pleasures. The end of analysis is consequently conceived as working through this fantasy, so that the analysand is able "to secure a bit more satisfaction from the little pleasures of quotidian existence, once these pleasures are not completely overshadowed by the unattainable standards of a nonexistent enjoyment."[7] Deleuze's criticism of psychoanalysis as calling for an "infinite resignation" here seems apropos.[8] But it is by no means certain that, for Freud and Lacan, we are pushed forward in fruitless strivings by the inadequacy of our pleasures or the bounty promised by our dreams.[9] While Lacan's thesis that jouissance is *partial* is typically understood as meaning that it is only ever a meager part of an ideal—lost, forbidden, unattainable—Whole, it also designates something quite different: a volatile excess that drives and is driven beyond itself. To use one of Lacan's neologisms, enjoyment ex-ists, it is a tension and not a state, ideal or otherwise. Jouissance is not lacking but too much, a dangerous surplus that has to be somehow managed, domesticated, or artfully dealt with.

A (very) brief history of pleasure

If Deleuze makes the philosophical decision to consign the word *pleasure* to the dustbin of worthless, uncreative concepts (the name of a "false problem"), this may be seen as part and parcel of his emphatic anti-Platonism. It was Plato, after all, who defined *hēdonē* as a process of filling a lack (*plerosis*), and Socrates who proclaimed that desire wants what it does not have. For Deleuze, this Platonic scheme casts a dark shadow over the history of the concept: "Western philosophy has always consisted of saying [...] desire is desire for what one does not have; that begins with Plato, it continues with Lacan."[10] As Deleuze specifies, this scheme consists of three essential moments: (1) Lack gives rise to desire, which opens onto a "field of transcendence" as the striving for some satisfying object; (2) what desire ultimately aims at is something unreachable, a purely transcendent, absolute Otherness, hence; (3) any satisfaction it does attain can only be ephemeral, an illusion of fulfilment, a passing relief.[11] Pleasure is thus accorded a very low level of reality—it is essentially relief from distress—and is even deemed by Plato to be "ontologically false," a kind of swindle or unkept promise. What really drives life is pain, the pain that sets desire into motion and the pain of desiring. In modern times, the most famous proponents of this tragic view are Schopenhauer, Freud (more on him later), and Sartre, but one of Deleuze's favorite authors, William Burroughs, also proves perfectly Platonic on this score: "I experienced the agonizing deprivation of junk sickness, and the pleasure of relief when junk-thirsty cells drank from the needle. Perhaps all pleasure is relief."[12]

Historically speaking, the first systematic critique of this theory of pleasure-desire is found in Aristotle's *Nichomachean Ethics*. Contra Deleuze one could argue that Western philosophy has always been split between two paradigms of pleasure, the Platonic and the Aristotelian, and that the tradition's reflections on pleasure have consisted mostly in an elaboration and/or combination of these opposing views.[13] Put briefly: Aristotle criticizes the negative definition for failing to do justice to the richness of the phenomenon, leaving incomprehensible the intimate connection between pleasure and "our human nature."[14] Instead of defining pleasure in terms of a restorative process (filling a lack, remedying a deficiency, the return to equilibrium), Aristotle makes it a supplementary perfection of being. Pleasure is what completes the unimpeded exercise of a faculty; it supervenes like the "bloom in those who are vigorous"[15] upon the free performance of an activity; it is bound up with the living being's self-actualization. Far from being a mere escape from suffering, pleasure is a heightened state of health and vitality: it is pure as such, neither mixed with nor conditioned by pain. What sets life into motion is not the desire to overcome a lack, but rather a manifold of activities—*energeiai*, positive "energies"—that enjoy being active and expanding the scope of their power.

Oddly enough, Deleuze's own position might be closer to Plato's than that of Aristotle, at least according to the subversive reading of Plato proposed in *The Logic of Sense*. There Deleuze undertakes a reversal of Platonism via a reinterpretation of Plato's notion of becoming. To recount the main points: for Plato becoming is a category subordinate to being, in accordance with the logic "shipbuilding goes on for the sake of ships": a process of becoming terminates with the completion of the goal for the sake of which it was undertaken.[16] Such is the metaphysical scheme in which Plato situates pleasure: pleasure is essentially a transition from lack to fulfilment, and once the filling is complete pleasure is over too. However, Plato also delineates a realm of "pure becoming" consisting of movements without end or limit (*apeiron*). This is a domain of chaos and disorder—the "bad infinite"—which cannot be conceived without falling into contradiction. Something that grows absolutely larger, for example, without fixed measures to gauge the movement, also grows simultaneously smaller. The flow of time is in a way short-circuited: "[A]t the same moment [...] one becomes larger than one was and smaller than one becomes. This is the simultaneity of a becoming whose characteristic is to elude the present."[17] "Now" Alice is bigger than she was before, but already she is tinier with respect to her infinite growth. This pulling in two opposite directions at once is the paradox of pure becoming—the "mad" element that disrupts official Platonism. Now, although the idea is elaborated primarily in the *Philebus*, a dialog on pleasure and the good life, Deleuze never connects the paradox of pure becoming with the concept of pleasure. Plato himself, though, gives a simple example of it: scratching. As everyone knows, the more you scratch the more you have to scratch: itching is enjoyable, but it also exacerbates the underlying irritation making it necessary to scratch further.[18] Pleasures like this are marked by an inner tension (*suntasis*).[19] In extreme cases (Socrates is speaking in a veiled way about sex), "it finally drives the person totally out of his mind, so that he shouts aloud like a madman."[20] Here Plato comes very close to Nietzsche's thesis that "all pleasure includes pain—if pleasure is to be very great, the pains must be very protracted and the tension of the bow tremendous."[21] However, there is one crucial difference: while pleasure-in-becoming remains for Plato a mere pseudo-pleasure, impure, inherently thwarted, Nietzsche argues that pleasure's excess over itself *is* its very "positive" nature. The admixture of pain which according to Plato ruins pleasure, is what from a Nietzschean perspective constitutes its real force or explosive dynamism.[22] In this sense, the categories of lack and surplus are not simple opposites, but in dialectical tension: the poverty of a lack that can never be filled *converts* with the richness of a force that always wills more. In both cases one is dealing with a boundless, infinite movement, an existential restlessness, though viewed from incompossible perspectives.

If Deleuze turns out to be close to a certain Plato, one can also observe an unexpected affinity between Lacan and Aristotle. While Deleuze places Lacan in a Platonic lineage, it is actually Aristotle that serves as

Lacan's primary reference in his conceptualization of jouissance. This may be surprising given Lacan's insistence on lack—the subject, he repeats, is coextensive with a *manque-à-être*—and the transcendence of the object of desire. Nevertheless, in the crucial seminars VII and XX Aristotle is given the feature role, and already in his 1956 address "Freud and the Century" Lacan remarked that he had been "reading an old text by Aristotle, the *Nichomachean Ethics*, with the intention of redis-covering the origin of Freudian themes on pleasure in it."[23] Why this choice? First, *negatively*, the reference to Aristotelian ethics allows Lacan to sharply demarcate the psychoanalytic conception of the human being and its modernity. For Aristotle, proper education, following the paths laid down by nature, can lead to self-realization and happiness; in contrast, in the Freudian universe nature is no longer a reliable guide for action: the human being is "polymorphous perverse," not spontane-ously oriented by its own good or that of the others. As opposed to an ethics of self-perfectioning Freud theorizes the discontent in the human condition. Second, *positively*, Lacan focuses on Aristotle because he is the first philosopher to put pleasure at the center of the philosophy of being. What interests Lacan is the great ontological dignity accorded to pleasure as the "bloom" or "radiance" of fully realized being, the "energy" driving the cosmos. In his late work Lacan similarly speaks of a "jouissance of being" and jouissance as the "sole substance admit-ted by psychoanalysis."[24] However, this all-pervading enjoyment is no longer Aristotle's pure pleasure, but closer to what Freud called "primary masochism."

Does Freud have a positive conception of pleasure?

A quick glance through Freud's work suffices to confirm Deleuze's basic point: Freud does indeed, over and over again, define pleasure in a negative way, as the discharge or extinction of psychical tension. As Lacan once ironically observed, the pleasure principle is in fact "the principle [...] that pleasure should cease."[25] At the beginning of his career Freud dubbed it the "unpleasure principle" and this is the more accurate term: what lies at the base of human existence is not a positive enjoyment or gratification but the flight from unpleasure (it is for this reason that it is incorrect to label Freud's theory hedonistic). From the start, however, the "unpleasure principle" is beset by a certain ambigu-ity. Is the psyche's fundamental aim to maintain itself at a relatively low level of tension (principle of constancy) or does it wish to rid itself of tension altogether (principle of neuronal inertia)? While the first describes the functioning of a homeostatic system, the second is obviously more uncanny. It would seem to imply if not outright physical death, then a kind of mental death, a monotonous "dead life" wherein psychic processes have been largely dulled and emptied out. Again, to cite William Burroughs: "If all pleasure is relief from tension, junk affords relief from the whole life process [...] junk suspends the whole cycle of tension, discharge and rest. [...] Boredom, which always indicates an undischarged tension, never troubles the addict. He can look at his shoe for eight hours."[26] But if the psyche naturally aims at such a navel-gazing, tensionless "Nirvana," how then to account for the fact of mental activity at all? Is the psyche only moved by the desire to purge itself of all desires?

Deleuze has nothing but contempt for this doctrine that makes "desire to be a dirty little thing [...] that wakes us up in a most disagreeable manner."[27] Indeed, his critique of Freud's negative conception of pleasure is shared by many. It is even one of the oldest criticisms directed against psychoanalysis. As the psychologist Karl Bühler argued early on: "The old and venerable formula [linking pleasure with tension reduction] does not contain the whole truth about the relation between the pleasure principle and activity."[28] "Beyond the pleasure principle," he asserts, lies the most elementary sense of pleasure, evident to anyone who has ever seen a child frolicking, but which somehow eluded Freud. Namely, the pleasure that belongs to play and rhythmic activity. Instead of being solely regulated by the need to discharge tension, psychic life is in the first place sustained by what Bühler calls *Funktionslust* (functional pleasure), the joy that springs from "life with its changes and movements of vital processes."[29] Now the obvious question is: what prevented Freud from realizing this? Why did he stubbornly cling to such a narrow and phenomenologically dubious definition of pleasure? The answer becomes clearer if one takes into account the role "functional pleasure" later played in revisionist psychoanalysis. The call for a positive concept of pleasure, tied to the flourishing of psychic life, has largely served a normalizing function in psychoanalytic theory, promoting the idea of a conflict-free, healthy development.[30] Against this rosy picture of the "joy of life" Freud insisted on the hard reality of pain, need, and dissatisfaction. And while Deleuze and Guattari's notion of positive desire hardly intends such a normalization (quite the contrary), their argumentation occasionally appeals to the same kind of phenomenological common sense. "The satisfaction the handyman experiences when he plugs something into an electric socket or diverts a stream of water can scarcely be explained in terms of 'playing mommy and daddy', or by the pleasure of violating a taboo."[31] It's simply the pleasure of tinkering, without ulterior motive.

A closer reading of Freud's work reveals that, in spite of his consistent identification of pleasure with tension reduction, his views on pleasure are much more nuanced and varied than the standard account allows. Without going into a detailed examination here, suffice it to mention that Freud does know that there is pleasure inherent to activity, though he relegates it to secondary importance;[32] that he describes infantile sexuality in terms of an organ-pleasure irreducible to the satisfaction of needs; and that he explains adult sexuality according to the split between *Vorlust*, the pleasure that accompanies sexual excitation, and *Endlust*, orgastic release. Already in *The Three Essays on the Theory of Sexuality* Freud struggles with the contradiction in his economic theory of the libido that some tensions are patently enjoyable. His provisional solution is to argue that excitation can be a source of pleasure as long as it is part of a larger movement that leads to eventual discharge. However, by the time of "The Economic Problem of Masochism" this answer no longer holds and the conceptual impasse threatens to explode his entire economic scheme. This essay marks a crucial turning point in Freud's metapsychology. In his earlier work, the pleasure principle constituted the primary threat to psychic integrity, through a catastrophic reduction of tension. In the new scheme, the pleasure principle now has a *protective* function, militating against its dangerous build-up. What has changed in the interim is the *absolutization of Vorlust*: no longer subordinated to or aimed at end-pleasure, it seeks only its own intensification. This is what Freud calls primary or erotogenic masochism.

Benno Rosenberg has forwarded a very interesting interpretation of Freud's theory of primary masochism, linking it to the fusion and defusion of the life and death drives.[33] The crux of his argument is that primary masochism is a Janus-faced phenomenon. On the one hand, the eroticization of tensions serves as a defense against their massive expulsion: to live means to find pleasure in the drives that move one from within and to maintain a certain level of libidinal energy. Yet this pleasure cannot be assumed as a natural given: the drives first manifest themselves as a menace to the psyche, which must be more or less contained and defused if mental processes are to develop. If this minimum of psychic integration is not effected, the drives becomes pure harbingers of death, seeking total discharge.[34] In this sense, masochism is the very "guardian of life." On the other hand, the protective dimension of masochism comports a new danger, that of the unrestrained intensification of the drives: this is a masochism that is *too* successful, engendering a potentially harmful surplus of pleasure; in Rosenberg's terminology, a "mortifying masochism." The psyche is thus precariously balanced between two equally unhappy alternatives: the catastrophic elimination of psychic tension (expulsion of the drives, the dismantling or unbinding of the psychic apparatus) and its self-destructive exacerbation.

The masochistic paradigm

The uniqueness and radicality of Freudian psychoanalysis can be summarized in terms of the way its upsets the classic psychiatric scheme of normality and pathology.[35] According to Freud, there is no bright line separating the "healthy" and the "sick," only gradual variations along a continuum; instead of psychopathology being an accidental deviation from the norm of mental health, it is normality that is a domesticated form of madness. A corollary to this is the so-called crystal principle: in the same way that crystals break and cleave along pre-established yet invisible fault lines, so too does man "break" according to fractures which secretly traverse his existence.[36] The study of mental illness thus provides the key to understanding the structures of human existence in general. Or in the words of Henri Michaux: "More than the all too excellent mental skills of the metaphysicians, it is the dementias, the backwardnesses, the deliriums, the ecstasies and agonies, the breakdowns in mental skills which are really suited to 'reveal' us to ourselves."[37]

We may therefore ask: What can the study of psychopathology teach us about the nature of enjoyment? This question lies at the crossing of the "critical and the clinical," the philosophical tradition's reflections on drive and desire and the clinical investigation of mental illness. During roughly the same time period, Deleuze and Lacan address this question through two very different optics. Deleuze privileges perversion, in particular masochism, as the key to understanding desire, whereas Lacan makes hysteria the centerpiece of his theory of jouissance in relation to social discourse.

Apart from schizophrenia (which we will examine below), Deleuze illustrates his positive notion of desire via three main examples: the "non-orgasmic" sexuality of ancient China (Robert Van Gulik's *Sexual Life in Ancient China*, just translated into French at the time, serves as the major reference), courtly love (recall Nietzsche's high estimation of the "gay science" of the troubadours), and (especially) masochism. Although Deleuze and Guattari sometimes profess allegiance to the libidino-revolutionary theories of Wilhelm Reich, their approach to desire is the absolute inverse of Reichian orgasmotherapy: orgasm

(*Endlust*) is to be avoided at all costs, in favor of the "joy immanent to desire" (radicalized *Vorlust*).[38]

Sexual life in ancient China

"There's a book from which one can learn many things, entitled *Sexual Life in Ancient China*."[39] What interests Deleuze in Van Gulik's classic study are the various techniques of *coitus reservatus* by which the man retains his semen and draws the feminine essence *Yin* into himself. As he puts it, if the "Western problem" is "how to extract sexuality from genitality," that of the Chinese is "how to extract sexuality from the orgasm."[40] Taoist sexuality is praised as a self-contained, uninterrupted process: the Chinese sexual manuals prescribe a "field of immanence of desire traversed by flows."[41]

The analysis of Chinese sexuality furnishes an excellent illustration of one of Deleuze's fundamental points, that desire is not "a natural or spontaneous reality" but is "always assembled and fabricated."[42] This argument distances Deleuze from the proponents of *Funktionslust*: it does not belong to spontaneous nature of desire to be active, self-affirming, and so on, rather this positive dimension must be engendered, constructed, and cultivated by a specific practice. Indeed, the only thing natural to desire is the stupid, rotten—one is tempted to say brute biological—"fact" that it must end: the stomach is filled, the penis ejaculates, desire is quelled and exhausted. The moral tone of Deleuze's argumentation should not be overlooked. Pleasure or orgasm as the interruption of a process is, as he writes, "completely deplorable!"[43] Desire is constructed precisely as a victory over this vulgar nature.

It is worthwhile mentioning another aspect of Chinese eroticism, also noted by Van Gulik, which may be more relevant to our supposedly "hedonistic" times where enjoyment is less a risky transgression than a positive injunction. Namely, the role of the courtesans. Instead of providing a readily accessible means for sexual gratification, high-class prostitution was a refined way for aristocrats to *escape* from the incessant pressures of courtly sexual life.[44] Polygamy and the strict regimentation of conjugal life had the effect of making physical pleasure into a burdensome obligation. In these circumstances, paid consorts offered respite from the nobleman's conjugal duties, the possibility of spontaneous female companionship outside the confines of the normal voluptuous regime. Here the idealized version of Oriental sexual wisdom runs up against the reality of sexual commerce at the court. This search for refuge from the pressures of sex might well be seen as the underside of Deleuze's celebration of Chinese eroticism as purely flowing energies, the eternal embrace of Yin and Yang, unconstrained by Western categories of lack, castration and the law.

Courtly love

"This makes it clear without further ado why love *as passion*—it is our European specialty—absolutely must be of aristocratic origin: it was, as is well known, invented by the poet-knights of Provence, those splendid, inventive men of the *'gai saber'* to whom Europe owes so much and, indeed, almost itself."[45] For Nietzsche, courtly love is the expression par excellence of the aristocratic mode of valuation that knows how to esteem service and submission, as opposed to the gregarious will to universal equality, and that delights in a "useless passion" against any idea of the good. "The noble human being," he writes, "enjoys practicing severity and harshness upon himself and feels reverence for all that is severe and harsh."[46] And who could be a more cruel and exacting master than the Lady sung by the troubadours, "La belle dame sans merci?" Deleuze's reading of courtly love focuses on dispelling what he deems a fatal misinterpretation. Courtly love has nothing to do with the supposedly unattainable object of desire. The imposed tests and ordeals that postpone desire's consummation are "not a method of deprivation" but "the constitution of a field of immanence."[47] "Ascesis," Deleuze states perfectly in line with Nietzsche, "has always been the condition of desire, not its disciplining or prohibition."[48] The asceticism of courtly love, its severity and harshness, are means for provoking and intensifying desire as such—or as Walter Benjamin put it, "What is it that courtly *Minne* seeks [...] if not to make chastity, too, a transport?"[49] Crucial here is the distinction Deleuze proposes between void and lack: "The plane of consistence or of immanence, the body without organs, includes voids and deserts. But these are 'fully' part of desire, far from accentuating some kind of lack in it. What a strange confusion—that of void with lack."[50] If lack refers to the transcendence of something missing, the void works rather as a kind of internal creative principle: not an absent or ungraspable thing, but like a bend in space around which desires turns. Far from being a ballad of eternal frustration, desire is positively "assembled" and "machined" in and through the figure of the sovereign Lady.

On this point Deleuze's interpretation of courtly love dovetails with that of Lacan, who also underlines that the techniques of courtly love "belong to the sphere of foreplay," the paradox of Freudian *Vorlust* which "persists in opposition to the purposes of the pleasure principle."[51] Moreover, Deleuze's distinction between void and lack echoes

Lacan's own remarks to the effect that there are "detours and obstacles which are organized so as to make the domain of vacuole stand out as such."[52] Indeed, Lacan's "lack" can easily be read as Deleuzian void, positively productive of desire (think of the *objet a* as *cause* of desire). Nevertheless, Lacan insists that courtly love be understood from the perspective of the signifier, as a symbolic practice. What difference does this make? First, Lacan argues that courtly love is not—unlike Eastern erotic practices—a "lived substance." It is rather a poetry, a fiction, a pure artifice composed and recited by court players who were, in the meanwhile, busy with their little affairs with village girls and so on (for example, the first known troubadour, Guilhem IX of Aquitaine, was in fact a Don Juan-like womanizer, even while preaching fidelity in his poetry to the one and only Lady).[53] Second, if this poetic practice constitutes in Lacan's eyes a "paradigm" of sublimation, this is not only due to its cultivation and stylization of desire, but because in its hyperbolic elevation of the Lady something of desire's traumatic core shines forth: in the symbolic fiction the Lady is emptied of personal qualities and becomes an "inhuman partner," a hollowed out place—the void—around which the libidinal economy turns. What is exemplary about courtly love is the way it makes space in culture for the aesthetic disclosure of something inadmissible, traumatic, repressed. What it offers is not an ecstatic elegy to the flows of desire but a sideways ("anamorphotic") glance at the void from a safe distance.

Masochism

Masochism takes its name from the Austrian writer Leopold von Sacher-Masoch. Freud uses the term to designate three distinct phenomena: (1) pleasure-in-excitation (primary or erotogenic masochism); (2) the unconscious satisfaction provided by guilt feelings and self-punishment (moral masochism); (3) the sexual perversion in which pleasure is contingent upon pain and humiliation inflicted by another (what Freud calls feminine masochism). It is this last which occupies Deleuze, who develops an original theory of masochism by returning to its literary source. Sacher-Masoch was the author of a considerable body of fiction, including the grandly conceived series *The Legacy of Cain* which was meant to set forth his view of human history. This work is a veritable theodicy in which the murder committed by Cain and Christ's sacrifice are put back-to-back, the first as the entrance of sin into the world (Cain's six-fold legacy to humanity is love, property, the state, war, work, and death—causes of man's suffering), the second as act of redemption. Echoes of Schopenhauer's philosophy of renunciation are to be found throughout. In Sacher-Masoch's vision woman figures as the instrument of man's salvation, precisely through her cruelty: masochism continues the exaltation of "La belle dame sans merci" in a new modern context. One of Sacher-Masoch's last novels, *The Mother of God*, provides a particularly clear insight into this religious-erotic universe—Deleuze ranks it among his finest.[54] An Adamite sect is ruled by the beautiful Mardona, a woman filled with mercy and love, yet also cold and hateful. The young Sabadil is in love with her, and the story of their relationship is in essence a complicated retelling of the Passion. In the end Mardona asks him to consent to be tortured and nailed to the cross, yet in this Passion Play the Father is decidedly absent: it's the Mother who crucifies the Son, in order that he may be resurrected as her son alone, a parthenogenetic rebirth. As Deleuze states, "The final objective of Masoch's work expresses itself in the myth that embraces both Cain and Christ: Christ is not the son of God, but the new Man; his likeness to the Father is abolished, he is 'Man on the Cross, who knows no sexual love, so property, no fatherland, no cause, no work...'"[55] Put otherwise, what masochism aims at is a radical transcendence of human nature, the "construction and assemblage" of a new (asexual, deterritorialized) Man. This theological dimension, while not as present in his most famous novel *Venus in Furs*, forms the constant background of Sacher-Masoch's fiction.[56]

Deleuze isolates a number of specific features that define masochism, or rather the "masochistic style" insofar as he conceives the clinical entity as a distinctly aesthetic phenomenon. These include the humor of over-conformity, a dialectical sensibility (the female "master" is theatrically directed by the male "slave"), an artistic and mythological imagination, the psychical processes of fetishism, disavowal, and idealization, and the juridical form—the contract—that binds the partners. Above all what characterizes this style is *suspense*, an aesthetics of arrested gestures, threatened punishments, and delayed satisfaction. In masochism's ultimate dialectical reversal, the postponement of pleasure becomes the higher and more intense pleasure of postponement. Deleuze will continually emphasize this point: the core of masochism is "waiting or suspense as a plenitude, as a physical and spiritual intensity."[57] The drama of delay serves to break the link between desire and pleasure, and beyond that the order of genital sexuality, allowing the masochistic to attain a cool "supersensuality." Insofar as the father represents genital sexuality (orgastic pleasure, the interruption and death of desire) he is expelled from the masochistic universe, literally beaten out: "far from feeling that he has sinned against the father, it is the father's likeness in him that he experiences as a sin which must be atoned for."[58] In its aesthetic cultivation of desire, pervert masochism effectively rejoins masochism in the non-pervert sense of the immanent joy of desire, pleasure in tension without discharge. Despite the term being problematic, Deleuze's theory of masochism could well be viewed as a theory of sublimation, a positive transformation of the drives and a redemptive "rebirth" of the subject. As with his interpretation of *Bartleby*, another avatar of the non-patriarchal order, in this sublimation the anti-oedipal theme receives pride of place. What is said of Melville applies equally well to Masoch. "The dangers of a 'society without fathers' have often been pointed out, but the only real danger is the return of the father."[59]

Though Lacan praises Deleuze's book on masochism, calling it the best on the subject,[60] his own perspective on masochism cannot really be reconciled with it. What Lacan applauds is Deleuze's sharp deline-ation of masochism from sadism and his withering critique of that psychoanalytic chestnut "sadomasochism." However, for Lacan all per-version, masochism included, must be thought in terms of *defense*. The pervert's positive satisfaction is essentially duplicitous: what looks like unrestrained pleasure from the outside is in fact an ambivalent strategy for keeping a threatening jouissance at bay.[61] Rather than an overcom-ing of the paternal law, masochism constitutes a desperate attempt to shore up symbolic authority—the pervert masochist plays at the edge of a game where his appointed "master" is pushed to the point of laying down the law, putting a halt to the torments. Beyond making himself the tool of the Other's enjoyment, what the masochist ultimately (and unconsciously) seeks is the Other's anxiety.[62] This is obviously a very different clinical portrait than the one Deleuze paints. What interests Deleuze in literary masochism is the transformation in the *quality* of enjoyment, the construction of a plane of immanence that breaks with vulgar (genital) satisfaction. Lacan, in contrast, selects hysteria as the sole pathology worthy of being considered a "discourse," thereby focus-ing on the signifying elements which frame the subject's jouissance. If hysteria is a provocation that at the same time safeguards the master's (master signifier's) power, there is as it were a redemptive dimension to hysteria, if the hysteric's questioning can be radicalized to the point of passing through the "Other supposed to know," that is, realizing there a fundamental lack. It will come as no surprise to see Deleuze offering a strikingly different interpretation of hysteria. Hysteria, he explains, is a malady of the fragmented body whose vital forces seek to escape through one its organs, like the Burroughs character who strains to empty himself through his cock or the Bacon painting where the figure tries to slip through a syringe.[63] In this account there is no question or provocation addressed to the Other, but rather an anarchic redistribution of organs and intensities—that is, a decidedly schizophrenic take on the "hysterical reality of the body."[64]

The schizophrenic paradigm

From *Anti-Oedipus* onwards desire is thought according to the paradigm of schizophrenia, and Deleuze's earlier theory of masochism is subsequently recast in a more psychotic mode. Masochism is now seen as a sub-species of psychosis: "the masochist uses suffering as a way of constituting a body without organs and bringing forth a plane of consistency of desire."[65] Deleuze had argued previously that the pervert lives in a "world without others."[66] The case of *Equus eroticus* described in *A Thousand Plateaus* bears this out. The masochist does not imitate but becomes a horse: in the erotic scenario it is not a question of identification (mimesis) but the circulation and assemblage of de-subjectivized drive intensities (becomings). Nor are the mistress-rider's legs the disciplinary implements of a person. Or rather, "Legs are still organs, but the boots now only determine a zone of intensity as an imprint or zone on a BwO."[67]

However altered the theoretical landscape may be, in the move from the masochistic to the schizophrenic paradigm there is an underlying consistency. Just as Deleuze does not interpret masochism as a defensive structure (that is, an unconscious strategy for coping with and containing a threatening "enjoyment") but as a *positive* expression—a transformation or even liberation—of desire, so too is schizophrenic delirium understood as an intrinsically creative production. Indeed, the schizophrenic is the desiring being par excellence: it is schizophrenia, the most radical fracture of the psyche, that best reveals the chaotic machinations of desire. In this, Deleuze and Guattari follow a trend in post-Freudian research, comprised primarily by Melanie Klein, Wilfred Bion, and Jacques Lacan, that sought to refound psychoanalytic theory on the basis of psychosis rather than neurosis, Freud's own main field of study. It is no coincidence that these are the three principal analysts who embraced the controversial idea of a death drive operating "beyond the pleasure principle." Their experience with psychosis led them to posit a fundamental fault, gap, or rupture in psychic life, a trauma coextensive with the psyche's existence that must be dealt with (that is, defended against) in one way or another if mental processes are to be sustained and elaborated. Such is perhaps the simplest way to understand Lacan's difficult notion of *jouissance*: life must live from an energy that at the same time threatens to destroy it. Deleuze and Guattari, on the other hand, while affirming that madness pertains to the very heart of human existence and thus cannot be considered an accidental deviation, conceive of schizophrenia not so much in terms of trauma as extravagant vitality or exuberance. There is, as it were, a "good" madness, which expresses "the internal explosive force that life carries in itself."[68] If this folly takes a destructive turn, or put crudely: if the person can't handle the trip, this must be understood as an accidental circumstance, a poisoning caused by external relations, and not an intrinsic "death bound" tendency of the drives themselves. "Psychoanalysis ought to be a song of life, or else be worth nothing at all."[69]

The object without the Other?

From Deleuze and Guattari's own writings, as well as recent commentaries, it should be clear that there is no question of simply opposing psychoanalysis and schizoanalysis. If anything, Deleuze and Guattari see themselves as faithful *because* they are iconoclastic adherents to Lacan's program against the stale sloganeering of his disciples. "Lacan himself says 'I'm not getting much help'. We thought we'd give him some schizophrenic help." Deleuze continues: "And there's no question that we're all the more indebted to Lacan, once we've dropped notions like structure, the symbolic, or the signifier, which are so thoroughly misguided, and which Lacan himself has always managed to turn on their head to bring out their limitations."[70] *Anti-Oedipus* might well be viewed as a monstrous offspring of Lacanian psychoanalysis, in the sense that Deleuze conceived his philosophical enterprise as creative buggery, producing "children" of great thinkers that were misshapen and improbable, but nevertheless their own.[71] Jacques-Alain Miller has claimed that *Anti-Oedipus*, with its critique of naïve oedipalism and its humor-laden praise of madness, was indeed recognized by Lacan as a "delirious progeny."[72]

Broadly speaking, *Anti-Oedipus* engages Lacan in a double manner, vehemently rejecting the so-called orthodox aspects of his theory (the bad "Lacanism" of lack and the signifier), while elaborating what Deleuze and Guattari take to be his most original and productive concepts (notably, the *objet a*). "Lacan's admirable theory of desire appears to us to have two poles: one relation to 'the object small *a*' as a desiring-machine, which defines desire in terms of real production, thus going beyond any idea of need and any idea of fantasy; and the other related to the 'great Other' as a signifier, which reintroduces a certain notion of lack."[73] This brief statement sums up the essentials of Deleuze and Guattari's approach. Lacanian theory is effectively bifurcated: the imaginary and the symbolic (along with the concept of fantasy) are denigrated, even tossed overboard, and the real developed in a new (delirious) direction. For Deleuze and Guattari the real is the only "real" domain; the imaginary and symbolic are realms of illusion and alienation, falsifying the chaotic dynamics of real experience, that is, the machinic productions (couplings and un-couplings, syntheses and disjunctions) of the unconscious. "*Anti-Oedipus* was about the univocity of the real, a sort of Spinozism of the unconscious. [...] The people who hate '68, or say it was a mistake, see it as something symbolic or imaginary. But that's precisely what it wasn't, it was pure reality breaking through."[74] As they state unequivocally: "For the unconscious itself is no more structural then personal, it does not symbolize any more than it imagines or represents; it engineers, it is machinic. Neither imaginary not symbolic, it is the Real in itself, the 'impossible real' and its production."[75] Correcting Lacan on this last point, they explain that the real is the domain where "everything becomes possible" since it is a "sub-representative field": only in the symbolic is "the fusion of desire with the impossible is performed, with lack defined as castration."[76] This critique of the "theater" of representation in favor of the "factory" of the unconscious, this discourse on the mechanics of the real as it is "in itself" apart from its imbrication in other registers, the repeated qualification of the real as a "sub-representative field," a field of forces and intensities bereft of signification (where the question "how does it work?" replaces "what does it mean?")—all this points to, as Jacques Rancière has observed, a Schopenhauer-style metaphysics of the Will rumbling beneath the realm of Representation.[77] The (libidinal) object without the (signifying) Other—this could well serve as motto for Deleuze and Guattari's selective appropriation of Lacan: a theory of pre-personal intensities and desiring machines *in opposition to* the subject split by language, the order of signifiers (the Other) in which it finds its identity as barred, inconsistent, lacking. Such is the "reverse side of the structure" uncovered by *Anti-Oedipus*.[78]

There are two passages in particular in Lacan's oeuvre that may be marshalled in support of this approach, both from what is usually considered the middle period of his teaching. *First* is his characterization of the drive in Seminar XI as a montage of heterogeneous fragments, a kind of "surrealist collage": "If we bring together the paradoxes that we just defined at the level of *Drang*, at that of the object, at that of

222 Is Pleasure a Rotten Idea?

the aim of the drive, I think that the resulting image would show the workings of a dynamo connected up to a gas-tap, a peacock's feather emerges, and tickles the belly of a pretty woman, who is just lying there looking beautiful" (large portions of *Anti-Oedipus* might be read as an extended riff on this passage).[79] As Lacan elaborates in that seminar, the drive should be conceived as a headless (acephalous) circuit turning around a partial object, a "radical structure in which the subject is not yet placed."[80] *Second* is the distinction between drive and desire proposed in the *écrit* "On Freud's 'Trieb' and the Psychoanalyst's Desire": "[D]esire comes from the Other, and jouissance is located on the side of the Thing"; "the drive divides the subject and desire, the latter sustaining itself only by the relation it misrecognizes between this division and an object that causes it. Such is the structure of fantasy."[81] Though not maintained in his later work (or at least not in the same form), this distinction would appear to provide a relatively clearcut scheme for understanding the relationship between jouissance and subjectivity. On the one hand, enjoyment is linked to the Thing and its corporal representatives, the various *objets a*: this is the "immanent" domain of the drive, radically closed in on itself in an autoerotic loop. Desire, on the other, is bound up in an intersubjective dialectic whose very essence is interpretive openness: desire is desire of the "transcendent" Other, turning around the unfathomable question "what does the Other want?" These two levels meet in the fundamental fantasy, which provides a kind of (unconscious) answer to the enigma of the Other's desire by ciphering it in a bizarre bodily scenario—fantasy is the imaginary side of the partial objects, i (a). By doing so, however, it obscures what Deleuze and Guattari would call the real desiring production, so that the subject "misrecognizes" its non-fantasmatic real "cause." Much more important than the trumpeted critique of Oedipus and allegorical-style interpretation (truck = Daddy, etc.), *Anti-Oedipus* is, in Lacanian terms, a theory of the drive against desire (to avoid possible confusion: what Deleuze and Guattari call *desire* is referred to by Lacan as *drive*).

Deleuze and Guattari refer to Serge Leclaire's essay "La réalité du désir" as crucial to their understanding of Lacanian psychoanalysis and an important influence on their own theory of desiring machines. It is therefore instructive to review Leclaire's main line of argument. Taking up Freud's distinction between the plasticity and adhesiveness of the libido—in spite of the libido's incredible openness, it tends to get stuck on the same dumb satisfactions that repeat throughout a person's life— Leclaire describes a realm of "pure singularities," fixed elements that compose the final vocabulary of the subject's desire: the odor of a woman's neck, the modulation of an echoing voice that seems to say "You," the hint of acidity in baked apples, the fullness of the hand as it seizes a ball, a beauty mark.[82] He calls this collection of irreducible elements the "pure being of desire," a "fiction" of the unconscious in-itself without conscious or preconscious entanglements. This is the most primordial level of the psyche, the "reality of desire." We encounter it when, in the course of analysis, certain ideas or impressions no longer participate in the sphere of meaning, when a psychic content falls out of the play of connections, associations and substitutions that constitute meaningful discourse. Such elements insist in psychic life, they are stubborn, they do not budge, ("on bute indéfiniment sur le même ensemble de 'pures singularités'"), but one can no longer say why: they cannot be exchanged for other signifiers or explained or further analyzed. They are *basic* (molecular) terms. Though they have no relation to one another they form a definite ensemble; as Leclaire writes, they are "soldered" together precisely by their "absence of link."[83] They are nonsense but also pure sense, *meaningless* and at the same time *too meaningful*, in Freudian terms: too charged with affect to participate in the movement of representations, their intensity bends and warps the functioning of other mental processes, in Lacanian terms: both radical lack *and* surplus, *objets a*. Deleuze and Guattari enthusiastically approve "the rule of the right to nonsense as well as to the absence of link," repeating with Leclaire "you will not have reached the ultimate and irreducible terms of the unconscious so long as find or restore a link between two elements."[84] This point deserves to be underlined: although *Anti-Oedipus* can be read as a poetic elegy to the infinite plasticity of the libido, it is in fact what Freud called points of *fixation* (not flow!) that are at the heart of the desiring machines. Rather than pure chaos or flux, what interests Deleuze and Guattari are the ultimate and irreducible elements that fall outside the ever-shifting network of libidinal relations. They go on to ingeniously reinterpret Leclaire's "pure being of desire" in Spinozistic-Leibnizian terms, reading the "absence of link" that defines unconscious singularities in terms of the metaphysical concept of "real distinction": the ultimate desiring-elements are like the infinite attributes of God that are strictly independent of one another yet participate in a common divine substance. "Likewise for the partial objects and the body without organs: the body without organs is substance itself, and the partial objects, the ultimate attributes or elements of substance."[85] Spinozism of the unconscious: the body without organs refers to the abstract body-substance qua pure intensity, the partial objects comprise its specific elements (desiring machines), and both stand opposed to the "organism," that is, the organization of desire according to the (oedipal) dialect of subject and Other.[86] But this creative reinterpretation entails one crucial difference with the original. Whereas Leclaire carefully qualified his "pure being of desire" as a fiction, since one can never seize it directly but only through its belated effects on other mental processes, Deleuze and Guattari insist that it is the real itself.[87] Leclaire's "pure being of desire"—what we called, using a phrase of Richard Rorty's, the "final vocabulary" of desire—thus becomes "a pure dispersed and anarchic multiplicity, without unity or totality, and whose elements are welded, pasted together by the real distinction or the very absence of distinction."[88]

In what is certainly one of the most interesting critical responses to *Anti-Oedipus* from the psychoanalytic milieu, Leclaire himself contests this use of Lacan. What he considers most problematic in Deleuze and Guattari's theoretical edifice is precisely their conception of the *object*. How can the object be understood once it is cut off from imaginary and symbolic mediation? As Leclaire argues, *Anti-Oedipus* presents the real as ground and the imaginary and symbolic as superstructures (adopting, as we noted, a quasi-Schopenhauerian division between will and representation); yet in Lacan the *objet a* "belongs in a fourfold structure that includes the signifier, which is dual (S1 and S2), and the subject (crossed-out S)."[89] Is this a residual conservatism on Lacan's part, an indication that he didn't go far enough in his "auto-critique" of psychoanalysis? One thing is clear: in Lacanian theory one cannot divorce the object from the Other, the dynamism of the drives from the differential structure of language (indeed, our earlier interpretation of Lacan is misleading for this very reason). The partial object only derives its extraordinary intensity because of the role it plays in an intersubjective exchange, for example, the breast in relation to the mother's desire, shit as object of a gift economy, the gaze and voice as elusive snares circulating between the subject and the Other, the phallus as marker of sexual difference. The drives are mediated by a movement of demands and counter-demands.[90] Instead of directly plunging into the real, Lacan advances a logic of "extimacy": the object cannot be conceived outside an intersubjective relation, yet is never fully absorbed by that relation; it belongs to the universe of signifiers as something that exceeds it, an intimate exterior ("transcendence within immanence"). Daniel Smith has recently proposed a distinction between two ways of understanding the real: either as an internal limit to symbolization, a moment of rupture or negativity, or as the positive "inorganization" of partial objects, becomings, and desiring machines.[91] But this alternative is misleading.

What Lacan endeavored to think was how language *introduces* difference (a cut, fissure, lack) into the world, and how this symbolic difference *positively* affects and structures human drives and desire. It is the rupture created by the signifier that accounts for the extraordinary exuberance of the drives, the speaking being's polymorphous perversity—this is without a doubt Lacan's most important and original thesis.[92] The debate between Deleuze, Guattari, and Lacan might thus be characterized as that between, on the one hand, a direct ontological claim about the deepest strata of reality, and on the other, an attempt to derive the real (according to a retroactive temporality) through the intervention of negativity—in other words, a new version of Spinoza versus Hegel?[93]

Mental breakdown and the nature of the drives

The clearest account I know of *Anti-Oedipus* is provided by Deleuze himself in his seminar of May 27, 1980. In what follows I will examine a few key points in this critical self-assessment.[94]

At the beginning, Deleuze acknowledges one of the critiques of *Anti-Oedipus* to have touched him: the problem of the romanticization of madness. The celebration of schizophrenia as authentic existence or redemption from alienated social reality is something one can find in authors like R. D. Laing, David Cooper, and Norman Brown, but Deleuze was more nuanced with regard to this "praise of folly."[95] He opens the seminar with a review of different psychiatric and analytic approaches to schizophrenia. The personological perspective, in which schizophrenia is conceived as a degradation of the personality caused by accidental damage, is rejected as simply presuming the unity of the person. The structural approach, which he identifies with Lacan, is much closer to his own orientation, insofar as it consider madness not as an accidental deviation but an "essential event."[96] The third defines mental illness as a *process* and presents a generalized theory of psychosis where the neuroses are determined as "stopping points" on a "potential becoming-psychotic."[97] He links this approach with Karl Jaspers and the anti-psychiatry movement, adding that *Anti-Oedipus* develops it in a new way. A process, he explains, is a movement without a pre-existing trajectory, a voyage that finds its way as it goes along, a "line of flight" (*ligne de fuite*), according to the well-known term, though not in the sensing of escaping "to" somewhere but a kind of perpetual escape. It is "destructured," in flux, a positive flow not contained or defined by external parameters. Now, it would not be difficult to show that Deleuze's critique of structuralism here is based on a naïve equation of structure with static being, as if structure were fundamentally incompatible with "dynamic" situations or unable to account for change. However, I wish to focus on another problem. Deleuze later specifies that a "line of flight" is *normally* (I emphasize) a "line of life" (*ligne de vie*), an affirmative creative power, and yet it also contains within itself the danger of becoming a pure pathway of destruction (*ligne de mort*): "[L]e danger propre aux lignes de fuites, et il est fundamental, il est, c'est le plus terrible des dangers, c'est que la ligne de fuite tourne en ligne d'abolition, de destruction. Que la ligne de fuite qui normalement et en tant que processus est une ligne de vie et doit tracer comme de nouveaux chemins de la vie, tourne en pure ligne de mort."[98] This ambivalence is consistently underlined in Deleuze and Guattari's descriptions of madness. To cite a few passages: the schizophrenic process is "a kind of intrusion, the arrival of something for which there is no possible expression, something wonderful, so wonderful in fact [...] that it runs the risk of coinciding with collapse."[99] "We make a distinction between schizophrenia as a process and the way schizophrenics are produced in clinical cases that need hospitalizing. [...] The schizophrenics in hospitals are people who've tried to do something and failed, cracked up."[100] Most commentaries focus on the mechanics of creation in Deleuze's philosophy, the dynamics of becoming, the revolutionary potential of schizophrenia, and so on, but perhaps the more interesting question is: how does Deleuze account for the dark side of creative Being, the possibility of collapse, of failure, the crack up? How does a "line of life" get transformed into a "line of death?"

To sketch the basic outlines of this problem: in accordance with our previous discussion, the terms process, line of flight, and line of life may be seen as names for the psychoanalytic concept of drive. Lacan himself argues, in Deleuzoguattarian fashion, that the best translation of *pulsion* (Trieb) is *dérive*: the drive goes adrift.[101] However, unlike the authors of *Anti-Oedipus* he immediately associates this drift with death. Alongside Deleuze and Guattari's schizophrenic critique of Oedipus, Lacan's later work proposes a generalized theory of psychosis and a pluralization of the names-of-the-Father.[102] Yet he insists on the fundamentally destructive nature of jouissance: the symptom (or "sinthome") is a defensive formation, a way of holding things together, a knot that renders more or less liveable what would otherwise be sheer traumatism. In brief, "normality" is a gentrified form of madness, life a containment and structuration of destructive forces, the dream a tempered nightmare. Despite certain points of convergence between Lacanian psychoanalysis and schizoanalysis, Deleuze's way of conceiving the "line of death" departs decisively from this scheme.

At a certain point in the seminar Deleuze reiterates his claim that there is no lack or negativity in desire, and recapitulates his theory of masochism as breaking the link between desire and pleasure. The masochistic, he says, is someone who is horrified by the prospect of interruption: he looks for ways to prolong and delay desire, seeking to liberate sexuality from the punctual satisfaction of orgasm (genital sexuality as represented by the Father) in order to cultivate the joy immanent to desire. Now if pleasure is a "rotten idea," because it marks the termination of a process, then death is an even more revolting notion. "When I hear the idea that death can be a process, my whole heart, all my affects, bleed."[103] Death is not a process, it is not a drive, it is not the ineluctable destiny of one's being-toward-death, it is not the limit that inhabits and gives form to temporal life from the inside.[104] On the contrary, it is something the befalls the living being, as it were, by accident. On this point Deleuze relies squarely on Spinoza. Proposition 4 of Book III of the *Ethics* reads "No thing can be destroyed except by an external cause," and in the proof of III, 6 Spinoza states "no thing can have in itself anything by which it can be destroyed."[105] This affirmative *conatus* which "endeavors to persist in its own being" and which can only be extinguished by an external force (a bad encounter, a shock from the outside) lies at the core of Deleuze's conception of the drive: the drive is fundamentally a "line of life" which knows nothing of death or self-destruction. What could be further from the lesson of psychoanalysis, or at least the psychoanalysis of the mature Freud of Thanatos and the "discontent in civilization," carried on by Klein and Lacan? How to account, within a vitalist metaphysics, for all the self-imposed miseries and defeating behaviors that make up the everyday matter of the psychoanalytic clinic? For a Spinozism of the unconscious, this proclivity to self-sabotage, these various "lines of death," must be explained not in terms of some structural defect, but according to the contingent occurrence of bad encounters, a kind of poisoning. In "apparent phenomena of self-destruction [...] what is involved is always a group of parts that are determined to enter into other relations and consequently behave like foreign bodies inside us."[106] In the case of suicide, "the disturbed group gets the upper hand and, in a different relation, induces our other parts to desert our characteristic system."[107]

Is there an inherent tendency of the psyche to destroy itself? Or are the forces that move the psyche from within essentially good and life-sustaining, however prone they are to corruption and contamination? The major topics that occupy Freud's late theoretical work—guilt, masochism, and the death drive—can be seen as responding fundamentally to a crisis in the clinical practice: why aren't the patients getting better? Why does the therapeutic process seem almost endless? How is it that people get so stuck on the very illnesses they suffer from and constantly complain about? Freud's metapsychology is at the same time a theory of the limit of psychoanalytic praxis: however much the therapy is able to "further the analysand's eros" (to cite one of Lacan's formulas for the aim of analysis), it necessarily runs up again a "hard rock," some kind of built-in discontent which goes against the grain of the self-preservative conatus.[108] Later analysts, who have reformulated Freudian theory on the basis of psychosis, have offered different ways of understanding this fundamental psychic impasse. Rosenberg, for example, takes the lesson of Freud's economy to be that the tension of the drives is originally a danger and source of unpleasure fit only for evacuation: in order to live the psyche must come to enjoy in its own drive-tensions, a condition that is far from being self-evident. Or for Bion, thinking is not simply the joyful activity of producing and linking ideas—rather, thinking is motivated in the first place by the need to cope with the pressure of thoughts.[109] Or as one of Philip K. Dick's characters, himself no stranger to the world of schizophrenia, states: "The basis of life is not a greed to exist, not a desire of any kind. It's fear, the fear which I saw there. And not even fear; much worse. Absolute *dread*. Paralyzing dread so great as to produce apathy. [...] All the activity of life was an effort to relieve this one state."[110] On the other hand, Deleuze's Spinozistic rejection of modern philosophies of finitude, which locate death as a limit inside of life, might unexpectedly fit very well Lacan's own characterization of the libido as immortal substance, "life that has need of no organ, simplified, indestructible life."[111] If the schizophrenic process comports within itself the danger of ruin, perhaps it is due to the fact that this "profound and almost unlivable Power"[112] can quickly threaten to become too much (*pace* Spinoza) for the finite mode it traverses. In that case, the idea that pleasure and death are rotten because they imply a stop may be turned around: "Death belongs to the realm of faith. Of course, you have good reason to believe that you are going to die—it comforts you. If you didn't believe that, would you be able to support the life that you have?"[113]

Notes

1. "The idea of pleasure is a completely rotten (*pourrie*) idea." "Dualism, Monism and Multiplicities (Desire-Pleasure-*Jouissance*)" Seminar of March 26, 1973, translated by Daniel W. Smith, *Contretemps*, 2 (May 2001), p. 96.

2. Gilles Deleuze, "Desire and Pleasure" translated by Daniel W. Smith, in *Foucault and His Interlocutors*, edited by Arnold Davidson (Chicago: Chicago University Press, 1997), p. 189.

3. "There is, in fact, a joy that is immanent to desire as though desire were filled by itself and its contemplations, a joy that implies no lack or impossibility and is not measured by pleasure since it is what distributes intensities of pleasure and prevents them from being suffused by anxiety, shame, and guilt." Gilles Deleuze and Felix Guattari, *A Thousand Plateaus*, translated by Brian Massumi (Minneapolis: University of Minnesota Press, 1987), p. 155.

4. See Monique David-Ménard, *Deleuze et la psychanalyse* (Paris: PUF, 2005); Christian Kerslake, *Deleuze and the Unconscious* (London: Continuum, 2007); Slavoj Žižek, *Organs Without Bodies: On Deleuze and Consequences* (NY: Routledge, 2004); Daniel W. Smith, "The Inverse Side of the Structure: Žižek on Deleuze on Lacan," *Criticism*, 46.4 (Fall 2004), pp. 635–50; and Sophie Mendelsohn, "Père, impair et passe" in *Fresh Théorie* (Paris: Éditions Léo Scheer, 2005), pp. 455–66.

5. Lacan, *Le Séminaire livre X L'Angoisse*, edited by Jacques-Alain Miller (Paris: Seuil, 2004), p. 67.

6. "Deleuze and Guattari Fight Back..." in *Desert Islands and Other Texts 1953–1974*, translated by Michael Taormina (NY: Semiotext(e), 2004), p. 221. Henceforth cited in the text as "Deleuze and Guattari Fight Back." Originally published in *La Quinzaine Litteraire*, 143 (June 16–30, 1972), 15–19.

7. Adrian Johnston, *Time Driven: Metapsychology and the Splitting of the Drive* (Evanston: Northwestern University Press, 2005), p. 338.

8. "Deleuze and Guattari Fight Back...," p. 223.

9. *The* great theorist of this position is Giacomo Leopardi, who does not hesitate to draw the radical conclusion that pleasure does not exist: it is a mere phantom of the mind, not an actual feeling. "[P]leasure is a theoretical subject, not a real one; a desire, not a fact; some sort of feeling man conceives in his mind but does not experience; or, to be more exact, a concept, not a feeling. Don't you realize that at the same time you enjoy pleasure [...] since you cannot be satisfied with it in each of its moments, you are constantly waiting for a greater and more real enjoyment that may contain the sum total of all that particular pleasure? And, meanwhile, you seem to keep looking forward to the future moments of that same pleasure? And this always end before the fully satisfying instant arrives..." "Dialogue Between Torquato Tasso and His Familiar Spirit," *Operette Morali: Essays and Dialogues*, translated by Giovanni Cecchetti (Berkeley: University California Press, 1982), p. 173.

10. Deleuze, Seminar of March 26, 1973, p. 101.

11. Deleuze, Seminar of March 26, 1973, pp. 101–2.

12. William S. Burroughs, *Junky* (London: Penguin, 1977), p. xvi.

13. For a detailed comparative reading of Plato and Aristotle's theories of pleasure, see Chapter I of Gerd Van Riel's *Pleasure and the Good Life: Plato, Aristotle, and the Neoplatonists* (Leiden: Brill, 2000).

14. Aristotle, *Nichomachean Ethics*, Book X, 1172a19.

15. Aristotle, 1174b33.

16. Plato, *Philebus*, 54b.

17. Deleuze, *The Logic of Sense*, translated by Mark Lester, edited by Constantin V. Boundas (London: Athlone, 1990), p. 1.
18. "When the irritation and infection are inside and cannot be reached by rubbing and scratching, there is only a relief on the surface." *Philebus*, 46d-e.
19. *Philebus*, 46d, 47a.
20. *Philebus*, 47a.
21. Nietzsche, *The Will to Power*, translated by Walter Kaufmann and R. J. Hollingdale (NY, Vintage: 1968), §658 [1885].
22. We might also mention that this emphasis on the explosive becoming of the will puts Nietzsche at odds with what he takes to be Spinoza's conservatism: "Spinoza's law of 'self-preservation' ought really to put a stop to change: but this law is false, the opposite is true. It can be shown most clearly that every living thing does everything it cannot to preserve but to become *more*—" Nietzsche, §688 [March–June, 1888].
23. Lacan, *The Seminar of Jacques Lacan. Book III The Psychoses 1955–1956*, edited by Jacques-Alain Miller, translated by Russell Grigg (NY: Norton, 1993), p. 235.
24. Lacan, *The Seminar of Jacques Lacan: Book XX Encore 1972–1973*, edited by Jacques-Alain Miller, translated by Bruce Fink (NY: W. W. Norton, 1998), p. 70.
25. Lacan, *The Seminar of Jacques Lacan: Book II The Ego in Freud's Theory and in the Technique of Psychoanalysis 1954–1955*, edited by Jacques-Alain Miller, translated by Sylvana Tomaselli (NY: Norton, 1988), p. 84.
26. William Burroughs, *Naked Lunch* (NY: Grove Weidenfeld, 1959), p. 35. Burroughs also writes: "A junky does not want to be warm, he wants to be Cool-Cooler-COLD. But he wants The Cold like he wants His Junk—NOT OUTSIDE where it does him no good but INSIDE so he can sit around with a spine like a frozen hydraulic jack ... his metabolism approaching Absolute ZERO," pp. xvii–xviii. Although Deleuze cites this passage as an example of the zero-intensity of the body without organs, Burroughs is obviously very close to Freud, with their shared definition of pleasure as tension reduction. In both cases, the strictly negative conception of pleasure leads automatically to the thought of a "death drive", that is, to a peaceful Nirvana lying "beyond" the cycle of lack and fulfilment, a consummate satisfaction (for Burroughs: junk) that would halt desire's relentless march not temporarily but for all eternity.
27. Deleuze, Seminar of March 26, 1973, p. 101.
28. Karl Bühler, "Displeasure and Pleasure in Relation to Activity" in *Feelings and Emotions: The Wittenberg Symposium*, edited by Martin L. Reymert (Worcester: Clark University Press, 1928), p. 196.
29. Bühler, p. 197, 199. Bühler elaborates this notion in Chapter IV of his *Die Krise der Psychologie* (Jena: G. Fischer, 1927).
30. The list of authors in psychoanalysis, psychology, and neurology that have made use of the idea of functional pleasure is quite long: Kurt Goldstein, Ernst Kris, Otto Fenichel, Jean Piaget, Erich Fromm, Arnold Gehlen, Jean and Evelyne Kestemberg, and Abraham Maslow to name some of the most important.
31. Deleuze and Guattari, *Anti-Oedipus*, p. 7. Deleuze and Guattari's theory of desire is linked with Jung's conception of libido as "general interest," as

opposed to Freud's intrinsically sexual force. On this connection with Jung see Kerslake, *Deleuze and the Unconscious*, p. 74.

32. See "Jokes and Their Relation to the Unconscious" in *The Standard Edition of the Complete Psychological Works of Sigmund Freud*, translated by James Strachey (London: Hogarth, 1955) vol. VIII, pp. 95–6. Hereafter *SE*; and *Three Essays on the Theory of Sexuality*, *SE*, VII, pp. 201–4.

33. Benno Rosenberg, *Masochisme mortifère et masochisme gardien de la vie* (Paris: PUF, 1999).

34. "Certain psychotiques asilaires, comme nous en conaissons tous, ont besoin de se masturber du matin au soir pour réduire drastisquement la tension d'excitation insupportable pour eux (et l'angoisse qui l'accompagne) et sont en cela très proches d'une *définition quantitative du plaisir comme besoin de réduction drastique de la tension d'excitation...*," Rosenberg, p. 62.

35. On this point, see Philippe Van Haute, "Psychoanalysis and/as Philosophy? The Anthropological Significance of Pathology in Freud's *Three Essays on the Theory of Sexuality*," *Philosophy Today*, 50 Suppl. (2006), pp. 90–7; and Alphonse de Waehlens, "Anthropologie, Psychiatrie, Psychanalyse: Quelque réflexions sur leurs rapports" in *Études d'Anthropologie Philosophique* (Leuven: Peeters, 1980), pp. 19–32.

36. See "The Dissection of the Psychical Personality" in *SE*, XXII, pp. 58–9.

37. Henri Michaux, *The Major Ordeals of the Mind and the Countless Minor Ones*, translated by Richard Howard (London: Secker & Warburg, 1974), p. 7.

38. Deleuze criticizes Reich precisely for this reason in Seminar of March 26, 1973, p. 96.

39. Deleuze, Seminar of March 26, 1973, p. 92.

40. Deleuze, Seminar of March 26, 1973, p. 98.

41. Deleuze, Seminar of March 26, 1973, p. 100.

42. Gilles Deleuze and Claire Parnet, *Dialogues II*, translated by Hugh Tomlinson and Barbara Habberjam (London: Continuum, 2002), p. 103.

43. Deleuze, Seminar of March 26, 1973, p. 98.

44. Jean-Claude Guillebaud, *La Tyrannie du plaisir* (Paris: Seuil, 1998), pp. 134–5. Guillebaud cites Van Gulik as his source. See Robert Van Gulik, *La vie sexuelle dans la Chine ancienne* translated by Louis Évrard (Paris: Gallimard, 1971 [1961]), pp. 231–3.

45. *Nietzsche, Beyond Good and Evil*, translated by R. J. Hollingdale (London: Penguin, 1990), §260.

46. Nietzsche, §260.

47. Deleuze and Parnet, p. 100.

48. Deleuze and Parnet, pp. 100–1.

49. Walter Benjamin, "Surrealism" in *Reflections* translated by Edmund Jephcott (NY: Schocken, 1978), p. 181.

50. Deleuze and Parnet, p. 90.

51. Lacan, *The Seminar of Jacques Lacan Book VII: The Ethics of Psychoanalysis 1959–1960*, edited by Jacques-Alain Miller, translated by Dennis Porter (NY: Norton, 1992), p. 152.

52. Lacan, *Ethics of Psychoanalysis*, p. 152.

53. See Chapter 7 of Marc De Kesel, *Ethics and Eros: Reading Jacques Lacan's Seminar VII*, translated by Sigi Jöttkandt (Albany: SUNY Press, 2009).

54. Deleuze, "Coldness and Cruelty" in *Masochism*, translated by Jean McNeil (NY: Zone, 1991), p. 97.
55. Deleuze, "Coldness and Cruelty," p. 100
56. See Jacques Le Brun, *Le Pur amour de Platon à Lacan* (Paris: Seuil, 2002), pp. 249–65.
57. Gilles Deleuze, "Re-presentation of Masoch," *Essays Critical and Clinical*, translated by Daniel W. Smith and Michael A. Greco (London: Verso, 1998), pp. 53–4.
58. Deleuze, "Coldness and Cruelty," p. 101.
59. *Gilles Deleuze*, "Bartleby; or, the Formula," *Essays Critical and Clinical*, translated by Daniel W. Smith and Michael A. Greco (London: Verso, 1998), p. 88.
60. In his unpublished Seminar XIV, *La logique du fantasme* (1966–7), session of April 19, 1967.
61. Lacan, Seminar x, p. 176.
62. Lacan, Seminar x, p. 192.
63. Deleuze, *Francis Bacon: The Logic of Sensation*, translated by Daniel W. Smith (Minneapolis: University of Minnesota Press, 2003), p. 17.
64. Deleuze, *Francis Bacon: The Logic of Sensation*, p. 42.
65. Deleuze and Guattari, *A Thousand Plateaus*, p.155.
66. See "Michel Tournier and the World Without Others" in *The Logic of Sense*, translated by Mark Lester & Charles Stivale (London: Athlone, 1990), pp. 301–21.
67. Deleuze and Guattari, *A Thousand Plateaus*, p.156.
68. Deleuze, "Bergson's Conception of Difference" in *The New Bergson*, translated by Melissa McMahon, edited by John Mullarkey (Manchester: Manchester University Press, 1999), p. 5.
69. Deleuze and Guattari, *Anti-Oedipus*, p. 331.
70. Deleuze, "*On Anti-Oedipus*" in *Negotiations*, translated by Martin Joughin (NY: Columbia University Press, 1995), p. 14.
71. Deleuze, "Letter to a Harsh Critic," in *Negotiations*, p. 6.
72. "*L'Anti-Oedipe* est une variation sur un thème de Lacan, la critique de l'oedipianisme naïf, enrichie d'un éloge, non sans humour, de la schizophrénie. C'est d'ailleurs une progéniture que Lacan a reconnue, tout en la taxant de délirante." Interview with François Ewald, *Magazine Littéraire*, 271 (November 1989), p. 24.
73. Deleuze and Guattari, *Anti-Oedipus*, p. 27n.
74. "On Philosophy" in *Negotiations*, pp. 144–5.
75. Deleuze and Guattari, *Anti-Oedipus*, p. 53.
76. Deleuze and Guattari, *Anti-Oedipus*, translated by Robert Hurley, Mark Seem, and Helen R. Lane (Minneapolis: University of Minnesota Press, 1983), pp. 27, 300, 306.
77. Jacques Rancière, "Deleuze, Bartleby, and the Literary Formula" in *The Flesh of Words*, translated by Charlotte Mandell (Stanford: Stanford University Press, 2004), pp. 150, 154, 156, 157. It would also be interesting to compare Deleuze and Guattari's philosophy of desiring machines with the "material phenomenology" of Michel Henry, with its unrelenting critique of representation and its emphasis on the immanent domain of affectivity. It is provocative to think that Deleuzoguattarian pagan vitalism might find its uncanny counterpart in Henry's Christian cult of Life.

78. Deleuze and Guattari, *Anti-Oedipus*, p. 309. At stake here is the philosophical genealogy of psychoanalysis: is psychoanalysis the inheritor of vitalist theories of the passions and the will (as Michel Henry argues), or does it rather derive from the subversive underside of the rationalist tradition, the Cartesian cogito (the position of Lacan)?

79. Lacan, *The Four Fundamental Concepts of Psychoanalysis*, edited by Jacques-Alain Miller, translated by Alan Sheridan (NY: Norton, 1981), p. 169.

80. *The Four Fundamental Concepts of Psychoanalysis*, pp. 181–2.

81. Lacan, "On Freud's 'Trieb' and the Psychoanalyst's Desire" in *Écrits*, translated by Bruce Fink (NY: Norton, 2006), p. 724.

82. This is Leclaire's set of examples, the descriptions slightly shortened. Serge Leclaire, "La réalité du désir' in *Écrits pour la psychanalyse, 1 (1954–1993)"* (Paris: Seuil, 1996), p. 149.

83. Leclaire, p. 150.

84. Deleuze and Guattari, *Anti-Oedipus*, p. 314.

85. Deleuze and Guattari, *Anti-Oedipus*, p. 309.

86. Žižek's witticism, "organs without bodies" thus already belongs to Deleuze and Guattari's overarching scheme. In Lacanian terms, the relationship between the Body without Organs and partial objects ("organs without bodies") would appear equivalent to that between the Thing and the *objets a*.

87. Deleuze and Guattari, *Anti-Oedipus*, p. 314.

88. Deleuze and Guattari, p. 324

89. "Deleuze and Guattari Fight Back...," p. 224

90. The most detailed analyzes of how partial objects function in an intersubjective dialectic are contained in Lacan's Seminar VIII, *Le Transfert* (Paris: Seuil, 2001), pp. 237–312.

91. See "The Inverse Side of the Structure: Žižek on Deleuze on Lacan."

92. The crucial seminar on this subject is the unpublished *Seminar IX L'Identification* (1961–62). Anticipating Deleuze's major study, there Lacan links together *difference*, as introduced by the unary trait, the most primitive symbolic element, and *repetition*, the peculiar insistence of human drives which break with the cycle of need and satisfaction. What repeats is difference as such, the rupture instituted by the autonomous order of language with the pre-symbolic real.

93. The most interesting, and for me unexpected, passages in Guattari's *The Anti-Oedipus Papers* are his critical remarks on Lacan's unary trait in the direction of set theory. "The single trait is not sufficiently deterritorialized yet. It should be the *sign-point* of set theory, a never-ending axiomatization, that extends the deterritorialization process into math and science. Behind the letter: not being, but the real, the cobbled-together real, the real of scientific objects." Felix Guattari, *The Anti-Oedipus Papers*, edited by Stéphane Nadaud, translated by Kélina Gotman (NY: Semiotex(e), 2006), p. 129. Does this not (at least vaguely) anticipate Alain Badiou's own set theoretical formalization as a step beyond Lacan's logic?

94. A transcript of this seminar (entitled "Anti-Œdipe et autres réflexions") is available at <http://www.univ-paris8.fr/deleuze/> [accessed July 14, 2009].

95. Lionel Trilling concludes his *Sincerity and Authenticity* with an eloquent critique of this romanticization of madness: "[N]o expression of disaffection from the social existence was ever so desperate as this eagerness to say that

authenticity of personal being is achieved through an ultimate isolateness and through the power that this is presumed to bring. The falsities of an alienated social reality are rejected in favor of an upward psychopathic mobility to the point of divinity, each one of us a Christ—but with none of the inconveniences of undertaking to intercede, of being a sacrifice, of reasoning with rabbis, of making sermons, of having disciples, of going to weddings and to funerals, of beginning something and at a certain point remarking that it is finished" (Cambridge: Harvard University Press, 1972), pp. 171–2. Does this not capture the basic point of Peter Hallward's criticism of Deleuze in *Out of the World: Deleuze and the Philosophy of Creation* (London: Verso, 2006), that in the end Deleuzian philosophy, precisely as a critique of alienated reality, amounts to an abandonment of the world and its complex interrelations ("reasoning with rabbis" and so on) in favor of a quasi-mystical, theophanic, "mad" illumination?

96. "Anti-Oedipe et autres réflexions."
97. "Anti-Oedipe et autres réflexions."
98. "Anti-Oedipe et autres réflexions."
99. "Capitalism and Schizophrenia" in *Desert Islands*, p. 240.
100. "On Anti-Oedipus" in *Negotiations*, p. 23
101. Jacques Lacan, *Le Séminaire livre XXIII: Le sinthome 1975–76*, edited by Jacques-Alain Miller (Paris: Seuil, 2005), p. 125.
102. Sophie Mendelsohn argues that Deleuze and Guattari's critique of oedipalism is fully integrated in Lacan's last teachings on the sinthome. See "Père, impair et passe." On the other hand, one should ask what happens to the earlier structural approach in the new generalized theory of psychosis: the advantage of the former is the identification of specific mechanisms (repression, disavowal, foreclosure) at the root of different pathologies.
103. "Anti-Oedipe et autres réflexions."
104. On this last point, see Georg Simmel, „Zur Metaphysik des Todes" [1910] in *Das Individuum und die Freiheit* (Berlin: Wagenbach, 1984), pp. 29–35.
105. Spinoza, *Ethics*, translated by Samuel Shirley (Indianapolis: Hackett, 1992).
106. Deleuze, *Spinoza Practical Philosophy*, translated by Robert Hurley (San Francisco: City Lights, 1988), p. 42.
107. Deleuze, *Spinoza: Practical Philosophy*, p. 42. A highly ironic restatement of this Spinozistic principle is found in the writings of Pessoa's most depressing character, the Baron of Teive. The idea that "life is the law of all existence" and so "death must always result from an outside intervention" once saved the Baron from suicide, since he could not stand the idea of acting on himself as "someone else's instrument" (perhaps this theory is right, he wonders, and there is no such thing as an "authentic" suicide...). This speculation, however, proves to be only a temporary stopgap: the Baron eventually offs himself after concluding that it is impossible to create superior art—a deadlock he perceives as inherent and not accidental. *The Education of the Stoic: The Only Manuscript of the Baron of Teive*, translated by Richard Zenith (Cambridge: Exact Change, 2005), pp. 20–1.
108. "When we think of the facts of masochism, of the unconscious need for punishment and of neurotic self-injury, which make plausible the hypothesis of there being instinctual impulses that run contrary to

self-preservation, we even feel shaken in our belief in the general validity of the commonplace truth on which the theoretical structure of Individual Psychology is erected." "Explanations, Applications, and Orientations," *SE*, XXII, p. 142.

109. "[T]hinking is a development forced on the psyche by the pressure of thoughts and not the other way round." W.R. Bion, "A Theory of Thinking" in *Second Thoughts* (London: Karnac, 1993), p. 111. Deleuze endorses a similar conception in his reading of Artaud (the "terrible revelation of a thought without image") in *Difference and Repetition*, translated by Paul Patton (London: Continuum, 1994), pp. 146–8.

110. Philip K. Dick, *We Can Build You* (London: Harper Collins, 1972), pp. 77–8.

111. Lacan, *The Four Fundamental Concepts of Psychoanalysis*, p. 198.

112. Deleuze, *Francis Bacon: The Logic of Sensation*, p. 39.

113. Recording of Lacan's conference at the Université Catholique de Louvain, October 13, 1972.

12

Nationalist Ext(im)asy: Maurice Barrès and the Roots of Fascist Enjoyment

Gil Chaitin

French fascists of the twentieth century such as Pierre Drieu La Rochelle and Robert Brasillach were great admirers of Barrès in their youth,[1] and Georges Valois, leader of the first French fascist party, Le Faisceau, looked on Barrès's nationalism as the major precursor of his movement, as did several others who slid from integral nationalism to fascism in the 1920s (e.g., Taittinger, Renaud, La Rocque, Doriot).[2] It was Barrès, after all, who invented the term "National Socialism," and his brand of nationalism included the "leader principle" along with a heavy dose of mob violence, xenophobia and anti-Semitism. For the same reasons, recent anti-fascist scholars, such as Soucy, Sternhell and Carroll (who takes his cue from Lacoue-Labarthe and Nancy's *Nazi Myth*),[3] have examined his writings in order to discover the roots of the later movement in the ideology of the virulent revolutionary nationalism he developed around the turn of the century, just before and during the Dreyfus Affair (1897–1902).

Paradoxically, while Sternhell and Soucy contend that it was Barrès's abandonment of rationalist humanism that made him the bridge between nineteenth-century conservatism and twentieth-century fascism, Carroll takes just the opposite view, that it is the persistence and exacerbation of the philosophy of the subject that explains his fall into totalitarianism. From the one perspective it is his betrayal of the tradition of the Enlightenment, from the other his fidelity to that heritage, which precipitates him into the abyss of proto-fascism. While both these explanations have much to recommend them—there certainly was an important strain of irrationalism in Barrès's politics of cultural heredity, the strong leader and the masses, on the one hand, the assertion of the prerogatives of the autonomous subject in his identification with national heroes, the valorization of sameness evident in the insistence

236

on national unity and totality leading to racism and xenophobia on the other—each suffers from the flaw of over-generalization. The major tenets of Barrès's "irrationalism" were in fact commonplaces of the rationalist scientism of his times. Comte, Taine, Durkheim, Tarde, Le Bon, Ribot, Soury, all believed in some form of hereditary determinism as well as in the subordination of the individual to the group. Like Schopenhauer, Hartmann, Wundt, Exner and Lichtenberg among German thinkers of the period, the last three also upheld the anti-Cartesian view that affect and instinct take precedence over individual reason and that thought itself is the product of the impersonal forces of a collective unconscious, a stance they condensed in the pre-Lacanian catch phrase *"Il pense en moi."*[4] Moreover, the anti-individualist social theories of that same positivism were combined in a strange alliance with a certain philosophy of the subject derived straight from Kant and the Enlightenment via Condorcet, Quinet, Proudhon and Renouvier among others, in order to serve as the ideological basis of the very Opportunist Republic Barrès's nationalism and later fascism were designed to overthrow.[5] To put it bluntly, there was a republican irrationalism that nevertheless did not condone mob violence, and a patriotic subject of national unity that did not sanction legalized racism, anti-Semitism and xenophobia.

The problem, then, is that while each of these theories brings out aspects of Barrès's ideology that might otherwise remain hidden from view, neither distinguishes adequately between proto-fascism and republicanism, since the very traits they emphasize, even those that appear to be mutually contradictory, were in fact constitutive of republican ideology. Such a differentiation can be effected, I would suggest, by examining Barrès's texts from the time of the Dreyfus affair in light of Lacan's notion of "extimacy," his neologistic mode of escaping from the polar opposition of the interior and the exterior that so often haunts the discourse of identity at the heart of republican, nationalist and fascist ideology.[6]

What makes Barrès's texts of this period especially interesting, and frightening, are his perceptions of the more or less covert fears and gratifications that constitute the emotional force of the striving for identity in fin-de-siècle nationalism beyond, and often against, the self-interest advertised in political campaigns and the rights and duties described in political philosophies. While Barrès articulated the main themes of his program in the polemical prose of his *Scenes and Doctrines of Nationalism*, a collection of speeches and articles written between 1898 and its publication in 1902, I would argue—and this is my second thesis—that it is in his fiction, much more than in his political pamphlets, that Barrès

allows the full range and complexity of the tendencies that make up
nationalist identity, and, above all, the contradictions within them, to
surface and interact freely. And it is likewise in the novels that what
distinguished his nationalist solution from that of others and made it
especially dangerous emerges most clearly.

In the three volumes that form the *Novels of National Energy*, *The
Uprooted* (1897), *Appeal to the Soldier* (1900), and *Their Faces* (1902),[7]
the seductive power of Barrès's nationalism is not simply asserted or
described as in his political and journalistic pamphlets; it is dramatized
as scenarios of jouissance. In particular, it is in the development of the
main character, Sturel, that Barrès brings out the hidden implications
of his program. As the title of the first book of the series indicates, the
plot is primarily designed to enact before the reader the concrete effects
of the "uprooting" produced by the philosophical doctrines expounded
by professor Bouteiller on the lives of seven of his pupils from Lorraine,
who decide to seek their fortunes in Paris after graduating from the
lycée in Nancy where he teaches. Two of them, Racadot, grandson of
a serf freed during the Revolution, and Mouchefrin, whose father is
a poverty-stricken photographer, end up very badly, murdering a beautiful young Armenian woman named Astiné Aravian for her jewels.
A third, Renaudin, son of a petty civil servant and a scholarship student
like Mouchefrin, engages in the most unsavory journalistic practices of
the period, and in a later volume of the trilogy is nearly killed in a duel
provoked because of his betrayal of the cause of General Boulanger. The
four others, Roemerspacher, Sturel, Saint-Phlin and Suret-Lefort, with
higher social status, some independent means and greater intellectual
ability, are successful in varying degrees, but only after suffering from
their transplantation to the metropolis. Moreover, they all share at
least some complicity in Racadot and Mouchefrin's crime; none more
than Sturel who was formerly Astiné's lover and yet refused to come
to her rescue when his two friends were hauling her off to her death.
The question of the teacher's responsibility is thus at the heart of this
novel, more specifically, the effect of the ideology he teaches on the
identity and ethical commitments of his pupils. By recounting the lives
of a whole group of characters subjected to this teaching and then interacting with each other and with the culture and society of the times,
Barrès indicates his polemical aim, to impugn the social and political
institutions of the Republic that promulgated those views.[8]

A cursory reading of the opening chapter gives the impression that the
ideological argument of the novel will consist of what was by the end of
the century the standard right-wing attack against the universalism of

the Republic in the name of particularism. On the one hand, Kantian universalism with its categorical imperative and rationalist abstraction:

> [Bouteiller's] behavior, like his teachings, [rest] on the Kantian principle that he formulated as follows: "I must always act in such a way that I can will that my action will serve as a universal rule" (p. 504). Thus he made his pupils into citizens of humanity, emancipated men, initiates of pure reason.
>
> (p. 510)[9]

On the other, the empirical consideration of the particular conditions of real life, everything that Kantianism allegedly ignores:

> [A]ll the conditions of existence, which differ with each milieu. Each individual is constituted by realities that cannot be contradicted (p. 502). [E]verything in life that is varied, dissimilar, spontaneous in a thousand different directions.
>
> (p. 505)

Members of "humanity" should be understood here in Taine's terms (which echo those of de Maistre and Tocqueville): paper constructs, "abstract men, empty simulacra, philosophical puppets";[10] while "citizen" indicates people who have lost their selves, their ties to their ancestors, to the land where they were born and raised, and to their cultures; they are victims of synthetic theory and artificial law, imposed upon them by means of physical or mental violence. The "purity" of reason consists, in the eyes of Kant's adversaries, in turning one's back on the natural, social and cultural conditions of real life.

Bouteiller teaches his charges that it is not possible to tell whether our sense of space and time or our idea of causality correspond to anything real; what they receive from this notion is "the most acute sense of *nothingness*" (p. 500; my emphasis). While the professor later tries to show them that Kant's categorical imperative reestablishes the certainty his critique of pure reason had destroyed, his students retain only the first part of the lesson. The narrator wonders whether this overdose of negation might not lead them to devise for themselves "a kind of cruel nihilism" (p. 500), and the author reinforces this impression in a crucial scene later in the novel by attributing the same idea to a voice of authority, the fictionalized philosopher Taine (p. 595). The uprooting for which Barrès wants to indict the Republic is thus not just a matter of physical displacement but above all one of mental upheaval. Like

Socrates, the professor has undermined his students' childhood beliefs, the cultural *doxa* of their social classes and family milieus. The worst effect of Kantianism on the adolescents from Lorraine is that, in robbing them of their certainty, it also deprives them of their identity, insofar as the latter is determined by that *doxa*. The result is that they are reduced to the status of abstract individualities whose identity is devoid of any positive content and is therefore totally defined by the desires of self-assertion and self-perpetuation.

When they arrive in Paris, then, they decide that they must commit themselves as a group to an important project, but they have no idea of what that project might be. The choice of launching a newspaper stems neither from an inner impulse nor from a shared goal but from the observation of the enormous power of the press both to sound and to shape public opinion. In the ensuing pages, the story revolves around the conflict between two ethics designed to fill the void left by Kantian "nihilism": the realist ethic of acceptance symbolized by the plane tree which Taine uses as a metaphor of organic self-assertion combined with submission to external necessity, and the romantic ideal of the intellectual (this was written before the Dreyfus case had become a *cause célèbre*) who, unafraid of life, is willing to take risks and confront unexpected dangers, and for whom thought has value only insofar as it stimulates action, inspires and mobilizes creative energy (pp. 600–4). The debate is focalized chiefly through the character of Sturel, the romantic who persistently refuses to accept social and political realities. While his comrades from school take decisive steps that tend to stabilize their identities, until the very end of the trilogy Sturel refuses to compromise. Racadot and Mouchefrin, characterized as victims of social and economic, as well as intellectual uprooting, rebel openly and are punished for their crime; Renaudin and Suret-Lefort take the opposite tack, selling out, albeit in different ways, to the bourgeois system of money and power that rules the Opportunist Republic; Saint-Phlin and Roemerspacher, on the contrary, overcome their prior rootlessness and its evil effects, resisting the temptations of the Republic by espousing different versions of Barrès's own anti-parliamentary, nationalist ideology.

One might be tempted to conclude, and many critics have taken this step, that the latter two represent the author's ideal. After all, as one commentator argues, "It is this true disciple of Taine [Roemerspacher] who receives the hand—symbolic reward—of the sweet Mme de Nelles [the former Mlle Alison], the young woman from Lorraine whom Sturel was unable to keep."[11] No doubt. But marriage is also the best way to kill desire, by subjecting it to the law. Even if we did not have the evidence of Barrès's diary and magazine articles, in which he repudiates what he takes to be the servile aspect of the philosopher's conservative ethic of acceptance,[12] the parallel in the novel between settling down into marriage and settling into a fixed political program, especially one based on accepting acceptance, is too evident to be discounted. By not marrying the local girl, by not staying in Lorraine with his friend Saint-Phlin, Sturel alone remains the man of desire, in the Lacanian sense, on the sexual as on the political level.

It is true that in the final pages of the trilogy, Sturel at last grudgingly reconciles himself to the idea of acceptance that constitutes the heart of nationalist ideology, according to Barrès's famous exclamation in *Scenes and Doctrines of Nationalism*: "Nationalism is the acceptance of a determinism."[13] But he does not do so in the spirit of a Roemerspacher or a Saint-Phlin; on the contrary, he defiantly refuses to give up his desire, his idealism (pp. 1208–9). Combining autonomy and necessity, individualism and collectivism, regionalism and nationalism, he concludes:

> My heroic resolutions have value only if they derive from a profound inner necessity, from something ethnic [...]. If I maintain my tradition [...] if I am the son of my dead and the father of their grandsons, I may not realize the plans of my race, but I will keep their potential alive. My task is clear: [...] to be Lorraine so that it may traverse intact this period in which decerebrated and dissociated France seems to be undergoing a general paralysis.
>
> (p. 1211)

Sturel's tour de force here, or perhaps his sleight of hand, is to harmonize the apparent contradictories that have plagued not only himself but the entire novel. He has accomplished this feat merely by reversing the valence of an adjective, thus shifting the position of a single key term in his description of the self. He now agrees with the lesson of Taine's tree parable, that "the individual Ego is supported and nourished by society," as Barrès put it in his *Response to Mr. René Doumic*.[14] But his new version differs from Taine's by the sole word "inner." The necessities to which Taine's tree yielded were conceived as external to that organism, environmental factors such as space, sunlight and soil. For that reason, Ringer observes that the metaphors of organic growth in the tree allegory bear only a superficial resemblance to the German conception of *Bildung*, for the diversity of individuals implied is that of "conditioning environments" rather than of "self-defining individuals."[15] The compulsion that Sturel ultimately accepts is, on the contrary, understood as an inner force. Taine's tree developed according to its own internal law, but only insofar as its milieu permitted. Sturel imagines that the ancestral determinism to which he acquiesces is his internal law.

Barrès's nationalism is indeed the acceptance of a determinism, but it is a determinism that aims to preserve the autonomy of its adherents. The contradictory nature of these two requirements is evident, yet they do have a certain hidden coherence. In *Appeal to the Soldier*, Saint-Phlin explains his notion of the link between freedom and belonging to one's group:

> Listen, Sturel, after exercising many forms of freedom, you recognize that the best and the only one is precisely the ease enjoyed by him who voluntarily strengthens his natural ties with a region and with the employments befitting his station in life; that is, when, banishing the anxieties of our nomadic imaginations, we accept the condition of our development.
>
> (p. 948)

The ease (*aisance*) which Saint-Phlin celebrates indicates the meaning of freedom for the Barresian nationalist—the sense of following one's own nature combined with a feeling of release from any form of external restraint. Ironically, then, for the outspokenly anti-Kantian Barrès as for Sturel, it is a more or less perverse variation of the Kantian notion of the moral subject that makes it possible to resolve the apparent contradiction between determinism and liberty in nationalism.[16] In Kant, the subject is free to the extent that it obeys the law of reason, a law it gives to itself, determining its own action in competition with, if not in downright contradiction to, the external law of physical determinism. Likewise for Barrès in his nationalist phase, insofar as one's ancestors are experienced as forming the core of one's inner being, accepting the law of their "determinism" is the ultimate expression of the freedom of the self.

In this conception, freedom and identity are inextricably bound together, for both are conceived as matters of autonomy and hence in opposition to the Other. Identity is nothing other than that inner law of development of which Taine spoke in his tree parable. For the Kantian subject that law is the rule of practical reason; its identity as "human" derives from exercising its freedom, understood as the power of ethical self-determination, because it is the use of reason that distinguishes human beings from other entities not only as a theoretical question of definition but as a matter of actual resistance to an otherwise iron law of external, natural causality. In short, its identity is its freedom. As with Barrès's definition of the social self, by shifting the locus of the law from outer to inner, it transforms being dominated into resisting domination, or even dominating the other outright. That transformation, however, is accompanied by another switch, of equal importance. The position of dominator can be successfully reversed only because the change of site also effects a shift in the distribution of the role of otherness. Carroll remarks perceptively that for Barrès the ostensible others which the self is, its ancestors or fellow countrymen, are not really other, for they are felt to be "affinities,"[17] that is, the same as the self (p. 27).[18] In like manner, Kant argues that the voice of reason which speaks in the human conscience is in fact our own voice. In other words, both the Kantian and the nationalist identify with the law to which they subject themselves.[19]

Barrès's discovery of the social self at the base of the individual ego was not the result of disinterested introspection or scientific observation, as his conservative admirers often make out. Nor did he simply stumble upon the America of the social self while looking for the individual Indies. In fact, as with the character Sturel, there was no smooth transition from belief in the one to allegiance to the other. His change of heart responded rather to the urgent search for a way to avoid falling irreparably over the edge of a curiously flattened landscape of the mind into the fathomless abyss of the void. While formerly his protagonists believed there was an authentic, natural, inner self, hidden beneath the façade artificially imposed by society and waiting to be unearthed and cultivated, now he claimed to have discovered that, when the various layers of the self are peeled away through continued analyzes, eventually one finds nothing, absolutely nothing.

> In *The Uprooted*, the free man discerns and accepts his determinism. A candidate for nihilism pursues his apprenticeship, and, from analysis to analysis, he experiences the nothingness of the Ego [...].[20]
>
> [I] noticed that the "Ego," when subjected to any kind of serious analysis, vanishes completely [...]. But the "Ego" vanishes in a still more terrifying manner if we take cognizance of our automatism [...]. We are not the masters of the thoughts that arise within us. They are ways of reacting in which very ancient physiological dispositions find expression [...].[21]

At stake in Barrès's denial of the power of individual consciousness here is not merely the latter's claim to independent reason, however crucial that may be, but rather his hold on existence itself. It is this distress, this dread of the total loss of self which imparts such dire urgency to that lust for being that Barrès knew as the Spinozan desire to "persevere in our being" and that we most often call euphemistically the quest for identity.

That it was the shadow of annihilation which gave Barrès's long-standing nationalism its peculiar virulence at the end of the century we know from the fact that while he mentioned the cult of the soil and the dead as a possible solution to the disarray he claimed to perceive in himself and his country at the time of *The Uprooted*, it was the demise of his father the following year, in 1898, which plunged him into the turmoil that frightened him into fully embracing that ideology.[22] Reinforced by the death of his mother a few years later, this reaction was a kind of rejection of mourning, a desperate attempt to "save" his parents from the grip of death,[23] just as the earlier theoreticians of political reaction in France, De Maistre and Bonald, wanted to rescue the *ancien régime* from the oblivion threatened by the Revolution.

What is surprising at first sight about this conversion is that it was not his own mortality but that of his father and mother that precipitated his new ideological commitment. Upon further reflection, however, this motivation appears entirely consistent with the quest for identity he had been pursuing since his first novel, *Under the Eyes of the Barbarians* (1888), in which he compensates for his aggression against the fathers—society and its authorities and even its concept of reality—with the final plea for a "master [...] axiom, religion or prince of men."[24] The same oscillation between belligerent rebellion and obsequious veneration is manifest in his pronouncements during the intervening years, first assuring his readers that the dead are poisoning the younger generation, then extolling the virtues of a strong national leader such as Boulanger or Napoleon. The combination of guilt, for his hostile wishes, and fear, of the loss of his protector, instills in him the intransigent need to maintain this particular Other, regardless of the preliminary cost to the self.

Nevertheless, it was not guilt and fear alone that motivated Barrès's conversion to rootedness, as he explained retrospectively in his account of the motives that impelled him to champion the anti-dreyfusard cause.

> When the Dreyfus Affair arrived, my father was dead. I think that everything I said at that hour was an expression of these roots.[25]
>
> I realized that I was them [my parents] and that it was my destiny, my necessity to keep them [alive] as long as I could [...]. The whole universe could go to hell, as long as I was in agreement with their memory [...].[26]

Like Lacan's Antigone,[27] Barrès saw his opposition to the Jewish captain as the expression of his unyielding devotion to his family. The soil and the dead his nationalism strove to preserve were first of all his own parents and the land where he was born. For him the Dreyfus affair was a battle between Creons who were pitting the universalizing laws of abstract truth and justice against the ineffable, but all the more intensely felt, singularity of his loved ones. And it is this non-universalizable principle that, he claimed, should govern politics.[28]

By appealing at once to the filial devotion and to the sense of individuality of his countrymen, Barrès sought to give social and political resonance to what would otherwise have remained a purely personal reaction to a private event. In this way, he attempted to arouse the visceral feelings of the masses, to convince them that they were being uprooted by republican values designed to sever them from their parents, their families, their homes and their selves, both physically, as in the case of the ever-growing urban proletariat streaming into Paris from the provinces, and morally, in that of the peasants whom the Republic was subordinating to the central government and trying to wean from clericalism if not religion in general. At the same time, he hoped to unite all those who felt that their identity and their very existence were under siege by the Republic, especially those who could no longer have confidence in the universalist humanism so closely associated with its quasi-official doctrine, which Barrès attacks as Kantianism. For many intellectuals, especially decadent and symbolist writers, the "relativism" of a Renan made it impossible to accept those abstract principles. Catholic leaders, of course, objected vehemently to the attempt to coerce adhesion to those values through universal education. For others, the regime had not done enough to overcome the demoralization occasioned by the defeat at the hands of the Prussians in 1870. And a large number were simply repelled by the venality and corruption of the bourgeois Republic with its apparently unending parade of scandals. Dissatisfied with the universal yet unable to live in the relative, many longed for a seemingly impossible remedy for their malaise, a non-universal absolute.

Barrès's method for squaring this particular circle was, as Rambaud expresses the matter, the oxymoronic procedure of "making his relativism absolute."[29] The fear of the nothingness of the self was, it turned out, groundless, precisely because that void was undergirded by the firm ground of society. As such it provided a stable platform from which everything appears in its true being. Unlike the Lacanian heroine, who insists on burying her brother properly, Barrès maintained his stance not through the acceptance of death, but, on the contrary, in order to deny it. Each time he insists on the annihilation of the self, he adds that underneath its nothingness lies society, the collectivity which supports and thereby reassures the disappearing self:

> For a long time I pondered deeply the idea of the "Ego" using only the method of the poets and mystics, inner observation, and descended through layers of sand offering no resistance until, at the bottom, I found the collectivity as support.[30]

In his scheme of things, the Ego and society are involved in a pact of mutual protection from death. The individual agrees to accept as her entire destiny the perpetuation of the life of the community, while society serves not only as a support underneath the nothingness of the conscious self but also as a kind of manhole cover shielding from view the even darker abyss of physiological heredity and processes whose ancient instinctual compulsion threatens to annihilate the ego "in a still more terrifying manner."

In order to negate the death of his parents while maintaining contact with the living, Barrès defined society in accordance with the ideological move typical of reactionary thought of the nineteenth century: assimilating society to the ancestors, and the self to both. Barrès found his barrier against death first through the dissolution of his individuality in the relative eternity of ancestral continuity:

> We are the extension and the continuity of our fathers and mothers. [...] "I am they themselves [my father and mother]." [...] The individual disintegrates in order to recover himself in the family, the race, the nation, the thousands of years which the grave cannot nullify.[31]

The populism of the collective unconscious he had earlier proclaimed in *The Garden of Berenice* opened up a second avenue into the disintegration and subsequent rehabilitation of the ego, merging with the all-encompassing spatiality of the collectivity, the "herd" (*troupeau*), as Barrès himself called the crowd in his reminiscences about his involvement in the Boulangist movement.[32] In either case, whether by fusing with the spatial or with the temporal collectivity, Barrès managed to convert the death of the ego into a merely provisional condition, a way station on the road to the total recovery of the self.

The Barresian, then, must cling to his national identity for dear life because group identity was his dear life; paradoxically the only way to save the innermost core of his being was to position it outside of his self. Ringer was therefore only half right to contrast Barrès's doctrine to the German idea of *Bildung*, for the French writer does not simply abandon the ideal of the development of the inner self; he concludes rather that the inner self is, at the same time, outer. Unable to endure the tension this confrontation with extimacy entails, however, he immediately recuperates the otherness within by making it over into a new dimension of the same. This oddly Kantian conception entailed a new duty, designed to replace Kant's categorical imperative. In Saint-Phlin's words: "each one of us must turn inwards towards his hereditary reserves to seek his rule" (*Their Faces*, p. 1172). In order to maintain its integrity, that social self which, according to Barrès, forms the base of the individual self, must adopt as its first rule the duty to resist domination by what it conceives to be the external. And this duty not only justified the xenophobia and racism typical of nationalism, it obligated its adherents to safeguard the purity of the nation by extirpating all foreign elements from the greater body of which they strove to be a part. Otherwise, as Sturel puts it in *Appeal to the Soldier*: "I feel that French nationality—the substance that supports me, without which I myself would vanish—is diminishing, disappearing" (p. 901).

At this stage of the argument, we seem to have reached the same conclusion as the humanist or post-structuralist critics: by assimilating himself in irrational fashion to the group of identical fellow countrymen, the Barresian nationalist strives to affirm his identity by excluding, even attacking, those he defines as foreign, as other, and therefore as enemies. According to this logic, the pleasures of racism and xenophobia would arise from satisfying the self-preservative instincts. By emphasizing the role of annihilation as an intermediary between the moment of loss and the recuperation of self through national identity, however, we have isolated a factor which cannot be subsumed under that category, since that nothingness indicates the presence of *otherness within the self*. To exterminate the other is then tantamount to destroying the self, and this intimates a darker species of pleasure, one better characterized as *jouissance*.

Enjoying your thesis

The terms in which Barrès describes his dissolution within the Boulangist herd make it clear that this experience provided him with exquisite gratification: "I savored deeply the instinctive pleasure of being in a herd." He promises a similar *jouissance* to those who participate in his ideology of "the soil and the dead"; after affirming that each of us is an extension of our forebears, that we are they, he prefaces his remarks about the death-defying continuity of the family, race and nation with the assurance: "Those who are convinced [that they are their parents] [...] derive [from this awareness] a delightful giddiness in which the individual disintegrates in order to recover himself in the family, the race, the nation, the thousands of years which the grave cannot nullify."[33] In either case, whether fusing with the spatial or the temporal collectivity, it is by reveling in the death drive that his nationalism professes to abolish death.

The same enjoyment of the crowd is nowhere more evident than in the mob scene that Sturel witnesses around the Lyons train station in Paris (*Appeal to the Soldier*, p. 787).[34] Dismissed from his post as Minister of War, forced to leave Paris and go into exile, General Boulanger is hailed by a mob of screaming supporters and carried off in a whirlwind of humanity. In a description whose images and ambiguous focalization are reminiscent of Hugo or Zola but whose tone betrays a rapt admiration for sheer power alien to his predecessors, Barrès metaphorizes the crowd into an "immense wave," an "animal" with "formidable undulations," and explains: "Obscure sentiments, inherited from their ancestors, words that these combatants would have been unable to define, but through which they recognized each other as being brothers, created that delirium [...] [those] forces of the national unconscious," while Sturel "remained for a few moments, enjoying the emotion incited within him by these torrents of humanity" (p. 787).

This scene is the counterpart to the climactic sequence of *The Uprooted*, in which the public outpouring of emotion during the funeral ceremonies of Victor Hugo sends thrills running up and down Sturel's spine, while he alternately represses and broods over his collusion in the crime of Racadot and Mouchefrin. By its open evocation of death, both in the apotheosis of the dead national hero's body at the foot of the Arch of Triumph and in the intermittent recalls of Astiné's gruesome murder, the chapter describing Hugo's memorial services, tellingly entitled *"La vertu sociale d'un cadavre,"* elicits much more forcefully the delectation that constitutes the reward for those who allow themselves the luxury of dissolving into the mob. The exhibition of Hugo's corpse in front of that "door to the void," as the Arch of Triumph was called in those days when the city ended there, brings home to the people of Paris the reality of death whose thought they usually try to elude, for, they reflect, if even the great man can die, then so will we. Thus transformed into the gateway to "nothingness and mystery" (p. 728), the Arch becomes the visible image of that wintry fear of death and the unknown at the bottom of every effort to grasp at a solid identity. Like the turning tide, in reaction to this dread the crowds of people flooding the *Champs-Élysées* from the *Place de la Concorde* to the Arch of Triumph soon become drunk with their own elevation of the poet to the status of a god and devote a veritable orgiastic cult to the product of their creation.

> Like every cult of the dead, these funeral ceremonies heightened their sense of life. The grand idea the crowd formed of the corpse [...] swept a strange ardor into their veins. The benches along the *Champs-Élysées*, the shadows in the bushes became one immense orgy that lasted all the way to dawn.
>
> (p. 728)

The similarity of these scenes of pro- and anti-republic mass demonstrations makes almost palpable the continuity between that Republic and its Boulangist and nationalist enemies. On one level, the enjoyment of belonging to the herd responds to the craving for adherence to a tangible group—whether crowd or ancestors—produced by the sense of powerlessness and the evacuation of identity resulting from the impersonal universalism of the discourse of the Republic. The means chosen for satisfying this need, however, shows that it is an ironic, populist exaggeration of the republican ethics of universality, in that the latter depends on and enforces the sameness of all citizens as of humanity in general, erasing all boundaries between the individual and the group. A kind of living parody of republican universalism, nationalist mass demonstrations, like the Boulangist rallies that preceded them, were in part a performance, for the benefit of the republican Other, of the inadequacy and the persistent externality of republican identity for those who felt that in reality they were excluded from participating in it. Precursors of the political theater so closely associated with fascist politics, in Italy as in Germany, these demonstrations hover between being conventional protests and the exhibitions of rapt acquiescence of the 1920s and '30s. They follow the more or less covert lesson taught in the schools, by the behavior of the pupils and the tacit encouragement of the authorities, embodiments of the democratic superego: conform to the group or suffer exclusion and humiliation.[35] In exchange for the renunciation of all particularity, individuals receive the sensation, if not the reality, of control and group identity. This enjoyment compensates for their sense of impotence in the face of a distant, vast and impersonal bureaucracy on the national level, a perception of real powerlessness that is magnified a thousandfold by the promise of power—the citizen as *sovereign*—held out in all the Republic's civics textbooks.

The other death evoked in this chapter is that of Astiné. It opens with Sturel's mortal battle with himself over the guilt he feels for his implication in the murder and the sense of obligation he harbors toward his friend Mouchefrin. The ostensible purpose for the juxtaposition of the two fatalities is of course to provide Sturel with a determining reason to conclude his otherwise inextricable vacillation between loyalty to a former friend and the obligation to denounce a criminal. The national grandeur and unity manifested in the civil ceremonies of Hugo's funeral chase away his somber thoughts of death, replacing them with an acceptance of Taine's message: "After marching all day with organized France [...] he has discovered the great spring of which his life is just a tiny stream" (p. 737). Now able to step back from his individual predicament and see things under the aspect of eternity, feeling the mysterious unity of life that Hugo displays in his poetry and the crowd manifests in its exhilaration, Sturel renounces all desire to seek remedies or wreak vengeance for "the atrocity that was committed."

Carroll and Reid discern another function in this combination of plot elements: the assassination of Astiné and the trial of Mouchefrin and Racadot, which surround the narrative of Hugo's burial, represent a purification of the nation, the brutal eradication of the "foreign," whether external or internal, being a necessary preparation for the exaltation of Hugo as national hero.[36] No "sacrifice," as the narrator later calls the failure of the two criminals, is too great in the service of the noble goal of national unity. Since that unity is threatened by everything alien, whether it be the Greek and German philosophy of "nihilism" Bouteiller teaches, the Jews who have "invaded" Lorraine after the German annexation of Alsace, or, above all, the values represented directly by Astiné—the feminine that weakens men, stories that arouse the imagination, and, of course, exoticism, "his *bête noire*, Romanticism accompanied by its orientalist hodgepodge."[37]

Foreignness is such a great danger, Barrès laments, because, whereas in previous times France was strengthened by integrating foreigners into herself, "Nowadays, these vagabonds are transforming us in their image" (*Uprooted*, p. 661). This interpretation is just the forerunner of the noxious antisemitism Barrès will take over from Soury during the heat of the Dreyfus Affair,[38] when he will trumpet the defamations later repeated by the Nazis, that the Jew is not a human being at all and therefore has no claim to be treated according to ethical or legal standards. He should instead be put on display in an ethnology department.[39]

Beyond the exclusion and extermination of the alien, another dimension of the crime bears close scrutiny: Sturel's profound complicity in it and the enjoyment his vicarious participation betrays. It is he who, out of selfish motives, unwittingly precipitates the bankruptcy of Renaudin's newspaper, the event that eventually leads the two young men to commit the murder. Although Sturel is not present at the moment when the two crush Astiné's skull, the author takes great pains to make the reader understand that he could have saved his former lover from her destruction, but failed to help her in order not to compromise himself in the eyes of Thérèse Alison, the young woman he was then courting, and her mother (pp. 702–3).

The message these scenes convey is that Sturel inadvertently but inevitably must do everything in his power to rid himself of Astiné in order to be able to possess Thérèse. On the level of political ideology his behavior signifies, as the critics point out, the removal of the foreign and the return to the regional, the national, Thérèse being from Lorraine. The accidental nature of his involvement in the motivation of Racadot's crime, the quasi-hypnotic character of his paralysis at the time of Astiné's need, and above all the fact that he never recalls either event during his anguished debate with himself in the aftermath of the crime, all this intimates the presence of an unconscious motive as well. A great part of Astiné's attraction for her young lover derives from the stories of her oriental origins she recounts to him. The names of the areas where her family had lived, the Euphrates, Mesopotamia, Persia, awaken deep stirrings within him, for when he was four or five, his imagination was created through listening to stories of these legendary places (p. 545). In his memoirs, Barrès reveals that it was his own mother who performed this service for him in reality by reading him *Richard the Lion-Hearted in Palestine* when he lay ill as a child. At that moment, "my imagination took hold of a few delightful figures that would never leave me again: young angelic women, the Orient, were to lie dormant in the depths of my mind along with my young mother's voice, to be reawakened at the time of my adolescence."[40] Astiné, the widow, the older, experienced woman who initiates Sturel into sexuality, the "oriental" whose very exoticism recalls the most intimate memories of the child, is thus an avatar of the mother from whom Sturel must liberate himself in order to reach the emotional autonomy without which he will never attain the identity he seeks.

The private oedipal situation is thus transposed onto the politics of nationalism, although it should be noted that this is not a necessary connection, desire for the exotic woman having already served in *Enemy of the Laws* the contrary ideological aim of attacking "narrow" nationalism.[41] The same motif of separation from the matrix, which seems so contradictory to nationalist immersion in the group, recurs twice in the space of a few pages, the first time in the narrator's commentary on the lesson Hugo offers Sturel in his poetry, the second in the narration of Sturel's visit to Mouchefrin's room the night of Hugo's burial. On the one hand, he casts the murderer outside the pale of the human race, describing him as "a reptile striving to attain to being, to differentiate himself from the slime, the fevers, the chaos in which he moves" (p. 733). On the other, like Michelet, he exalts the power of the word, of Hugo's poetry, to make us participate in the fraternal communion of our common heritage as we rose out of the darkness of undifferentiated nature (p. 729), just as he had admired Michelangelo's Promethean figures "who tear themselves free of their block of marble."[42] Fraternity in the collectivity is therefore the remedy to non-differentiation, in the same way that belonging to society is meant to protect us from the abyss of pure nature that represents dissolution into the nothingness which preceded the first glimmerings of identity.

The nationalist and oedipal themes of xenophobia and separation are not the only significant aspects of Astiné's slaying, however. Its other face is the mask of enjoyment. The entire murder scene is tinged with sexual overtones. Mouchefrin especially, who has earlier tried in vain to make the Armenian woman his mistress, is excited by frustrated desire, whipped up into a frenzy by Astiné's insulting sneer at his size as he pulls her along: "—You can see very well that you are still too little to hold on to women except by their skirts" (p. 704).

> Creature of luxury, she has inflamed their blood with desire, with her disdainful body. She is being killed by two poor men who are also proud males. These two characteristics, when they don't exclude each other, form a most dangerous species.
>
> (p. 705)

The narrator takes obvious delight in the detailed, sensual and rhythmic description he gives of her dead body:

> *Ce beau corps, cette gorge de vierge qu'elle avait gardée, et que baigne le fleuve d'un sang encore vivant, ces jambes adorables[...] . Ce cadavre, ce*

sang et ces beautés découvertes [...] c'est l'éternelle Hélène [...] qui [...] attise dans notre sein une ardeur que rien ne satisfera.[...]. Pour que soit complète l'atmosphère de volupté, il ne manque pas au tableau l'appareil du carnage.

(p. 706)[43]

At the same time, as Suleiman and Reid have argued, Barrès tries to exorcize the temptation of sadism and disorder by throwing all the blame, scientifically—"We are botanists" (p. 708)—on the two allegedly primitive characters and the universalizing education that has deracinated them from the social ties that prevent other men from acting out their violent instincts (p. 738).[44] "Frightful debauchery," "The deeply horrible thing is that this spectacle is utterly exhilarating! Men love to bite, and their mouths go dry with desire at the sight of appalling things" (p. 705). No other characters being present at the fatal moment, it must be to the reader that the narrator addresses his exclamation; Barrès thus invites his public to participate imaginatively in the sadistic pleasure aroused in contemplating this sight. Despite the narrator's overt disavowal of Racadot and Mouchefrin, then, he makes their act appealing to the reader in order to demonstrate the kind of covert gratification he can expect from participation in nationalist pogroms designed to exterminate the foreign. As her decapitation testifies, Astiné is the figure of "castration" in the Lacanian sense of the term. The graphic description of her murder represents a kind of sexual climax, a covert satisfaction of incestuous desire that combines the refusal to renounce the maternal object and to take on the mutilation of the self such renunciation entails, with the attempt to throw all the suffering of being onto the other, all of this staged for the benefit of the Other,[45] a position occupied in this case by the politicized readers who together form the Nation.

Suleiman makes the interesting suggestion that the strong emotional reaction evoked by these descriptions overflows, as it were, the didactic intention of the author manifested in the analytic tone of his scientific explanations.[46] Certainly, the charm Astiné exercises on the reader as on Sturel is not dissipated by the narrator's classification of her as the evil alien, the virus or poison (Barrès's terms for her, e.g., p. 554) which must be removed in order to restore the national organism to health.[47] In fact, as strange as it might seem, each time the narrator mentions her lingering seductive power over the young man it is to support rather than negate the ideological value system he promulgates elsewhere in the text. For the lesson that Astiné had taught Sturel is the same one he learns from the crowds at Hugo's funeral and from the poet's writings, the very notion of acceptance that is supposed to constitute the heart of Barrès's nationalist doctrine (p. 730).

Nihil humani me alienum puto

As Suleiman points out, Astiné's influence on Sturel, like Bouteiller's, persists through the later volumes of the trilogy, long after her murder.[48] A few years, and several hundred pages after her death, Astiné's ghostly presence reasserts itself. Sitting in a café, plotting vengeance for the Panama scandal with the anarchist Fanfournot, Sturel ponders the similarity between the members of parliament who profit from graft in that scandal and the anarchists who steal Panama bonds to finance their political activities. The two groups use identical pretexts to justify their appetites. Overcome by the atmosphere of the place, Fanfournot's stories, and too much absinth, Sturel plunges into a kind of trance, in which he contemplates "this abject society of enjoyment" under the same aspect of eternity he had reached during Hugo's burial. Individuality, however real, becomes irrelevant in this perspective; all people are united in their fundamental animality, in the very instincts the narrator invoked in describing Racadot and Mouchefrin attacking Astiné: biting, grasping, tearing apart (p. 1146). Lurking beneath the pleasant glow that society projects over life, Sturel muses, reign the "Mothers" of Goethe's *Faust* Part Two, and this idea inevitably calls to his mind the image of Astiné with her "proud humility" and her "clairvoyant slave's resignation" (pp. 1146–7). Like her, the Mothers, as Mephisto explains to Faust, counsel total acceptance; to which Faust replies that he will not seek salvation in lethargy (quoted on p. 1147). With a shudder, Sturel pulls himself up out of his stupor, having understood that everything is necessary (p. 1147). But just as Barrès never loses his fascination with and taste for the "Orient" or for romanticism, despite his sometimes violent criticisms of both,[49] so he will memorialize the call of the earth in his political slogan of "the earth and the dead."

In this whole scene Sturel is described as a drowning man being sucked down into the depths of a whirlpool whose overwhelming force derives from the almost irresistible attraction of the sheer nothingness of the pre-human, pre-social self attached to Astiné and the earth Mothers. It is the surreptitious fascination of that nothingness, designated under the term "nihilism," that unites the apparently disparate and unmotivated set of associations the text attaches to Astiné. Her assassination aims not only at eliminating everything foreign; it also strives to eradicate that which is most intimate, precisely because this ownmost being [*la nature propre*] of Sturel is actually the alien, "that intimate part of Sturel that is properly [*proprement*] Astiné" (p. 730). During the murder and again in the description of the Hugo ceremonies, the narrator insists that Astiné lived on in Sturel. She had deposited in him elements forever amalgamated with his own nature (p. 730). Nihilism, the fascinating seduction of nothingness, is "Astiné's poison acting in his blood! Wherever he goes, he carries her within him" (p. 703). It is this nothingness that forms the core of Sturel's identity and constitutes at the same time the rationale for Barrès's "scientific" condemnation of Astiné and the voluptuous charm that causes both the rhetoric and the ideology of the text to overflow the "scientific interpretation" of her role.

The motto of the Barresian nationalist (with apologies to Terence) thus could be: "I think the nothingness of humanity is the foreign within me." This extimacy is not quite the same thing as the assertion that "the individual is nothing without the group." Like Barrès and the Nationalists of those days and our own, the critics would like to make a neat division between inside and outside: between the others who are in fact the same (see Carroll, p. 27)—Barrès's "affinities"—and the Others who are genuinely alien, foreign. The problem is that the enemy also resides within the self, not just outside it. And it does so due to the subject's own desire. Astiné's murder aims at eliminating everything foreign, as the critics rightly observe, but to do so would be to eradicate that which is most intimate within Sturel. The nationalists' bargain is the reverse of Faust's pact with the devil: he was eager to sell his soul for one moment of total fulfilment, while they are willing to kill their desire in order to acquire a solid identity (see Lacan's analysis of university discourse in *L'envers de la psychanalyse*). Willing, but, at least in the exemplary case of Sturel, not able.

For, to eliminate "that intimate part of Sturel that is specifically Astiné" (p. 730) would be to eliminate the desiring core of his self. Secretly convinced that the Other, the foreigner holds the key to *jouissance*, the nationalist Sturel—the "true French"—cannot live with her, yet he (and they) cannot live without her. The nationalist solution to this paradox—which is the main paradox of present-day multiculturalism and its discontents—is instead to embalm her within him, to preserve her, but as dead.

From this perspective, a third reading of the function of the juxtaposition of the two deaths emerges: Sturel is able to exorcize the foreign only by making it an essential "part" of himself. It is not simply that the nationalist subject defines himself by his difference from the other, as some postcolonial theory has it; rather, by the paradoxical logic of the extimate, the act of murder functions to immortalize the (M) Other, preserved *in vitro*, so to speak. As Sturel watches Astiné about to be hauled off to her death, the narrator opines:

> In truth, at this date, if she has fulfilled her own [*propre*] destiny, she can benefit from a continuation of her life in Sturel. And perhaps it is her appetite for self-destruction, her perpetual gift of herself in the midst of her debauchery, that make this rare woman worthy of surviving herself.
>
> (p. 703)

The permanent installation of Astiné in Sturel's mind is a refusal of mourning, in every way comparable to the institution of Barrès's nationalist identification with the race in reaction to the death of his parents, and to the intoxication with death that characterizes the *jouissance* of Barrès's nationalism.

After her death, through her murder, Astiné is transported from the real to the symbolic, becoming the element of suture for the discourse of rootedness and nationalism. Once dead, she functions as the signifier of the excluded element—the foreign, the Other, the *nihil*—the signifier that makes it possible to incorporate the alien into the nationalist system as that which is excluded from nationalism, and that, like Frege's empty set in the realm of the logic of number theory, is required to allow that system to achieve closure.[50] Her use as suture constitutes the desperate attempt to assimilate the unassimilable, to guarantee the unity so obviously contradicted by her very existence. Unlike a purely logical system, however, a political engine like nationalism must constantly be fed and stoked in order to be maintained; hence the insatiable need, characteristic of fascism, for ever more victims to persecute and eventually to exterminate. An infinite series of human signifiers representing the Other, the foreign, the exotic must be lined up and purged, but not in order to purify the system totally, getting rid of them once and for all. Rather, they must be inhumed and embalmed within the system, like dead butterflies skewered onto the pages of an entomologist's album. For ultimately, the closure and the sense of autonomy achieved by killing desire are illusory: the sense of incompletion and the recognition of loss inevitably return, to haunt the nationalist and to reactivate the secret allure of nothingness. Rootedness may very well have "provide[d] an intellectually respectable solution to the problem of nihilism and decadence which plagued so many intellectuals at the fin de siècle" (Soucy, p. 113), but it did so by enshrining the very nihilism whose troublesome persistence it was meant to eliminate.

In the final analysis, acceptance and nihilism are not simple binary opposites in the nationalist system, but participate in a three-tiered system, whose elements are the individual Ego, the hereditary collective self, and the nothingness threatened by physiological "animal" instinct and passion. The latter, the realm of the Mothers, is the nucleus of what Lacan calls the traumatic real within the symbolic, in that it is the element that society cannot represent, precisely because in this system nihilism is the destruction of society's beliefs and values. It is no doubt for that reason that Sturel must enter a trance-like state when he contemplates that domain. Society, therefore, the nationalist symbolic, acts as a shield from that traumatic real. At the same time, the nationalist imagines that it is the Republic that is forcing him to renounce the object of his desire. Barrès's solution allows him to keep that object alive, but as impossible to attain, a kind of permanent and ineffectual non-acceptance of current social arrangements that harnesses revolutionary energy directed against the Republic for the purposes of reaction typical of fascism.[51] Just as Astiné is worthy of surviving herself insofar as she accepts, and even seeks, her self-destruction, so the acceptance of the dissolution of the self in the herd is designed to guarantee the self-assertion and self-perpetuation of the nationalist identity against all "foreigners" and thereby against the true annihilation encapsulated within the foreign. In sum, it is precisely by accepting his self-destruction—his dissolution into "society," the symbolic understood as the collectivity—that the nationalist can ensure his survival, that is, can avoid his annihilation by the absolute otherness of "instinct and passion," the object within.

Notes

1. This article is based on research completed at the Institute for Advanced Study in Princeton, with funding from the National Endowment for the Humanities. Robert Soucy, *Fascism in France: The Case of Maurice Barrès* (Berkeley, CA: University of California Press, 1972), p. 18, p. 162, pp. 283–99.
2. Soucy, p. 20.
3. Soucy, p. 20. Zeev Sternhell, *Maurice Barrès et le nationalisme français* (Paris: Armand Colin, 1983); David Carroll, *French Literary Fascism: Nationalism, Anti-Semitism, and the Ideology of Culture* (Princeton: Princeton University Press, 1994); Philippe Lacoue-Labarthe and Jean-Luc Nancy, *Le mythe nazi* (La Tour d'Aigues: Éditions de l'Aube, 1991).
4. See Édouard de Hartmann, *Philosophie de l'inconscient*, translated by D. Nolen (Paris: Germer Baillière, 1877), I, p. 45 (the first French translation from the German of Hartmann's *Philosophy of the Unconscious*); also Jules-Auguste Soury, *Campagne nationaliste*, p. 60, cited in Sternhell, p. 258. In his diary,

Barrès cites Soury on this topic (*Mes cahiers 1896–1923* (Paris: Plon, 1994 [1963]), p. 53), and returns to it several times in *Le roman de l'énergie nationale* [*The Novels of National Energy* trilogy], in *Maurice Barrès: Romans et voyages,* edited by Vital Rambaud (Paris: Robert Laffont, 1994), p. 660, p. 757, and p. 1197, as well as in *Scènes et doctrines du nationalisme* (Paris: Trident, 1987) [*Scenes and Doctrines of Nationalism*].

5. Thus Jules Ferry, two-time President of the Council (akin to Prime Minister) and Minister of Public Instruction in the 1880s, following the positivist theories of Auguste Comte and his disciples, as well as of Spencer's *On Education* (translated into French in 1878), justified teaching secular morality in the new primary schools he fought to establish throughout France with views identical to those of so-called "irrationalism": The heart is more powerful than the intellect; the "instinct" of sympathy, which is the basis of morality, is as natural an affection as selfishness; sentiments must be actively cultivated and developed; and the goal of ethical instruction in the schools is to teach the individual to subordinate himself to the group, and above all to national unity in order to combat "intellectual anarchy." The men and women he appointed to direct those schools and to formulate their curricula were, for the most part, neo-Kantians with more or less strong Protestant leanings, rather than positivists.

6. See Jacques-Alain Miller, "Extimacy," in *Lacanian Theory of Discourse: Subject, Structure, and Society,* edited by Mark Bracher (NY: New York University Press, 1994), pp. 74–87, for a detailed explication of this term.

7. The French titles are, respectively: *Les déracinés; Appel au soldat;* and *Leurs figures.* All citations from these novels are from the Rambaud edition of *Romans et voyages,* with page references given in parentheses in the text.

8. Fritz Ringer, *Fields of Knowledge: French Academic Culture in Comparative Perspective 1890–1920* (Cambridge: Cambridge University Press, 1992), p. 130.

9. All translations from the French, of Barrès and other writers, are my own.

10. Hippolyte Taine, *Origines de la France contemporaine, La révolution,* vol. 2, *La conquête jacobine* (Paris: Hachette, 1881), p. 9.

11. Pierre-Henri Petitbon, *Taine, Renan, Barrès: Étude d'influence* (Paris: Belles Lettres, 1935), p. 90.

12. *L'oeuvre de Maurice Barrès,* edited by Philippe Barrès, vol. 13 (Paris: Au Club de l'Honnête Homme, 1968), p. 138, entry of November 13, 1897; *La Revue Blanche* (Summer 1897), p. 267.

13. *Scènes et doctrines,* pp. 12–13.

14. "Réponse à M. René Doumic," in *Romans et voyages,* p. 181; first published in *La Revue des Deux Mondes,* January 15, 1900.

15. Ringer, p. 133.

16. We know that this notion comes down to Barrès through his early reading of Kant's pupil, Fichte (See Ida Marie Frandon, *Barrès précurseur* (Paris: Fernand Lanore, 1983), p. 51).

17. Barrès, "Réponse à Doumic," p. 181.

18. The ideological interchangeableness of left and right in certain of their critiques of liberalism is nowhere more visible than in this profession of national identity, apparently so characteristic of the right. In fact, Pierre Leroux, the socialist thinker who so profoundly influenced George Sand,

proclaimed in Book Five, Chapter 12 of *De l'humanité* (1840), entitled "La solidarité des hommes est éternelle": "Nous sommes non pas seulement les fils et la postérité de ceux qui nous ont précédés, mais au fond et réellement ces générations elle-mêmes." In this passage, Leroux is objecting to Constant's contrary assertion, about the lack of ties among generations and races, in *De la religion*.

19. See Barrès, *Scènes et doctrines*, p. 51.
20. 1904 "Préface" to *Un homme libre*, in *Romans et voyages*, p. 93.
21. "Réponse à Doumic," p. 182.
22. *Romans et voyages*, p. 1351, n. 48.
23. *Mes mémoires* in *L'oeuvre de Maurice Barrès*, vol. 13, p. 26.
24. *Sous l'oeil des barbares* in *Romans et voyages*, p. 86.
25. *Mes cahiers*, p. 50.
26. *Mes cahiers*, p. 43.
27. See Jacques Lacan, *The Seminar of Jacques Lacan, Book VII, The Ethics of Psychoanalysis*, edited by Jacques-Alain Miller, translated by Dennis Porter (NY: W. W. Norton, 1992).
28. *Scènes et doctrines*, p. 14.
29. Vital Rambaud, "Barrès et 'le sens du relatif'" in *Mesure*, 4 (October 1990), p. 192.
30. "Réponse à Doumic," p. 181.
31. "Réponse à Doumic," p. 182.
32. *L'oeuvre de Maurice Barrès*, vol. 13, p. 24.
33. "Réponse à Doumic," p. 182.
34. See Soucy, p. 118.
35. See Slavoj Žižek, *The Metastases of Enjoyment* (London: Verso, 1994), pp. 55–6, for a compelling description of what Lacan calls the "obscenity of the superego."
36. Carroll, p. 39; Martine Reid, "L'orient liquidé (Barrès, *Les déracinés*)," in *Romanic Review*, 83.3 (May 1992), pp. 379–88.
37. Reid, pp. 386–7.
38. Sternhell, p. 253.
39. Barrès, *Scènes et doctrines*, p. 153.
40. *L'oeuvre de Maurice Barrès*, vol. 13, p. 8.
41. *L'ennemi des lois*, in *Romans et voyages*, pp. 307–8.
42. Barrès, *Du sang, de la volupté et de la mort*, in *Romans et voyages*, p. 449.
43. Here is a literal translation of the passage that conveys its sense if not its sensuality. "That beautiful body, that virgin's breast she had preserved and which is bathed in a river of still living blood, those adorable legs [...]. That corpse, that blood and those uncovered beauties [...] she is the eternal Helen ... who fans in our breast the flames of an ardor that nothing will satisfy [...]. To complete the voluptuous atmosphere, not even the trappings of carnage are missing from this tableau."
44. Susan Suleiman, *Authoritarian Fictions: The Ideological Novel as a Literary Genre* (NY: Columbia University Press, 1983), p. 208; Reid, pp. 383–7.
45. See Jacques Lacan, "Kant with Sade," translated by James B. Swenson, *October*, 51 (Winter, 1989) 55–75, p. 65.
46. Suleiman, p. 209.
47. Reid, p. 387; Carroll, p. 39.

48. Suleiman, p. 125.
49. See Reid, p. 387.
50. The elements in Frege's set are those things that are identical to themselves; everything real presumably. The empty set contains those things which are not identical to themselves, that is nothing, which is why it is empty. But if it contains nothing, nevertheless it is itself something, a signifier, a set, the first element in that other set, the series of integers; it is the zero term that acts as the starting point necessary to launch the infinite series. See Jacques-Alain Miller, "Suture," translated by Jacqueline Rose, *Screen*, 18 (1978) pp. 24–34.
51. Soucy, p. 206.

13
Topography of the Border: Derrida Rewriting Transcendental Aesthetics

Joanna Hodge

I will rapidly mention the first seven *aporias* that concern the theme of this conference. Each of them puts to test a *passage*, both an impossible and a necessary passage, and two apparently heterogeneous borders. The first type of border passes among *contents* (things, objects, referents, territories, countries, states, nations, cultures, languages etc.) or between Europe and some non-Europe, for example. The other type of borderly limit would pass between a *concept* (singularly that of duty) and an other, according to the bar of an oppositional logic. Each time the decision concerns the choice between the relation to an other, who is its other (that is to say, an other that can be opposed in a couple), and the relation to a wholly non-opposable other, that is, an other that is no longer its other. What is at stake in the first place is therefore not the crossing of a given border, rather, at stake is the *double concept of the border*, from which this *aporia* comes to be determined.

—(*Aporias*, pp. 17–18)

Setting the scene

This opening citation is taken from the paper Derrida delivered to the Cerisy conference, 'Passages to the frontiers: concerning Jacques Derrida', held in 1992, and subsequently published as *Aporias: Awaiting One Another/Death at the Limits of Truth*.[1] There, Derrida invokes his own previous study, 'The Other Heading: Memories, Responses,

Responsibilities', delivered in Turin in 1990, and published with additional explanatory notes in 1991.[2] These two papers provide the primary points of orientation for a discussion of a Derridean topography
of the border, understood as a rewriting of a transcendental aesthetics.
This notion of a 'topography of the border' takes up and recasts the
figure of a topolitology, of the secret, of the command, of the promise,
of the threshold, developed in the discussions of negative theology, and
brought to a certain form in 'How to avoid speaking: Denials', first presented in Jerusalem in 1984.[3] This earlier discussion of the logic of the
boundary, as threshold, in a topolitology, is concerned with the arrival
of a divine interruption, and with marking a boundary between secular
and sacred experience, whereas with the notion of topography, there
is to be marked a shift to a concern more for a demarcation between
the political and philosophical, than between ontology and theology,
or religion and philosophy. This shift permits an identification also of
Derrida's preoccupation with connections and parallelisms between the
delimitations of Kant's critiques, and the delimitations of sense undertaken in the name of psychoanalysis. My discussion of this topography
of the border seeks in the first instance to focus attention on a relation
of transformation between Derrida's intervention in philosophy, and
Kantian critique, between Derrida on borders and passages, and Kant
on critical delimitation. This reveals a third figuration, as intermediary,
in the guise of Husserl's phenomenology, for, with Kant, Husserl is committed to a certain transcendentalism and, with Derrida, to rethinking
the relation between sense, as meaning, neutral between languages, and
sense, as embedded in specific discursive formations.

The question to which my juxtaposition of terms, transcendental aesthetics, and topography of the border, responds is that of thinking the
multiple *aporia*, delineated by Derrida, through an analysis of a double
concept of the border, and, as it turns out, a double concept of duty. The
double concepts of the border and of duty are as indicated in this citation double in a double sense, for while in the first instance they are set
up as a closed opposition between two terms which exhaustively delimit
each other, there is then also a shift of levels in which a series of further
non-opposable terms arrive for consideration. There is the other which
may be opposed in a couple, and a third, a wholly non-opposable other,
that is the 'other that is no longer its other'. This is the structure of the
three more or less than one, invoked by Derrida on various occasions,
to mark up the non-dialectical nature of the first presumed opposition.
The structure of these *aporia*, I suggest, is best determined in terms of
the problem of how to think time, as famously posed by St. Augustine,

in *Confessions* 11, 13–18: 'if no-one asks me about it, I know what it is, but when they ask, and I wish to explain it, I do not know', a quotation positioned by Edmund Husserl's editors at the start of the 1928 edition of his *The Phenomenology of Internal Time Consciousness*.[4] The notion of *aporia* here in play then is not held in place by reference back to its classic point of deployment in the philosophical tradition, in the Socratic dialogues, since for the Socratic dialogues there is a different set of questions, concerning a series of demarcations between reason, political life and religious orientation, between notions of *theoria, praxis, poiesis* and piety. The arrival of Christianity reveals the curiously permeable boundary for the Greeks between deifying natural forces, the oceans, the thunder of the mountains, and deifying cognitive faculties.

Derrida introduces a distinct modification of the notion of the aporetic, which brings to the fore the puzzle for thinking philosophical conceptuality in relation to two, or three, or more, or less, versions of monotheism, underlined by continual returns to a reading of St. Augustine, as both his compatriot, from the Northern African littoral, his predecessor, his foe and his close confederate. My discussion then is framed by the relations between Derrida and Augustine, between Derrida and Kant, between Husserl and St. Augustine, and, by implication, the relation between Derrida and Husserl.[5] The notion of duty and the notion of the promise as deployed by Kant are taken up and transformed in the process of Derrida taking up and transforming Kant's transcendental aesthetics, which defends the presumption that a thinking of a relation between space and time is basic. The *aporia* of Derrida's title start out as a problem of thinking limits and ends, and beginnings, and their derivation from the terms of discussion of space and time set out by Kant in the *First Critique*. These *aporia* modulate into the problem of how to think duty and responsibility, in a space neutral between a context devoid of religious commitment, and a context permeated with religious commitment. The problem is one of thinking the transition between the concept of necessity, as developed in Kant's *First Critique,* and the concept of duty, as developed in his moral philosophy, while maintaining a neutrality with respect to the religious commitments which, for Kant, motivate while not providing conceptual or ontological grounding for that transition. The double concept of the border thus turns into a questioning of philosophy, in relation to politics, within a framework where religious orientation is taken for granted; and a questioning of philosophy, for which religious orientation cannot be taken for granted.

The double concept of the border is articulated by Derrida at first in terms of two dimensions, as both empirical and conceptual determinacy.

The first is developed in relation to territories, between Europe and 'some non Europe', and between domains of entities, enumerated by Derrida as things, objects or referents; and the second is marked up in terms of conceptual determinations, in the first place through the notion of duty. This notion of duty makes implicit appeal to the notion of duty, as deployed by Kant, in the development of his distinctive transcendental account of morality, in the *Critique of Practical Reason* (1788), the *Groundwork for a Metaphysics of Morals* (1785), and in the doctrines of right and of virtue developed in the *Metaphysics of Morals* (1797). In *Aporias*, Derrida traces the emergence of his own preoccupations in the following way:

> In more recent texts ('*Passions*' and '*Donner la Mort*') I have pursued the necessarily aporetic analysis of a duty as *over-duty* (*sur-devoir*) whose *hubris* and essential excess dictate transgressing not only the action that *conforms to duty* but also the action undertaken *out of the sense of duty*, that is, what Kant defines as the very condition of morality.
>
> (*Aporias*, p. 16)

Derrida here marks up a shift from using the Greek term, *hubris*, of getting above oneself, in seeking to transgress the limit between mortals who must succumb to fate and divinities who live through fate, and the Kantian notion of a transcendental concept of duty. Derrida subjects the concept of duty to an analysis, whereby its meanings proliferate beyond the position secured for it within moral philosophy by Kantian critique. In parallel with the disruption of this concept of duty, the notion of the border is also subjected by Derrida to a torsion between an empirical determinacy and a process of conceptual or transcendental determination. It will turn out that this doubling of the empirical and transcendental, along with this invocation of rewriting transcendental aesthetics, puts into question Derrida's relation to Husserl, and reveals an open-endedness to his encounter with Husserl's enquiries, in addition to marking up his responses to Kant.[6] Indeed Derrida's increasingly explicit relation to Kantian critique can be thought sometimes to mask his ongoing engagement with the phenomenology of Husserl, which emerges again into view in the second essay of *Rogues: Two Essays on Reason* (2004): 'The "world" of the Enlightenment to come (exception, calculation, and sovereignty)'.[7]

In terms of Kantian critique, the notion of duty must be thought in sequence with the notions of virtue and happiness, of finite and non-finite ends and intentions, and of freedom, as transcendental ideal, framed by recourse to the two remaining ideas of reason, an immortality of the soul and the idea of God. The continuity of the enquiries between *First* and *Second Critiques* is marked up by Kant in the Preface to the *Critique of Practical Reason*:

> Now practical reason itself, without any collusion with the speculative, provides reality to a supersensible object of the category of causality, i.e. to freedom. This is a practical concept and as such is subject only to practical use; but what in speculative critique could only be thought is now confirmed by fact. The strange but incontrovertible assertion of the speculative *Critique*, that the thinking subject is only an appearance to itself in inner intuition, now finds its full confirmation in the *Critique of Practical Reason;* the establishment of this thesis is here so cogent that one would be compelled to accept it even if the first had not already proved it.[8]

For Derrida, in *The Other Heading,* and in all the seminars from 1984 on, developing the theme at the *École des Hautes Études*, the notion of duty becomes connected up to a different series of terms: remembering and promising, hospitality and foreignness, critique and deconstructive genealogy, universality and specific idiom, event, futurity, as *a-venir*, decision and responsibility. With such a proliferation of themes, it is difficult to know what line of enquiry to follow. One clue here is the juxtaposition of the notions of the *a-venir*, and of the regulative idea, otherwise known as the 'Idea in the Kantian sense', as openings on to a thinking of the shape of futurity.

While the regulative idea is set up as a determinacy towards which actual deployment tends, the *a-venir* suggests by contrast that determinacy would arrive as an interruption of a sequence of time, not as its fulfillment. Thus there is implicit a contrast between time, as series brought to a completion in attaining the ends set out in advance, and a time as necessarily incomplete, interrupted and interruptive of any thinking of conceptual completions. In the essay in *Rogues*, Derrida indicates parallels and lacks of fit in the notions of time elaborated in the conjunction of teleological thinking and architectonic construction in Kant's writings, and the slightly different articulation in Husserl's writings of finality, in relation to meaning fulfillments, and system. Determinacy thus may have a counter-factual status, as the impossible completion of the series, held in place in a simple time horizon, and it may, according to the temporal structure of the *a-venir*, have a temporality distinct from that of any such time series. The arrival of transcendental determinacy in empirically given natural time series must have the latter status, for the temporality of transcendental determinacy is distinct from that of the natural time series. It should be noted that the concept of duty is deployed by Kant within the domain of a pure practical reason, whereas the regulative ideas are first introduced in the context of the *Critique of Pure Reason* (1781, 1787). Since the scope of pure reason and of pure practical reason are for Kant quite distinct, there is a question about what if any modifications of the concept of an 'Idea in the Kantian sense' might take place, if it is transposed from the domain of the former, the *First Critique* to that of the latter, the *Second Critique*. This is a topic which exercised Hegel in his extensive readings of and responses to Kant, and must here be left to one side.

Crossing borders

The crossing of given borders appears to have a simpler form than that of the passage from the problem of crossing given empirical borders, to the level of determination of transcendental concepts. For the latter is no longer a passage within the empirical, but rather a passage from the empirical to a transcendental level of reflection, or determination. However, it then becomes clear that even the empirical passage, if sense is to be made of it, presupposes the application of transcendentally determined concepts. Thus even at the empirical level there is no simple opposition and delimitation of two terms. For it is at the level of the transcendental that the meanings taken for granted at the empirical level are to be constituted, and analysed as in process of formation and determination. It is in these processes that sense and meanings get to be attached to notions of borders, passages, crossings and limits. Thus there are three distinct domains of enquiry here: the empirical, in which given concepts are deployed, a transcendental level of constitution, and that of the moves from the one to the other. Crossing actual borders takes place in a domain of experience, while the delimitation of domains of experience is simultaneously empirical and transcendental in nature. The specification of concepts appears to presuppose a pure domain of transcendental, or, perhaps, absolute meaning, however these meanings are, for Husserl at least, given only in empirically determinate contexts of lived experience.

Discussion of the status of such first level passages, and of a passage from the empirical to the transcendental, and of the difficulty of distinguishing between the two, is explicitly connected up by Derrida to a questioning of Heidegger's distinction in *Being and Time* (1927), between the vulgar, derivative notion of time, and the supposed existential, primordial notion of time, and the supposed passage from one to the other. Clarification of the vulgar, empirically given notion of time is taken by Heidegger to depend on a clarification of the existential structures of time, but there turns out to be a problem with supposing the latter to be available for thematization and amenable to conceptualization. Phenomenological enquiry classically takes the form of identifying what is made available pre-predicatively, or pre-ontologically, in advance of there being explicit procedures for individuation and identification, and then seeks to provide a thematization of what is given at that pre-predicative level. However, the structures of existential temporality appear to resist the degree of stabilization required for demonstrating conceptual determinacy, for they arrive, according to Heidegger in his analyses in Division Two of *Being and Time,* in the mode of the *Augenblick,* the twinkling of the eye, in which the secular world is transformed into one of salvation. In secular terms, empirical evanescence is given transcendental determinacy. Thus the temporality of their arrival itself has the form of a transition, by contrast to the mode of arrival of Husserlian essences, which is achieved through the double process of bracketing naturalist assumptions about what there is and the processes of variation and reduction. The problem for Husserl is of an apparently incompletable passage from a pre-predicative givenness, to a determination of essences; for Heidegger, the problem is that of insufficient stability in the supposed existentials which are to delimit the otherwise unstable notion of the horizon in which this meaning determination is supposed to take place. There is also apparently a reliance on a theological image to permit an articulation of the mode in which they might all the same be registered. As a result, the empirical concept cannot be shown to be derivative from a prior existential concept or grounding, since that concept or grounding can only be intimated, not demonstrated. In short it is not a concept, but a residue of theology. 'What', Derrida asks, 'if there was no other concept of time than the one that Heidegger calls "vulgar"'? (*Aporias*, p. 14). He then repeats the question in relation to Heidegger's distinction, from the beginning of Division Two of *Being and Time,* between a biological or physiological, and an existential concept of death:

> What if consequently opposing another concept to the 'vulgar' concept were itself impracticable, non-viable, and impossible? What if it was the same for death, for a vulgar concept of death? What if

> the exoteric *aporia* therefore remained in a certain way irreducible,
> calling for an endurance, or shall we rather say an experience other
> than that consisting in opposing, from both sides of an indivisible
> line, an other concept, a non-vulgar concept, to the so-called vulgar
> concept?
>
> *(Aporias*, p. 14)

The existential attestation of finitude, given in the existential determination of death, is supposed to provide a delimitation of Dasein, such
that, from its position as finite in the world, it can all the same aspire
to conceptual determinacy at an empirical and at an absolute, transcendental or, as Heidegger prefers, the existential level. This existential level
should then provide an intensification of an empirical notion of experience, as one in which its own ontological conditions are simultaneously
given. It appears, however, that the temporal conditions for this cannot
be determinately specified.

Derrida draws attention to this doubling of the notion of experience:
alongside Kant's empiricist notion of experience, there is a transcendental notion of experience, which Derrida calls an endurance, in
which the passage from empirical to transcendental levels is hypothesized, as Sisyphean, and never completable. Oddly, Derrida does not
also mark up the connection to Husserl, although Heidegger himself
indicates that the distinction between derivative and primordial time
is derived from Husserl's analyses, from the discussion of time in *On
the Phenomenology of the Consciousness of Internal Time* (1899–1917),
and indeed from the subsequent *Bernauer Manuscripts Concerning Time*
(1917).[9] For Husserl, as Heidegger is well aware, the naturally given
and scientifically constructed notions of time are derivative from
a consciousness of internal time, the status of which Husserl found
difficult to display, but which provides for him the unifying structures
for all intending. Analysis of this inner time consciousness reveals an
order and orderliness, constituted by the operations basic to Husserl's
phenomenology, of meaning intending and meaning fulfillment. This
order emerges out of what Husserl describes as the primordial streaming of absolute consciousness, and the question in dispute between
Husserl and Heidegger is whether this streaming is thinkable without
hypothesizing the primacy of Dasein. The dispute between Husserl and
Derrida concerns the shape of this streaming: is it linear and continuous, or is it looped and constructed around a series of lacunae, including the immemorial past, hypothesized by Levinas, and reconsidered
by Blanchot?[10]

Derrida appeals to a distinction between an exoteric *aporia*, the impossibility of choosing between a vulgar and a primordial concept of time, or of death, and an esoteric *aporia*, in which there is no such choice, since the two registers are interdependent. It is with this latter move that he retrieves the concept of experience from its immobilization within a system of metaphysically grounded oppositions and hierarchies, and rewrites it as the notion of endurance, traversal, or passage.

> The affirmation that announced itself through a negative form was therefore the necessity of experience itself, the experience of the *aporia* (and these two words that tell of the passage and the non-passage are thereby coupled in an aporetic fashion) as endurance or as passion, as interminable resistance or remainder.
>
> (*Aporias*, p. 19)

This reveals an unstated connection back to his readings of Nietzsche in the seventies, which engage the problems of doing justice to Nietzsche's thinking of overcoming and transition, while acknowledging Heidegger's imposition on the Nietzschean figures. While Nietzsche describes the possibility of a human self-transformation, in the figure of a transitional humanity, *Übermensch*, Heidegger's readings of Nietzsche repeat the movement of overcoming, in the thought of a winding up of metaphysics, overcoming a customary subordination of sensibility to intelligibility, but thereby reaffirming a movement of return to a Greek origin for philosophy, which Derrida seeks to resist. The notion of overcoming is transformed by Derrida into the notions of the excess of duty, an over-duty, and the excess of living, the living-on, *sur-venir*, in which these processes are both intensified and suspended, because thought as incompletable or unattainable.

The temporality of a border crossing is a point in a natural time series; the time of the Kantian critical delimitation is that of a methodological, transcendental interruption. The determination of the possibility of empirically given time, the time of the passage, is this time of endurance, of passion, or, indeed, of a Husserlian passive synthesis. Thus there is a distinction to be marked between an instant of self-affirmation, as an interruption of a natural time series, and a time of endurance, as duration, and as a disruption of that naturalized time series. This notion of experience as endurance is quite distinct from that theorized by Kant in the *Critique of Pure Reason*, and the imputed topography of the border gives a transcendental aesthetic for this alternate form of experience, by contrast to the transcendental aesthetic provided by Kant for the notion of experience, as repeatable experiences of actual and possible objects. In place of the modalities of the actual and the possible, Derrida installs the alternate modalities of chance, of the perhaps and the maybe, again in part as provided by Nietzsche's analyses. In place of the Kantian account of time, in which such an experience of actual and possible objects of experience may be organized, there is a hypothesis of the time of the interruption, and disruption, in the thought of an *a-venir*, which intimates a futurity, which does not proceed in accordance with models already set out, and in which chance, the perhaps and the maybe can occur, if unpredictably.

Kant introduces his notion of experience at the opening of the 'Analytic of Concepts', in the *Critique of Pure Reason*, as combining two heterogeneous elements, and in terms of a distinction between the inner articulation of faculties, and an openness to receiving impressions of what there is in the world:

> We can, however, with regard to these concepts, as with regard to all knowledge, seek to discover in experience, if not the principle of their possibility, at least the occasioning causes of their production. The impressions of the senses supplying the first stimulus, the whole faculty of knowledge opens out to them, and experience is brought into existence. That experience contains two very dissimilar elements, namely, the matter of knowledge (obtained) from the senses, and a certain form for the ordering of this matter (obtained) from the inner source of the pure intuition and thought which, on occasion of the sense-impressions, are first brought into action and yield concepts.[11]

It is worth remarking that while Husserl disputes the separation between empirical sensation and transcendental intuition, Derrida disputes the distinction between inner and outer sources for sensory or intuitable contents. This experience of objects of experience and of possible objects of experience takes place within a spatio-temporal framework, stabilized by the move made in the opening sections of the *First Critique*, giving a number of definitions of space, of time and of the relations between them: that they are two, that there is one, and only one, relation between them, and that they provide *apriori* forms of intuition, which in turn provide access to the evidences of sensation.[12] Thus a transcendental faculty, intuition, with its *apriori* forms, is brought to bear to frame empirical contents, given in sensation, which then conform to the structures provided by this faculty and its forms, and are articulable as processes of reception and registration. Derrida's attitude to this stabilization is indicated in his treatment of it in *The Truth in*

Painting (1978), which suggests that Kant's account of space and time in the 'Transcendental Aesthetic' at the beginning of the *First Critique* is retrospectively disrupted by the developments of alternate accounts of space, of time, and of the relation between them, in the *Third Critique*, especially but not only in relation to the analysis of the sublime, of magnitude and of might, in the *Critique of Aesthetic Judgment.*

The *Critique of Teleological Judgment,* concerning the relation between mechanism and finality, sets two notions of time alongside each other; that of an efficient causality, in which events are arranged in a series, made up of discrete sequences; and that of finality, in which there is a hypothesis concerning the durations of time required for the completion of certain identifiable processes, which may or may not fall into the time of the series, hypothesized in accord with a notion of cause as efficacy, and of efficacy as mechanical. This then leaves open the possibility of a priority of a thinking of time as external to the processes ordered within it, and of a thinking of time as organic to the articulations in question. This opening can but does not have to be tied into a discussion of the differences between a messianic break in time, and the completion of time implied in the full notion of messianism, the former operating as a formal indication of the latter.[13] The consequence of Derrida's questioning is to put up a further series of alternative accounts of the relation between space, time, human understanding and the relations between them, from that proposed by Kant at the beginning of the *First Critique*, from the one implied in the *Second Critique*, and in the various complications of the relations between space and time opened out by Kant, in the *Third Critique*. The methodologically challenging, disjointed reading of Kant's *Third Critique*, offered in the first part of *The Truth in Painting*, explores the possibility of generating figurations of truth through framings other than that of the Transcendental Aesthetic, placed at the beginning of Kant's *First Critique*, and other than the processes of the cumulative interpretation of text, the definition of terms and the development of cumulative argument. This line of thought clearly continues into the discussion of differences between messianism and messianic time, in *Specters of Marx: The Work of Mourning, The State of the Debt and the New International.*[14] However, it might be thought that Husserl has already committed himself to a rethinking of the relation between space and time, on the one hand, and the operations of understanding, on the other, in his insistence on modifying the Kantian notion of intuition.[15] Space and time are no longer separately determined, but are articulated through the temporally extended relation, indeed the duration marked out by the connection between meaning intention and meaning fulfillment. Time becomes internal to the articulation of meaning itself, not as a single linear series, but as a series of loopings of relations of satisfaction and non-confirmation of meaning intentions by the evidences provided by what Husserl calls intuition, but which takes a very different form from that hypothesized by Kant.

Genealogies for aesthetics

There are then three main elements to the discussion underway in this essay: there is an indication of what it might mean to find a transcendental aesthetic in Derrida's writings. There is an outline of a double genealogy for this notion of a transcendental aesthetics in the writings of Husserl (1859–1938) and of Kant (1724–1804). Finally, there would be a demonstration of the working through of Kantian and Husserlian themes in Derrida's writings, to test out the hypothesis that there is, indeed, such a re-working of transcendental aesthetics for Derrida, with respect to this double genealogy. In this essay there is a discussion of the first two, but not of the latter working through, since detailed textual reading is required to show the evidence supporting the claim. At this stage it is more important to show the outlines of a certain stretching and twisting of the notion of transcendental aesthetics, between Kant and Husserl and between Husserl and Derrida, which aligns to a certain stretching and twisting of the notions of space and time, and of their interconnections, which is flagged up by Kant as the principle concern of such an aesthetic. Thus it will turn out that the term '*différance*', neither a word nor a concept, is a place-holder for this rethinking of Kant's transcendental aesthetics, since it indicates a proposal to rethink space and time, and the relations between them. For Derrida, but not for Kant, and maybe not for Husserl, transcendental aesthetics thus understood is already a question of ethics, since for Derrida, the return to Kant disrupts the delimitation between metaphysics, thought in relation to questions of knowledge, and metaphysics thought in relation to questions of morality.

It is also important to mark up the differences, already drawn by Kant, between aesthetics, as concerned with analysis of the sensory experiences, specifically connected to the appreciation of art, as a distinct but subordinate area of sensory experience, and transcendental aesthetics which, as Kant states in the opening sections of the *First Critique*, is concerned with the *apriori* aspects of sensibility, and with the faculty of intuition, which provides the means for registering the effects presented in sensibility at all. The latter thus has much broader scope than the former. Thus for Kant space and time are the *apriori* forms of intuition, while formal intuition provides the *apriori* forms of sensibility. While for Kant artworks, and aesthetics in the more restricted sense, may have a connection to ethics, via the function of beauty as a symbol of moral value, there will be a different connection for Kant from transcendental aesthetics to ethics, one which is to be marked out in terms of a transition out of the domain within which ethical claims and ethical deliberation occur, within a finite time of human experience, prompted by the irruption into it, interminably, of non-delimitable claims, and non-finite values.[16] This in effect is the arrival of Levinasian questioning into the stabilizations effected by the Kantian schemas.[17] This line of thought requires a discussion of the mediation between the finite time-space, traced out in the transcendental aesthetic of the *First Critique*, marking differences between the finitude of a derivative intuition, and the non-finitude of an originary or intellectual intuition, opening from the finite time-space of the syntheses of faculties, on to a time space of the soul, as locus or bearer of these faculties, and of their finite duration, in embodiment. The soul, as transcendental idea, postulated for enquiry in the *First Critique* becomes a concept for the enquiry developed in the *Second Critique*, since the analysis of the conditions for moral deliberation demonstrates to Kant's satisfaction at least that there are freedom, an immortal soul, and a divine source and origin for them both.

For Kant, a connection from a transcendental aesthetics to ethics comes to the fore only once the relation between the value free concerns of enquiry about objects of experience, and the interplay of duty and virtue in a transcendental binding of the drives has placed the formal aesthetic of the *First Critique* back into the context of a pure practical aesthetic of the drives, given in the *Second Critique*. This is, as it were, an efficient aesthetic, which provides an account of the structures of self-determination and of motivation to virtuous action and restraint, provided in outline in the *Second Critique*, in part three of the 'Analytic of Practical Reason'. The *Third Critique* could then be thought to provide accounts of a material aesthetic and of an aesthetic of finality. For Kant, in the *First Critique*, a transcendental aesthetic is concerned with the distinctive time-space of human thought and experience; in the *Second Critique* aesthetics becomes a question of affirming a binding of the drives, in a *Triebfeder*, a drive wheel bringing together the actual passions into a determination of the will, in line with the indications of duty and of the categorical imperative. This then links the empirical dimensions of human feeling into a set of transcendental constraints.

For Husserl, by contrast, the task of reason in clarifying the origins of meaningfulness is hypothesized as a feature of the moral destiny of human beings. Thus, for him, the role of transcendental aesthetics in the determination of meaning already provides some connection to questions of ethics. What remains to be set out is the connection between Derrida's rewriting of transcendental aesthetics as a topography of the border and the ethics of undecidability. This can now be located as an ethics, which accepts a splitting between transcendental and empirical levels, but which affirms an impossibility of a determination at the empirical level by transcendental conceptions. This topography concerns the questions of limit, crossing, border, and passage, and the questions of the living on, and intensification, in the *survivre*, and also intimates the operations of a suspension and affirmation of the death drive, as set out in Derrida's discussions of Freud and of Blanchot. The notion of suspension, or bracketing here affirms, and intensifies, what it puts to one side, as opposed to a notion of a suspension, or bracketing, which irreversibly puts processes out of play. It is arguable that for Husserl, too, bracketing is more a question of intensification than of neutralizing.

Husserl introduces the notion of a transcendental aesthetic explicitly only relatively late in his trajectory, and it would be the task again for another occasion to show that the problematic of such an aesthetic has been in evidence from *Logical Investigations* (1900, 1901) onwards. It comes less obliquely into play alongside the introduction in *The Idea of Phenomenology* (1907), and, more emphatically still, in *Ideas One* (1913), in the language of a transcendental turn and of transcendental enquiry, through the procedure of bracketing naturalization, in order to attend to formal, necessary, and transcendental structures. For Husserl, there are at least three levels of articulation in a transcendental aesthetic. There is the enquiry into the inter-connectedness of sensory experience, which permits him to develop an account of kinaesthesia, the structural system, or movement of apperception in relation to perception, whereby the evidences of the five senses are bound together and set up as a set of processes delimiting possible articulation as meaningful wholes. There is the concern to show that there is a single form, into which all egoic activity falls, and this form Husserl calls time, although it is a form of time or temporalization which has bracketed time as naturally given series. Third, there is his concern to show that there are inter-subjective correlations. Thus, Husserl opens out the differences between there being a unity of the manifold, *tout court*; there being a unity of the manifold informing the experiences of given empirical human individuals; and there being a unity of the manifold underlying and permitting communicativity between distinct human individuals, and indeed between distinct historical epochs, introducing a fourth layer: the forming of an intergenerational manifold. As a consequence of putting in question the unifiability of the former levels or stages of the construction, Derrida also puts in question the presumptions attaching to the latter. In this he follows up questions to Husserl's account of time posed by Levinas, in *Time and the Other* (1947) and in *Existence and Existents* (1948), in terms of an irretrievable immemorial time, not recuperable within such a unified manifold.[18]

For Derrida, these considerations concerning the time-space of individual and of collective humanity open up a questioning of ethics, since they pose the threefold problem, of there being ethical claims on any individual, in excess of a capacity to perform; of there being a problem relation between the instances of human beings; and a problem status for the notional ideals 'the human', and 'humanism' which, for Derrida, remain in contention throughout his writings, both on account of their radical indeterminacy and on account of a lack of attention bestowed to this indeterminacy. This is most notably in evidence in the early essay 'The Ends of Man' (1966), which engages with the humanism implicit in Kant's moral philosophy, but it is also to be found in all his writings on Heidegger, under the title '*Geschlecht*' (1983, 1986, 1989), where Derrida meditates on the manner in which for the most part the limit between who is to count as human and who is not; and what is to count as human and what is not, remains to the sidelines of enquiry, apparently unworthy of remark.[19] It is in the fourth of these papers, the third of which remains unpublished, that Derrida introduces the notion of a philo-polemology, a love of the study of conflict and antagonism, as a means of reading Heidegger's relation to the philosophical inheritance. This love of the study of conflict urges a return to Heidegger's controversial questioning of the human in the 'Letter on Humanism' (1946), and its conjunction with the manner in which the twentieth century has born witness to an unparalleled inhumanity, from human to human.[20] It also permits a return to the relation between Heidegger and Husserl, as deeply contested. For Derrida himself, the topic of boundaries and limits in relation to thinking the human is pervasive. It returns in the notion of limitrophy, the cultivation of limits, on the border, or *limes*, in the more recent publications, the paper, and posthumous texts: 'The Animal That Therefore I am (More to Follow)' (1997), in *L'animal autobiographique* (1999), and *L'animal que donc je suis* (2006).[21]

Repeating the exergue

Rather than pursue these connections, this perhaps is the moment to return to the exergue:

> I will rapidly mention the first seven *aporias* that concern the theme of this conference. Each of them puts to test a *passage*, both an impossible and a necessary passage, and two apparently heterogeneous borders. The first type of border passes among *contents* (things, objects, referents, territories, countries, states, nations, cultures, languages etc.) or between Europe and some non-Europe, for example. The other type of borderly limit would pass between a *concept* (singularly that of duty) and an other, according to the bar of an oppositional logic. Each time the decision concerns the choice between the relation to an other, who is its other (that is to say, an other that can be opposed in a couple), and the relation to a wholly non-opposable other, that is, an other that is no longer its other. What is at stake in the first place is therefore not the crossing of a given border, rather, at stake is the *double concept of the border*, from which this *aporia* comes to be determined.
>
> (*Aporias*, p. 17–18)

It is striking that this text suggests both two, and three, and then more, and less, than three distinct delimitations of borders. There are borders, as conceptual delimitations between distinct kinds of contents, and there are borders, as physical, geographical demarcations on maps, at airports, between nationalities. These are grouped together, but they seem to move imperceptibly from the order of the conceptual to that of the symbolic. There is then the invocation of a conceptual border, as implying an oppositional logic between duties and non-duties, and a distinction between duties to oneself, and duties to another. This then implies a further distinction between oneself, and others as nameable and recognizable, and further unnameable and unrecognizable others. This series of shifts is best taken as entirely deliberate, for it underlines the movement marked up in the immediately preceding remark, from the same paragraph, on the same page:

> The formulation of the paradox and of the impossible therefore calls upon a figure that resembles a structure of temporality, an instantaneous dissociation from the present, a *difference*, in being-with-itself of the present, of which I gave then some examples. These examples were not fortuitously political. It was not by accident that they

concerned the question of Europe, of European borders and of the border of the political, of *politeia* and of the State as European concepts. Nine or eleven times, they involved the same aporetic duty; they involved ten-plus or minus one-commandments, considered as examples in an infinite series, in which the ten could only count (as) a series of examples.

(*Aporias*, p. 17)

This suggests that the ambiguity with respect to number is deliberate, marking up the manner in which the determination of quantity is more usually permitted to take precedence and pass unnoticed, with certain consequences for how time and concepts, and the connections between them are to be thought. This suggests that time, and space, and time and space might be both more and less than three.

Provisional summary and transition to a return to Husserl

Classically, then, transcendental aesthetics is a term invented by Immanuel Kant to designate the enquiry into the *aprioris* of thinking about space and time. In the *Critique of Pure Reason* (1781, 1787), Kant argues that space and time are the forms of pure intuition, and he argues that they are two, that they are pure forms, that their relation is one of independence from one another, and that they are the necessary forms for the deployment of intuition, holding in place the manifold of intuition, within which for Kant appearances are ordered. However, when in the *Second* and *Third Critiques*, he presents alternate accounts of the relations between, and functions of the faculties, sensibility, intuition, understanding and reason, it turns out, as indicated, that the transcendental aesthetics of the *First Critique* is not his final word on the question of the relation between space and time. Furthermore, as Derrida's insistent reading has shown, Kant's writings on history and politics, on the cosmopolitical, on hospitality and on evil, deepen the disruption of any supposed exhaustiveness in the account of space and time, as offered in the *First Critique*. For in those writings time is revealed to be both the horizon for the fulfillment of the destiny of humanity and the medium for the arrival of the sign of hope, concerning the possible improvement of the human condition. This emerges in the texts *Religion within the Bounds of Reason Alone* (1793) and *The Conflict of the Faculties* (1798), and in Derrida's readings of them. The proposal then is to read Derrida's analyses of space and time, from *différance*, to *restance* and *destinerrance*, and the analyses of hospitality and of spectrality, through the thinking of borders and their instability, provided in *The Truth in Painting* (1978), *The Other Heading; Reflections on Today's Europe* (1991) and indeed in *Aporias: Dying, Awaiting One Another at the Limits of Truth* (1993), as a systematic questioning of and displacement of Kant's notion of transcendental aesthetics, in favour of what I here call 'topography of the border'.

This has various virtues as a reading: it does justice to the innovations of Derrida's reading, as presented in *The Truth in Painting*, of Kant's *Third Critique*, as a quite deliberate disruption of the schemas of the *First Critique*, working at several levels. It affirms a connection between that reading of Kant, and the reflections on political topography, as carried out in the Seminar, from 1984 onwards, and it prepares the way for a consideration of Derrida's meditations on death, in relation to Hegel, to Heidegger, Levinas, Freud, and Blanchot. It also has the virtue of connecting Derrida's thinking of space and time and death, as a series of returns to his responses to Husserl on genesis and passive synthesis, and to Husserl's suggestions, in both *Formal and Transcendental Logic* (1929) and *Cartesian Meditations* (1931), of the need to rewrite transcendental aesthetics, in line with the impact on the critical thinking of Kant of the invention of the phenomenological programme. In the Fifth Cartesian Meditation, Section 61, Husserl writes the following:

> The extraordinarily vast complex of researches pertaining to the primordial world makes up a whole discipline which we may designate as 'transcendental aesthetics' in a very much broadened sense. We adopt the Kantian title here because the space and time arguments of the critique of reason obviously, though in an extraordinarily restricted and unclarified manner, have in view a noematic Apriori of sensuous intuition. Broadened to comprise the concrete Apriori of (primordial) nature, as given in purely sensuous intuition, it then requires a phenomenological transcendental supplementation by incorporation into a complex of constitutional problems.[22]

Thus, for Husserl, the *aporias* identified by Derrida are to be resolved by excavating this structure of *aprioris*. Here in the *Cartesian Meditations*, Husserl is preoccupied with the co-incidences between distinct, monadically constituted transcendental subject poles. This induces him to consider the deployment of a notion of empathy in order to grasp the phenomenon of pairing, in which the evidences of activity of empirical subjectivity induces me to ascribe to the other an activity of a transcendental grounding, binding those activities together into a coherent unity. However, already in *Logical Investigations* (1900, 1901) there are explorations of the operations of association and imaginative variation as binding together the brute sensory sequences of exposure to empirically given data.

In the papers gathered together in *The Crisis of European Sciences and Transcendental Phenomenology* (1936), Husserl advances towards a cross temporal notion of a transcendental aesthetic, permitting the experiences and thoughts of whole generations to be bound together, as continuing series of responses, with an internal system of transmission of, distortion of, and reaffirmation of originary meaningfulness, as then set out in these *aprioris*. This, very roughly, is a schematization of three of the layerings in what Husserl calls a transcendental aesthetics: internal to the constitution of individual egos, in the relations between what comes to be called passive and active synthesis; working through to establish inter-subjectivity and objectivity in a recognition of and understanding of a constitution in parallel of other subject egos; and a further layer, permitting the trans-historical transmission across groups of individuals. This shows both a tangential connection back to the Kantian notion of transcendental aesthetics, and its degree of separation from it. Husserl's main suggestion is that Kant's transcendental aesthetics is still dependent on a naturalized and derivative notion of time, which must be subjected to the procedures of bracketing and reduction, to reveal its origins in the processes of meaning formation. Derrida's readings of Husserl then suggest that an instability or incompletability of such procedures of reduction reveals a far more complex structure of time than that supposedly entertained by either Husserl or Kant. For the instability and incompletability of the procedures of reduction entail that no two attempts to arrive at a monadic ego structure arrive at identical and stable results, even in relation to the same empirically given ego. This repeats at the transcendental level the same result as that of attempting to write the same autobiographical account of oneself twice over.

This account of a topography of the border reveals this border to be a borderline concept between the Kantian notion of the limit and the Derridean concept of passage. This puts in play a double concept of transcendental aesthetics, one aspect of which replays a set of Aristotelian distinctions between formal and efficient, between material and final causalities and determinations of concepts. The other aspect is intimated by the transformation at work on some of the central concepts of Kant's enquiries, in the movement between the texts of Husserl and Derrida. *Différance* as a new name for transcendental aesthetics reveals an inseparability between formal and material determinations with respect to any thinking of temporality. Transcendental aesthetics as *différance* then reveals a priority to transformation and passage, as the movements through which meaning arrives, as opposed to the Kantian categorial schemata and Husserl's account of habituation. The dynamics of writing become the privileged site for identifying these movements as opposed to mapping them through a series of processes of retracing the outlines of static geometrical figurations. It would then be possible to argue that Husserl should have chosen not the origin of geometry as an exemplary case of meaning formation, affirming a continuity with the enquiries of Kant, but rather the emergence of the meaning formations making the articulation of calculus possible.

Notes

1. See *Le Passage des frontieres: Autour du travail de Jacques Derrida*, edited by Marie Louise Mallet, (Galilee, Paris 1993), and in English as *Aporias: Awaiting One Another/Death at the Limits of Truth*, translated by Thomas Dutoit (Stanford: Stanford University Press, 1993), henceforth cited as *Aporias*.
2. See *The Other Heading: Reflections on Today's Europe*, translated by Pascale Anne Brault and Michael Naas (Chicago: University of Chicago Press, 1992).
3. See 'How to Avoid Speaking: Denials' in *Derrida and Negative Theology*, edited by Harold Coward and Toby Foshay (Albany: SUNY Press, 1992). See also my differently inflected discussion of some of these issues and texts in Joanna Hodge, *Derrida on Time* (London: Routledge, 2007), especially Chapter 4, Section II and Chapter 5.
4. Edmund Husserl, *The Phenomenology of Internal Time Consciousness* (1928), edited by Martin Heidegger, translated by James Churchill (Bloomington: Indiana University Press, 1964). The critical edition of 1966 is translated as *On the Phenomenology of the Consciousness of Internal Time* (1893–1917) (HUA 10) translated by John Barnet Brough (Dordrecht: Kluwer Academic Publishers, 1991).
5. For the readings of Husserl see Len Lawlor, *Derrida and Husserl: The Basic Problem of Phenomenology* (Bloomington: Indiana University Press, 2001), Joshua Kates, *Essential History: Jacques Derrida and the Development of Deconstruction* (Evanston: Northwestern University Press, 2005) and see also Hodge, *Derrida on Time*.
6. For a different account of his responses to Kant, see my 'Introduction: Kant par excellence' in *Kant after Derrida*, edited by Philip Rothfield (Manchester: Clinamen, 2003), pp. 1–17.
7. See Derrida, *Rogues: Two Essays on Reason*, translated by Pascale Anne Brault and Michael Naas (Stanford: Stanford University Press, 2005).
8. See Immanuel Kant, *Critique of Practical Reason*, translated by Lewis White Beck, The Library of Liberal Arts (Indianapolis: Bobbs Merrill, 1956), AK 5. p. 6. The standard way of referring to works by Kant are by means of the Akademie Ausgabe volume and page numbers.

9. For a preliminary discussion of these, see my 'Excesses of Subtlety: The Current Reception of Edmund Husserl', *Journal of the British Society for Phenomenology*, 35. 2 (May 2004), 208–213. See also Toine Kortooms, *The Phenomenology of Time* (Dordrecht: Kluwer Academic Press, 2002). The later text, the Bernauer Manuscripts, puts in question the supposed securing of the account of time in a notion of absolute consciousness, since there is a lack of hyletic data to support any such hypostatising of the latter.

10. For the negotiation between Levinas and Blanchot on the arrival of the divine as the source of interruption, or the arrival of the mode of the neuter, see William Large, *Emmanuel Levinas and Maurice Blanchot: Ethics and the Ambiguity of Writing* (Manchester: Clinamen, 2005).

11. Kant, *Critique of Pure Reason*, translated by Norman Kemp Smith (NY: St. Martin's Press, 1965), A 86, B 118, p. 121.

12. For discussion of Irigaray's work as a disruption of Kant's transcendental aesthetics, along these lines, see my 'Feminism and Utopia: Irigaray reading Kant' in 'Gender and Philosophy', *Women: A Cultural Review*, 14. 2 (Summer 2003), 195–209.

13. For a discussion of Derrida's troubled relation to Walter Benjamin and his notion of the messianic, see my 'The Timing of Elective Affinity: Walter Benjamin's strong aesthetics' in *Walter Benjamin and Art*, edited by Andrew Benjamin (London: Continuum, 2005), pp. 14–31.

14. *Specters of Marx: The State of the Debt, the Work of Mourning, and the New International*, translated by Peggy Kamuf (NY and London: Routledge, 1994).

15. For further discussion of this see my essay, 'Husserl on Apriorism and Authenticity,' in *Husserl and the Logic of Experience*, edited by Gary Banham (London: Palgrave Macmillan, 2006).

16. Kant, *Critique of Judgment*, translation and introduction. by J. H. Bernard (NY: Hafner Press, 1951), Section 59.

17. For Levinas' discussion of this see his *God, Death and Time* (1975), translated by Bettina Bergo (Stanford: Stanford University Press, 1998).

18. For a discussion of Levinas' enquiries in relation to those of Husserl and Kant, and on a thinking of ethics and time, see my 'Ethics and Time: Levinas between Husserl and Kant,' *Diacritics, a Journal for Contemporary Criticism*, 32.3–4 (Winter 2002), 107–34. See also Robin Durie 'Speaking of time...: Husserl and Levinas on the Saying of Time', *Journal of the British Society for Phenomenology*, 30 (January 1999), 35–58.

19. For 'The Ends of Man', see Jacques Derrida, *Margins of Philosophy* (1972), translated by Alan Bass (Brighton: Harvester Press, 1982), pp. 109–35. The *Geschlecht* papers are to be found in *Between the Blinds*, edited and translated by Peggy Kamuf (Brighton: Harvester, 1991); in *Deconstruction and Philosophy: The Texts of Jacques Derrida*, edited by John Sallis (Chicago: The University of Chicago Press, 1987); and *Reading Heidegger: Commemorations* (Bloomington: Indiana University Press, 1993). For the beginnings of a reading of these, see Hodge, *Derrida on Time*, Chapter 5.

20. See Martin Heidegger, *Off the Beaten Track* (*Holzwege*, 1950), translated by Julian Young (Cambridge: Cambridge University Press, 1998).

21. See Derrida, 'The Animal That Therefore I Am (More to Follow)', translated by David Wills, *Critical Inquiry*, 28 (Winter 2002), 369–418; the conference

proceedings; *L'animal autobiographique: Autour de Jacques Derrida*, edited by Marie-Louise Mallet (Paris: Galilee, 1999), and Jacques Derrida, *L'animal que donc je suis*, edited by Marie-Louise Mallet (Paris: Galilee, 2006).

22. Edmund Husserl, *Cartesian Meditations* (1931, HUA 1, 1950), translated by Dorion Cairns (The Hague: Martinus Njhoff, 1960), p. 146.

Index

Disgrace (Continued)
South Africa, 'the new'   155,
157–8, 170n. 6
Spivak, Gayatri Chakravorty
on   156–7, 161–3, 168–9,
169–70n. 6
Dolar, Mladen   132, 135
act, Hegelian   133
ambivalence, Hegelian   133
craniology, Hegelian   133–4
Hegel, rejection of heterogeneity
by   133
observing reason   135
"Phrenology of Spirit, The"   132–3,
135, 149, 150n. 3, 151n. 5
physiognomy, Hegelian   135
Dupuy, Jean-Pierre   3, 40
duty, *see* Derrida, Jacques; Kant,
Immanuel

economy, the   63
Eliot, George
Ellenberger, Henry F.   *see* Sloterdijk,
Peter
enjoyment, *see jouissance*; Lacan,
jouissance
Evans, Dylan   181–2
event   4
Ewald, François   232n. 72
exception, state of, *see* Agamben,
Giorgio

Fenves, Peter, *see Schwärmerei*
Ferry, Jules (Minister of Public
Instruction)   258n. 5
Findlay, J. N.   151n. 8
Foucault, Michel   35–6, 46
Frege, Friedrich Ludwig
Gottlob   260n. 50
Freud, Sigmund   84, 228
"Beyond the Pleasure
Principle"   95, 183, 185, 187
"Child is Being Beaten, A"   191
coincidence in   177
criticism of   182
deferred action,
see Nachträglichkeit
"Dynamics of Transference,
The"   183, 194n. 15

"Economic Problem of Masochism,
The"   212
fantasy in   191–2
"Fetishism"   186
group psychology   94
*Group Psychology and the Analysis of
the Ego*   95–6
identification   95–6, 110n.57
insect communities   94
masochism   216
primary   212
mob formation   95
Nachträglichkeit   180–1, 183–4
perversion   87
pleasure in, *see* pleasure, Freud on
radicality of   213
"Remembering, Repeating and
Working-Through"   182–3, 189
repetition   183–4, 186–9
repression   182
telepathy   94–5
*Three Essays on the Theory of
Sexuality*   212
Totem and Taboo   96
trauma, on, *see Nachträglichkeit*
working-through   189
see also Schwärmerei, Freudian

Geulen, Eva   47, 51n. 30
Girard, René   78n. 35
Grether, Reinhold   75n. 4
Grunberger, Béla   78n. 36
Guattari, Félix   81n. 56
Anti-Oedipus Papers, The   233n. 93
see also Deleuze and Guattari

Habermas, Jurgen   59
Hallward, Peter   234n. 95
Hazlitt, William   84,103n. 13
Hegel, G. W. F.   1, 5, 84
allusion, literary, in   144–6
consciouslessness   140–1
consciousness: dialectical
progression of   140, 144–5,
148; ethical   137; shapes
of   140, 145; survival
144–5, 147
craniology: dialectic of   131,
133–4, 144, 149; dialectical

Lightning Source UK Ltd.
Milton Keynes UK
UKHW021955231020
372136UK00003B/186